SONORAN DESERT JOURNEYS

SONORAN DESERT
JOURNEYS

Ecology and Evolution of Its Iconic Species

THEODORE H. FLEMING

THE UNIVERSITY OF
ARIZONA PRESS

TUCSON

The University of Arizona Press
www.uapress.arizona.edu

We respectfully acknowledge the University of Arizona is on the land and territories of Indigenous peoples. Today, Arizona is home to twenty-two federally recognized tribes, with Tucson being home to the O'odham and the Yaqui. Committed to diversity and inclusion, the University strives to build sustainable relationships with sovereign Native Nations and Indigenous communities through education offerings, partnerships, and community service.

ISBN-13: 978-0-8165-4729-6 (paperback)
ISBN-13: 978-0-8165-4730-2 (ebook)

Cover design by Leigh McDonald
Cover illustration by Theodore H. Fleming
Designed and typeset by Leigh McDonald in Adobe Jenson Pro 10.5/14

Library of Congress Cataloging-in-Publication Data
Names: Fleming, Theodore H., author.
Title: Sonoran Desert journeys : ecology and evolution of its iconic species / Theodore H. Fleming.
Description: Tucson : University of Arizona Press, 2022. | Includes bibliographical references and index.
Identifiers: LCCN 2022014546 (print) | LCCN 2022014547 (ebook) | ISBN 9780816547296 (paperback) |
    ISBN 9780816547302 (ebook)
Subjects: LCSH: Natural history—Sonoran Desert. | Desert animals—Sonoran Desert. | Desert plants—
    Sonoran Desert. | Sonoran Desert—Environmental conditions. | BISAC: NATURE / Essays |
    NATURE / Environmental Conservation & Protection
Classification: LCC QH104.5.S58 F585 2022 (print) | LCC QH104.5.S58 (ebook) | DDC 508.72/17—dc23/
    eng/20220613
LC record available at https://lccn.loc.gov/2022014546
LC ebook record available at https://lccn.loc.gov/2022014547

Printed in the United States of America
♾ This paper meets the requirements of ANSI/NISO Z39.48-1992 (Permanence of Paper).

"We are all potential fossils still carrying within our bodies the crudities of former existences, the marks of a world in which living creatures flow with little more consistency than clouds from age to age."

—Loren Eiseley, *The Immense Journey*, 6

CONTENTS

PREFACE

THIS BOOK was inspired by three books that I read as an undergraduate at southern Michigan's Albion College (1960–64): *The Immense Journey* by Loren Eiseley (1957), *A Sand County Almanac and Sketches of Here and There* by Aldo Leopold (1949), and *The Meaning of Evolution* by George Gaylord Simpson (1949). Eiseley (1907–77) was an influential paleontologist, anthropologist, and essayist who wrote poetically about science and evolution. From his book, which is a collection of essays about evolution, human or otherwise, I gained an impressionistic view of the history of life on Earth and how, through immense spans of time, animal life had emerged from aquatic depths to eventually colonize and radiate spectacularly on land.

For most of his career, Aldo Leopold (1887–1948) was a well-known wildlife biologist at the University of Wisconsin. His book is a beautifully written account of memorable incidents in his early adult life as well as the history and natural history of his Sand County farm in southern Wisconsin. It ignited in me a desire to become a close observer of the natural world. The final section of this book is titled "The Upshot" and deals with broader aspects of conservation ethics. It contains his famous essay "A Land Ethic," which is often considered to be the basis for the modern conservation movement in the United States and elsewhere. In that essay, Leopold states that the "land ethic simply enlarges the boundaries of the [human] community to include soils, water, plants, and animals: the land" (1949, 204). This straightforward idea is often forgotten in our capitalistic world, in which man and the natural world are often viewed as two separate entities.

George Gaylord Simpson (1902–84) was perhaps America's premier vertebrate paleontologist in the twentieth century. He had an impressive ability to translate his deep knowledge of vertebrate fossils, mostly mammals from southern South America, into a sweeping and detailed view of how vertebrate life on Earth has evolved. He was another wonderful writer who was able to communicate his knowledge and ideas into highly regarded books such as *The Major Features of Evolution* (1953), which found a wide scientific audience. His *The Meaning of Evolution*, however, was written for a general audience and was therefore less technical than his other books. In it he plays the role of a historian of life who "takes not only knowledge of fossils but also a tremendous array of pertinent facts from other fields of earth sciences and of life sciences and weaves them all into an integral interpretation of what the world of life is like and how it came to be so. Finally, he is bound to reflect still more deeply and to face the riddles of the meaning and nature of life and of man as well as problems of human values and conduct" (Simpson 1949, 3). In this pursuit, he was following directly in the footsteps of Charles Darwin a century later.

I was already an enthusiastic young naturalist when I entered Albion, but these books fired my imagination and interest in the study of natural history and the evolution of life on Earth as a life's profession. Fortunately, I was able to pursue that passion by earning a PhD in zoology at the University of Michigan (1969) and then spending nearly forty years as a faculty member at the University of Missouri–St. Louis (1969–78) and the University of Miami in Coral Gables, Florida (1978–2008). My adventures as a tropical ecologist and student of plant-visiting bats in Panama, Costa Rica, Australia, and Mexico are recounted in two books: *A Batman in the Tropics, Chasing El Duende* (2003) and *No Species Is an Island* (2017).

Here I will step away from my formal research studies to explore in some detail the lives of some of the animals and plants that I either find interesting or have encountered regularly while living in retirement in Tucson, Arizona (as Simpson did in the 1970s and early 80s). All of these animals are vertebrates because I've always been fascinated by reptiles, birds, and mammals. Among these species are desert spiny lizards, Cooper's hawks, hummingbirds, and nectar-feeding bats. Two of the plants include the saguaro cactus, the iconic plant of the Sonoran Desert, and the desert mistletoe. I've chosen these plants because they play an important role in the lives of several desert-dwelling birds and mammals. What I'm interested in exploring here, however, is not just their natural history, which is generally quite well known, but their evolutionary histories and biogeography. What kinds of journeys have these and many other animals and plants and their ancestors taken in space and time to arrive together in my backyard or, a bit more widely, in the Sonoran Desert of southern Arizona, the major geographic focus of this book? How long have these species been living together here? How many of them are restricted, at least in part, to this unique habitat and how many others are habitat generalists whose broad geographic ranges happen to include this desert? And finally, what is their conservation status? To what extent are the lives of these and other Sonoran Desert species endangered, primarily as a result of human activities, including climate change?

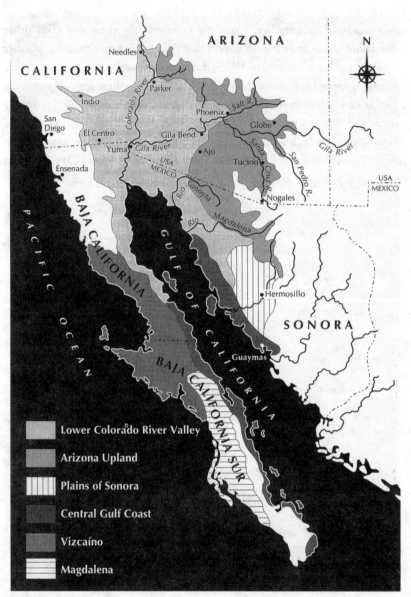

MAP 1 Map of the Sonoran Desert showing its six biotic subdivisions. From Dimmitt (2015) with permission.

INTRODUCTION

THIS BOOK is about two "immense journeys"—one dealing with the natural world and the other dealing with our understanding about the evolution of this world. The word *immense* is generally defined as "extremely large or great, especially in scale or degree." I'm sure we can all agree that the evolution of life on Earth has been, as Loren Eiseley says, an immense journey in time and space. And I'm using this word in this sense, to some extent. Thus, while it hasn't occurred over a period of billions of years, the evolution of many of the species of animals and plants that currently live together in the Sonoran Desert has certainly occurred over millions of years. Compared to our life expectancies, these time spans are definitely immense. But in addition to the relatively long evolutionary histories of many (but not all) of these species, I'm also interested in exploring the immense intellectual/scientific journey that we've taken to understand the evolution of life on Earth. This journey perhaps began with Aristotle over 2,000 years ago and started to accelerate rapidly in the eighteenth and nineteenth centuries with the work of Carl Linnaeus and Charles Darwin. Please remember that in the middle of the eighteenth century, most people in the Western world believed that species were the special creations of God and that Earth was only a few thousand years old. I consider the gap between that thinking and our current understanding of Earth's geological and evolutionary history to also be an "immense journey."

Much of this history was not known, at least in its current details, when I was a college student over fifty years ago, and I am fascinated by how much we have learned about the history of the natural world in the past half century. Whereas Loren Eiseley could only write poetically about evolutionary histories, we now have very powerful tools for actually determining this history in ever-increasing detail. Hopefully, this new knowledge will not eliminate the wonder that still surrounds the evolution of life on Earth. The world still needs (perhaps more than ever) wonderful scientists/poets such as Eiseley, Leopold, and Simpson to remind us how special our place in the universe is. We tend to take for granted the existence of the animals and plants that we see around us every day. I suspect that we seldom take the time to consider how improbable—in the context of the universe we live in—organisms such as rattlesnakes, spiny lizards, humming-birds, nectar-feeding bats, and saguaro cacti are. So what's their story? How did we uncover their stories? How did they come to live together and survive in this climatically harsh southwestern desert?

My geographical focus in this book will be on the Sonoran Desert where I live. This desert is the most tropical of North America's four deserts (the Great Basin Desert, the Mojave Desert, the Chihuahuan Desert, and the Sonoran Desert). It encompasses an area of about 223,000 km^2 and is located in Arizona and the northwestern Mexican states of Sonora, Baja California, and Baja California Sur (map 1). Its vegetation is diverse, and it contains six currently recognized subdivisions. Tucson lies in the Arizona Upland subdivision and will be my major focus in this book. I have conducted most of my fieldwork in the Central Gulf Coast subdivision and have traveled widely in this desert, but most of the ecological research that I will discuss here has been conducted in the northern portions of this desert as well as in parts of the Mojave and Chihuahuan Deserts. Similarly, my treatment of conservation issues associated with the Sonoran Desert will concentrate on its northern subdivisions.

As a technical note, I will follow scientific convention in presenting all measurements in metric units. Appendix 1 contains metric-to-English conversion values.

SONORAN DESERT JOURNEYS

1

OUR IMMENSE JOURNEY TO CLASSIFY AND DETERMINE THE HISTORY OF LIFE ON EARTH

WHAT'S IN A NAME?

OUR PROPENSITY as humans is to give everything and everyone we encounter a name. These names can either be informal or formal, but in any case they are important because they always say, "I exist. Someone has signified that I exist." The lack of a name doesn't necessarily mean that something doesn't exist (e.g., only about two million of the estimated ten million species alive on Earth today actually have a formal scientific name, but they most assuredly exist), but having a name in most cases is concrete evidence that something does exist. This is not true, however, about imaginary things (e.g., gods) that only exist in our minds. As a historical note, eighteenth-century Europeans were fascinated with naming all of the new plants and animals that were coming from the burgeoning far-flung explorations of the world. But it wasn't until the publications of Carl Linnaeus (also known as Carl von Linné) in the middle of that century that scientific naming became an orderly process.

We have also always had a propensity to group or classify things, whether they are animate or inanimate. Early humans must have developed "lists" of local edible and inedible foodstuffs, thus likely naming and classifying organisms in their environments based on their food value. Contemporary non-Western cultures have been doing this for millennia. For example, the Seri Indians of northern Sonora, Mexico, where I conducted my desert studies, have names for many Sonoran Desert plants, especially those that are important sources of food, fiber, and building materials. But, as Roberto Molina, one of their elders, once told me, their knowledge of bats, my research animals, is limited, and they have only one name for the different kinds of bats they encounter in their ceremonial caves.

Naming and classifying organisms in a systematic fashion—the current domain of taxonomists—dates from the work of the Swedish physician and naturalist Carl Linnaeus (1707–78). His work culminated thousands of years of attempts to create order in a world of ever-increasing knowledge about Earth's biological diversity (biodiversity). Among the early Greeks, for instance, the philosopher Theophrastus (372–287 BC), one of Aristotle's students, attempted to classify plants on the basis of their growth habit (e.g., trees, shrubs, herbs, grasses) and medicinal value. And Aristotle (384–322 BC) himself can be considered to be the father of biological classification by placing different kinds of marine and terrestrial animals into groups based on their morphological characteristics.

As men began to explore the world more widely, beginning with ocean-going sailing ships in the fifteenth century AD, collections of plants and animals began to accumulate, originally in private collections rather than in state or national institutions. As Richard Conniff (2009) details in his book *The Species Seekers: Heroes, Fools, and the Mad Pursuit of Life on Earth*, for a period of about two hundred years beginning in the eighteenth century, naturalists around the world began a frenzied search for new species. According to Conniff, "they regarded the hunt for new species as one of the great intellectual quests in human history" (2009, 2). It wasn't until the late eighteenth and nineteenth centuries, however, that state-run museums such as the British Museum of Natural History (from 1881) or the U.S. National Museum of Natural History (from 1856) began to properly house, curate, and study these collections within a scientific framework.

As a result of these worldwide explorations, Europeans were introduced to many unusual and exotic animals. As a spectacular example, imagine what the King of Spain must have thought when one of Magellan's sailors presented to him in 1521 the skins of two birds-of-paradise that he and his crew had received as gifts from the sultan of one of the Spice Islands. With their long, luxuriant, yellow flank feathers; long and wire-thin inner tail feathers; brown back and yellow head; and iridescent green throat, these gorgeous crow-sized birds became an instant hit with Europeans. But more astounding than their beautiful plumage was the fact that these specimens lacked wings and feet—the standard way that New Guinean natives prepared these birds as gift offerings. Noting the absence of these appendages, Europeans surmised that they were supernatural birds that had descended directly from the Garden of Eden, hence the name birds-of-paradise. They also guessed that they now spent their entire lives floating in the air and feeding on dew or fresh air. It wasn't until the end of the sixteenth century that intact examples of these birds reached Europe, dispelling forever the myth of their heavenly lifestyle.

As our knowledge about Earth's biodiversity increased, it became increasingly clear that there was a serious need to devise a rigorous system of naming and classifying these organisms and to begin to understand how different kinds of plants and animals were related among themselves. Early attempts to do this included a cumbersome system of applying polynomial names to them based on abbreviated descriptions. For example, the plant we now know as *Plantago media* (the hoary plantain of central Europe) was originally named *Plantago foliis ovato-lanceolatus pubescen tibus, spica cylindrica, scapo tereti*—probably a reasonable description of it but quite unreasonable for remembering and cataloging. The modern system of naming and classifying species began with Carl Linnaeus with the publication of two seminal works: *Species Plantarum* (1753) and *Systema Naturae* (tenth edition, 1758). In these works, Linnaeus introduced a system of binominal nomenclature in which species were given two names, usually derived from Latin or Greek: a genus name followed by a species name, e.g., *Homo sapiens*. In modern nomenclature, our scientific name is *Homo sapiens* Linnaeus (or simply *L.*) (1758). This name includes the person or persons who originally described the species and the year it was described. Also in modern taxonomy, a type specimen upon which the species was originally described and a type locality where that specimen was collected is usually designated. In the case of *H. sapiens*, Linnaeus himself was the type specimen and Uppsala, Sweden, was the type locality. Needless to say, Linnaeus was not actually placed in a museum collection after his death.

As we all know, in addition to advocating a binominal nomenclature, Linnaeus devised a system for classifying or grouping organisms based on their anatomical similarities. This system originally included the descending hierarchy of kingdom, class, order, genus, and species. This so-called Linnaean hierarchy was later expanded to include two more levels and now is kingdom, **phylum**, class, order, **family**, genus, and species. Thus *H. sapiens'* place in this hierarchy is Animalia, Vertebrata, Mammalia, Primates, Hominidae, *Homo, sapiens*. In his classification of 1758, Linnaeus recognized two kingdoms, Plantae and Animalia, and six classes of animals: Mammalia, Aves, Amphibia, Pisces, Insecta, and Vermes; class Mammalia included eight orders and thirty-nine genera. At that time, the category *genus* was very broadly construed and often represented the next higher category of *family* as it is used today. His order Primates, for instance, included four very broadly defined genera, many of which we now consider to be separate families: *Homo*, *Simia*, *Lemur*, and *Vespertilio*, which included seven species of bats (!). For birds, he recognized six orders and sixty-three genera in groupings that differ wildly from their modern classification. His order Picae, containing seventeen genera, for instance, included hummingbirds, parrots, toucans, and crows, among others!

Linnaeus originally recognized only two kingdoms, plants and animals, but this would obviously change as we learned more about the details of life's biodiversity. When I began teaching general biology in the early 1970s, for instance, Robert Whittaker's five kingdoms had just come into vogue. In 1969, Whittaker, an American ecologist and broad thinker, listed these kingdoms as Monera (including all prokaryotic organisms such as bacteria that lacked an organized cell nucleus) and four groups of eukaryotes (i.e., organisms with a cell nucleus), Protista, Fungi, Plantae, and Animalia. Reflecting Whittaker's ecological focus, each of these groups fed in a fundamentally different manner. Less than a decade later, however, a radical new view of the organization of life appeared, mainly as the result of research by Carl Woese, an American microbiologist and biophysicist (1928–2012), on the characteristics of the 16S ribosomal RNA (rRNA) gene and the composition of cell walls of different kinds of bacteria. In 1977, Woese and George Fox proposed that the kingdoms of life on Earth are organized into three major domains— Archaea (prokaryotic extremophiles whose cell wall composition, rRNA, and energy metabolism differ from that of true bacteria), Bacteria, and Eucarya—and six kingdoms: Archaea, Bacteria, Protista, Fungi, Plantae, and Animalia. Archaea are a group of ancient bacteria that sometimes live under extreme environmental conditions such as deep-sea hydrothermal vents. They are considered to be the forms of life most likely to be found on Mars. Not all Archaea are extremophiles, however, and they are now known to live in many kinds of aquatic and terrestrial environments, including our own intestines.

Finally, Michael Ruggiero and colleagues (2015) proposed that life exists in seven kingdoms and added Chromista, a group of unicellular and multicellular eucaryotes that sometimes have chloroplasts that contain chlorophyll c but lack chlorophyll a and b as well as certain unique cell wall characteristics, to the six previously recognized kingdoms. The Chromista are a very heterogeneous group of organisms (familiar examples include *Paramecium* and the malaria parasite *Plasmodium*) whose diversity suggests that we still don't have a final answer regarding how many kingdoms of life have evolved on Earth.

AND THEN CAME CHARLES DARWIN

In the eighteenth century, during Linnaeus's time, species were considered to be the static, unchanging creations of God. This was Linnaeus's view of the biodiversity he was naming, and because of his high scientific stature, this view was readily adopted by theologians. One hundred years later, however, our understanding of the nature of species and of the history of life on Earth was revolutionized by the genius and insights of Charles Darwin (1809–84), rightly considered to be the father of evolutionary biology. His "abstract"—*The Origin of Species by Means of Natural Selection or the Preservation of Favored Races in the Struggle for Life*—published in late 1859 after about two decades of intense thought, research, and scholarship completely changed our understanding of the processes that have created life on Earth. As a result, over one hundred years later, Darwin's *Origin* inspired the prominent twentieth-century population geneticist and evolutionary biologist Theodosius Dobzhansky (1900–1975) to state in 1973 that nothing in biology makes sense except in the light of evolution. Thanks to Darwin and his insights, we now know that organic evolution and its primary driver, natural selection, have been operating for as long as life has existed on Earth, that is, for at least 3.8 billion years.

Examining Darwin's life and scientific contributions has spawned a cottage industry of scholarly interest and many books, but I will primarily restrict my treatment of his life and scientific milieu to information found in another of Loren Eiseley's (1958) books, *Darwin's Century*, which I also read, along with *The Origin of Species*, as a college undergraduate. In that book, Eiseley recounts the events and thinking about evolution that preceded Darwin's tremendous contributions. Referring to the importance of the work of Linnaeus and others that were concerned with naming and classifying species, he wrote: "An orderly and classified arrangement of life was an absolute necessity before the investigation of evolution, or even its recognition, could take place" (Eiseley 1958, 15).

So the century between *Systema Naturae* and *The Origin of Species* was a crucial period in Western thought in which many of the elements needed for a theory of evolution to develop were being recognized, though their overall significance relative to evolution was usually not appreciated. In the middle of the eighteenth century, at the time of Linnaeus, the European worldview embraced *catastrophism* to explain Earth's geological history and *progressionism*, whose centerpiece was the Scala Naturae, to account for Earth's biodiversity. Another important aspect of this worldview was that the Earth was young—only about 6,000 years old.

Catastrophism attempted to explain geological strata and the occurrence of fossils in them either as the result of sedimentation after the Great Flood or as a series of upheavals that created new layers of rocks and their fossils. This geological view was challenged by James Hutton (1726–97), a Scottish geologist, physician, and naturalist, who published the *Theory of the Earth* in 1788. In his book, Hutton proposed that erosion, uplift, and volcanism can account for many of Earth's geological features. Based on his explorations of the Scottish Lowlands and coasts, he noted that these processes were slow and took immense periods of time, hence Earth had to be old. His view was that of *geological uniformitarianism* rather than catastrophism. Hutton is now considered to be the father of historical geology.

Progressionism viewed nature as static, immutable, and created (or at least commanded) in a short period of time by God; no extinctions existed in this view. Its Scala Naturae ordered all of life into a straight-line progression from the simplest unicellular organisms through increasingly more complex animals until it finally reached humans, which were deemed to be the ultimate goal of life's development. This view was challenged by the French paleontologist and comparative anatomist Baron Georges Cuvier (1762–1832). With his vast knowledge of comparative anatomy of contemporary animals, he was able to reconstruct ancient vertebrates from their fragmentary fossil remains. To be able to do this, he proposed the "principle of correlation," that is, the body plans of ancient animals were similar to those of current species. He wrote: "We will take what we have learned of the comparative anatomy of the living and we will use it as a ladder to descend into the past" (quoted in Eiseley 1958, 85). His work defied the idea of a Scale of Nature by pointing out that some animal groups (e.g., mollusks and mammals) are so different that they cannot be placed on such a single ladder. From this, Eiseley reasonably concludes that Cuvier's view was that "Life [is] a bush, not a ladder" (quoted in Eiseley 1958, 88).

Moving into the first third of the nineteenth century, the thoughts and writings of at least three additional Europeans—Compte de Buffon, Erasmus Darwin, and Jean-Baptiste Lamarck—set the stage for the emergence of Darwin's theory of evolution. Compte de Buffon (1707–88), a French naturalist and author of the widely regarded multivolume *Histoire naturelle*, recognized a long list of the elements that Darwin would use to develop his theory of evolution. Among these were (1) most species are endowed with high fecundity and are usually faced with limited environmental resources; as a consequence, they always face a struggle for existence; (2) species possess heritable variation that creates material for selection (e.g., in domestic plants and animals); (3) similarity of structure among animals suggests relatedness; (4) hints of long geological time (about 72,000 years in Buffon's view) and geological uniformitarianism; and (5) the importance of biogeography for showing distant relationships—for example, between new- and old-world species.

Darwin's grandfather, Erasmus Darwin (1731–1802), was a physician and a keen observer of nature. He embraced the general idea of evolution and had advanced ideas about sexual selection, which his grandson would later use, and the inheritance of acquired characteristics, an idea that was better developed by the French naturalist Jean-Baptiste Lamarck (1744–1829). Lamarck had a fuller view of evolutionary change than Erasmus Darwin. He knew that a long time was required to produce Earth's biodiversity; and most famously, he postulated that use and disuse of structures within animals caused morphological changes; that is, an unconscious desire for perfection caused organisms to adapt to their environment and to acquire new characteristics. Both men were influenced by Buffon and reflected a growing interest in evolution that was an emerging idea in the intellectual milieu of their time. Finally, in his highly influential book *Principles of Geology* (1830–33), Charles Lyell (1797–1875), an English geologist and former lawyer, provided a summary of these ideas that was closely studied by Darwin during the five-year, around-the-world voyage of the *Beagle*. Eiseley states, "It is no wonder that Darwin, years after, expressed agreement with Judd [a British writer on evolution] that without the *Principles of Geology* the *Origin of Species* would not have been written" (1958, 160).

The life and scientific contributions of Charles Darwin have been studied in minute detail; hence there is no need to recap them here. But I do want to address the impact that his employ as the geologist and naturalist aboard the *HMS Beagle* had on his conversion from the conventional views of his day about the origin of life on Earth to a radically different view. We need to remember that Darwin was only twenty-two years old when he joined that five-year expedition. Although he had relatively little formal training as a scientist, from an early age, and most certainly during his college years at Cambridge, he had tremendous enthusiasm for natural history, especially beetles, and the geology of the English countryside. He was also an avid reader and was inspired by the writings of Alexander von Humboldt and his explorations of South and Central America. Fortuitously, he was given a copy of the first volume of Lyell's *Principles of Geology* just before departing on the *Beagle*. As a result, he was quite well prepared intellectually to take full advantage of the adventures and sights he was about to experience in his explorations, primarily in South America. He would receive a copy of the second volume, which contained Lyell's views on evolution, while he was in Montevideo, Uruguay.

The *Beagle* arrived in the Galapagos, a series of eighteen major volcanic islands located on the equator, about 900 km off the coast of Ecuador, on September 15, 1835. During its six-week stay, Darwin made extensive observations and collections of plants and animals from four main islands—Chatham, Charles, Albemarle, and James—but made a nearly unfortunate mistake based on his current thinking: he failed to note carefully the islands from which many of his specimens, particularly the birds, came. In his previous wanderings in southern South America, especially in the Andes, he had noted gradual latitudinally or altitudinally based changes in the features of clearly "allied" species of animals, which suggested to him the occurrence of adaptive variation, not separate creation. A similar "succession of types" was also becoming clear to him and others in the similarity between the fossils and their living relatives that he encountered. As a result of these observations, just before arriving in the Galapagos, Darwin, who had had a lifelong interest in geology, began to realize that perhaps animals, and not geology, held the key to understanding how evolution operates on Earth. Darwin's failure to clearly label the locations (which islands) his collections came from in the Galapagos reflects the fact that he hadn't expected to find much geographic variation in this small, isolated group of islands of rather similar climate and geology compared with the effect that vast environmental differences had on plant and animal life in South America. How could finches, mockingbirds, and tortoises evolve into a set of very distinctive species under the same physical conditions on different islands that were within sight of each other? It wasn't until the British ornithologist John Gould pointed out to Darwin in March 1837 that the finches and mockingbirds that he had collected on different islands appeared to represent different species that he began to think seriously about the origin ("transmutation") of species. Shortly thereafter, Darwin began a two-decade-long study of this problem.

Although the existence of evolution was becoming well accepted by many European scientists by the middle of the nineteenth century, the mechanism behind this process was still unknown. As we know, it was Charles Darwin and another extensively traveled British naturalist and animal collector, Alfred Russel Wallace (1823–1913), who jointly proposed in 1858 that this mechanism is natural selection. Darwin had come to recognize this mechanism by 1844, when he wrote an unpublished manuscript that would eventually form the basis of the *Origin*. In 1855 Wallace, who had been corresponding with Darwin about their common interests in evolution, wrote an essay, "On the Tendency of Varieties to Depart Indefinitely from the Original Type," in which he described but didn't name a mechanism whereby better fit individuals persist and less fit individuals perish, eventually causing new species to arise. He sent this essay to Darwin in early 1858. Realizing that he and Wallace had independently come up with the idea of natural selection and not wanting to be scooped by him, Darwin shared this essay with his friends Charles Lyell and Joseph Hooker. They proposed that Wallace and Darwin jointly present this essay along with an unpublished essay and letter of Darwin's describing his ideas about natural selection to London's Linnean Society, the world's oldest scientific society, on July 1, 1858. Their ideas attracted little attention initially. But the following year Darwin finally published an expanded version of his 1844 essay as the *Origin of Species*. Its first printing of 1,250 copies sold out immediately, and his radical ideas about how species arise gained immediate scientific and public attention.

As an aside, in November 2003 I participated in a symposium on bat-plant ecological interactions at the Linnean Society in central London. I was thrilled to be speaking in the same venue that had hosted the Darwin-Wallace presentation on natural selection some 147 years earlier. In fact, we speakers stood under framed portraits of those two scientific giants as we presented our talks. As I spoke, I tried to picture the meeting in this lecture hall as it was in July 1858. That audience likely consisted mostly of older men (no women), some clean-shaven but many others bewhiskered and all dressed formally in woolen suits, vests, and ties, as they listened to speakers literally reading their papers. In contrast, our meeting consisted of a mixture of male and female grad students and academics. Some men were clean-shaven, but others were bewhiskered, and everyone was dressed casually. Most of us spoke without notes from a series of PowerPoint slides. Nonetheless, one of my esteemed British colleagues still followed the old tradition of carefully reading his paper. During the meeting we were also invited to visit the Linnean Collection in the basement of the building. This collection includes some of Linnaeus's specimens of plants, insects, fish, and shells, in addition to his correspondence, manuscripts, and a library of 1,600 books. I was fascinated to note that his fish specimens were preserved flat as skins with some skeletal elements, much as plant specimens are mounted on herbarium sheets. In most museum collections today, fish are usually preserved whole in fluid-filled jars.

HOW FAR OFF WAS THE BISHOP OF USSHER'S CALCULATION OF THE AGE OF EARTH?

Darwin's theory of evolution required large amounts of time to produce Earth's present and past biodiversity. Robert Hutton's and Charles Lyell's books, which advocated a uniformitarianism view of Earth's geology, had given him and others long stretches of time, but they did not contain estimates of how old Earth actually is. Earlier attempts at this suggested that Earth was at most a relatively few thousands of years old. For example, the Irish Bishop James Ussher calculated in 1650, using known historical events and biblical accounts, that Earth was about 6,000 years old. By Cuvier's time in the early nineteenth century, this estimate had increased to about 72,000 years.

The geological science of stratigraphy, which is the study of the deposition and layering of sedimentary and volcanic materials, dates from the work of William Smith (1769–1839), a British surveyor and engineer. Ahead of his time, Smith used vertebrate and invertebrate fossils to define different geological strata and argued that geographically distant strata containing the same fossils were similar in age. His principle of faunal (or floral) succession in which similar fossils replace or succeed each other in vertical layers ultimately led to the formulation of a geologic timescale in the nineteenth century. Interestingly, Smith did not ascribe differences between fossils in different strata as the products of evolution. Instead, he held to a theological interpretation of the origins of life.

The geological timescale will be important in our discussion of the evolution of Sonoran Desert species and is therefore briefly described here (table 1). As in the Linnean hierarchy, geologists have devised a classification system representing different stages of Earth's geological history. Major units in this classification in descending length of time include eons, eras, and periods. Multicellular life arose about six hundred million years ago (Ma) and defines the Phanerozoic Eon—the eon of visible life. The Phanerozoic is divided into three eras: Paleozoic (ca. 600–ca. 260 Ma), Mesozoic (ca. 260–66 Ma), and Cenozoic (66 Ma–present). Of major interest to students of the evolution of current plants and animals is the Cretaceous Period at the end of the Mesozoic Era (ca. 140–66 Ma) and the seven epochs of the Cenozoic Era (table 1). At an age of about 150,000 years, our own species evolved in the Pleistocene, a time of dramatic climatic change involving major glacier advances and retreats.

Accurate estimates of the actual age of Earth begin with the work of Ernest Rutherford on radioisotopes in the early twentieth century. Discovery of

TABLE 1 The Geological Society of America's Geologic Timescale

ERA	PERIOD	EPOCH	AGE (MA)
Cenozoic	Neogene	Pleistocene	2.6–present
		Pliocene	5.3–2.6
		Miocene	23.0–5.3
	Paleogene	Oligocene	33.9–23.0
		Eocene	56.0–33.9
		Paleocene	66.0–56.0
Mesozoic	Cretaceous	Late	100.5–66.0
		Early	145.0–100.5
	Jurassic	Late	163.5–145.0
		Middle	174.1–163.5
		Early	201.3–174.1
	Triassic	Late	237.0–201.3
		Middle	247.2–237.0
		Early	251.9–247.2

Note: Ages are in millions of years (Ma).

radiation (energy)-emitting elements dates from the late nineteenth century from work of the French physicist Henry Becquerel and the Polish physicists Pierre and Marie Curie in the early twentieth century. From their work, it was soon discovered that many chemical elements such as carbon can exist as different isotopes that differ in the number of neutrons in their atoms (e.g., ^{12}C, ^{13}C, and ^{14}C). Physicists also discovered that some of these isotopes are unstable or radioactive (i.e., they release energy, e.g., ^{14}C) and that some even change into different elements (i.e., they release both energy and particles). Thus, uranium-238 (U-238) releases two protons and two neutrons plus energy to become thorium-234 (Th-234) which decays into protactinium-234 which is also unstable. Eventually, through a series of thirteen steps, U-238 becomes stable lead-206 (Pb-206). The rate of decay of unstable isotopes can be calculated as half-lives (i.e., the amount of time it takes for half of a collection of radioactive atoms to decay into a stable form). For example, the half-life of ^{238}U is 4.47 billion years and that of ^{14}C is 5,700 years. ^{235}U decays into ^{206}Pb with a half-life of 704 Ma. So rocks containing both uranium isotopes can be quite accurately dated using these different half-lives. In addition to U–Pb dating, other radiometric methods include potassium 40–argon 40 (with a half-life of 1.3 billion years); rubidium 87–strontium 87 (with a half-life of 50 billion years);

and U-235–Th-230 (half-life = 80,000 years). As a result of these methods, we now know that Earth is about 4.54 billion years old, which is about one-third of the estimated age of the universe. This is certainly enough time for life in all of its present and past diversity to evolve. It should be noted that there still are people today who adhere to the biblical creation story and believe that Earth is only 6,000 years old. This makes me wonder whether these people also still adhere to medical practices that were in vogue during biblical times rather than embracing current medical advances that are the products of recent scientific research. Unless you're comfortable about being called a hypocrite, I personally don't think you can have it both ways. The same goes, of course, for those people who cling to the biblical version of the creation of life.

NATURAL SELECTION IN ACTION

In Darwin's time and even today we often think that evolution is a slow process and that its basic mechanism, natural selection, is too subtle to be seen. But this isn't necessarily true. As many evolutionary biologists have shown in the past seventy-five years or so, it is a process that can be readily observed or experimentally demonstrated if you work with the right organisms. Lizards of the genus *Anolis* and guppies living in Trinidad (e.g., *Poecilia reticulata*) have been very instructive model systems. Before describing three very different examples of the results of natural selection in action that have occurred over recent, short periods of time, I want to briefly describe how selection works. To visualize this, picture a hypothetical bell-shaped curve that represents the frequency distribution of variation—for example, body size and its underlying genetic variation—in a population. When, for whatever reason, selection imposed by both biotic and abiotic environmental factors favors average body size in the population, those individuals will have the highest reproductive success, the usual currency of selection, and larger or smaller individuals on the tails of the curve will have less reproductive success. In this scenario, average body size will not change from one generation to the next, and we call this *stabilizing selection*. In contrast, whenever selection favors individuals on either tail of the bell curve, that is, individuals that are either smaller or larger than average, we call this *directional selection*, and average size, for example, in a population will change from one generation to the next. Body size in this example will either increase or decrease through time as a result of directional selection. A third possibility is *disruptive selection* in which individuals in the two tails of the distribution both have higher reproductive success than average individuals. In this case, populations will be polymorphic rather than monomorphic with respect to the trait under selection.

Our first example deals with directional selection and features the house or English sparrow (*Passer domesticus* L., 1758). House sparrows are rather recent non-native additions to the avifauna of North America. They were first released in New York City's Central Park in 1852, and from there they dispersed widely throughout North and Central America as far south as Panama by the end of the twentieth century. They reached Vancouver, British Columbia, by 1900, Death Valley by 1914, Mexico City by 1933, and Costa Rica by 1974. They were introduced into Hawaii from New Zealand in 1870–71. And as Richard Johnston and Robert Selander (1964) first reported in the journal *Science*, this species has undergone significant evolution (but not speciation) in many of its morphological features, including the color of its plumage and general body size, in North and Central America in less than one hundred years. Thus, birds living in the cold, wet Pacific Northwest are much darker than those living in the hot, arid U.S. Southwest. Northern birds are also significantly larger in terms of wing length and body mass than birds living at lower latitudes. Further analyses of the skeletons of house sparrows by Johnston and Selander found that although northern birds were larger than southern birds, they had shorter legs, wings, and tails relative to their overall size than their southern relatives. These trends in plumage color and body and limb size are the same as trends seen in many native North American birds and conform to three well-known ecogeographic rules. *Gloger's rule* states that birds and mammals living in cold, damp locations are darker than those living in hot, dry locations; humans are an exception to this. *Bergmann's rule* states that birds and mammals living in northern latitudes are larger than their more southern relatives. And *Allen's rule* states that birds and mammals living in cold climates have shorter limbs and other appendages (e.g., ears and tails) relative to their overall body size than those living in warm climates. Each of these rules reflects selective pressures to reduce loss of body heat in cold climates and to reduce ambient heat gain in hot climates. Geographic variation in coloration and size in birds and mammals clearly reflects adaptive responses to geographic variation in climatically derived selective pressures. In many cases this variation occurs within species and doesn't necessarily reflect the evolution of new species.

What is surprising about geographic variation in many features of house sparrows is how rapidly it has occurred. Johnston and Selander estimated that these changes have occurred at most in about 110 generations (i.e., in as little as fifty years). In places like Vancouver, British Columbia, they have occurred even faster. These changes obviously reflect the power of evolution via strong directional selection to rather quickly adapt organisms to their local environments. The house sparrow example shows us that it doesn't necessarily take millennia for significant adaptations to evolve in a vertebrate species. Vertebrates are rather large on the scale of life on Earth, and yet in some cases they can respond quite rapidly to environmentally (or human) induced selection pressures. This suggests that global warming will definitely have important evolutionary consequences for many species, including some of those living in the Sonoran Desert.

Since rapid evolutionary responses to selection pressures can occur in vertebrates, it should come as no surprise that tiny organisms such as bacteria, protozoans, and viruses with large populations, lots of genetic variation, and fast life cycles can evolve very rapidly (i.e., on the order of a few years or less) if they are subjected to intense selective pressures such as antibiotics. For example, *Staphylococcus aureus*, the bacterium that causes MRSA (methicillin-resistant *S. aureus*), was a rather innocuous source of skin infections prior to the introduction of penicillin in the 1940s. Within a decade, however, certain strains of *S. aureus* had evolved resistance to penicillin. Within a year after the introduction of methicillin in 1961, a stronger antibiotic chemically related to penicillin, methicillin-resistant strains of *S. aureus* had appeared. And now this bacterium is resistant to vancomycin, a much more powerful antibiotic than either penicillin or methicillin, and other antibiotics. MRSA bacteria cause serious health problems in hospitals, in communities outside of hospitals (e.g., in school locker rooms), and even in antibiotic-treated livestock. The evolution of drug-resistant strains of *S. aureus*, which involves a process known as horizontal transfer among different kinds of bacteria of resistance genes that reside in tiny cellular particles called plasmids, is thus a very dramatic illustration of the power of natural selection to cause rapid evolution.

House sparrows and *S. aureus* illustrate the action of natural selection in human-associated organisms, but I want to conclude this section by highlighting another, perhaps less dramatic, example of natural selection in nature. This comes from the work of Mauro Galetti and collaborators in Brazil's Atlantic Forest. Once a 1.5 million km² tract of forests and savannas located in southeastern Brazil and renowned for its high biodiversity, this region has recently lost nearly 90 percent of its forest cover as a result of deforestation. Remaining forest remnants have been reduced to island-like fragments that are separated from each other by extensive tracts of cattle pastures and agricultural fields of sugarcane, coffee, soybeans, and other crops.

Galetti's study focused on the effects of forest fragmentation and the hunting of large fruit-eating birds on seed size of a common palm tree (*Euterpe edulis*). In intact forests, the major dispersers of its seeds are toucans, toucanets, and cotingas—all large birds capable of easily swallowing and dispersing large palm seeds with diameters of ≥ 12 mm. In forest fragments in which these frugivores have basically disappeared, however, only smaller birds such as thrushes are available to eat palm fruits, but they can only swallow seeds with diameters of < 12 mm. As a result, in forest fragments lacking large frugivores, palm seeds are now significantly smaller (by almost 1 mm in diameter) than in fragments still containing large frugivores. Small frugivores are providing directional selection for smaller seeds whereas large frugivores provide stabilizing selection for larger seeds. These researchers estimate that these changes in seed size within forest fragments have occurred in less than one hundred years. And, although small, these changes will have at least two significant effects on the population ecology of this palm. First, thrushes are less-effective dispersers of palm seeds than toucans so that this palm will produce fewer seedlings than if the large frugivores dispersed them. And second, even if they are successfully dispersed, small seeds produce small seedlings that are more prone to desiccation under dry conditions and have higher overall mortality rates than larger seedlings produced by large seeds. Overall, forest fragmentation and the loss of large frugivorous birds will clearly have negative ecological effects on this common palm.

Two of these three examples attest to the power of natural selection to change the phenotypes (outward appearances) and their underlying genotypes in natural populations of animals and plants. The third example shows how rapidly micro-organisms can respond genetically to strong human-induced selection. Thus, beware of cleaning agents such as Lysol that claim to kill (only) 99.9 percent of "germs." It's the remaining 0.1 percent that we have to worry about because the surviving bacteria will undoubtedly become more resistant to cleansers through time. These examples obviously represent a very small tip of the huge iceberg of evidence now supporting the universality of natural selection and its role in driving the evolution of life on Earth. As my colleague John Thompson has stated in his recent book *Relentless Evolution*, evolution is indeed relentless and has been so for as long as life has existed on this planet (i.e., at least 3.8 billion years). It's the creative force behind nearly all of Earth's species and their adaptations.

BUT WHAT ABOUT THE ORIGIN OF SPECIES, DARWIN'S "MYSTERY OF MYSTERIES"?

Where in fact do species come from? This was the main question motivating Darwin to write the *Origin of Species*. We know that natural selection is the main driver of evolutionary (ultimately genetic) change within species, but what processes produce new species? Why does our planet currently contain about 10,000 species of birds, 5,400 species of mammals, and over 300,000 species of flowering plants rather than far fewer species? Before we address these questions, we need to define what we mean by a species. In 1942 the ornithologist and evolutionary biologist Ernst Mayr proposed that species are groups of actually or potentially interbreeding populations that are reproductively isolated from other such groups. Although the appropriateness of this definition for all forms of life has been widely debated over the years, it is the one that is still reasonable for most species of vertebrates and flowering plants.

To begin to understand the process of speciation, let's return to the Galapagos Islands and its group of thirteen or fourteen species of birds known as Darwin's finches. Darwin was certainly fascinated by their morphological diversity, especially in overall size and the range of beak sizes and shapes. About this he wrote: "Seeing this gradation and diversity of structure in one small, intimately related group of birds, one might really fancy that from an original paucity of birds in this archipelago, one species had been taken and modified for different ends" (Darwin 1839, 328). These "modifications" included a variety of strong-billed, ground-feeding, seed-eating species; a finch specialized for feeding on the flowers of tree cacti; a finch that uses tools such as cactus spines to pry insects out of tree bark; and a thin-billed, warbler-like species. On purely morphological grounds, most of these species are certainly distinct, although recent research by Peter and Rosemary Grant indicates that certain species can in fact exchange genes and are not totally reproductively isolated yet. This might be because speciation in these birds has occurred only in the last 3 Ma or less.

In addition to lots of genetic variation, the likely key ingredients for speciation in these birds (and in many other organisms) include geographic isolation, different environmental conditions on different islands, and competition for limited resources within islands. Geographic isolation (or allopatry, living apart) can occur when the geographic range of a species is split by a geological feature such as a river or mountain or when individuals disperse to a new habitat such as an island and lose genetic contact with the parent population. In the absence of additional gene flow via dispersal, genetic differences between isolated populations can then arise as a result of random genetic drift, which can occur in small populations, or from adaptation via natural selection to new environmental conditions. If genetic divergence is strong enough, then if the two populations ever become sympatric (i.e., living together in the same region) again, they may not be able or even have the desire to interbreed. Competition for limited resources (e.g., food or mates) can select for further differences between these sympatric species. This latter scenario suggests that geographic isolation might not even be necessary for a population to diverge into two reproductively isolated populations or species. Very strong disruptive selection would be necessary for speciation to occur in sympatry, however. As a result, allopatric speciation is much more common in animals and plants than sympatric speciation.

In the case of Darwin's finches in the Galapagos, Peter Grant has visualized three main events that have led to the production of its current thirteen species: (1) initial colonization of the archipelago by an ancestral species from South America; (2) establishment of allopatric (geographically separated) populations via occasional dispersal between islands; and (3) reestablishment of sympatry. In allopatry on separate islands, populations become adapted to their local ecological conditions, especially food supplies that include an array of seeds that differ in size and hardness, and may or may not acquire enough genetic differences to prevent interbreeding with populations on other islands; speciation would be complete should this occur. If populations should become sympatric again, selection against any hybrids formed by interbreeding would complete or reinforce the speciation process. Competition for resources among sympatric species could also result in directional selection and further morphological divergence between species. Additional species result from repetition of steps (2) and (3). As a result of these processes, from three to ten species currently coexist on the seventeen major islands.

I visited the Galapagos Islands for a week or so in October 2012 and marveled at the many wonderful animals, plants, and landscapes in eastern parts of this archipelago. Being a dedicated photographer and knowing that most of the animals there are extremely tame, I took only one DSLR camera with an 18–200 mm lens with me; this lens was totally adequate to photograph many of the animals we encountered. During the visit I was able to see several species of Darwin's finches, including ground feeders, tree feeders, the cactus feeder, and, on one occasion, a warbler finch. I loved walking through the streets of Puerto Ayora, the islands' capital, and seeing black-plumaged small ground finches searching for seeds instead of the ubiquitous English sparrows we're used to seeing in cities and towns throughout North America. Tree cacti, friendly Galapagos sea lions, marine and land iguanas, and giant tortoises were all part of a truly memorable experience.

ANCESTRY 101

No life on Earth was created de novo. All creatures past and present on Earth have a history, and in the twenty-first century, we can begin to trace our own and other histories through information contained within our DNA molecules. But tracing true evolutionary histories—something that Darwin could really only dream about—has only recently begun to rely on these molecules. Indeed, realization that DNA is the molecule that contains genetic information, its structure, and how it codes for proteins and other macromolecules only dates from the mid-twentieth century—within my lifetime. Prior to the 1970s and 80s, non-molecular methods, usually involving morphology, were the main tools used by systematic biologists to assess evolutionary relationships among species and to create hypotheses about their evolutionary history. Here I will give a brief history of the methods scientists have used to determine the evolutionary histories of particular groups of organisms. We will use these methods to determine the histories in the Sonoran Desert species accounts that follow.

The rich (but threatened) biodiversity that we see on Earth today is the result of the adaptive radiation of many lineages of animals and plants. This radiation can be viewed from a variety of different perspectives that coincide with Linnaeus's taxonomic hierarchy. Thus, we can consider the radiation of phylum Vertebrata into different classes such as bony fish, amphibians, reptiles, and so forth; the radiation of classes into many different orders and families; and the radiation of families into a variety of different subfamilies. And so on. All of these radiations, of course, ultimately involve speciation and the spread through time and space of groups of related species into available ecological space. During this process, some lineages flourish and others do not. But as George Gaylord Simpson (1953, 227) reminds us in *The Major Features of Evolution*: "The actual phylogenetic process is not first a radiation of phyla, then of classes in each phylum, then of orders in each class . . . [it] is simply a divergence of populations, which are or are becoming separate species, into different adaptive zones." It is

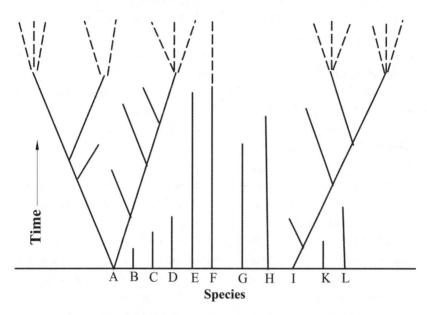

FIGURE 1 Darwin's hypothetical diagram showing the fate of particular species' lineages (A–L) through time. The time frame here is thousands of generations. At each point in time, species A and I are represented by more surviving lineages than the other species. Redrawn from *The Origin of Species* (Darwin 1859).

only by taking a long-range perspective that we recognize these radiations as ultimately becoming different phyla, classes, orders, and so forth.

Darwin (1859, 119), of course, was aware that the proliferation of related species can result in an adaptive radiation, though he didn't actually use this term, and gives us a graphical representation of it in the *Origin* (fig. 1). Because of its branching pattern, this diagram vaguely resembles a phylogenetic tree, but it is only meant to show the history of a group of related species in a large genus, some of which prosper and leave descendants (e.g., species A and I) while many others become extinct. The time frame here is thousands of generations in which the ultimately successful lineages (A and I) initially produce new varieties and eventually new species that, in this example, replace them. This diagram is purely hypothetical, and it would take many future generations of evolutionary biologists to create phylogenies (i.e., evolutionary histories) of real organisms.

Until quite recently, morphology (*sensu lato*), including anatomy and embryo-logical development patterns, provided most of the data used to identify, classify, and determine evolutionary relationships among vertebrates and other organisms. For example, morphological features of birds that have been used in their classification are myriad and include anatomical details of feathers, feet, skulls, postcranial skeletons, muscles, and internal soft anatomy. The large order Passeriformes (perching birds or songbirds), for instance, has been traditionally divided into two suborders—the suboscines and oscines—based on differences in the anatomy of their voice box or syrinx. Oscines have a more complex syrinx than suboscines; as a result, they are better songsters. Morphological features of mammals that have been useful in their classification include a similar suite of external and internal characters of both soft and hard tissues. For example, in a recent classification of phyllostomid bats (American leaf-nosed bats), Andrea Wetterer and her colleagues (2000) used 136 morphological characters ranging from the scaling patterns of hair to anatomical features of the female reproductive tract. In general, teeth have been especially important in mammalian classification and have been the source of much fossil material because of their hardness and resistance to the destructive forces of time. Because mammals possess hard teeth and robust skeletons and are often much larger than birds, their fossil record is much richer than that of birds.

Morphology was still king in systematics when I entered graduate school in the fall of 1964. By then I had decided to become a mammalogist rather than a herpetologist, my first love, and was assigned an office in the Division of Mammals in the University of Michigan's Museum of Zoology. My graduate adviser was Dr. Emmett T. Hooper, an eminent student of the classification and systematics of new-world rats, mice, and voles in the family Cricetidae. At that time, he was determining evolutionary relationships within groups of these animals based primarily on the morphology of the glans penis of males. One of my first research projects as a beginning graduate student in a Birds of the World class was to help classify closely related species of shorebirds on the basis of their thigh musculature. I also worked on the anatomy of the inner ears of voles as part of Hooper's taxonomic studies.

But by the mid-1960s methods of identifying and classifying species and working out their evolutionary relationships had begun to change dramatically, stimulated in large part by rapid advances in molecular biology and genetics resulting from the publication of the structure of DNA by James Watson and Francis Crick in 1953. These studies opened up a whole new array of "characters" at the molecular level that could be used in evolutionary studies. Gene sequences, rather than (or in addition to) morphology have now become the preferred method of reconstructing the evolutionary histories of many groups of organisms. An important reason for this is that morphology alone can sometimes be misleading about relationships, primarily because of the well-known process of *convergent evolution*. This process often involves superficial morphological resemblances between unrelated or only distantly related organisms. Classic examples include new-world kangaroo rats and old-world jerboas. Both groups are desert-dwelling rodents with elongated hind limbs for jumping and long tails, but they belong to very distantly related families. Similarly, new-world cacti and certain groups of old-world euphorbs (family Euphorbiaceae) both resemble "cacti" in having succulent stems and spines, but again they belong to completely unrelated families of flowering plants. A more subtle example comes from the new-world bat family Phyllostomidae (American leaf-nosed bats), a group that contains species that I have studied for over fifty years. Throughout the twentieth century, this family contained a subfamily Phyllostominae of insect-eating and carnivorous species. But recent molecular studies have shown that this subfamily is not monophyletic, that is, not all of its species share a common ancestor. Instead, this subfamily is polyphyletic, that is, its species are derived from different ancestors. As a result, species that do share a common ancestor have been placed in different subfamilies, even though some species groups closely resemble each other morphologically. Similarly, as can be seen in current bird field guides, many passerine bird families containing species that resemble each other have recently been reconstituted on the basis of molecular evidence. For example, Darwin's finches used to be classified in family Emberizidae—new-world sparrows and old-world buntings—but are now placed in the tanager family Thraupidae.

To avoid the trap of convergent evolution or, more generally, *homoplasy* (i.e., widely shared features such as four legs in many terrestrial vertebrates or the possession of fur in most mammals), modern methods used for determining evolutionary relationships between species rely on shared, derived (i.e., not ancestral) characters or features. The occurrence of shared, derived characters in a group of species implies that they all share a common ancestor. For example, Darwin's finches are considered to belong to the same monophyletic group as certain Caribbean seed-eating birds because they all produce domed nests, a derived, not ancestral, form of nest-building in songbirds. Distinguishing derived from ancestral characters usually involves comparing monophyletic groups with other closely related groups. Characters that are shared widely among different groups are likely to be ancestral whereas those unique to the group of interest are likely to be derived.

Historically, ancestral or derived morphological characters have been the basis for inferring relatedness between organisms, but with the advent of DNA-based studies in the latter part of the twentieth century, "ancestral" or "derived" nucleotide sequences have now become important characters in phylogenetic analyses. A large literature on using molecular data to infer evolutionary relationships now exists, but the logic behind this approach remains the same: unique, shared derived sequences are much more informative about relationships than are widespread (i.e., ancestral) sequences.

A few words about our new evolutionary workhorse DNA are in order here. Prior to early 1953, the structure of the macromolecule DNA, which had been identified in 1944 as being the molecule containing genetic information, was unknown. However, based on X-ray crystallography images created under the direction of Rosalind Franklin in Maurice Wilkins's lab in King's College, London, Francis Crick and James Watson, working in the Cavendish lab at Cambridge, were able to deduce that DNA was a double helix (i.e., double-stranded) molecule whose intertwined strands are held together in ladderlike fashion by complementary pairs of molecules called nucleotides (or bases). These so-called base pairs include adenine paired with thymine (A-T) and guanine paired with cytosine (G-C). Each separate strand of DNA can thus be symbolized by its sequence of nucleotides (e.g., AATGCGTAC . . .). The other strand has the complementary sequence of nucleotides (e.g., TTACGCATG . . .). Genes, which are discrete sections of DNA that code for particular proteins, are located in chromosomes and can also be characterized by their nucleotide sequences.

We usually think of DNA as occurring in the nucleus of the cells of animals, plants, and fungi. But this is not entirely correct. Certain other cellular organelles or plastids (e.g., mitochondria in animals and chloroplasts in plants) also contain significant amounts of DNA. Mitochrondrial DNA (mtDNA) in animals, for example, occurs in a single circular molecule containing about 17,000 base pairs coding for thirteen proteins in humans and other mammals. These proteins control a cell's metabolic activities and the production of the important energy molecule ATP (adenosine triphosphate). MtDNA and other plastid-associated DNAs differ from nuclear DNA (nucDNA) in that it is usually passed from one generation to the next via maternal inheritance. That is, whereas the nucleus receives half of its chromosomes and genes (i.e., its DNA) from males and half from females during sexual reproduction, female mtDNA does not recombine with male mtDNA, which is destroyed shortly after fertilization takes place. As a result, mtDNA mutates (evolves) faster than nucDNA because it doesn't undergo recombination, and it has less ability to repair mutations than nucDNA. The higher rate of evolution of the gene sequences of mtDNA makes it an especially useful source of data for evolutionary studies.

Methods for determining DNA sequences were developed in the 1970s, and the first fully automated sequencing machine dates from 1987. Sequencing DNA and its sister molecule RNA and determining their nucleotide (base pair) sequences is now routine. Phylogenetic studies currently use the sequences of several to many mitochondrial and nuclear genes (and increasingly, entire genomes) to characterize a species. The degree of sequence differences between species is then used to assess their relatedness under the assumption that relatedness is positively correlated with sequence similarity. Sequence differences usually arise from mutations caused by nucleotide substitutions or nucleotide insertions or deletions, among other processes. Furthermore, if we assume that rates of nucleotide substitutions roughly occur in a clocklike fashion (which has been widely debated), then percent sequence differences between related species can be used to estimate their time of divergence from a common ancestor. Using this method, divergence rates between the genes of closely related species of birds or mammals based on mtDNA are generally around 1–2 percent per million years.

Determining nucleotide sequences quickly and efficiently changed dramatically with the invention of the polymerase chain reaction (PCR) in 1983. PCR was invented by Kary Mullis (1944–2019) while working at the Cetus Corporation in California. The idea for it came one night while he was driving in his little Honda car along a logging road up to his mountain cabin. After thinking about this all night, the next morning he knew that his world (and the world of molecular genetics) had just changed. As the "inventor" of PCR, Mullin was awarded a Nobel Prize in chemistry in 1993. PCR has become critical for amplifying particular genes many times (thousands to millions) before sequencing them. For a brief description of this process, see box 1.

Modern sequencing techniques of single genes or entire sets of genes (i.e., genomes) for groups of species generate enormous amounts of data, so it should not be surprising that it takes powerful computers to analyze these data. The rise of DNA-based phylogenetic studies has thus occurred in parallel with the rise of powerful computers and a multitude of complex analytical programs. Some of these programs have delightful names such as PAUP, MESQUITE, BEAST, and DIVA. With these computational tools, researchers can now routinely conduct many kinds of phylogenetic studies using their desktop or laptop machines, something that would have totally amazed Charles Darwin. Large-scale genetic analyses such as those associated with the Human Genome Project, which dealt

BOX 1 The Nuts and Bolts of the Polymerase Chain Reaction (PCR)

PCR is a method for amplifying specific segments of DNA many times prior to sequencing. Ingredients involved in PCR reaction mixture include (1) a target DNA sequence (i.e., a specific gene or part of it up to 40,000 base pairs long); (2) two sets of custom-made extension primers (very short DNA sequences) that bind specifically to one end of the target sequence on each of the two single strands—these primers are necessary for replication of the target sequence to occur; (3) a thermally stable DNA polymerase enzyme such as Taq (derived from *Thermus aquaticus*, a thermophilic eubacteria found in hot springs such as those in Yellowstone National Park) for replication of the target sequence; and (4) a supply of nucleotides, which are the building blocks of copies of genes as well as new strands of DNA. The PCR process then involves three steps: (1) denaturing or separating a double-stranded DNA molecule by heat; (2) annealing the extension primers to sites flanking the target sequence to be amplified; and (3) primer extension in which new strands containing the target sequence are created. In each round of the cycle, the amount of target sequence is roughly doubled in the reaction mixture. As a result, after about twenty cycles, the target sequence predominates in the mixture and can then be sequenced as nearly pure DNA.

with three billion nucleotides contained in about 19,000 genes, usually require supercomputers for their computations.

In 1992–93, I spent part of a sabbatical year working in the newly established molecular genetics lab at the University of Arizona. There I learned how to extract and amplify mtDNA from tiny tissue samples that had I collected from nectar-feeding bats during concurrent field work in Mexico, Venezuela, and Arizona. During that year I became very adept at using micropipettes to create the solutions used in DNA extraction and PCR. It was always very satisfying to see a small clump of pure DNA, looking like a wad of rubber cement, precipitate out of solution in a small test tube. But I left the sequencing of my PCR products to my friend Jerry Wilkinson at the University of Maryland. In subsequent years, my graduate students were able to complete the entire process from DNA extraction to its sequencing in a new lab at the University of Miami. This enabled us to conduct evolutionary studies of several species of plant-visiting phyllostomid bats from the West Indies, including the Bahamas, Venezuela, and Mexico.

I will finish the immense intellectual and technical journey that I've described in part one of this book by reviewing our current understanding of the evolutionary history of Darwin's finches based on molecular genetics and morphological data. This journey began with the discovery and naming of these birds, which started with the voyage of the *Beagle*. Shortly thereafter, the British ornithologist and bird artist John Gould examined Darwin's bird and mammal collections, which had been deposited at the Zoological Society of London. In papers published in 1837 and 1841, Gould described and named nine species of Darwin's finches, including a close relative, the Cocos Island finch. The other five species were named somewhat later; the final two species were named in 1897 by the American ornithologist Robert Ridgway.

I became interested in these birds as a college undergraduate when I read David Lack's (1947a) classic book *Darwin's Finches* for a class on evolution. David Lack (1910–73) was one of Britain's leading ornithologists of his generation. He spent five months in 1938–39 studying the behavior and ecology of Galapagos finches in the field and then as museum specimens at the California Academy of Sciences for half a year in 1939. His landmark book provides a thorough discussion of breeding behavior, interspecific competition for food (though he didn't actually determine diets in relation to food supplies), and speciation in these birds. His conclusion about their evolution was depicted in a relatively speculative and nonrigorous (by modern standards) evolutionary tree of these birds (fig. 2).

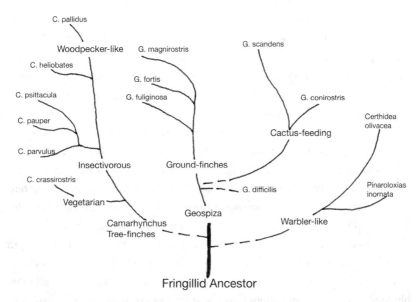

FIGURE 2 David Lack's suggested evolutionary tree (phylogeny) of Darwin's finches based on morphological similarities (or dissimilarities). This is an example of how phylogenies were portrayed prior to the emergence of DNA-based phylogenies in the latter part of the twentieth century. Redrawn from Lack (1947a).

After World War II, David Lack became the director of the Edward Grey Institute of Field Ornithology (EGI) at Oxford University, a post he held until his death in 1973. With Lack at its helm, the EGI became an internationally renowned center for the study of the ecology and behavior of birds. In 1977–78, I spent my first academic sabbatical there becoming immersed in the newly emerging field of behavioral ecology, which I wanted to apply to the study of tropical plant-visiting bats. I had a thoroughly enjoyable time working with John R. Krebs and Nick Davies, two rising stars of this new field. Shortly after my young family and I became settled in Eynsham, a small village outside of Oxford, I met Peter and Rosemary Grant, who were just finishing up a sabbatical at the EGI and were about to head to the Galapagos Islands for the beginning of their forty-plus years of studying Darwin's finches. The Grants had also been living in Eynsham, and to celebrate the end of their sabbatical, they invited Marcia and me, along with John Krebs and his wife and a few other Oxford couples, to join them in a farewell dinner. This meal typified the warmth that Oxford academics and friends often extended to their visitors.

As a coda to my Oxford sabbatical, many years later I reunited with Nick Davies, by then a distinguished professor of behavioral ecology at Cambridge University, on an Oxford-Cambridge trip to the Galapagos Islands in 2012. Nick was the resident naturalist on the trip, a post he had held on several previous trips, and gave us excellent lectures each night on Darwin's finches plus his own world-class research on bird behavior. It was wonderful to spend days with Nick and his grown daughter Alice exploring the islands and watching its amazing wildlife together. It was hard not to feel the presence of Charles Darwin on this excursion.

Our current understanding of the evolutionary history of these iconic birds, based to a large extent on the long-term research of the Grants plus their students and colleagues, is summarized in figure 3. This phylogeny is based on the sequences of two mtDNA genes. All recent molecular-based analyses indicate that these birds, along with the Cocos Island finch, form a monophyletic group (i.e., they all share the same common ancestor) and that the thin-billed warbler finch (*Certhidea olivacea*) is its basal or oldest member; the heavy-billed *Geospiza* ground finches are its youngest members. The biogeographic source of these birds has been the subject of much debate, but a recent phylogenetic analysis based on DNA sequences of one mitochondrial gene (cytochrome B) and morphology indicates, surprisingly, that these finches are members of a group of small seed-eating, finch-like birds from islands in the Caribbean. They are not simply immigrants from nearby South America. In addition to showing a high

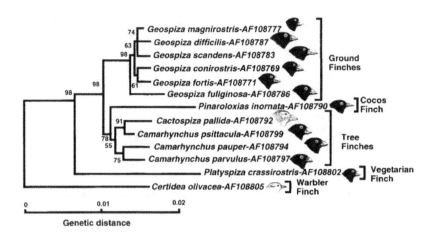

FIGURE 3 An mtDNA-based phylogram (i.e., an evolutionary tree) of Darwin's finches showing the degree of genetic similarity (or dissimilarity) between these species. Compare this diagram, which is from Sato et al. (1999), with that of Lack's evolutionary tree (fig. 2). Both diagrams agree that a warbler-like bird was basal in this group and that the *Geospiza* finches are the most advanced. But the DNA-based phylogram gives a much more precise picture of the degree of relatedness between species. The evolutionary position of the Cocos Island finch differs especially noticeably in the two trees. Figure courtesy of National Academy of Sciences, USA.

degree of genetic relatedness, these birds also share a unique (derived) behavioral trait: they all create domed nests for their eggs, a nest type that is unusual in birds. In addition, this group displays a higher degree of diversity in beak morphology than other related groups, suggesting that they have a particularly labile set of regulatory genes that code for beak development. Evolutionarily labile beaks and a propensity to island-hop apparently set the stage for the colonization and subsequent evolution of Darwin's finches.

In summary, the history of the Galapagos finches indeed involves a rather long journey in space—from Caribbean islands to the Galapagos (a distance of about 750 km)—if not in time. The Galapagos Islands are volcanic in origin and are known to be only about five million years old. So their finches can be no older than this. In fact, their radiation has probably occurred within the last 1.5 Ma, and to judge from the fact that hybridization is currently still occurring between some species, speciation in these birds is still an ongoing, incomplete process. Although Charles Darwin was unaware of the complex history of these birds, he certainly recognized their evolutionary significance once John Gould informed him of his taxonomic conclusions. And the rest, as the cliché says, is history.

2

IMMENSE JOURNEYS

An Exploration of the Natural History and Evolution of Some
of My Favorite Sonoran Desert Animals and Plants

A SENSE OF PLACE: EVOLUTION OF
THE SONORAN DESERT

I LIVE IN Tucson, Arizona, in the northeastern edge of the Sonoran Desert. The most subtropical of western North America's four deserts, this desert occurs in the southwestern United States, including the southwestern third of Arizona and adjacent California, and most of the Mexican states of Sonora and Baja California and Baja California Sur (map 1). It lies between the latitudes of about 27°–35° north and longitudes 110°–116° west. These latitudes are critical because they straddle latitude 30° north (the "horse latitudes") which is a region of descending dry air and high atmospheric pressure. High summer temperatures and little annual rainfall characterize these zones. Many deserts of the world occur at or near this latitude north and south. Annual rainfall in the Tucson area averages about 30 cm and occurs in two principal seasons: the summer monsoon with rain coming from warm tropical oceans (especially the Sea of Cortez) and winter rains coming from the cold Pacific Ocean. Prior to the onset of the monsoon (typically around July 4 in Tucson), summer temperatures can be very hot (sometimes > 40°C), winters are relatively mild and usually frost-free. As a result of its geographic location (which includes the Sea of Cortez and its many islands) and substantial topographic diversity, a high diversity of animals and plants occurs in this desert. People coming to the Sonoran Desert for the first time are often surprised to see how verdant and full of life many areas actually are. Its biodiversity currently includes about 130 species of mammals,

500 species of birds, and over 2,000 species of plants, including at least 4 species of tall columnar cacti.

To me, living in the Sonoran Desert is basically an aesthetic experience created by a pleasing combination of geological and biological features. On the geological side, the predominant landscape is the basin and range province—a series of granitic or volcanic mountains surrounded by desert flatlands. Tucson, for example, lies in a valley surrounded by four mountains: the Santa Catalinas to the north, the Rincons to the east, the Santa Ritas to the south, and the Tucsons to the west. This landscape gives one a feeling of vast vistas that contrast strongly with the much more restricted views of the landscapes I experienced growing up in southern Michigan and living for thirty years in southern Florida. Both of those regions lack significant elevational relief and broad vistas except at the edges of large lakes and the ocean where the only vista is that of a vast expanse of water.

But I'm not a geologist, and so my attention has always been focused on the biological features of this region. Driving east from Southern California along Interstate 10, for example, one suddenly encounters a dramatic new biotic landscape as soon as you enter Arizona. Widely spaced giant saguaro cacti rapidly appear in the landscape, creating a very low-density forest unlike any other found in North America. Scattered among the saguaros also at low density are many legume trees of rather short stature—scraggly mesquites, pale green palo verdes, and gray-green-canopied ironwoods. Whiplike ocotillos add to this strange landscape. Except for the saguaros, the open canopy of this forest is only a few meters tall. Much of the ground is bare and gravelly, but it also includes a low density of several kinds of opuntia and cholla cacti in addition to shrubs of various species, including creosote bushes. Closer inspection of these plants reveals that nearly all of them are well armed with spines or thorns, which makes moving through thick stands of this vegetation a very prickly business. Especially fearsome are patches of teddy bear chollas (*Cylindropuntia bigelovi*), those cute-looking but fiercely armed cacti. I've walked through those patches both day and night, each time holding my breath and stepping very carefully to avoid accumulating their loose stems on my shoes and pants. Spines and thorns present a strong warning of "Don't eat me" to mammalian herbivores, but some of them, including javelinas, mule deer, and pack rats, munch away anyway.

At first glance, animal life seems to be rather scarce in this habitat, but first impressions can be misleading. When you walk slowly through the desert in the spring, you gradually become aware of lizards dashing rapidly between plants;

songbirds and woodpeckers flying to and from their nests in shrubs, trees, sagua-ros, and even clumps of spiny chollas; hawks and vultures circling overhead or perched on saguaros; and rabbits and ground squirrels hopping or scampering away at your approach. With luck, you might even encounter several noteworthy reptiles, including the slow-moving desert tortoise, an extremely fast black-and-salmon-colored coachwhip snake, and a pink and black Gila monster waddling along. After dark, most kinds of snakes; a host of seed-eating rodents; several species of owls; and mammalian predators such as gray foxes, coyotes, and bob-cats become active.

In addition to changes in temperature and rainfall, seasonal biological changes in the Sonoran Desert are notable. These include colorful bursts of flowers in the spring, fierce lightning-filled monsoon storms in the summer, colorful fall foliage of sycamores and cottonwoods along intermittent streams, and occasional thin sprinklings of snow on the tops of mountains in winter. In some years of particularly wet winters, carpets of beautiful flowers cover the desert floor in the spring and create a Monet-inspired landscape. Yellows and oranges produced by brittlebush, desert marigolds, Mexican poppies, and globe mallows are the predominant flower colors at this time of the year. These colors reflect the high abundance and diversity of their major pollinators—native bees and non-native honeybees. Reds and pinks are produced by hummingbird-pollinated ocotillos and penstemons. And blues and purples produced by lupines and scorpion flow-ers attract a diverse array of insect pollinators. Among the desert trees, dull yellow or brilliant yellow flowers adorn mesquites and palo verdes, respectively, and flowers of ironwoods are delicate pink. Finally, saguaro cacti are covered with bouquets of large night-opening, creamy white flowers in May and June. At night these flowers are visited by nectar-seeking bats. During the day, they are visited by various species of bees and birds, including their major pollinators, white-winged doves.

Because of our relatively short lifetimes, geologically speaking, the world around us seems to be relatively unchanging and it may seem like the Sonoran Desert has always been where it currently is. But this, of course, is very short-sighted. From a geological perspective, Earth and its geological and biological features are always changing, as Robert Hutton and Charles Lyell had surmised in the eighteenth and nineteenth centuries. Most dramatically, we now know that Alfred Wegener (1880–1930), the German meteorologist and geophysicist, was right. After noting the potential jigsaw puzzle-like fit of certain continents (e.g., Africa and South America), he proposed in 1912 that continents move slowly around on Earth's surface. Continents are not fixed in space; over time they drift. Today, many lines of physical, geological, and geochemical evidence indicate that continental drift and its underlying mechanism is real and has been a crucial part of Earth's history for hundreds of millions of years. Complete acceptance of this, however, didn't really occur until the late 1960s while I was still in graduate school. I vividly remember the excitement that arose when fossils of *Lystrosaurus*, a dog-sized, large-headed reptile of Early Triassic age, were found in Antarctica. The occurrence of these fossils plus others, including *Glossopteris* plants and *Cynognathus* reptiles, in India, Africa, China, *and* Antarctica strongly suggested that certain continents had been much closer together some 250 million years ago than they are today.

Incidentally, it is ironic to note that my paleontological hero, George Gaylord Simpson, strongly dismissed the idea of continental drift for years. Indeed, many evolutionary biologists of his generation advocated that land bridges that have long since disappeared can account for faunal and floral resemblances between different continents. With continental drift, however, the existence of missing land bridges is no longer necessary to explain the distribution of life on Earth. On this topic, one of Simpson's Harvard colleagues, the entomologist Philip Darlington Jr. (1957, 606), wrote in *Zoogeography: The Geographical Distribution of Animals*: "I have tried to keep an open mind on this subject [continental drift] . . . to see if I can find any real signs of drift in the present distribution of animals. I can find none. So far as I can see, animal distribution now is fundamentally a product of movement of animals, not movement of land." But what about the distributions of ancient plants and animals? Do they not indicate that continental positions and connections have changed substantially through time? I'm happy to note that Simpson changed his mind about this near the end of his life.

In terms of Earth history, the current biological makeup and geographic extent of the Sonoran Desert is very young indeed. It's somewhere between about 9,000 and 4,500 years old. But many of its antecedents are much older; many of its plant lineages, for example, including legume trees and cacti, have deep historical roots within the new-world tropics and some have existed for all or much of the Cenozoic Era (i.e., the last 66 Ma). Tom Van Devender, a colleague of mine here in Tucson, is one of the leading students of the history of this desert. His research indicates that this habitat is dominated by a unique combination of legume trees (e.g., mesquites, ironwoods, and palo verdes) and columnar cacti and that many of its desert-adapted plants and animals probably evolved in the Late Miocene, circa 8 million years ago. During the Pliocene and Pleistocene (i.e., the last five million years), its areal extent expanded and contracted as a result of strong worldwide climatic fluctuations. Van Devender has suggested that tropical thorn scrub (TTS), rather than tropical dry forest (TDF), is the "mother" of the Sonoran Desert. TTS, with its plants of shorter stature than those found in TDF, developed along the Pacific coast of Mexico during the Miocene (about 15–8 Ma) after uplift of the Sierra Madre mountains restricted TDF, an older and geographically more widespread habitat, to Mexico's Pacific lowlands. More arid adapted than TDF, TTS was widespread over much of the area now covered by the Sonoran Desert during the Pleistocene, and it is likely where many Sonoran Desert plants, including columnar cacti such as organ pipe (*Stenocereus thurberi*) and senita (*Lophocereus schottii*) and tree ocotillo (*Fouquieria macdougalii*) evolved. Other plants likely evolved in the Sonoran Desert from ancestors deeper in Mexico; these include saguaro (*Carnegiea gigantea*), foothills palo verde (*Cercidium microphyllum*), and desert ironwood (*Olneya tesota*). Tropical thorn scrub currently occupies the lowlands in the eastern half of Sonora before being replaced by TDF in far southern Sonora. I worked with plants and animals in TDF, which occurs along the Pacific lowlands of Mexico and Central America, in northwestern Costa Rica for many years before switching to the Sonoran Desert in 1989. So in a sense, I was preadapted to feel comfortable in this vastly more open habitat.

An important source of information about the relatively recent vegetational history of the area now occupied by the Sonoran Desert comes from an unusual source—pack rat middens. These middens, which are well preserved in dry caves, are piles of sticky, viscous pack rat urine and feces that accumulate over many years, trapping and preserving plant and animal micro- and macrofossils such as pollen, seeds, leaves, and bones along the way. They can be carbon-dated and provide a time frame for changes in plant and animal communities going back about 50,000 years. Tom Van Devender studied these middens for his doctoral dissertation at the University of Arizona in the early 1970s. Interestingly, George Gaylord Simpson was on the faculty of the University of Arizona's Department of Geosciences at the time and was a member of Tom's doctoral committee. When I asked Tom about his impressions of Simpson, he said that he was short, had a beard, and walked with a cane; Simpson was in his early seventies at the time. Though he was soft-spoken, Simpson commanded a lot of respect as a scientific giant, according to Tom.

Analyses of pack rat middens indicate that from 45,000 to 11,000 years ago, the area currently occupied by the Sonoran Desert was covered by north temperate forests composed of pines, junipers, scrub oaks, and Joshua trees. They also indicate that by 11,000 years ago saguaro and the common shrub brittlebush (*Encelia farinosa*) were early members of the current Sonoran Desert and that many other species arrived to form desert scrub about 9,000 years ago as cooler-tolerant plant species retreated upland. The Sonoran Desert plant community that we currently live in dates from about 4,500 years ago. Finally, these middens reveal that during the Pleistocene, cool woodlands replaced desert lowlands in our area for about 90 percent of the time; the Sonoran Desert has occupied these lowlands for only about 10 percent of the time. With global warming, the southwestern United States is expected to become even warmer and drier than it currently is. If true, this will undoubtedly have a significant effect on the future success and distribution of our desert-adapted flora and fauna, as I discuss near the end of this book.

THE BIG PICTURE, BOTANICALLY AND ZOOLOGICALLY SPEAKING

Before we examine in detail the natural history and evolutionary history of certain Sonoran Desert animals and plants, I'd like to step back and briefly review the "gross" evolutionary histories of flowering plants (angiosperms) and three vertebrate classes, Reptilia, Aves, and Mammalia. These histories are based on the fossil record as well as on modern morphological and molecular genetic analyses. They provide the framework for more detailed accounts of the evolutionary histories of particular groups of plants and animals that follow.

THE RISE OF ANGIOSPERMS

Loren Eiseley's *The Immense Journey* contains a chapter titled "How Flowers Changed the World," in which he dramatically wrote: "Somewhere, just a short time before the close of the Age of Reptiles, there occurred a soundless, violent explosion. It lasted millions of years, but it was an explosion, nevertheless. It marked the emergence of the angiosperms—the flowering plants. Even the great evolutionist, Charles Darwin, called them 'an abominable mystery,' because they appeared so fast" (1957, 63). This "explosion" occurred in the Early Cretaceous, about 130 million years ago at a time when abundant fossil remains of these plants began to show up. Older Cretaceous rocks lacked any fossil evidence of angiosperms. Then they suddenly popped up everywhere. How could this happen? What did it say about Darwin's gradualist view of the pace of evolution? In his review of Darwin's correspondence with other scientists studying the evolution of angiosperms in the 1870s, William Friedman (2009), a botanist at the University of Colorado, wrote that it was the conundrum caused by the apparently rapid rise of angiosperms that was Darwin's "abominable mystery," not the emergence of flowering plants themselves.

In chapter five, Eiseley (1957, 63) continued: "Flowers changed the face of the planet. Without them, the world we know—even man himself—would never have existed." Insects, birds, and mammals all owe their existence, either directly or indirectly, to the evolution of the reproductive innovations of angiosperm plants. Prior to their rise, gymnosperms of various lineages were the dominant land plants. These lineages probably evolved from different ancestors but are united by the production of "naked seeds" that are borne unprotected on reproductive branches or in cones. In addition to seeds, gymnosperms were the first plants to produce pollen, the male sex cells that fertilize female sex cells (ovules) during pollination. Wind is the most common method of pollen dispersal in these plants. Angiosperms, in contrast, produce their seeds in protective vessels (*angeion* in Greek) that we call carpels or ovaries, which are part of the female structures in typical flowers. Pollen grains of angiosperms are produced by male structures called anthers that are usually found together with female structures in a typical angiosperm flower. Whereas some angiosperms rely on wind (or water) to disperse their pollen, the vast majority of them rely on animals, initially insects such as beetles, to move their pollen from one flower to another. It is important to note that the pollen grains of both gymnosperms and angiosperms have an extremely hard outer shell, the exine that is chemically very resistant to destruction. As a result, pollen grains and their exquisite architecture are extremely important in the fossil records of higher plants.

Currently including over 300,000 species, angiosperms first appeared in the fossil record in the Cretaceous Period about 145–100 Ma (but possibly much earlier). By about 95 Ma, they were the dominant plants on land, having replaced gymnosperms in many lowland tropical locations. Several life history features are thought to have given angiosperms an overall adaptive advantage over gymnosperms. These include insect pollination, rather than the more capricious wind pollination, that promotes genetic outcrossing; faster life cycles that promote rapid population growth; and small, easily dispersed seeds that promote rapid colonization of disturbed habitats.

The rise of molecular genetics in the 1980s has resulted in a rather detailed picture of the evolution of flowering plants. Beginning in 1998, the Angiosperm Phylogeny Group (APG), a worldwide consortium of systematic botanists, has endeavored to create a classification of the orders and families of angiosperms reflecting their evolutionary history. Four iterations of this classification have appeared (in 1998, 2003, 2009, and 2016). The third iteration (APG III) is shown in figure 4; APG IV is not much different from this version. Five major lineages occur in this classification. These include basal angiosperms (e.g., magnolias and avocados), monocots (e.g., bananas and orchids), basal eudicots (e.g., buttercups and cacti), and two groups of advanced eudicots, asterids (e.g., tomatoes and sunflowers) and rosids (e.g., roses and legumes). With eight orders and twenty-eight families, basal angiosperms, which is simply a group of families with many "primitive" floral features that don't necessarily share a common ancestor, contains the lowest taxonomic diversity and the two lineages of advanced eudicots, both of which are truly monophyletic groups, contain the highest taxonomic diversity (e.g., fourteen orders and 105 families in asterids and seventeen orders and 125 families in rosids).

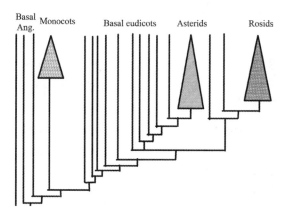

FIGURE 4 A diagram showing the evolutionary relationships between orders of flowering plants (angiosperms) based on APG III, which was published in 1999. Five major lineages are shown in this phylogeny (basal angiosperms, monocots, basal eudicots, asterids, and rosids). Monocots, asterids, and rosids are monophyletic (familes in their orders share a common ancestor) whereas the other lineages are not monophyletic. The three species of Sonoran Desert plants treated in this book are members of the basal eudicots (saguaro and desert mistletoe) and rosids (foothills palo verde).

The APG classifications do not contain a timescale that tells us when all of these orders and families first arose. For example, did most of the families in these lineages first evolve in the Cretaceous or did they first appear in the Cenozoic (i.e., within the last 66 Ma)? Ideally, ages of plant orders and families should be based on fossil evidence. However, as was true in Darwin's time but is certainly less true today, the fossil record of angiosperms is still somewhat spotty, so fossils alone cannot necessarily provide us with an accurate time line for the evolution of many groups of flowering plants. As a result, many botanists have turned to molecular genetics to provide this time frame. Reliance on molecular genetics alone to determine evolutionary ages can also be controversial, so its results must often be viewed cautiously. Nevertheless, in the PCR era, DNA sequences are much more common and more accessible than fossils, so it's not surprising that they have been used extensively to reconstruct the evolutionary histories of all kinds of organisms, including angiosperms. Whenever possible, however, molecular phylogenies are usually calibrated with fossil evidence.

Figure 5 shows the distribution of the estimated ages of 107 angiosperm families (of a total of 405; 26 percent) based on time-calibrated phylogenies that come from table 1.3 of our book *The Ornaments of Life* (Fleming and Kress 2013). These 107 families contain species whose pollen or seeds are dispersed by birds and mammals. This distribution has a single peak that occurs in the time

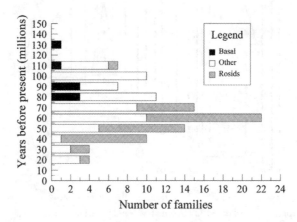

FIGURE 5 A diagram showing the estimated ages of 107 angiosperm families grouped by position in the APG evolutionary tree that provide flowers or fruit for plant-visiting birds and mammals. Figure 4 and data used to create figure 5 both come from Fleming and Kress (2013) with permission.

interval of 60–69 Ma, at the end of the Cretaceous Period and beginning of the Cenozoic Era (table 1). This distribution is quite symmetrical with fifty-two families appearing before 69 Ma and fifty-four families appearing after it. These data suggest that about half of this group of flowering plants had evolved by the Early Cenozoic Era. As might be expected, the few families of basal angiosperms in this group are older than most families of rosids, a more recently evolved group of plants. Nonetheless, by the Late Eocene Epoch (about 35 Ma), nearly all floras on Earth were basically modern in their flowering plant compositions.

So the immense journey taken by flowering plants has occurred over a time period of at least 130 Ma. And where did this journey begin? Because of the absence of angiosperms in the fossil record until late in the Early Cretaceous, Darwin suggested that they first arose and slowly evolved in a landmass that no longer exists, perhaps in the Southern Hemisphere. This idea, of course, has been discredited. With the recognition of plate tectonics and continental drift, we now have a picture of what continental distributions looked like when angiosperms were beginning to radiate in the Early Cretaceous. Late in the Triassic Period, at about 200 Ma and likely before angiosperms had begun to evolve, continental land masses were configured in two supercontinents: Laurasia (North America and Eurasia) in the north and Gondwanaland (South America, Africa, India, Australia, and Antarctica) in the south. By 145 Ma in the Late Jurassic, Gondwanaland had begun to break up as India and Australia-Antarctica separated from South America-Africa. By the end of the Cretaceous at 66 Ma, when angiosperms were radiating extensively, South America had begun to separate from Africa, but it still had a connection with Antarctica. India was drifting north toward the underbelly of Asia. For most of the Cenozoic, South America, like Australia, was an island continent and remained separated from North and Central America until about 4 Ma with the closing of the Panamanian Portal.

Now let's superimpose the biogeography of angiosperms onto these earth movements. In the early 1970s, it was thought that angiosperms first evolved in West Gondwanaland before Africa and South America had separated. Not surprisingly, with the discovery of more fossil material and many more detailed phylogenetic studies of plant families, the picture now is more complex. To be sure, many families likely evolved in tropical Gondwanaland, especially in Africa/South America. But many other tropical and subtropical families are now known to have had a Laurasian ancestry. Regardless of where they initially evolved, past and present distributions of all of these families are the products of several different processes, including vicariance (e.g., splitting of geographic ranges when continents such as Africa and South America drifted apart), long-distance overland migrations (e.g., between Eurasia and North America), and long-distance over-water dispersals (e.g., from Africa to South America and vice versa). As a result, current angiosperm families exhibit many different distribution patterns, including cosmopolitan distributions (e.g., the daisy family Asteraceae), pantropical distributions (e.g., the avocado family Lauraceae), and regional endemic distributions (e.g., the pineapple family Bromeliaceae in the New World). Despite being firmly rooted in the ground, angiosperms and other plants have displayed an impressive ability to move around on the face of the Earth. For flowering plants, much of this mobility has been provided by the evolution of modern groups of seed-dispersing birds and mammals beginning in the Late Cretaceous and Early Cenozoic.

THE RISE OF REPTILES

As a college undergraduate I had wanted to be a herpetologist, but I'm afraid I was born way too late. I missed the golden age of these vertebrates by hundreds of millions of years. Fossil evidence indicates that reptiles evolved from amphibians about 300 Ma. Amphibians, of course, were the first vertebrates to move onto land at about 365 Ma, but their reproduction has always been tied to water. As most school kids know, with the evolution of the shelled egg and its water-conserving amniotic membranes, reptiles were the first vertebrates whose reproduction was totally divorced from water. Among terrestrial vertebrates, they were also the first to "invent" internal fertilization. And of course they were the dominant land vertebrates in terms of abundance and size for about 200 million years—a most impressive degree of evolutionary success indeed. Plus we can't forget that reptiles (broadly defined here to include synapsids and true reptiles) gave rise to mammals about 200 million years ago and birds about 150 million years ago.

Many books celebrate the diversity of reptiles during the Mesozoic Era, and it is worthwhile to scan current dinosaur "encyclopedias" to see their wonderful recreations of what many of these fossil beasts large and small might have looked like in real life. These books give us a glimpse of how fantastic vertebrate life must have been like back then. Figure 6 provides an overview of the evolution of class Reptilia. A variety of early forms, including terrestrial pelycosaurs, therapsids, pareiasaurs, and captorhinids, were present in the Permian and Triassic Periods. Archosaurians (the "ruling reptiles" or dinosaurs) and Lepidosaurians (squamates—snakes and lizards) began to radiate in the Triassic. As a result, the Jurassic and Cretaceous Periods were times of high reptilian diversity. In addition to herbivorous and carnivorous dinosaurs, these periods also included marine kinds (e.g., plesiosaurs and ichthyosaurs) and winged fish-eating ptero-dactyls as well as early mammals and birds, turtles, crocodilians, lizards, and snakes. By the beginning of the Cenozoic Era, however, only mammals, turtles, crocodilians, birds, lizards, and snakes had survived.

Turtles have an extensive fossil record and have long been considered to be the oldest of living reptiles. Fossil turtles date from at least the Upper Triassic (about 207 Ma) when they had a cosmopolitan distribution across Pangaea. But recent molecular and morphological studies have challenged the evolutionary position of turtles as being among the most primitive reptiles. On the morphological side, turtles have always been considered to have anapsid skulls, that is, skulls that lack any openings in the temporal region. Fossil reptiles have traditionally been classified as having anapsid (no temporal opening), synapsid (a single tem-poral opening), or diapsid (two temporal openings) skulls. Mammals evolved from synapsid ancestors (therapsid and cynodont reptiles). And dinosaurs and squamate reptiles evolved later from diapsid ancestors. The progression from no to two skull openings is usually seen as a trend toward lightening the skull and providing more space for larger jaw muscles. But recent morphological work suggests that turtles actually have diapsid, not anapsid or secondarily anapsid, skulls and that turtles did not evolve long before archosaurs or lepidosaurs. In fact, molecular evidence suggests that turtles are the sister group of archosaurs, including dinosaurs, crocodilians, and birds. This rather radical repositioning of turtles in the evolutionary tree of amniote vertebrates is still controversial and will not be resolved without further research on both the morphological and molecular side of things. Despite all of this, turtles, currently classified in thirteen living families and 356 species, still plod or paddle along knowing that they've been around for hundreds of millions of years and are likely to continue doing so for the foreseeable future.

With over 10,000 species in about 58 families, lizards, snakes, and amphis-baenians (worm lizards)—the so-called squamate reptiles because they possess movable upper jaw bones—are classified in subclass Lepidosauria, which might be the sister group to the dinosaurs (subclass Archosauria) (but see above). Squamates separated from their lepidosaurian ancestors at about 169 Ma and thus have also had a long history. Based on fossil evidence, geckos are among the oldest lizards, first appearing in the Middle Jurassic along with skinks and snakes. These groups likely first evolved in Gondwanaland before dispersing worldwide. As seen in Figure 6, snakes, which are basically legless lizards, are embedded in the current phylogeny of squamates. Iguanian lizards, a large group in North America today, particularly in the arid southwest, appeared somewhat later, in the Cretaceous. Today and in the past, the highest diversity of both lizards and snakes occurs in tropical regions, and, as in many groups of plants and animals, their species richness decreases as latitude increases. Currently in North America, lizard diversity is highest in the more arid west and snake diversity is highest in the more humid east.

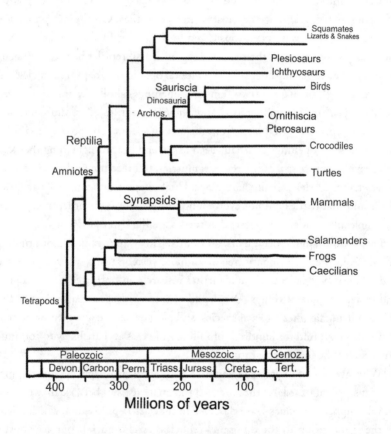

FIGURE 6 A recent phylogeny of the reptiles based on morphology and DNA data (wherever possible). This figure, which is redrawn from Pough et al. (2016, fig. 2.7), shows putative evolutionary relationships and the ages (in Ma) of these lineages. Abbreviations: Archos. = Archosaurians, Carbon. = Carboniferous, Cenoz. = Cenozoic, Cretac. = Cretaceous, Devon. = Devonian, Jurass. = Jurassic, Tert. = Tertiary, Triass. = Triassic.

We're all familiar with seeing images of the skeletons of huge dinosaurs and their relatives and paintings of what the Late Mesozoic world looked like when these behemoths wandered the world's landscapes and seascapes. But we need to remember that these fossils are likely to be a biased picture of what the vertebrate world actually looked like back then. We know from the frequency distributions of modern vertebrate faunas that small species far outnumber large species. This was also likely true back in the Mesozoic: small species of reptiles, including lizards and snakes, and also birds and mammals, likely outnumbered large species; the fossil record supports this. When dinosaurs and other reptiles died out, many more of the big ones with their huge appetites and large home ranges likely disappeared than the small ones with their more modest appetites and smaller spatial needs. Having lived in the shadows of large reptiles throughout the Mesozoic, most mammals were small. As Steve Brusatte says in *The Rise and Fall of the Dinosaurs*, "No mammal living with the dinosaurs got bigger than a badger. They were bit players in the Mesozoic drama" (2018, 247). But that was about to change in very dramatic fashion. Big dinosaurs lost, and small reptiles, birds, and mammals won in the lottery that is history of life on Earth.

This is because the evolutionary success of dinosaurs and many other kinds of reptiles, as well as many other organisms on Earth, unfortunately came to a violent end about sixty-six million years ago when a 10 km wide asteroid (or bolide) slammed into the Gulf of Mexico just north of the Yucatan Peninsula. Not for the first time, Earth suffered a cataclysmic event that caused widespread destruction on land and in the sea and that resulted in massive extinctions. The boundary between the Permian and Triassic Periods—the end of the Paleozoic and Mesozoic Eras—for instance, is marked by a time of violent volcanic eruptions that spewed large amounts of CO_2 into the atmosphere and massive amounts of molten lava across the land, resulting in another bout of mass extinctions worldwide. These dramatic events remind us that geological catastrophes—the kinds envisioned by Cuvier and many others in the seventeenth and eighteenth centuries—are an important part of Earth history. Uniformitarianism and catastrophism are not mutually exclusive processes. Both have had a profound effect on Earth's geological and biological history.

Like the acceptance of the reality of continental drift a decade earlier, the discovery of the cause of the Cretaceous mass extinctions, beginning in the late 1970s, is another example of a recent groundbreaking insight into Earth history. In her book *The Sixth Extinction*, Elizabeth Kolbert (2014) describes how the American earth scientist Walter Alvarez, working near Gubbio, Italy, discovered the element iridium (Ir) in a half-inch layer of white clay sandwiched between layers of limestone rocks that marked the end of the Cretaceous Period and the beginning of the Cenozoic Era (the so-called K/Pg boundary). This clay layer was highly enriched with Ir, a scarce element on Earth but one that's common in meteorites. Soon thereafter, Ir-rich clay samples at the K/Pg boundary were also discovered in Denmark and New Zealand. Working with his father, the noted physicist Luis Alvarez, and H. Asaro and H. Michel, Walter Alvarez (1980) published a paper in *Science* titled "Extraterrestrial Cause for the Cretaceous-Tertiary Extinction" based on an "impact hypothesis." This hypothesis proposed that sixty-five million years ago a large asteroid hit Earth with the energy of about one hundred million megatons of TNT, spewing Ir-rich dust around the world and setting fire to many terrestrial ecosystems. In addition to incinerating much of the terrestrial world, this dust also caused a worldwide "nuclear winter" featuring a prolonged period of dark, cloud-filled skies and cooler air temperatures.

This hypothesis, like that of Wegener, was initially met with widespread scorn from geologists and paleontologists. For example, in 1980 George Gaylord Simpson wrote that faunal turnover at the K/Pg boundary was a part of "a long and essentially continuous process"—clearly a uniformitarian point of view. (Sorry, but wrong again, George!) Over the next eleven years, however, further geological evidence emerged supporting this hypothesis. Finally, in 1991 the site of the asteroid collision was discovered (actually, it was rediscovered) near Chicxulub, Mexico, in the form of a 160 km wide crater under the northern Yucatan Peninsula. As a result of this impact and its aftermath, all dinosaurs (except birds and crocodilians) as well as most families of turtles, snakes, lizards, ancient birds, and mammals disappeared. By the luck of the draw, however, some organisms survived to create a brave new world. We wouldn't be here today if this catastrophe had not happened, just as the Permo-Triassic extinctions set the stage for the rise of dinosaurs. But one still has to wonder, when is the next geological catastrophe scheduled to occur? It was, after all, the fifth of Earth's known mass extinctions. The current elevated extinction rate of Earth's species is now being attributed to the rise and worldwide dominance of *Homo sapiens* and is being called the Sixth Extinction. But this doesn't preclude the occurrence of yet another geological catastrophe, does it?

Finally, I listen to Pandora radio, mostly jazz but also some pop, while processing my photographs. I find that two pop songs basically wrap up the events that occurred at the K/Pg boundary and its aftermath. In "Fire and

Rain" James Taylor alludes to cloudless days without end. However, that's not the scenario that emerged after the asteroid impact—quite the opposite: fire and rain. But, on a more optimistic note, in "Feeling Good," Anthony Newley and Leslie Bricusse write that it's a new day and a new life (for the survivors of this cataclysm).

THE RISE OF BIRDS

It has only been recently accepted that birds are really just feathered dinosaurs. With the recent discovery in China and elsewhere of ever-more-detailed fossils of early birdlike reptiles and reptilelike birds, it is now clear that birds evolved "from the ground up" from bipedal dinosaurian (theropod) reptiles in the Late Jurassic Period (around 150 Ma). Their current body plan of feathers covering a lightweight skeleton plus their high metabolic rates, internally produced body temperatures, and advanced cognitive abilities powered by large brains evolved over a period of about one hundred million years. Figure 7 shows some of the major anatomical features associated with this evolution during the Mesozoic Era. This scenario suggests that many of the advanced morphological features of birds (e.g., a hinge-like ankle, vaned feathers, and a wishbone) were acquired gradually and first appeared in dinosaurs, not in birds. It has even been suggested that certain well-feathered bipedal dinosaurs were likely able to fly (at least to a limited extent).

All living birds—over 10,000 species in about 200 families—and their recent ancestors are included in Neornithes, the so-called crown group containing all current families. This group contains three successively younger monophyletic lineages: Palaeognathae (tinamous and flightless ratites—ostriches, rheas, etc.), Galloanserae (geese, ducks, and gamebirds), and Neoaves (all other birds) (fig. 8). Among Neoaves, the order Passeriformes (songbirds) alone contains about 60 percent of all avian species in about 140 families and 6,000 species. The bulk of these three groups radiated rather quickly after the K/Pg boundary, perhaps from shorebird-like stock that managed to avoid extinction resulting from the asteroid impact. Given their current southern continent distributions (i.e., Australia, Africa, and South America), palaeognaths have long been thought to have evolved in Gondwanaland as it was breaking up. But recent phylogenetic studies dispute this, suggesting that flighted ratites evolved elsewhere before becoming flightless in Gonwanaland. Recent phylogenetic reconstructions based on DNA and morphology also suggest, surprisingly,

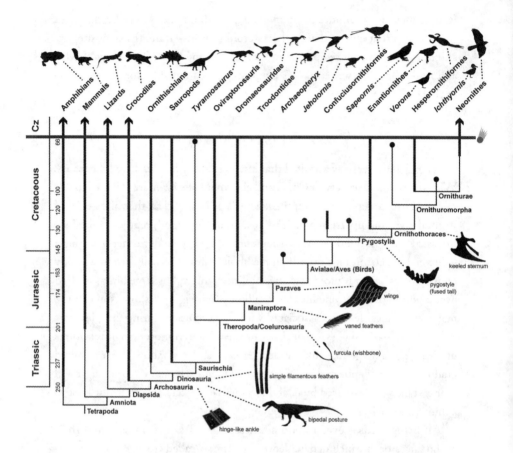

FIGURE 7 A simplified dated phylogeny of tetrapods showing the appearance of morphological features that characterize birds, showing that a number of important avian characteristics (e.g., hinge-like ankles, a furcular [wishbone], and vaned feathers) predate the evolution of true birds. From Brusatte, O'Connor, and Jarvis (2015) with permission.

that raptors and parrots may have been the birds that gave rise to the Passeriformes, which first evolved in the Australo-Pacific region about 47 Ma. From there passerines dispersed into Asia, Africa, Europe, and eventually North America, beginning in the Early Oligocene (ca. 34 Ma). Whether they dispersed into South America through Antarctica or from North America is currently under debate.

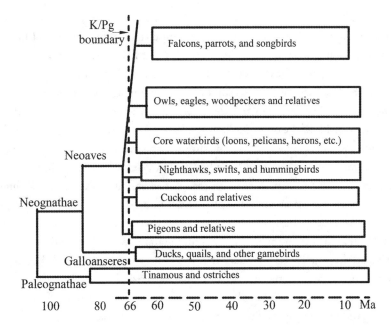

FIGURE 8 A highly simplified and dated genome-based phylogeny of modern birds, showing their three major divisions (Palaeognathae, Galloanseres, and Neoaves). The time line (in millions of years, Ma) is not to scale. Based on Jarvis et al. (2014).

THE RISE OF MAMMALS

If birds are just feathered dinosaurs, I suppose it's logical to assert that mammals are just hairy, milk-producing therapsid reptiles. In Darwin's time it was blasphemous in some circles to claim that humans are the direct descendants of apes. I fear that it's even more blasphemous to claim that we're really just brainy reptiles—second cousins only about several million times removed. We've had an immense journey through time from our synapsid forebears, indeed. Along with their sister group Sauropsida, which ultimately gave rise to the dinosaurs, early synapsid reptiles dominated the land worldwide during the Permian and Early Triassic Periods. Their dome-shaped skulls were characterized by a single temporal opening behind the eye socket and canine-like teeth; they probably preyed on amphibians and fish. Many groups of synapsids evolved in the Permian only to perish at the Permo-Triassic boundary, but an advanced group, the therapsids, survived and eventually gave rise to more mammal-like cynodont reptiles in the Late Triassic. In some therapsids, there was a change in the shape of the limb girdles that resulted in a significant change in the position of limbs from a sprawling position as found in turtles and lizards today to a position where the limbs were held closer to the body, as found in mammals. In cyno-donts, which are the direct ancestors of early mammals, skulls became more elongated and their large jaw muscles attached directly to the braincase rather than to the inside of the outer skull. By the Late Triassic, true mammals of small size (20–30 g) and characterized by dentition that was differentiated into molars and premolars and an enlarged brain had evolved. As we have seen, throughout the Mesozoic Era, mammals were generally small and lived amid an expanding array of dinosaurs of an enormous variety of body sizes and locomotory and feeding adaptations. Early mammals were endothermic insect eaters, had some ability to climb, and probably were nocturnal and hence color-blind. It wasn't until just after the K/Pg boundary that modern groups of mammals began to appear. At this time, in the absence of many marine and terrestrial reptiles, the stage was set for mammals (and birds) to begin to fill a wide variety of ecological niches. And both groups did this in rather rapid and spectacular fashion.

Currently, there are nearly 6,000 species of mammals classified in about 150 families. Rodents (order Rodentia with about 33 families and 2,300 species) and bats (order Chiroptera with 18–21 recognized families and 1,240 species) are the two most species-rich groups of mammals. Though they are not closely related, both rodents and bats likely first evolved in Asia (i.e., the former Laurasia) in the Paleocene and Eocene Epochs, respectively.

An overview of the Cenozoic mammalian radiation is shown in Figure 9, which is based on molecular data from living mammals and morphological data from both living and age-calibrated fossil mammals. This phylogeny shows that the earliest true mammals date from about 165 Ma in the Middle Jurassic. Living mammals are placed in the well-known sequence based on reproductive modes of egg-laying monotremes followed by the pouched marsupials and a diverse array of placentals; the latter two groups date from about 65 Ma. A recent recon-struction of an early placental mammal shows a squirrel-sized, fully furred ani-mal with a long, furred tail. Its skull is rather pointed, and its jaws are lined with well-differentiated incisors, canines, and molars; it was an insect eater. Among placentals, new-world armadillos, sloths, and their relatives occur at the base of this radiation followed by radiations within three major groups: Afrotheria (containing the orders of elephant shrews, aardvarks, hyraxes, elephants, and sirenians), Euarchontoglires (containing the orders of tree shrews, flying lemurs,

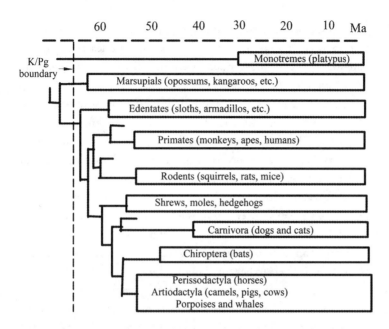

FIGURE 9 A highly simplified and dated phylogeny of orders of mammals based on molecular and morphological data, including the three traditionally recognized groups of mammals (monotremes, marsupials, and placentals [from edentates on]). Among the placentals, three major groups of orders are now recognized (Afrotheria, Euarchontoglires, and Laurasiatheria). See the text for the orders that occur in these three groups. Based on O'Leary et al. (2013).

primates, lagomorphs, and rodents), and Laurasiatheria (containing the orders of true shrews, pangolins, carnivores, bats, odd- and even-toed ungulates, and whales). Most of the orders and families in these three groups radiated explosively early in the Cenozoic.

WELCOME TO SOME OF MY FAVORITE SONORAN DESERT VERTEBRATES

Given its very young geological age—no more than about eight million years—it's not surprising that the fauna of the Sonoran Desert, except among certain reptiles and mammals inhabiting islands in the Sea of Cortez, doesn't contain a large number of endemic species whose distributions are limited only to this habitat. I'm not a botanist, so I find it daunting to attempt to identify the endemic plants in this biome in a flora of several thousand species. But by perusing range maps found in field guides to southwestern U.S. reptiles and mammals (e.g., *Amphibians and Reptiles in Arizona* and *The Mammals of Arizona*) as well as *The Birds of Sonora*, I have a pretty good feel for how many biome-restricted vertebrates live in the mainland Sonoran Desert. The bottom line is that there aren't many species of higher vertebrates whose ranges are restricted *solely* to this biome whereas there are many desert-adapted species whose ranges include the Sonoran Desert as well as the other North American deserts such as the Chihuahuan, Mojave, and Great Basin Deserts. In the case of its higher vertebrates, therefore, it is probably better to think of the U.S. Southwest and parts of northwestern Mexico as a relatively large region that has promoted the evolution of many arid-adapted animals in the past 15 Ma (i.e., since the mid-Miocene) or so. I assume the same is likely to be true about its flora.

In appendix 2, I provide a representative list of species of reptiles, birds, and mammals that are resident, at least seasonally in the case of many birds and a few mammals, in the Sonoran Desert as well as their migratory status, general geographic distributions, and current conservation status. This list does not include the many species of birds that merely pass through this region en route to their northern breeding or southern wintering grounds. It includes 33 species of reptiles, 50 species of birds, and 28 species of mammals. As expected, none of the reptiles are migratory, and most (82 percent) live exclusively in arid habitats. Among the birds, 14 species (28 percent) are migratory, and 25 (50 percent) occur in arid habitats. In mammals, 8 species (29 percent) are migratory, and 16 (57 percent) occur in arid habitats. Overall, 68 of these 111 species (61 percent) are associated with arid habitats, at least during their breeding seasons. These include most lizards and small species of birds and mammals. Widespread species of birds and mammals—the habitat generalists—tend to be larger in size than the arid habitat species. I will deal with the conservation status of these species later in the book. As a final comment, it is striking to me that most of these species are small: the largest reptile, the desert tortoise, is only about 380 mm long and only weighs up to about 2.2 kg; the largest bird is the great horned owl with a weight of about 1.4 kg; and the largest mammal is the mule deer weighing up to about 182 kg. During the Pliocene and Pleistocene, western North America had many more large vertebrates than it does now, some of which undoubtedly lived in arid lands. These included giant tortoises, large vultures, ground sloths, mammoths, mastodons, large carnivorous cats, bears, and wolves, as well as several species of horses, camels, and pronghorn antelopes. But most of them had disappeared by about 12,000 years ago. Causes of these extinctions—climate change and/or the hand and weapons of man?—have been widely debated for decades.

Before we begin to examine the lives of a series of Sonoran Desert animals and plants in detail, I want to step back once more to look at yet another "big picture" view of life on Earth. My theme for this interlude comes from a song by Jerome Kern and Oscar Hammerstein II from their 1927 Broadway show *Showboat.* Lyrics from "Can't Help Loving That Man of Mine" state that, as we all know, fish have to swim and birds have to fly.

What do these commonplace observations mean to you? To me, they point to the very obvious fact, which I'm sure we usually take for granted, that we live on a "Goldilocks" planet full of liquid water in which fish can swim and with a relatively dense atmosphere in which birds can fly. Water was where life first evolved. Without water, which only occurs in a liquid state in the relatively salubrious temperature range of 0°C–100°C, life as we know it would not exist. Water currently does not exist in a liquid state on our neighboring planet Mars, whose average surface temperature is a frigid -63°C compared with a balmy 14°C here on Earth. All living organisms on Earth contain lots of water. The water content of our bodies, for example, varies with age and gender and ranges from about 79 percent in infants to about 55 percent in adult females. Liquid water is obviously scarce in places like the Sonoran Desert, and as we will see, acquiring and conserving it is extremely important for organisms that live there.

Continuing with our brief comparison of physical differences between Earth and Mars, where some brave humans appear to be headed in the not-too-distant future, atmospheric pressure on the Red Planet, whose diameter is about one-half that of Earth, averages only a puny 7.5 millibars compared with a hefty 1,013 millibars at sea level on Earth—a 135-fold difference. Based on air density, the difference is about 170-fold. Although atmospheric pressure and air density on Earth decrease with increasing altitude, our atmosphere is still dense enough to allow an Airbus A320 jetliner weighing about 77,000 kg at takeoff to fly at a speed of 904 km/h at an altitude of 11.9 km. This airplane has a wingspan of about 34.1 m. Out of curiosity, I once asked Doug Altshuler, an expert on bird flight, what a hummingbird's wingspan would have to be for it to be able to fly on Mars. After a series of calculations, Doug's answer was that a Martian 4 g hummer would need wings that are about 58 cm long and 14.5 cm wide; for comparison, the wing length of a 4 g male broad-billed hummer is about 5.2 cm.

With a 58 cm long wing, however, our Martian hummer would be too large to hover, so it wouldn't really be a hummingbird at all. Aside from hummingbirds, Doug calculates that a 4 kg bird (about the size of a Canada goose) on Mars would have to have wings about 580 m long to be able to fly in its atmosphere! Needless to say, an Airbus A320 with an appropriate wingspan will never exist on Mars. Neither will hummingbirds and Canada geese!

A final major difference between Mars and Earth that has important biological consequences is the composition of their atmospheres. The Martian atmosphere contains 95.3 percent CO_2, 2.7 percent nitrogen, and 0.13 percent oxygen compared with 77 percent nitrogen, 21 percent oxygen, and 0.04 percent CO_2 on Earth—an enormous difference. Active multicellular life requires substantial amounts of oxygen for its metabolism, and hence it likely didn't begin to evolve on Earth until its atmosphere reached its current level of 21 percent O_2 about 500 Ma. With its current atmosphere, multicellular life cannot exist on Mars (without supplementary O_2). So why would anyone want to go and live there? With my lifelong fascination with reptiles, birds, and mammals, I certainly wouldn't.

To recap the obvious, we live on a planet that for much of its existence has been extremely favorable for the evolution of life. Its favorable features have changed (i.e., evolved) over time—for example, mean air temperatures and CO_2 levels have varied substantially through time and glacier-filled landscapes have come and gone—and continue to do so currently. Nonetheless, as a result of Earth's salubrious conditions, a truly amazing variety of organisms have lived here under a wide variety of physical conditions for almost four billion years. Since the mid-Miocene, deserts and other arid lands have presented a special series of challenges, including the low availability of water and extreme (summer) temperatures, for life on Earth. Let's now examine how some of my favorite Sonoran Desert animals and plants cope with these challenges. I used many Wikipedia accounts to obtain a general overview of each of these species and the evolutionary histories of their families before exploring the vast scientific literature that deals with them. One important source of detailed information about many species of birds is the website https://birdsoftheworld.org, which is operated by the Cornell University Laboratory of Ornithology. Individual accounts of many species of mammals can be found in the Mammalian Species series produced by the American Society of Mammalogists. I'm not aware of any comparable comprehensive biology-based websites for reptiles, but see the Reptile Database for accounts of the taxonomic histories of thousands of species of reptiles.

SONORAN DESERT REPTILES

With their scaly, nearly waterproof skin and low metabolic rates, reptiles would seem to be ideally suited for living in the desert. And this is certainly true. The herpetologist Eric Pianka, for example, has reported that the Earth's most diverse lizard fauna occurs not in any rainforest but in the Great Victoria Desert of Western Australia, where rainfall is erratic and averages 200–250 mm annually. Up to fifty species of lizards can occur together in the same habitat there compared with only six to seventeen species in desert or semidesert habitats in North America and the Kalahari Desert of southern Africa. I've chosen to highlight the lives of six representative Sonoran Desert species in this section: the desert tortoise, desert spiny lizard, tiger whiptail lizard, Gila monster, gopher snake, and western diamondback rattlesnake. I've had extensive contact with some, but not all, of them and have chosen them because they illustrate the range of adaptations and evolutionary histories found in some of the reptiles in this region. The same is true in my treatment of Sonoran Desert birds and mammals below.

DESERT TORTOISE

Gopherus agassizii (Cooper, 1861), Testudinidae. With adult females and males weighing 1.6–2.2 kg, this is one of the largest reptiles currently living in the arid Southwest. To the best of my recollection, I've only encountered one individual of this species in my desert fieldwork. This was in early May 1997 on a gravelly hillside in Organ Pipe Cactus National Monument in southwestern Arizona. Our contact was brief— only long enough for me to get down on the ground and take its photograph. We then went our separate ways—at vastly different speeds, of course. None probably live as free-ranging individuals in my neighborhood in the suburbs of northwestern Tucson, but a couple of our neighbors have adopted one or more of them through a program administered by the Arizona-Sonora Desert Museum. "Agnes" belongs to my neighbor Courtney and her family. Agnes has been in captivity with three different owners for over sixty years.

Thus, because she was already an adult when she became a captive, she might be as old as eighty years (a couple of years older than me!). Courtney tells me that Agnes sleeps from October to June and is then active, though she now seems to be slowing down a bit (as I am). Until recently Agnes was quite "playful"—I'm sure the definition of *playful* differs strongly for tortoises and puppies—and interacted with people. She produced seallike barking sounds and had a strong preference for junk food (i.e., kale, apples, and pears) rather than prescribed desert tortoise food. Given that her body is shell-bound, however, she'll probably never become obese on this diet.

This species has been the subject of many field and captive studies and its life history is very well known. A long-term study of desert tortoise behavior and ecology in far southwestern Utah published in 1948 gives us a good picture of many features of its life history. This study was conducted at the northeastern limits of this species' geographic range at a site in the Great Basin Desert whose sparse vegetation is dominated by Joshua trees and creosote bushes. In ten years, 281 tortoises were marked and recaptured over eight hundred times. From hatching, these animals are digging machines that have strongly scaled, spatulate front feet and elephant-like hind feet that they use to create two kinds of burrows. They generally spend the cool months (October–April) in extensive dens that can be 10 m long and house up to seventeen adults. During the warm/hot months, single individuals avoid high temperatures by resting in shallow burrows scattered around their home ranges. Although individuals of both sexes and all ages sometimes interact aggressively, primarily by biting and pushing, when they encounter each other, they are not territorial. At the Utah site, home ranges of both males and females overlapped with each other and averaged 4–40 ha in area; female ranges were smaller than male ranges. Within and outside their home ranges, all individuals have intimate knowledge of the locations of communal dens and burrows, sources of food (generally grasses and other green vegetation, including the red fruits of opuntia cacti), water (periodically available after rains), and mineral concentrations (needed for electrolyte balance). With an annual adult mortality rate of about 1 percent, these are exceptionally long-lived animals, so it is not surprising that they know their environments very well.

Avoidance of high air and substrate temperatures and dehydration are the major physical challenges these tortoises face during their active season. While moving about at this time of year, their body temperatures range from 25°C to 35°C and are close to surface temperatures. As ground and air temperatures increase during the day, they retreat to their cool, humid burrows to avoid over-heating and to reduce water loss via respiration. When they aren't estivating (sleeping) for long periods in their burrows during the summer, they become nocturnal. During their active season, they obtain much of their water from the vegetation they eat and store excess water in their large bilobed bladder; they conserve this water by urinating infrequently. Periodic rainfall is also import-ant for their water balance. During droughts they can lose up to 40 percent of their body mass, and the concentrations of chemical ions such as sodium and potassium in their blood and bladder fluids become elevated. When rainwater becomes available, they quickly drink copious amounts and empty their bladders of uric acid-rich water; ion levels in their bloodstreams return to normal, and excess newly acquired water is again stored in their bladders.

Reproduction is likely foremost on the minds of these tortoises as they leave their winter dens in the spring. During the active season, males are constantly looking for sexually receptive females. During courtship, males follow scent trails left by females to their burrows where they bite and ram them. During courtship females are always subordinate to males, and if they are being courted by more than one male, they will usually choose to mate with the largest one. Size and advanced age do have advantages for males in this species. Male size also matters in encounters with other males. Larger males are usually dominant over smaller males. I'll leave the actual tortoise mating act to my readers' imaginations, but it's probably not much more exciting than mating in elephant seals, which I've photographed several times. In the case of elephant seals, just picture passive sex in the midst of flying sand with a one-ton male holding a much smaller screaming female down with its trunk. Once they've mated, female tortoises dig a nest near a burrow or den in which they deposit a single clutch of four to five eggs; larger females produce larger clutches. Depending on amounts of rainfall and vegetative growth, females will produce up to three clutches a year in some populations. Gila monsters are avid egg eaters and actively search for tortoise (and bird) nests. Females are known to defend their nests against these lizards.

Compared with birds and mammals, which have sex-determining chromo-somes, reptiles play it pretty fast and loose with some aspects of reproduction, including the sex ratios of clutches of eggs and with the expression of sex or gender itself (see the tiger whiptail lizard account below). Regarding the sex ratio of clutches of eggs, turtles, most of which along with crocodilians lack sex chro-mosomes, are well known for the occurrence of environmentally determined sex ratios (EDR). The occurrence of EDR in clutches of crocodilians suggests that this might have also occurred in at least some dinosaurs. In turtles, the general saying is "Hot chicks and cool dudes" which means that clutches laid in warmer-than-average sites produce more (or only) females than males whereas the opposite is true for cooler than average nest sites. In crocodilians, males are hot and females are cool. In reptiles, long-lived taxa such as turtles and crocodilians are more likely to exhibit EDR than genetically determined sex ratios (GDR). The opposite is true in short-lived taxa such as lizards and snakes.

Sex expression in desert tortoises is environmentally determined. Experiments have shown that only males are produced in clutches incubated at 26°C–30.6°C whereas only females are produced in clutches incubated at 32.8°C–35.3°C. The "switch point" at which one sex or the other is produced is about 31.8°C. In addition, soil moisture at the incubation site influences hatchling survival. Hatchlings from nests incubated in dry sand at 28.3°C–33.0°C had higher survival rates than those incubated in dry sand at either 26°C or 35.3°C; hatchling survival from nests incubated in wet sand was lower at all temperatures. These results have important ecological and conservation implications. The sex ratios of hatchlings clearly depend on decisions made by females about potential nest sites. If they choose warm sites, their clutches will yield only females whereas they will yield only males from cool sites. Furthermore, soil moisture of nest sites can strongly influence hatchling survival. Therefore, to maximize their production of both males and females, it would seem that females should be choosy about where they lay their eggs. They cannot afford to pick only warm or cool sites to attain this goal. But because they are potentially very long lived, the decisions females make about "good" nest sites in any one year might not affect their lifetime production of both sexes. Placing their nests in a variety of different microclimatic sites each year (i.e., bet hedging) might be the best overall strategy for them.

The conservation implications of EDR in turtles are profound. Moving clutches of eggs to "safe" locations, as has been done many times for certain sea turtles (Chelydridae), can have unwanted results. For example, for many years the famed University of Florida herpetologist Archie Carr ran a conservation program for green sea turtles (*Chelonia mydas*) at Tortugero Beach on Costa Rica's Atlantic coast. To protect freshly laid clutches from predators such as raccoons, coati mundis, and humans, the eggs were removed from warm sunny beach sites and placed in cool, sandy soil in the shade. This was done before EDR was known to occur in turtles. As a result, this act of kindness produced only males (this was unknown because baby turtles are difficult to sex at hatching), and for years researchers were left to wonder why fewer and fewer adult females were returning to this beach to lay their eggs each year. Adult males always remain out to sea and mate with females as they travel to their nesting beaches. Being aware of the EDR situation, turtle conservation programs now take great care in how and where they incubate clutches of eggs.

What is the fate of desert tortoise nests and newly emerged hatchlings? Mortality rates tend to be high in the young of most animals, but the question remains, how high is it in this long-lived species? A two-year study of the fate of tortoise nests and hatchlings at a desert site in Southern California revealed that the diminutive kit fox (*Vulpes macrotis*), which can enter dens or burrows searching for nests, were major egg predators and destroyed 47 percent and 12 percent of nests in the two years; a total of 55 percent and 16 percent of eggs were destroyed. Surviving hatchlings weighed about 20 g at emergence and had soft shells that don't become completely ossified until tortoises are about five years old. Survival probability of these neonates was about 88 percent from hatching until they dispersed to their winter dens. Normally, new hatchlings are preyed upon heavily by ravens, but this was not the case in this study, though ravens were always present in the area. Their cryptic coloration and a tendency to hide under vegetation or in burrows that they've dug contribute to the high survival rate of these potentially vulnerable youngsters.

Finally, I should mention that desert tortoises have something in common with saguaro cacti (besides their ability to store water and being long lived): they both provide shelter and homes for many kinds of animals. As a result, both of these species provide important ecological services for other species in their ecosystems. In the case of desert tortoises, for example, their dens and burrows provide shelter for many insects and vertebrates, including many kinds of lizards and snakes such as Gila monsters and rattlesnakes, and mammals such as kangaroo rats, spiny pocket mice, and pack rats as well as rabbits and skunks. I don't think that it's a stretch to view saguaros and desert tortoises as "arks" for desert animals. They may not provide shelter for all of the desert's animals, but the ones they do shelter are often ecologically important members of their communities.

Turtles are an ancient group. Their fossils, even early ones, are unmistakable, and have been so since the mid-Triassic (ca. 228 Ma). A recent molecular genetics-based phylogeny of many species of turtles from all families and calibrated with many fossils indicates that their two major monophyletic lineages—Pleurodira (side-necked turtles) and Cryptodira (hidden-necked turtles, including tortoises)—first evolved in Gondwana and Laurasia (in the Oriental Region), respectively. This occurred as the supercontinent Pangaea was breaking up in the Early Jurassic Period. The family Testudinidae dates from the Late Cretaceous (ca. 74 Ma), and its ancestral home included the Oriental Region plus North America. The desert tortoise G. *agassizii* is a comparative youngster in its family, having evolved in North America from Oriental ancestors during the Miocene (ca. 18 Ma). In terms of its long-ago roots in Laurasia, tortoises and their ancestors have indeed had an immense evolutionary journey. Generally slow moving and exceptionally long lived, these animals are currently distributed across most of the world except Australasia. Collectively and individually, they have experienced much of what life on Earth has had to offer for tens of millions of years, and the end of their story is nowhere in sight.

Galapagos tortoises (*Geochelone nigra*) are also members of Testudinidae, and because they fascinated Charles Darwin, it is of interest to briefly recount their history. In the Pleistocene, giant tortoises like G. *nigra*, which can weigh up to 400 kg and be 1.9 m long, occurred on all continents except Australia and Antarctica. Sadly, owing to human exploitation, they now occur only on remote islands in the Indian Ocean and the Galapagos. Recent genetic analyses based on mtDNA indicate that this species originated in southern South America and split from its closest relative, the arid-adapted G. *chilensis*, some six to twelve million years ago. *Geochelone nigra* apparently colonized the Galapagos Islands by rafting from South America two to three million years ago. This is possible because these tortoises float well with their heads raised above water, and they can survive for long periods without feeding. The subsequent history of this tortoise in the Galapagos is complex and has resulted in the evolution of fifteen genetically and morphologically distinct taxa (subspecies) of which eleven still exist. Their two major morphological groups include the saddlebacks—tortoises with long necks and saddle-shaped shells—and the domed forms with short necks and more typical tortoise shells. The saddlebacks usually occur on small arid islands where their long necks help them feed on the pads and fruits of tree cacti. The domed kinds have shorter necks and live on larger islands amid lusher, more easily reached vegetation. Interestingly, at an age of about eighteen million years, our relatively small Sonoran Desert tortoise (G. *agassizii*) is much older than the giant Galapagos tortoises, whose current island home did not exist prior to about five million years ago.

DESERT SPINY LIZARD

Sceloporus magister Hallowell, 1854, Iguanidae. This rather large and handsome lizard is a member of family Iguanidae, a family containing eleven subfamilies, at least 700 species, and a worldwide distribution. Its subfamily, Phrynosomatinae, is endemic to North America, including Mexico, with a few species in Central America; it contains about 120 species. *S. magister* is one of the most common lizards in my neighborhood and has been a regular resident on our back patio since we moved here in 2008. About 142 mm long and weighing about 12 g, males are rather chunky and have very prominent keeled scales, a black band on their shoulders, and a bright blue-green throat patch and blue lateral patches during the breeding season. Females are slimmer, lighter brown, and less strongly marked.

Starting in the spring of 2016 through the summer of 2019, I began seeing regularly an adult male that I dubbed "Big Boy" on our patio close to the house. I know this was the same individual every year because of its appearance (its tail was regenerated) and, most convincingly, its behavior. It always hung out in the same spots day after day and year after year. If it wasn't near our patio's water faucet, where he began each morning after emerging from the space between a large cement planter and the wall of our house, I could find him across the patio sunning himself on a series of low bricks enclosing another set of plants. In both places, he would occasionally do a series of "push-ups" to signal to anyone watching that this was his territory. Our backyard is divided into two walled patios: an inner one near the house that is shaded by two very large Chilean mesquite trees and an outer, more open one that includes our swimming pool and a gazebo. Big Boy's territory only included the inner patio; he never tried to annex the outer patio where at least one other male spiny lizard lived into his territory.

Desert spiny lizards have been reported to be monogamous, and I'm pretty sure (in the absence of definitive paternity analysis data) that this was the case with Big Boy. An adult female, much shyer than her mate, would perch regularly on the large planter above Big Boy's favorite display site near the water faucet. She rarely ventured out into the patio away from the planter. Like Big Boy, she always used this same perch site year after year. This species is known to mate in the spring and summer and lay one or two clutches of up to a dozen eggs each. I never saw this pair mating. A few hatchlings would appear on the patio in the late summer, but they'd soon disappear. Our yard was never "crawling" with baby desert spiny lizards.

The social structure of this and many other species of *Sceloporus* lizards involves males that patrol territories during the breeding season, often giving deep push-up displays during and after changing locations; these displays are directed at both males and females. Females typically use shallow push-ups and head bobs as visual displays. During the breeding season, males chase other males and sometimes briefly wrestle with and bite them. They court females with deep push-ups while exposing their colorful throat and lateral patches. Females "sidle-hop" away from displaying males if they are sexually unreceptive. During the nonbreeding season in the summer and fall, these hormone-driven behaviors in males decrease in frequency. In all of these activities, these lizards strike me as being little robots, especially in comparison with the hyperactive migrant warblers that pass through our yard each spring. In 2020 Wilson's warbler with its jaunty black cap and shiny black eye set against a bright yellow face was the main migrant. In most years, the common migrants are yellow-rumped warblers. Regardless of species, these small birds are always quickly moving around the canopies of our two large mesquite trees looking for caterpillars and other insects while on the patio below the spiny lizards spend long periods of time doing nothing (except scanning) before quickly running to a new spot, doing a few push-ups, and then doing nothing again.

Within their territories, desert spiny lizards are sit-and-wait predators rather than being "always on the move" predators like whiptail (teiid) lizards. They often perch on trees while looking for prey and descend to the ground to grab their next meal. But I never saw Big Boy perch on the big mesquite tree near his favorite patio perch site. When he wasn't doing push-ups, Big Boy was always on the lookout for insect prey (and presumably also for mates, competitors, and predators). When he spotted a potential prey item in the middle of the patio or elsewhere, he would dash out and grab and swallow it whole. Through time, Big Boy seemingly became very comfortable around us as we sat in our shaded patio chairs and drank our morning coffee or ate our lunches. He would often approach and watch us with a gimlet eye. I was tempted to buy mealworms to feed him but never did, thinking that I didn't want him to become too dependent on an apparently endless food supply.

As I describe in the gopher snake species account, in 2017 two species of snakes (a gopher snake and a pair of common king snakes) began to use an upraised part of the cement patio floor near our house as a den site pretty much year-round. We seldom saw the gopher snake but saw the king snakes occasionally going into and emerging from this den. One lunchtime in 2018, we were watching Big Boy moving around the base of the mesquite tree near us when a king snake emerged from the den and began heading straight toward him. It kept getting closer to Big Boy who had moved behind a large flowerpot. I watched in fascination as the king snake actually touched the lizard's tail with its tongue and feared that Big Boy's days were finally over. But not to worry. When he was touched, Big Boy simply sprinted away and the snake didn't attempt to pursue him. This little drama struck me as though both animals knew each other, perhaps because they were neighbors, and thus had a special nonaggression pact. Why else would a king snake pass up a perfectly good meal? After all, they are certainly known to eat lizards as well as rattlesnakes.

As winter approached each year and days became cooler, lizards and snakes in our yard disappeared into their dens only to reemerge again in the spring. And for at least four years, I always looked forward to seeing Big Boy again each spring.

Lizards and other reptiles, of course, are cold blooded or more technically correct, they are *ectothermic*. This means that their body temperature is determined by external heat sources such as the sun or the substrate on which they are resting and not from their internal metabolism as in endothermic birds and mammals. As a result, their body temperatures and metabolic rates are positively correlated with ambient temperatures. There certainly are advantages and disadvantages to this kind of metabolism, the most common kind in almost all forms of life on Earth. I discuss this topic in more detail below. But on the plus side, the energy budget of an ectothermic lizard is only about one-tenth that of a similar-sized bird or mammal. As a result, it doesn't necessarily have to continually search for food. The occasional consumption of a large insect or caterpillar larva, which Big Boy did, will suit it just fine as a source of energy, nutrients, and water. And sporadic feeding exposes it less often to predators such as snakes, hawks, and roadrunners. On the negative side, it's at the mercy of the environment to maintain a high enough body temperature to be active. Lizards often shuttle between sunny and shady spots to regulate their body temperatures, and many studies have shown that lizards have preferred body temperatures, presumably one that optimizes conduct of their daily activities. I never measured Big Boy's body temperature but assume that it was probably stable during his diurnal activities because he spent time basking in the sun and retreating to shady areas among our plants every day. When perched on tree trunks, these lizards only have to move small distances between sun and shade to maintain a stable body temperature.

A major challenge for desert-dwelling organisms is water conservation and so it is of interest to know how water stressed a lizard such as *S. magister* is. Reptiles in general have a variety of means of conserving water that serves them well in arid environments. In addition to a relatively impermeable scaly skin, which is still a site of some water loss, these include the excretion of uric acid rather than urea to rid themselves of harmful nitrogenous wastes, production of dry feces, and temperature regulation. Produced by reptiles and birds, uric acid has low solubility in water and hence is a more efficient way of excreting nitrogenous waste products than urea, the main water-soluble nitrogenous waste product of mammals. While actively regulating their body temperatures, lizards can avoid desiccating conditions by moving from sunny spots to shade. A major source of water (and perhaps the only one) for many species of desert lizards is their insect food. Results of an experimental study examining survivorship and water loss in five species of North American arid-land lizards (four iguanids—desert iguana [*Dipsosaurus dorsalis*], zebra-tailed lizard [*Callisaurus draconoides*], fringe-toed lizard [*Uma scoparia*], and western fence lizard [*Sceloprorus occidentalis*]—and one teiid—tiger whiptail [*Aspidoscelis tigris*])—indicated that the four species living in deserts (i.e., all except *S. occidentalis*) were able to survive at 30°C either with food and water or with only food. These results showed that they were able to maintain water balance from food alone. Presumably the same is true for *S. magister*.

What is the sensory world of a lizard like? To what extent is it cognizant of the sights, smells, and sounds of its environment? Unlike snakes, lizards have external ears, so presumably they can hear airborne sounds to some extent. They can also detect substrate-produced sounds (vibrations) of approaching (large) animals, as snakes can. But, unlike birds, these kinds of lizards don't produce audible sounds, so they're not likely to communicate among themselves by sound alone. For example, when I was in the Galapagos among large groups of marine iguanas, the soundscape there was silence except for the crash of waves on the rocky shore. No grunting or snorting as you can hear, for instance, in a pond full of hippopotamuses.

Many lizards use scent for social communication. To detect chemicals, they have vomeronasal organs (like snakes and most other lizards) in the roof of their mouths, olfactory surfaces in their noses, and chemically sensitive tongues. Tongue anatomy in lizards (and snakes) is related to their foraging style.

Sit-and-wait predators such as desert spiny lizards and many other iguanids have thick, fleshy tongues whereas active hunters such as whiptail lizards (see below) and snakes have flexible, forked tongues. Because they sample scents by licking substrates or flicking their tongues, this mode of communication is obviously a very short-distance one in contrast to long-distance visual displays. Many iguanids have two sets of scent-producing glands: femoral glands located along the ventral surface of their thighs and proctodeal (anal) glands. Scent production by these glands occurs in males during the breeding season; female glands appear to be far less active than those of males year-round. Experiments with the western fence lizard (*S. occidentalis*) have shown that males will react by licking or tongue flicking to secretions obtained from male but not female glands and placed on sterile surfaces. After licking a scent-labeled surface, they do their characteristic push-up, even in the absence of any visual cues. The implication here is that males, but possibly not females, can mark their territories with scents like many mammals do. Because they are sit-and-wait predators, they do not use scent to find prey.

By far the most important sensory mode of *S. magister* and most other iguanids is vision, which is a long-distance detection and communication method. These lizards have keen eyesight—Big Boy could see small insects from many meters away—and color vision. Males have brightly colored patches on their throats, bellies, and sometimes their backs; they are much more colorful than the more cryptically colored females. Experiments have shown that *Sceloporus* males react to other brightly colored conspecifics (either males or artificially painted females) in an aggressive fashion whereas they undergo courtship displays to individuals (either females or artificially painted males) that lack bright colors. As a result, these lizards are constantly scanning their environments visually, looking for food, mates, competitors, and predators. And both males and females regularly undergo push-up displays. Their worlds are primarily visual.

Desert spiny lizards are one of eight species of *Sceloporus* in Arizona. A total of twenty-two species of this genus is found in the United States, and many additional species occur in Mexico and Central America as far south as Panama. Overall, the genus contains about eighty-six species and is one of the most speciose groups of lizards in North and Central America. A recent DNA-based phylogeny of *Sceloporus* and its close relatives indicates that basal members of the genus, *S. couchii* and *S. parvis*, are from central Mexico and that most species of the genus are located in Mexico. Close relatives of *S. magister* occur in Baja California. Judging from its advanced position in the clade of phrynosomatid iguanian lizards (i.e., the subfamily that includes horned lizards, *Sceloporus*, and members of the genus *Uta*), this genus evolved in Mexico in the mid-Eocene (ca. 42 Ma), and *S. magister* likely evolved in the mid-Miocene (ca. 15 Ma). Most members of the genus, including *S. magister*, are oviparous (i.e., egg layers), but advanced members are either ovoviviparous (females retain eggs and give "birth" to their young) or are actually live bearing (viviparous and without retained eggs). Ovoviviparous and viviparous species occur at high elevations in the tropics and subtropics and have a reproductive cycle involving fall mating, winter gestation, and spring births rather than spring matings and summer births found in oviparous species.

In summary, the desert spiny lizard's evolutionary journey has been rather modest in space (only from central or northern Mexico) and but not necessarily in time (from the emergence of desert scrub in the mid-Miocene). Many members (but certainly not all) of its clade are currently associated with arid or semiarid habitats in the northern Neotropics from Panama to southwestern Canada and have been so for tens of millions of years.

Finally, since I'm interested in highlighting the methods that are currently being used to study the evolutionary history of species as well as the results of those methods, I will briefly describe the nuts and bolts of a broad study of the evolution of phrynosomatid lizards published by John Wiens and his collaborators in 2012. This study sought to determine how climate (principally, annual rainfall) and evolutionary history interact to determine geographic patterns of species richness in this monophyletic clade. To do this, they first created a time-calibrated phylogeny of this group using DNA sequence data from eight nuclear genes and five mitochondrial genes for a total of 10,394 "characters" (nucleotides) from each of 137 species. Their time calibration was based on three dated fossils. Next, to determine the geographic ranges of these species and the climatic conditions within those ranges, they used two extensive online sources. Geographic range data came from online location records of preserved specimens in dozens of U.S. and foreign museum collections. And climatic data came from World-Clim (https://www.worldclim.org), a World Wide Web database of many climate variables from locations all over the world at a resolution of 1 km^2.

A study of this depth and magnitude could not have done a couple of decades ago because this amount of sequence data could not have been easily obtained and online access to museum records and extensive climate data did not yet exist. My bottom line here is that evolutionary history studies and hence our understanding of evolutionary processes have increased enormously in recent years. Charles Darwin started the ball rolling in this scientific endeavor in 1859 and just look at how far we have come since then. But better yet, think about how much more we will learn in the coming years. For one thing, studies of the entire genomes containing tens of thousands of genes and hundreds of thousands of nucleotides from a steadily growing number of species from throughout the evolutionary tree of life will give us an unprecedented look into the action of and interaction between specific genes that are involved in all of life's activities, including its evolution. On the downside, younger colleagues have told me that they find it hard to convince their advanced undergraduate and graduate students to go out in nature and study actual animals or plants anymore. Instead, they'd rather work in the lab with their DNA, often from tissue collections obtained by previous generations of field biologists (like me). How ironic will it be that as species disappear from the natural world, only their DNA will remain in frozen tissue collections in the world's museums (which are themselves becoming endangered)?

TIGER WHIPTAIL LIZARD

Aspidoscelis (formerly *Cnemidophorus*) *tigris* (Baird and Girard, 1852), Teiidae. This species is a member of another common family of lizards—Teiidae, the whiptails—that today occurs only in the new-world tropics and subtropics. Its sister family is Lacertidae, the most common group of lizards throughout the Old World, except Australia. Teiids and lacertids are not closely related to iguanian lizards and differ from them in many biological features. These include a long, slender body form, a long tail, small granular body scales, eyelids, strong legs, a preference for open habitats, and an active foraging lifestyle. Teiidae currently contains about 150 species in eighteen genera.

The tiger whiptail is a medium-sized whiptail (total length to 110 mm, mass about 17 g) with dark mottling and no longitudinal stripes on its back and sides. Males and females basically look alike, but the throats of males are mottled or solid black. Several individuals of this species lived on our back patio when we moved into our Tucson house in June 2008. But their numbers have declined since then to the point that it is now unusual to see one foraging in our backyard on a regular basis. They are not uncommon in our neighborhood, however. Despite my limited contact with them in Tucson, I've chosen to discuss this lizard because its lifestyle and that of its relatives contrasts very strongly with that of the desert spiny lizard.

Although I couldn't watch them closely at home, I regularly encountered whip-tails in my Sonoran Desert research. They were always moving quickly through my study area, foraging for insects or other small prey on the ground, around rocks, under litter, and among the roots of plants. They were also always very wary and quick to escape at my approach, so most of my contact with them consisted only of fleeting glimpses. This was also my experience with *Ameiva* lizards, another common genus in the Teiidae that is closely related to the *Aspidoscelis*/*Cnemidophorus* clade in tropical dry forest in Costa Rica. Ameivas were very common, rummaging around in the litter looking for insects and always on the go like the Energizer Bunny. But again, I only had a passing acquaintance with them.

Reproductively, the tiger whiptail is a typical lizard. It reproduces sexually with mating occurring in the spring and summer; females produce one or two small clutches of one to five eggs each year. But the really interesting thing about reproduction in whiptails is that six of the eleven species of Arizonan whiptails have given up sex altogether. Populations of these species (e.g., the Sonoran spotted whiptail, *C. sonorae*) contain only females, and they reproduce parthenogenetically; the babies are genetic carbon copies of their moms. This asexual mode of reproduction raises a fascinating evolutionary question: why give up sex with its obvious advantage of producing genetically variable offspring, especially useful in a changing world, to produce genetically invariable offspring? One obvious advantage of asexual reproduction is that females don't have to share space and resources with males, and they're not going to be hassled by males about sex. Another advantage is that the female population growth rate of an asexual species is theoretically twice as high as that of females in a sexual species. Furthermore, asexual species have greater potential to successfully invade new habitats because it only takes one individual to do this. But the question still remains: Are these advantages great enough to override the advantages of sexual reproduction? Furthermore, how do asexual species arise?

Asexual reproduction—parthenogenesis—is not uncommon in many groups of plants and animals, but it is not particularly common in higher vertebrates. In lizards, for example, it is only known to occur in certain geckos, lacertids, and skinks in addition to teiids (and not in iguanids). It rarely occurs in birds and never in mammals. Its occurrence and evolution in lizards have been widely discussed in recent decades. In the case of *Cnemidophorus* lizards (I will use this older name here to reflect its widespread use in the older literature), parthenogenetic species (technically they are considered to be "biotypes" because their individuals cannot interbreed) tend to be concentrated in the floodplains of the Rio Grande valley in New Mexico. More generally, parthenogens tend to occur in the major drainage systems of the southwestern United States. They usually occur in different habitats—often frequently disturbed habitats such as floodplains—than their bisexual progenitors.

In teiids, chromosomal and genetic analyses have indicated that unisexual species are produced when two sexual species hybridize. For example, unisexual *C. uniparens*, which is a grassland species living in central Arizona and along the Rio Grande in New Mexico, is the product of matings between two bisexual relatives, *C. inornatus* and *C. gularis*. Whereas both sexual species are diploid (i.e., they have two copies of every chromosome just as we do), the unisexual hybrid *C. uniparens* is triploid (i.e., it has three copies of each of its chromosomes) as a result of hybridization and then genetic backcrossing with *C. inornatus*. Its triploid daughters are produced from eggs that do not undergo meiosis, the process that normally produces haploid eggs and sperm in bisexual species. In certain unisexual species (e.g., *C. tesselatus*) both diploid and triploid forms are known as a result of matings between different sets of bisexual species, including the tiger whiptail.

Comparison of the mtDNA of unisexuals and their bisexual progenitors has been used to estimate the evolutionary ages of unisexuals. These analyses reveal that unisexual species are always very young, usually much less than one million years old. The implication here is that unisexual species come and go through time. Their persistence often depends on how long they can occupy disturbed habitats before they are outcompeted by or hybridize with bisexual species. Another indication that unisexuals are short lived, geologically speaking, is that none of them are known to have produced new unisexual species. That is, they have never begun to undergo an adaptive radiation.

Given their propensity to wander widely, whiptail lizards tend to occupy larger and more loosely defended territories during the breeding season than *Sceloporus* lizards. Field and experimental studies of these lizards indicate that they are generally active between 10:00 a.m. and 5:00 p.m. on most days during spring and summer; that this activity pattern is determined by an internal circadian rhythm; that when active they operate at relatively high body temperatures (36°C–41°C); and that they have definite thermal preferences determined by soil or other substrate temperatures. Despite living in somewhat different habitats, related bisexual and unisexual species usually have similar thermal preferences that differ from other such species groups, suggesting that the thermal niches of these lizards are inherited in conservative fashion.

Because of the absence of males, usually the more aggressive sex in many lizards and other reptiles, we can ask whether social relationships among individuals are the same or different in populations of unisexual and bisexual species. Are aggressive interactions such as biting and chasing more common in bisexual populations than in unisexual populations? Experiments addressing these questions have shown that, as expected, aggression is in fact more common in bisexual populations and that linear, dominance-based social hierarchies occur more often when males are present. When feeding in the presence of other unisexuals, unisexual individuals are infrequently hassled whereas this is not the case in groups of bisexual lizards; males, of course, are the hasslers. Furthermore, high intensity fights involving tumbling and biting were never seen in groups of unisexual individuals whereas they were common, especially when males were present, in groups of bisexuals. Overall, social relationships among whiptails are strongly influenced by degree of relatedness (much higher in unisexual populations) and the presence (or absence) of males. Unisexual populations are basically more pacific than bisexual populations. Field observations of populations of unisexual and bisexual species confirm these results: far less aggression occurs in the former kinds of species than in the latter ones. This makes one wonder about the evolutionary value of males. Except as sperm donors, what good are they? But please read on!

A final aspect of social relationships in populations of whiptail lizards is the reproductive response of females in the presence and absence of males. In bisexual species such as tiger whiptails, it is known that male courtship accelerates egg development and ovulation in females. But what happens in populations of unisexuals? It turns out that some reproductively inactive females in at least three unisexual species are known to exhibit "pseudosexual" behavior in which they court and mount reproductively active females the same way that males do in bisexual species. This male-like behavior also accelerates ovulation in unisexual females. It therefore appears that successful reproduction in populations of unisexual whiptails is facilitated by male-like sexual behavior on the part of some of its females.

Whiptail lizards and other teiids are active hunters whereas many iguanid lizards (e.g., *Sceloporus magister*) are sit-and-wait predators. Differences in these foraging modes should have important consequences for energy expenditure and rates of food acquisition in these two groups. A comparison of the daily energy expenditure and food intake between 16 g *A. tigris* and the 9 g zebra-tailed iguanid lizard (*Callisaurus draconoides*) confirms this. Energy expenditure of *A. tigris*, which spent 90 percent of its day actively foraging, was about twice as high as that of *C. draconoides*, which spent only 2 percent of its day in active movement. As a result, *A. tigris* consumed about 2.3 times more food per day than *C. draconoides*. It would be interesting to know if these two foraging modes result in different risks of predation. Are active foragers more heavily preyed upon than sit-and-wait foragers?

The evolutionary history of the *Aspidoscelis/Cnemidophorus* clade of teiid lizards has been the subject of several recent studies using molecular genetics and morphological data. Based on the fossil record and phylogenetic studies, the family Teiidae first evolved in South America in the Paleocene (about 65 Ma) and radiated there during the Eocene (about 45–40 Ma) as grasslands, their major habitat, began to expand. Cretaceous fossils of apparent teiids are also known from Romania and Mongolia, which suggests that this family may once have had a wider distribution than it currently has. Nonetheless, the clade including *Aspidoscelis/Cnemidophorus* evolved in South America in the Late Oligocene/Early Miocene (about 24 Ma) and dispersed to Central America in the Late Miocene (about 6 Ma). A detailed phylogenetic analysis of *Aspidoscelis* lizards suggests that the closest relatives of *A. tigris* include *A. guttatus*, *A. deppii*, and *A. hyperythrus*. These species occur either in central or southeastern Mexico (to Costa Rica in *deppii*) or Southern California and Baja California (*A. hyperythrus*). So *A. tigris* probably evolved in Mexico, not far from its current home.

In summary, the evolutionary journey of the tiger whiptail and its relatives began tens of millions of years ago in South America and ultimately ended up in Mexico and the southwestern United States within the last few million years. A notable feature of this journey has been the evolution of parthenogenetic (unisexual) taxa that currently represent about one-third of the "species" in the genus *Aspidoscelis*. This group of unisexual species is very young geologically speaking; they will likely have high extinction rates and are probably very short lived.

GILA MONSTER

Heloderma suspectum Cope, 1869, Helodermatidae. At a length of up to 560 mm and weighing up to about 700 g, this is the largest lizard in the United States. It is one of only two species in the new-world family Helodermatidae, which occurs in the southwestern United States, Mexico, and Central America as far south as Guatemala. With their stocky bodies, bead-like dorsal scales, and pink and black coloration, these lizards are easily recognizable. This family contains the only poisonous lizards in the world. Their poison glands are modified salivary glands located in the lower jaw, and their venom is delivered through grooved hollow fangs in the lower jaw. The venom is a mixture of peptides, enzymes, and toxins that can cause internal bleeding, among other effects. Although envenomation can be painful, it has rarely resulted in death in humans.

The name "Gila monster" comes from the Gila River basin in Arizona and New Mexico where it was once common. To early settlers of this region, I suppose this unusual lizard might have seemed like a monster, but it's really quite innocuous except when threatened and standing its ground before fleeing. Its scientific name is Greek: *Heloderma* means "studded skin" and *suspectum* reflects the fact that its scientific describer, Edward Drinker Cope, thought that it might be venomous. This wasn't known in 1869.

I've never encountered one of these unmistakable lizards in my neighborhood but have crossed paths with them a few times in the spring during my desert fieldwork and on hikes around Tucson. Although these lizards might appear to be rather sluggish, given their stocky build and relatively short sprawly legs, I've always been surprised by how quickly they can move when trying to escape from my seemingly nonthreatening approaches. As a result, I've never been able to get a decent photograph of them in the wild. An exception to this occurred on my first morning in Tucson before starting my first desert field season in Sonora, Mexico. While having breakfast on the patio of my host, the late Dave Hardy Sr., near Sabino Canyon, a gorgeous male Gila monster waddled up to us and calmly posed for his portrait. This was entirely appropriate because Dave, whom I had first met in Costa Rica three years earlier, was an avid professional-level herpetologist, though he was actually an anesthesiologist. Dave indicated afterward that this individual often visited him on cool spring mornings.

Like desert tortoises, Gila monsters spend most of their lives (90 percent or more) underground and out of sight. So encountering them above ground is fairly uncommon. Although they can appear above ground at any time of year, they're most active in the spring before the desert heats up. This is when they are in hunting mode. They're always on the lookout for eggs, whether they are reptile (e.g., desert tortoise) or bird's eggs. A friend once sent me a video clip of a Gambel's quail nest that he was monitoring in his garage. The clip showed a Gila monster slowly approaching the nest and then beginning to devour its eggs. Joe shooed the lizard off before it could consume the entire clutch. Although they spend most of the time moving around on the ground, they actually are competent climbers of bushes and trees and will go after bird's nests and their nestlings in trees. They're also dedicated consumers of any vertebrate that they encounter, including lizards, snakes, birds, and mammals. They've been known to eat prey as large as small rabbits.

Given their largely inactive lifestyle, Gila monsters don't need to eat many meals to meet their annual energy needs. It's been reported that they only need to eat four or five times a year to obtain enough food to store as fat in their large tails to last them through the year. In their book *Lizards: Windows to the Evolution of Diversity*, Eric Pianka and Laurie Vitt recount an amusing story that illustrates just how long these lizards can stay underground without feeding. They wrote: "A spectacular example of these lizards' capacity to go dormant took place in Arizona in the 1960s when an instant city called 'Sun City' was built in the Sonoran Desert. For a couple of years this small town received no appreciable rainfall, and residents irrigated their lawns and trees with groundwater pumped from deep below. When massive August rains finally did fall, Gila monsters began popping out of the ground in people's yards: they had been buried underground, inactive, living off the stored fat in their tails during the first few years of the city's existence!" (2003, 242). I guess this incident might be enough to convince some people to believe in spontaneous generation!

So how does this colorful lizard go about its daily activities and annual cycle? And how can this be monitored? Surgically implanted radio transmitters with long-lasting batteries that provide information about an animal's location and body temperature can be used to answer these questions in this relatively large lizard. Radio transmitters were in their infancy when my colleagues and I began to glue small ones to the backs of fruit-eating bats to study their foraging behavior in tropical dry forest (TDF) in Costa Rica in the mid-1970s. A lot has changed in this technology since then, and radio telemetry, including satellite-based telemetry, is now used routinely to study the lives of all kinds of animals in terrestrial and marine habitats all over the world.

In one field study of Gila monsters, three individuals were implanted with radio transmitters and a total of twenty-seven individuals were marked by toe clipping. They were studied for three years in a sandy canyon 2 km^2 in area in the Mojave Desert of southwestern Utah. Prey eaten by these animals included eggs of desert tortoises and mourning doves and young individuals of several mammals (e.g., desert cottontails, ground squirrels, and rock squirrels). Two large lizards weighing about 650 g each were seen eating 160–210 g of rabbits in one feeding—a large meal indeed and an example of binge feeding in this lizard.

As in desert tortoises, shelters are important in the lives of Gila monsters. Most shelters used by these lizards in the Utah study were located in rocky areas and were natural cavities that they sometimes enlarged by digging; they also sheltered in desert tortoise dens and pack rat nests. Body temperatures of these ectotherms while resting in shelters varied seasonally and ranged from about 12°C in the winter to about 27°C in the summer. When active away from shelters, their body temperatures averaged about 29°C, quite low for reptiles. Body temperatures of active tiger whiptails, for example, are about 40°C. Although several individuals sometimes used the same shelter either together or at different times, they did not overwinter in communal dens as desert tortoises do. Although Gila monsters are major predators of the eggs of desert tortoises, these two species sometimes inhabit the same shelters. These lizards are more likely to shelter with female tortoises than with male tortoises, raising the question, Why do female tortoises allow Gila monsters to share shelters with them? Are these species involved in some kind of mutualistic relationship in which the lizards provide protection for female tortoises and their nests in return for some (but certainly not all) of their eggs? Given the small clutch sizes of these tortoises, however, even the loss of one egg per clutch to Gila monster predation would seem to be a stiff price to pay for this putative protection.

Gila monsters are active for only a few hours during the day in March through May and again in October and November; they are mostly active around sunset in June through September. When active they don't move very far from their shelters—about 200 m but occasionally up to 1 km or more in the Utah study. Their top speed of movement is a whopping 0.25 km/hr. Sizes of home ranges of the three radio-tagged lizards in that study ranged from about 6 ha (in a female) to 63 ha (in a male) and overlapped extensively, as in desert tortoises. When males encounter each other, they interact in a very stereotyped fashion involving head displays, pushing, and straddling with the "superior" individual being on top. These interactions occur in slo-mo; they can last for several hours; and they apparently serve to establish dominance relationships. As in desert tortoises, the larger (stronger?) of two males usually "wins" these encounters. Scent marking by cloacal rubbing, a kind of chemical communication, around shelters by males has also been observed. This communication mode is known to allow individuals to identify each other and to assess their reproductive status in many animals. The occurrence of struggles for dominance and scent marking in males suggests that these basically solitary animals have a loose kind of social organization in which males at least know their status in relation to other males in the population.

Gila monsters, like all other desert animals, must maintain a safe body temperature (i.e., one that is neither too hot nor too cold) and conserve energy and water if they are to survive. How do they do this, and more importantly, how do modern physiological studies determine this? As we've seen, body temperatures can be measured directly via telemetry with temperature sensitive radio transmitters applied either inside or outside of an animal's body. But measuring rates of energy use (i.e., metabolic rates) and water influx rates in free-ranging animals requires a more involved process known as the "doubly labeled water" technique. This technique was invented in the 1950s but didn't become widely used by field biologists until the 1980s. Doubly labeled water is water (H_2O) in which its ^1H atoms have been replaced by its stable (nonradioactive) isotope deuterium ^2H or radioactive tritium ^3H; its ^{16}O atom has been replaced by its stable isotope ^{18}O. This water is then injected (or ingested in humans) into an animal and allowed to equilibrate with the body's water. Upon equilibration, which usually occurs rather quickly, a first blood sample is drawn; this is the baseline sample. Then the animal is released and allowed to resume its normal activities. After a period of time (usually twenty-four hours for small animals but much longer for larger animals such as Gila monsters), a second blood sample is drawn. The concentration of ^2H or ^3H and ^{18}O in these two samples is then measured and compared in the lab using a mass spectrometer, which basically counts atoms in a sample. (No one can say that this technique doesn't require sophisticated equipment!) The difference in the amounts of ^2H and ^{18}O in the two samples then tells us how much CO_2 has been released (a measure of metabolic rate called field metabolic rate or FMR) and the net influx of H_2O during the period of activity. We don't need to know the chemical details about why this is, but they are readily available in understandable form on the web (just google "doubly labeled water technique"). But trust me, they are straightforward but still pretty clever. As a hint about this, think about where the ^2H comes from compared with the ^{18}O.

The doubly labeled water technique has been used to measure FMR and water flux in Gila monsters living in the Mojave Desert near Las Vegas. Tritium ^3H was used instead of deuterium ^2H in this study. In these large lizards, FMR could be determined by multiple resamplings for a period of almost eighteen months. Results showed that this lizard is extremely frugal in its expenditure of energy; its FMR is only about 28 percent of the value expected for a lizard of its size. As expected, about 67 percent of its annual energy expenditure occurs during its rather limited period of activity; 33 percent occurs while animals are inactive underground. Also as expected, water influx rates peak during summer rains when animals actively search for sources of rainwater. At this time they ingest more water than expected for a lizard of their size—enough to help them maintain a constant body mass in the face of substantial changes in the availability of water during the year. This dependence on summer rains, however, will put these animals in a precarious position if climate change results in significantly lower rainfall in the Mojave Desert and elsewhere in the southwest. All in all, these animals possess impressive behavioral and physiological abilities to minimize their metabolic costs and water losses in a thermally hostile and water deficient desert environment.

The small lizard family Helodermatidae occurs only in the New World. It belongs to a clade of three families of lizards whose basal family is the old-world Varanidae (monitor lizards, found in the Gondwanan continents of Africa and southern Asia south into Australasia). Its sister family is the Anguidae (alligator lizards) whose distribution includes both the New World (North and Central America and the Caribbean) and the Old World (Europe, southern China, and Borneo and Sumatra)—basically a Laurasian distribution. A fossil helodermatid—a lovely lower jaw with sharp hollow teeth—from the Miocene of Florida suggests that this family has had a wider distribution in North America in the past. A recent molecular phylogeny of squamate reptiles suggests that Helodermatidae and Anguidae last shared a common ancestor in the Cretaceous (about 114 Ma). Subjectively, Gila monsters look and act like "old" reptiles, so it is not surprising that they may actually be old, geologically speaking. But the question remains, why has this family undergone such a modest proliferation of species compared with many other families of lizards and snakes? Their varanid (74 species) and anguid (130 species) relatives, for example, are much more speciose. Based on our current understanding, this lizard has to be the oldest vertebrate living in the Sonoran Desert.

GOPHER SNAKE

Pituophis catenifer Blainville, 1835, Colubridae. This handsome species is one of the largest snakes in Arizona, attaining a length of up to 2.3 m and weighing up to 960 g. It is quite cryptically colored with a light brown back, rusty brown dorsal blotches, and brown lateral patches. Superficially, it resembles a diamondback ratttlesnake, which it tries to imitate by sometimes rapidly buzzing its tail and elevating its head and hissing when approached. But I've never found these snakes to be particularly aggressive, even when gently picked up. This is a very broadly distributed species that occurs over most of North America from southern Canada into northern Mexico. It exhibits considerable morphological geographic variation, probably in response to geographic differences in the substrates (e.g., sandy desert vs. grassy prairie) where they live. As a result, seven subspecies are usually recognized in the western United States and Mexico. With about 1,800 species and a worldwide distribution, its family, Colubridae, is the largest snake family in the world.

On the wall of my study I've pinned three complete shed skins of this species. These skins are 1.2–1.6 m long, and they all came from our yard. Along with common king snakes (*Lampropeltis getulus*), gopher snakes are the only snakes we have seen in our yard. When we moved into our house in June 2008, there was an old redwood spa on our patio that housed pack rats and honeybees. At that time, gopher snakes often visited our yard to feed and shed their skins. After the spa was removed in 2009, gopher snakes visited our yard less often. Whenever I encountered one on our patio during the day, I would often get down on the ground to photograph it as it approached me. Completely unperturbed by my presence, the snake would continue slowly moving forward, sometimes under my arm if I was propped on my elbows or between my feet if I was standing. I never tried to catch them, though I've caught them in other places.

In 2018 a large gopher snake began to den under a concrete section of our patio floor that was being pushed up by the roots of one of our large mesquite trees. It would shed its skin on the rocks in front of the den. The only time we ever saw it, however, was when it was coiled up one morning in the crotch of our large mesquite tree about a meter above the ground. A pair of California king snakes also used the raised concrete slab as a den, and they also shed their skins on the same rocks. Unfortunately, this den was eliminated in the fall of 2019 when the concrete slab was demolished to remove the large mesquite roots that were growing under our house. The concrete slab was carefully broken up in pieces, and we saw the gopher snake resting beside two large empty leathery eggs under the last large piece. It apparently left the den that night. The morning after the slab was removed, we found a juvenile king snake crawling in the rocks just outside the den. The den had apparently served both species of snakes as a safe resting and hatching place during their active season and as a hibernaculum during winter. In the summer of 2020 at least two of those snakes, one king snake and a large gopher snake, briefly revisited our yard very close to where the den had been; the gopher snake returned on at least two occasions.

I saw rattlesnakes much more frequently than gopher snakes during my desert fieldwork, so I don't know how common they were at my Sonoran study site. Recent encounters of them in the field include a large individual that was resting quietly in grass and fallen leaves on the bank of the San Pedro River in March and another large individual along the creek that flows past the Santa Rita Lodge in Madera Canyon in April. We were drawn to this snake by a noisy mob of Mexican jays that had just witnessed this snake raid their nest. When we got there, it was quickly crawling away among rocks on the ground with two obvious large lumps in its midsection.

Being a snake—basically a legless lizard—must be an interesting way to interact with the physical and biological worlds. Unlike turtles, lizards, birds, and mammals, which run around on two or four legs and can avoid at least to some extent the thermal consequences of hot soil surfaces, snakes cannot do this. When they're moving on the ground, either by side-to-side undulations or by straight-ahead crawling, their body temperatures are bound to be strongly influenced by soil temperature, especially in the desert. But they can avoid these hot ground temperatures in a number of ways, including crawling into burrows, which most snakes don't produce themselves, staying in the shade of vegetation, or climbing into plants to name a few. To avoid high soil (and air) temperatures and to avoid being spotted by sharp-eyed avian or mammalian predators, snakes tend to be quite secretive, unlike many other kinds of reptiles, and hence they can be relatively hard to study. Nonetheless, there are herpetologists that are dedicated to the study of snakes and their behavior, physiology, and ecology in the lab and field.

Given their wide geographic distribution, gopher snakes have been studied in a variety of different habitats but apparently not very much in the Sonoran Desert. In the pine-oak woodlands of central California, for example, these snakes emerge from hibernation in March or April and are active during the day until hot, dry weather begins in the summer when they become crepuscular or nocturnal. For both males and females, finding food is their first priority, and they actively search for prey using vision and their chemically sensitive forked tongues and vomeronasal organ in the roof of their mouth to help them. Another priority for males, of course, is using chemical cues to find sexually receptive females. About three-quarters of the diet of these powerful constrictors is mammals, including both nestlings and adult rabbits, ground squirrels, and pack rats; bird eggs and nestlings as well as adults are also important in their diets. They eat more lizards in desert habitats than in other habitats. Average prey size is about one-third of the size of a snake (another example of binge feeding), and prey size tends to increase as snakes get bigger. Interestingly, gopher snakes of all sizes and ages seem to feed mostly on mammals; other related snakes sometimes eat lizards as juveniles before switching to mammals as adults. I presume that juvenile gopher snakes must eat very small mammals and birds.

Despite their relatively large size, gopher snakes have rather small home ranges. In the grasslands of central California, for example, the home ranges of four radio-tagged males were 0.9–1.8 ha in area and overlapped with each other, meaning that these individuals likely competed among themselves for food and mates. In a Great Basin valley in British Columbia, the home ranges of radio-tagged gopher snakes were somewhat larger and averaged about 11 ha (with a range of 5–25 ha depending on habitat); the maximum distance traveled by these snakes from their hibernation sites to their home ranges in the spring was about 2,400 m.

Once they reach reproductive maturity at an age of about three years, females lay one clutch containing ten to fourteen eggs each year. In central California, hatchlings can be found in September through November, and they are subject to substantial mortality from predators such as hawks, owls, coyotes, foxes, and king snakes. If they can survive this gauntlet of predators during their early years, adults have much lower mortality rates, and individuals can live a dozen years or more.

Finally, when gopher snakes are active, their body temperature is about 29°C. This is important because an experiment has shown that the strike speed and capture success of rodents by these snakes depends on their body temperature. Both of these increase with an increase in body temperature, and maximum capture success (81 percent) occurred at a body temperature of 27°C, which is close to observed body temperatures of active snakes in nature.

What is the evolutionary history of these snakes? The family Colubridae began its evolutionary journey at the end of the Mesozoic Era, probably in the Eurasian portion of the former northern supercontinent, Laurasia. From there it spread throughout the world except for most of Australia. Recent phylogenetic analyses indicate that it is perhaps the most recently evolved family of snakes; the family contains at least six subfamilies that are very diverse in all aspects of their biology. Gopher snakes belong to a monophyletic clade of new-world colubrines, the tribe Lampropeltini, whose basal members are racers and coachwhips. This clade probably arrived in the New World from Asia in the Early Miocene. It then radiated during the Miocene into its current assemblage of at least fifty-one species mostly in arid and grassland habitats, probably either on the Mexican plateau or in the southwestern United States. The genera *Pituophis* and *Pantherophis* (formerly *Elaphe*, rat snakes) are sister genera (i.e., they share a common ancestor) that apparently separated in the mid-Miocene (ca. 13.7 Ma). Early members of tribe Lampropeltini such as racers feed primarily on lizards (ectotherms), but advanced members, including *Pituophis*, feed mostly on mammals (endotherms).

In summary, gopher snakes are a middle-aged (for its clade) species whose most recent ancestors evolved in arid western North America and Mexico. Its deeper roots lie in Asia in the Old World. After colubrid snakes dispersed from Asia into North America, probably in the Early Miocene (around 24 Ma), a major climatic trend toward increasing aridity during the Miocene in North America and elsewhere set the stage for its evolution as one of North America's largest and most powerful nonpoisonous snakes.

WESTERN DIAMONDBACK RATTLESNAKE

Crotalus atrox Baird and Girard, 1853, Viperidae. This is North America's largest rattlesnake, sometimes reaching a length of 1.7 m and a weight of 2.7 kg. Its relatively large head with two light eye stripes, diamond-shaped dorsal patches, alternating black and white tail stripes, and, of course, a rattle at the tip of its tail make this snake unmistakable. It is a member of subfamily Crotalinae (the pit vipers), which occurs in the Old World from eastern Europe through most of Asia, including India, and in the New World from southern Canada to southern South America. Rattlesnakes are strictly New World in distribution, and the genus *Crotalus* contains about fifty species.

All pit vipers have a pair of long, hollow fangs attached to small movable maxillary bones located at the front of their upper jaws and large venom glands located at the back of their upper jaws. The fangs are folded against the roof of the mouth when not in use. The venom contains variable amounts of protein-digesting enzymes that come into action as soon as the venom is injected into a victim. They also possess heat-sensing pit organs located below their nostrils. These organs can detect infrared radiation (heat) produced by so-called warm-blooded prey such as birds and mammals. The occurrence of these organs suggests that pit vipers are specialized to feed on warm-blooded prey. After successful envenomation, these snakes locate their dead or dying prey using scent cues rather than heat cues.

At a length of up to 3.2 cm, western diamondback fangs are quite long. But this is all relative. My first night in Tucson in 1989, I stayed with Dr. Dave Hardy Sr., the professional-level herpetologist and physician whom I mentioned above. After dinner, he showed me a skull of this rattlesnake and a skull of the fer-de-lance (*Bothrops asper*), a pit viper that I knew very well from my previous fieldwork at the rainforest research station Finca La Selva in northeastern Costa Rica. Compared with rattlesnake fangs, the fer-de-lance fangs are humongous, though the snakes are about the same size. With this comparison, Dave was trying to assure me that I was about to start working in a habitat containing less fearsome pit vipers. He was right, of course. When I worked on bats there, I called La Selva "snake city" because two dangerous pit vipers—the fer-de-lance and bushmaster (*Lachesis muta*)—lived there. Whereas the fer-de-lance was a long, slender snake, the bushmaster was long and heavy bodied. It was called "mata buey" (ox killer) by Costa Ricans because of its very potent venom. Like rattlesnake bites, fer-de-lance bites are survivable (but very painful), as three of my biologist friends have shown, but this is not likely to be the case with bushmaster bites. Fortunately, each of the bushmasters that I encountered at La Selva was nonaggressive and nonthreatening.

As their name indicates, the most distinctive feature of these desert pit vipers is the rattle, which is a modified tail spine found in all vipers. A new segment is added at the rattle's base after each skin shed. Thus, the number of segments in an intact rattle indicates the shedding history of a snake, not its age; older segments at the tip of the rattle sometimes break off, so rattle size is not necessarily an indication of a snake's shedding history. The characteristic buzzing sound of the rattle is produced by the loosely interlocking segments rubbing against each other. In the field I could easily distinguish between the fast, high-pitched buzz of a small sidewinder (*Crotalus cerastes*) and the slower, lower-pitched buzz of a much larger diamondback. It is assumed that rattles evolved as an antipredator warning system. Some support for this can be found in two close relatives of C. *ruber* (the red rattlesnake of Baja California) that live on predator-free islands in the Gulf of California. These animals either lack rattles completely or have small, undeveloped rattles.

Diamondback rattlesnakes might live in our neighborhood, as they do in many areas around Tucson, but, as in the case of Gila monsters, I've never seen one here. However, I've encountered many individuals during my desert field-work and have seen a few on bike trails around the city and on the grounds of the Arizona-Sonora Desert Museum. They also reside in our local nature park, Tohono Chul. In a year of wandering around that park with my cameras, how-ever, I never saw one. But Larry, a fellow photographer who spends a lot of time in Tohono Chul, has seen them frequently and knows where they tend to hang out. Despite knowing where he always saw one individual, he managed to let his guard down once and ended up being bitten on his right ankle by it. He spent several days in the hospital with a badly swollen leg. It was a very unpleasant experience, he told me.

Despite walking past or stepping over them in my fieldwork, I have never had a dangerous encounter with one. I always stopped briefly to look at them, usually coiled up resting quietly under a bush or at the base of a tall cactus, before moving on. When I began going into caves looking for bats in the Sonoran Desert, I quickly discovered that cave entrances were common places for these rattlesnakes to hang out. I became so confident that these snakes were frequent cave dwellers that I once told my field crew to be careful upon entering a new cave, that there was sure to be at least one rattlesnake inside. Sure enough, after about ten minutes of exploration, we found one right in our midst. As usual, the snake was not agitated and remained resting quietly in place. Knowing that rattlesnakes like to hang out in or near bat caves, I was a bit worried about this as I crawled on my belly through a narrow 10 m long tunnel that led into a dark chamber filled with lesser long-nosed bats in Baja California Sur. But much to my relief, no snakes were present there that day.

My most memorable encounter with a diamondback rattlesnake occurred one afternoon in coastal Sonora as I wandered around in a large stand of tall cardón cacti collecting some of their flowers with a long pole. I was looking for my next group of flowers when a loud *buzzzzz* stopped me short. Practically at my feet was a round-tailed ground squirrel twitching in its death throes, having just been bitten by a large diamondback. The snake was coiled up a couple of meters in front of me and was clearly very agitated. It slowly crawled backward under a bush where it continued to rattle loudly. I resumed my flower search but returned to this spot about an hour later. The snake was still rattling away under the bush, and, unfortunately, the dead ground squirrel was now covered with ants. I left the area feeling very bad about apparently spoiling the snake's dinner. Since these snakes only feed a couple of times a year, however, and the squirrel was large, I'd like to think that the snake ignored the ants and ate it anyway.

Although diamondbacks can sometimes be found above ground in most months, even during warm periods in winter, in the Tucson area they are most active from early March to mid-October. Results of a three-year study of this species using temperature-sensitive radio tags in the foothills of the Tucson Mountains indicate that they spend the winter solitarily in rock shelters, burrows, and pack rat nests at a T_b of about 14.5°C. They are known to den communally in other areas. When they emerge in the spring, they move up to 2 km to creosote (*Larrea tridentata*) flatlands where they search for sexually receptive females, undoubtedly using odor cues, and food in home ranges that average about 5.4 ha. Individual home ranges are not exclusive, and the home ranges of both sexes overlap with each other. During the active season, their T_b is about 29.3°C, and they spend only about 1 percent of their time moving around, usually at sunset. For most of the active season, they remain alert but inactive in the shade of bushes, waiting for prey to come by. These sit-and-wait predators eat only two to three large prey per year for a total of about 95 percent of their body mass. Ground squirrels, other rodents, and birds are their main prey.

The reproductive cycle of diamondback rattlesnakes includes mating in March and April and then again in the fall; females store sperm from their fall mating over winter. Ovulation followed by fertilization occurs in early summer. Females are viviparous and give birth to two to seven babies in the late summer; litter size is not correlated with a female's size and represents about 32 percent of her mass. At birth, the sex ratio is about 1:1, and male neonates are somewhat longer and heavier than female neonates. Babies remain at their birth site for a few days until they undergo their first skin shed before dispersing. After giving birth, females do not breed again for at least two years while they rebuild their fat reserves. As a result, this species (and other rattlesnakes) has a "slow" life cycle compared with colubrids such as gopher snakes in which females reproduce every year. Data from a diamondback population in central Arizona indicate that males and females reach sexual maturity in their third or fourth summer, depending on their foraging success and growth rates. This is a long-lived species, and females can live for twenty years or more.

From an adult male's point of view, this life cycle has interesting population consequences. Although the sex ratio of the adult population is 1:1, the operational reproductive sex ratio (or OSR in the behavioral ecology literature) among adults is not 1:1. It is something like 1:0.5 or even 1:0.33 because reproductively active females are only one-half to one-third or less as common as reproductively active adult males each year. Whereas the resource competition sex ratio among adults is 1:1 (i.e., all individuals are competing for the same food resources), it is significantly less than this from a reproductive standpoint because females do not breed every year.

Whenever a population's OSR is less than 1:1, reproductively active females become a limiting resource for adult males, and males must compete among themselves for access to receptive females. In many species of vertebrates, this kind of competition results in sexual selection in which males are selected for characteristics that enhance their competitive ability; sexual selection was of great interest to Charles Darwin who published a book about it in 1871. Depending on species, these characteristics can include larger size than females, brighter colors, weapons such as antlers or large canine teeth in mammals, and so forth. In the case of rattlesnakes, we might expect males to be significantly larger than females. This is true in central Arizona and throughout its geographic range. Adult males are about 18 percent larger in length than adult females, and, unlike females, they continue to grow after reaching sexual maturity (at a length of about 80 cm).

Does size influence social dominance and reproductive success in males of *C. atrox*? If size matters, we would predict that the larger of two males should usually win during aggressive encounters. Males often engage in aggressive encounters with each other during the mating season. In these encounters, two males raise their heads and necks up to 50 cm above the ground and sway back and forth next to each other. Then one male hooks his neck around the other snake's neck (a behavior called "topping") and tries to force it to the ground. This goes on for some time until one male, usually the larger one, successfully forces the other male to the ground and the loser glides away. If a female is nearby, the successful or dominant male initiates courtship; subordinate males do not immediately initiate courtship with females after losing an encounter with another male. Courtship and copulation are slow processes in this species, and copulation can last for up to twenty-eight hours. Males often remain in the vicinity of receptive females for weeks during the mating seasons.

Do larger, presumably dominant males father more offspring than smaller, presumably subordinate males? Based on the results of a ten-year population study of C. *atrox* conducted near Florence, Arizona, the answer appears to be no. This question was addressed using paternity analyses based on a powerful DNA-based technique using microsatellites. These are small segments of DNA that contain "motifs" of six or more nucleotides that are repeated up to fifty times in a row; they are pieces of "junk" DNA that are found throughout an organism's genome and that have high mutation rates. Consequently, since the 1990s, "microsats" have become an important source of data for quantifying genetic variation in population genetics studies, including paternity analyses. Studies typically use twelve to twenty-four highly variable microsats, each with a different motif, in their analyses. From 2004 to 2008, my grad students and I used microsats to determine the population genetic structure and interisland gene flow in three species of plant-visiting bats in the West Indies.

Results of the Florence study are fascinating. It turns out that the mating system of C. *atrox*, like that of other species of snakes, is *polygynandrous* (*poly*=many, *gyn*=female, *andro*= male)—a system in which both males and females can have multiple mates in a season. Paternity analysis revealed that the small litters produced by females could have up to three fathers. Both large and small adult males were successful fathers, although large males spent more time than small males hanging around receptive females. Overall, spatial proximity (i.e., degree of home range overlap) rather than male size was an important predictor of paternity. During their long lifetimes, it may be that large males sire more offspring than small males, but results of this study clearly indicate that size and degree of social dominance in males isn't the only route to reproductive success.

A further kicker in this study that complicates our understanding of male mating success in C. *atrox* is the fact that females can store viable sperm for several years. Captive females isolated from males for several years can produce litters of viable offspring. This means that, theoretically, a female has a choice of which sperm to use to fertilize this year's litter—current sperm (from which male?) or stored sperm. All of this means that the best a male can probably do is try to inseminate as many females as he can each season. What happens after that is probably up to a female and her behavior and physiology. Who says sex is straightforward and boring in these "lower" vertebrates?

The Viperidae contains about 270 species and has a nearly worldwide distribution. It is the sister group of colubrid (nonvenomous) snakes such as gopher snakes and is thought to have evolved in Asia in the Early Cenozoic (ca.

47 Ma); it colonized the New World in a single dispersal event. Its subfamily Crotalinae (pit vipers) dates from about 31 Ma, and new-world crotalines date from about 22 Ma. Species of the genus *Crotalus* are advanced members of the monophyletic clade of new-world pit vipers. They likely began to diverge in the Late Miocene or Early Pliocene (ca. 5–6 Ma). A phylogeny of *Crotalus* based on mtDNA gene sequences suggests that *C. atrox* is one of the youngest members of its genus. As in the case of other arid-adapted reptiles (e.g., *Aspidoscelis* whiptail lizards), it likely evolved in northern Mexico. Thus, its evolutionary journey has been relatively short in both time and space. Since it is often very common in different habitats, this large-bodied pit viper has been evolutionarily very successful.

ECTOTHERMY VERSUS ENDOTHERMY

Let's now examine another important topic before we proceed on with Sonoran Desert birds and mammals. Here I will discuss a profound physiological difference between birds and mammals and reptiles, namely endothermy and how it evolved. Please consult box 2 for definitions of the metabolic terms used in this section. Before I proceed, I need to describe a basic difference between the energy metabolism of ectotherms and endotherms. In ectotherms, a species' body temperature (T_b) and its metabolic rate (MR) are usually positive linear functions of the temperature of its environment (T_a). In contrast, in endotherms T_b is independent of T_a, and their MRs are a nonlinear function of T_a and can be divided into three segments: (1) a thermoneutral zone (TNZ) in which MR is independent of T_a and is minimal (i.e., its BMR); (2) at T_as below the TNZ, MR increases as T_a decreases; and (3) at T_as above the TNZ, MR also increases as T_a increases. Outside their TNZs, endotherms have to expend energy either to warm (e.g., by shivering) or cool themselves (e.g., by sweating or panting) to maintain a constant T_b. The relationship between MR and T_a in endotherms thus looks somewhat like the letter U in which the TNZ is at the bottom of the letter and its arms are splayed out. Our TNZ is quite narrow (e.g., 28°C–32°C), but in general it increases with body size in birds and mammals. And, as you might guess, tropical endotherms have a much narrower TNZ than arctic endotherms. Thus, an arctic fox with a thick coat of winter fur has a TNZ that is 100°C wide (-30°C to > 30°C) whereas the TNZ of a tropical sloth is about 10°C wide (ca. 28°C to 38°C). Birds show the same trend.

BOX 2 Terms Used in Discussions of Energy Metabolism

AEROBIC RESPIRATION   Respiration in which cells break down sugars and fat to produce energy in the presence of oxygen. A multistep process that yields much more energy per unit of glucose broken down than anaerobic respiration. End products are CO_2 and H_2O.

AEROBIC SCOPE   Degree to which O_2-demanding activities can be increased above resting levels (e.g., 2X, 5X, etc.).

ANAEROBIC RESPIRATION   Respiration in which cells break down sugars and fats to produce energy in the absence of oxygen. Produces much less energy than aerobic respiration. Lactic acid and CO_2 are products of this process.

BASAL RATE OF METABOLISM (BRM)   The metabolic rate of birds and mammals when at rest in their thermoneutral zone (TNZ).

ECTOTHERMY   Body temperature (T_b) determined by environmental temperatures.

ENDOTHERMY   Body temperature determined by internal metabolic rate.

ESTIVATION OR AESTIVATION   Long-term dormancy associated with periods of excessive heat or drought. Includes moderate drop in metabolic functions, including heart rates, rates of respiration, and body temperature (T_b).

FIELD METABOLIC RATE (FMR) (=DAILY ENERGY EXPENDITURE [DEE])   The daily rate of energy expenditure of animals during normal activity.

HETEROTHERMY   Variable T_bs that can be caused by high muscular activity or periods of torpor or dormancy.

HIBERNATION   Long-term dormancy associated with periods of cold or food scarcity. Includes substantial reduction in metabolic functions, including heart rates, rates of respiration, and T_b.

HOMEOTHERMY   Constant T_bs.

STANDARD METABOLIC RATE (SMR)   The metabolic rate of a resting, inactive ectotherm.

THERMONEUTRAL ZONE (TNZ)   Range of environmental temperatures at which metabolic rates of birds and mammals are minimal (i.e., at BMR).

As we've seen, turtles, lizards, and snakes are ectotherms whose body temperatures are basically dictated by their environment as modified by their behavior. As a result, their energy budgets and activity levels are about an order of magnitude smaller and lower, respectively, than those of birds and mammals. As a commonplace example of this I can ask: Where does the most obvious vertebrate activity in my yard come from during the day? Clearly, it comes from birds—lesser goldfinches drinking and bathing in our fountain, northern cardinals and Abert's towhees flying to and from our seed feeder, a Bell's vireo continually calling as it searches for insects in the canopy of our mesquite trees, and hummingbirds constantly sparring around our bird feeders and flowering plants. Desert spiny lizards may be present on the patio floor and walls during the day, but they certainly don't command our attention like birds do. Mammals are not nearly as conspicuous as birds in our yard most of the time, but at certain times of the year, our patio is alive at night with groups of nectar-feeding bats silently (to us) visiting our hummingbird feeders.

We're all aware of the high activity levels of birds and mammals and often take this for granted, thinking, "Oh, that's just the way it is." But why are they so much more active and visible to us than reptiles? And how did their high levels of activity powered by endothermy and their higher brain power evolve? Why are there not more classes of hyperactive and brainy vertebrates in the world today? (No, I'm not wishing for a return of velociraptors of *Jurassic Park* fame!) Or, conversely, why have turtles, lizards, and snakes (not to mention amphibians) not evolved more active lifestyles powered by endothermy in the past 150 million years or so?

True endothermy, as opposed to transient endothermy (usually called heterothermy) that can occur during periods of high muscular activity as seen, for example, in fast-swimming tuna fish and their relatives, has apparently evolved only twice in vertebrates—in the therapsid reptiles that gave rise to mammals and in the theropod dinosaurs that gave rise to birds. So why is endothermy so uncommon in the world of vertebrates? What are the costs and benefits of ectothermy and endothermy?

Temperature regulation and metabolism in vertebrates have been studied by physiologists for almost a century, so the costs and benefits of ectothermy versus endothermy are well known. My comparison here will be between a lizard and a similar-sized rodent (e.g., the small desert pocket mouse [*Chaetodipus penicillatus*] that lives in our yard). Controlling for body size is important because many biological functions in animals either increase or decrease with size, usually expressed as mass in grams or kilograms. Home range size, for example, tends to increase with body size whereas population density (number of individuals per unit area) tends to decrease. We already know that it costs the lizard about one-tenth as much energy to maintain a high body temperature, say 37°C, as it does a rodent with a similar body temperature. But lizards only maintain such high body temperatures when they're active, which may be for only a fraction of the day. So their overall daily cost of living is substantially less than one-tenth that of the mouse, even if the mouse is active only at night; it still has to maintain a high body temperature whether it's active or not. As a result, a lizard's daily cost of living—and the amount of food that it needs to consume to remain in positive energy balance—is only a tiny fraction (about 3 percent) of that of the rodent. Furthermore, it's well known that the body temperatures and metabolic rates of birds are higher than those of similar-sized mammals, so endothermy in birds is even more costly than it is in mammals. Finally, because of the low metabolic cost associated with temperature regulation, lizards and other ectotherms can invest more of the energy they ingest in growth and reproduction than endotherms. That is, the *production efficiency* or percent of ingested energy that can be used for growth and reproduction in an ectotherm can be as much as twenty-five times higher than that of a similar-sized endotherm, which must spend nearly 99 percent of its ingested energy just to maintain its high body temperature.

In sum, there can be no doubt that endothermy in birds and mammals is energy-extravagant. To illustrate this, we can compare these animals' basal metabolic rate (BMR) with their active or field metabolic rate (FMR) (see box 2). The BMR of these vertebrates usually costs about 30 percent of their daily energy budget. Many studies have shown that values of FMR in birds and mammals are at least three to five times higher than their BMRs and that their FMRs are about seventeen times higher than the FMRs of similar-sized ectotherms.

This brief comparison suggests that in many respects, ectotherms have a more energetically advantageous lifestyle than endotherms. These advantages include the need for less food, hence less time spent foraging; less exposure to predators; and more energy for growth and reproduction. On the other hand, because of their high and constant body temperatures, endotherms have higher aerobic capacity (see box 2) and can be active over a greater range of temperature conditions than ectotherms. They can also digest and process their food faster. Furthermore, endotherms typically have larger brains and hearts than similar-sized ectotherms. The end result of these differences is profound: compared with ectotherms, endotherms are generally much more active, have a much greater metabolic scope of activity, and are "brainier." The advantages these differences confer on endotherms likely far outweigh the disadvantages associated with their much higher cost of living. Nonetheless, to judge by their number of species, terrestrial (and aquatic) vertebrate ectotherms have also been very successful evolutionarily. There clearly has been enough ecological space on Earth for both kinds of animals to prosper for hundreds of millions of years.

The question of whether non-avian dinosaurs were endothermic has been investigated and debated for many decades. However, I have chosen not to deal with this topic here but want to direct interested readers to read the excellent, extensive discussion of it in the Wikipedia account "Physiology of Dinosaurs."

Because of their high metabolic rates and high body temperatures, endotherms are constantly faced with a thermodynamic problem: they need to devise (evolve) some way of reducing their rate of heat loss to the environment. This problem is not as severe in ectotherms. I'm sure you can guess the main way birds and mammals have solved this problem—feathers and fur. A major function of feathers and fur is to provide an insulative covering that slows down rates of heat (and cutaneous water) loss. Without feathers or fur, birds and mammals would have to acquire even more energy every day to maintain their high body temperatures, which would make endothermy even more costly. So the big evolutionary question here is, which came first in birds and mammals and their ancestors, endothermy or an efficient insulative covering? To answer this, we need to learn something about the evolution of endothermy, which is clearly a derived metabolic system in vertebrates.

Barry Lovegrove of the University of KwaZulu-Natal in South Africa has conducted an extensive review of the evolution of endothermy in birds and mammals with particular emphasis on fossil evidence (and inferred behavior). In this respect he has followed the "principle of correlation" first proposed by Baron Georges Cuvier early in the nineteenth century (see page 8). As you may remember, Cuvier used his extensive knowledge of the comparative anatomy of contemporary animals to infer what their ancient fossil ancestors might have looked like. According to Cuvier, the present can be used as a ladder into the past. In similar fashion, Lovegrove has compared the anatomical features associated with endothermy in contemporary birds and mammals with those of their fossil relatives to infer when those features began to appear in the past. Some of these features include a four-chambered heart, increased brain size, and changes in limb stance (from sprawling to pillar-like support) in both groups; in mammals they include a secondary palate, heterodonty (teeth differentiated into canines, molars, etc.), and turbinate bones in the nasal cavity. As a result of his studies, he has proposed that the evolution of endothermy that we see today in birds and mammals proceeded in three main stages.

Stage I occurred in the Triassic Period (see table 1). Prior to this there is no (anatomical) evidence of endothermy in the reptilian linages leading to mammals and birds. Lovegrove infers that in the Triassic, the early stages of endothermy and elevated body temperatures (T_bs), possibly still involving behavioral rather than metabolic thermoregulation, likely began with the evolution of parental care and the higher activity levels associated with it. As we know, parental care is widespread in contemporary birds and mammals; it is uncommon or nonexistent in reptiles. Parental care requires much more energy and a more active lifestyle than reproduction in reptiles in which most females simply lay eggs or give birth to babies that are then left on their own for the rest of their lives. To appreciate this, all you have to do is watch the feeding activity of birds during their nesting periods. In Gila woodpeckers, for example, both parents are constantly flying back and forth and bringing food (often insects and bits of saguaro cactus fruit) to their nestlings early and late in the day. Similarly, mama hummingbirds (but never males) bring a beak full of tiny insects mixed with nectar to their two nestlings about every twenty minutes. Even more impressive is watching adult male Cooper's hawks bringing vertebrate prey (e.g., baby doves) to their fledglings well after they've left the nest. Because parental care usually increases the survival of nestlings and neonates, it has positive selective value, even though it requires a large energy expenditure on the part of adults. Increased aerobic capacity (see box 2) is an important feature of contemporary endotherms and is likely to have evolved in concert with the higher activity levels associated with parental care.

Stage II occurred in the Triassic/Jurassic Periods and produced many of the energy-demanding features that we see in birds and mammals today. In mammals, these included the evolution of small body sizes and fur (by about 230 Ma) and a nocturnal lifestyle. Feathers in birds (and in their archosaurian ancestors) evolved somewhat later (by about 150 Ma). In both groups, brain size increased and further metabolic and anatomical refinements, including larger heat-producing visceral organs such as livers, kidneys, and alimentary tracts, occurred that resulted in a high BMR, sustained endothermy, and a high body temperature.

The evolution of larger brains was an especially important trend. The brains of birds and mammals are now about ten times larger in volume than those of similar-sized reptiles, and this organ is expensive to maintain. For example, about 20 percent of a rodent's or human's daily energy budget is required just to keep brains functioning at maximum capacity. Thus, having a large brain is definitely a significant energetic investment. But the advantages of large brains are many, so selection for them, beginning in the Triassic, is easy to understand. However, it would seem that large brains are only energetically feasible in endotherms with their high BMRs and body temperatures and large energy budgets. So relative brain size has often been used to distinguish endothermy from ectothermy in fossils. Incidentally, dinosaurs were basically small brained and had brains that were similar to modern reptiles in relative size. As is the case in some endotherms today, herbivorous dinosaurs had relatively smaller brains than carnivores. Velociraptors and other archosaurian relatives of birds had somewhat larger brains compared with other similar-sized dinosaurs.

Finally, Stage III features a completely modern endothermic metabolism that became well established in the Cretaceous Period and Cenozoic Era with the evolution of muscle-powered flapping flight in birds and faster cursorial (toe-tip) running (from a slower plantigrade or flat-footed stage) in certain groups of mammals, including carnivores and large herbivores. As the Cenozoic Era dawned, high energy endotherms were fully prepared to radiate into Earth's ecological space that had been vacated by the demise of dinosaurs and many of their nonendothermic relatives.

Much of this scenario is built on our ever-increasing knowledge about the morphology and (inferred) behavior of fossil birds and mammals. And much of this information in recent years has come from the sophisticated use of biochemical analyses, electron microscopy, and computer technology as applied to fossils. For most of its history, paleontology relied solely on the careful morphological analysis of painstakingly acquired fossils. But that is now changing as the following two examples show. A group of Chinese scientists and colleagues have used biochemical analyses of the proteins α-keratin and β-keratin plus electron microscopy to confirm that the feathers of *Anchiornis*, a "near avian" dinosaur slightly older (ca. 160 Ma) than the oldest known bird *Archaeopteryx* (ca. 150 Ma), had the same biochemical and structural features as the feathers of true birds. As another example of the application of advanced technology to the study of fossils, South African and European researchers have used micro-CT scans of the brains (or their braincases) of several species of early therapsid mammal-like reptiles from the Late Permian (ca. 250 Ma) plus 3-D computer reconstructions to show that their brains were larger and more complex than those of other contemporary reptiles; they were beginning to approach in size the brains of early mammals.

Although most modern birds and mammals are fully endothermic, not all of them are. Heterothermy—the ability to reduce BMRs and T_bs daily or seasonally—occurs in a significant number of these animals. This physiological strategy occurs mostly in small species that undergo daily bouts of torpor, as in hummingbirds, certain rodents, and bats, or that hibernate or aestivate seasonally, as occurs in many small mammals (i.e., those the size of woodchucks or marmots and smaller). It is well known that on a mass-specific or per-gram basis, the metabolic rates of small birds and mammals are much higher than those of larger species. Thus, it should not be surprising to learn that heterothermy is an important method of saving energy in these animals. What is surprising, however, is that no birds, not even very small northern species such as chickadees and titmice, hibernate. While many of their small mammalian counterparts are hibernating in thermally or otherwise physically and biologically challenging habitats such as the Sonoran Desert and the Temperate Zone, small birds are still operating at high T_bs and high metabolic rates all year long.

SONORAN DESERT BIRDS

In this section, I have chosen to highlight ten species of Sonoran Desert birds based on my personal familiarity with them and/or their iconic status in this biome. These species cover much of the phylogenetic spectrum of modern birds, and their lives can teach us much about what it takes to prosper in this region.

GAMBEL'S QUAIL

Callipepla gambelii Gambel, 1843, Odontophoridae. Everyone living in or visiting the desert southwest should be very familiar with this elegant bird. Adult males look like avian Katsina dolls with their rusty caps, black faces set off by bold white lines, and curved head plumes; females are less gaudy and have smaller head plumes. Adults of both sexes weigh about 170 g. Once allied with pheasants in family Phasianidae, new-world quails are now considered to be a separate family (Odontophoridae) that contains about thirty species classified in nine genera and distributed in the Americas as far south as southern Brazil. Throughout their range they are important game birds and are avidly hunted and eaten.

I view Gambel's quail as an important harbinger of spring in Tucson because of the constant crowing of males, beginning in March and lasting through May. On many occasions at this time of the year, I have heard a male crowing on our patio well before sunrise. Outside of the nesting season, these birds are certainly still around but are much quieter as they go about their business of searching for food. But I always know it's spring when a pair of adults begins searching in our backyard for a nest site. They strut along our patio walls with the male leading the way and rummage around in our large pots full of plants. These searches will occur for several days, but in most years the pair will choose to nest somewhere else. Still, many households in our neighborhood end up with a quail nest in their yard. A neighbor once told me that she saw twenty-four chicks bail out of one of her flowerpots; this nest likely contained the eggs of more than one female. Baby quails, sometimes called "eggs with legs," begin to appear in May, but by the time the summer monsoons arrive in early July, their numbers have diminished considerably, and parents in our neighborhood are usually accompanied by only a handful of teenagers. I'm sure baby quails are savored by many predators, including snakes, roadrunners, hawks, owls, and a variety of mammalian carnivores, as much as people savor eating their parents.

Although they are common urban birds in Tucson and elsewhere throughout their range, which is pretty much restricted to the Sonoran Desert, Gambel's quails are basically shy birds that can easily blend into a shrub-filled landscape. When surprised, a group of quails, called a covey, is usually loath to fly, and instead they dash for cover, squawking excitedly as they go. At these times, they remind me of a bunch of circus clowns running helter-skelter like I remember from my childhood in Detroit. If they are rather far from cover, the birds will reluctantly fly on rapidly beating wings, but my impression is that they'd much rather run than fly for cover.

Over the years, quails have nested a few times in our yard, and it is at these times that I've been able to see a clutch of newly hatched chicks in action. Like most gallinaceous birds, baby quails are precocial and can run around and begin feeding right out of the egg. Mama quail seems to be in charge of them at this time, and she makes sure her babies minimize their exposure to predators by forcing them to run quickly across open areas from one hiding place to another. Once they've reached a safe hiding place, mom and her chicks become completely still and silent. It's a wonderful disappearing act; if you hadn't been watching them, you wouldn't know they were there. All the while, papa quail also keeps an eye on his babies from a nearby perch; he calls constantly to keep in contact with his family. Newly hatched chicks have outsize feet and legs and can run amazingly fast. Their bodies are covered with fluffy light-and-dark-striped down, and they already have a tiny mohawk projecting from their foreheads, a very early version of their eventual plumes. As a result, they're really cute. But I'm sure predators don't dwell on their cuteness when they're after a meal of very fast food.

Because they are important game birds, the ecology and behavior of Gambel's quails has been studied extensively for many decades. Reflecting this, they have been transplanted to many areas outside of the Sonoran and other deserts in the western United States, and their populations are managed by state departments of game and fish. Within its natural geographic range, they have a spotty distribution in many areas and are often restricted to habitats in major river drainages where there is plenty of vegetation and water. Soil types (granite-based soils are best), mild winter temperatures, and adequate annual rainfall appear to be important factors in determining the local distribution and abundance of these birds. Population fluctuations are not uncommon and tend to be related to rainfall and its effects on vegetation. Populations decline during periods of low rainfall. Winter rainfall of at least 127 mm is needed to support high population densities of these birds. Green vegetation that supplies essential vitamins and other nutrients are needed for successful reproduction. In southern Nevada, average brood or clutch size is much lower (e.g., about four) in years of low winter precipitation compared with wetter years (e.g., about ten); overall nesting success is also lower in dry years. Green vegetation and its associated insect populations are important sources of food and water for these birds.

Further evidence that winter rains and summer temperatures affect breeding and reproductive success in Gambel's quails comes from a twenty-two-year study near Oracle, Arizona. Results showed that intensity of male calling, which signifies upcoming breeding intensity, was affected more strongly by the number of midwinter rains (December–January) than by either early-winter (October–November) or late-winter (February–March) rains. Furthermore, reproductive

failure was associated with low total winter rainfall and high summer temperatures. Highest reproductive success occurred in years of cool summers and wet
winters. Climatic effects on both vegetation (less green vegetation in hot, dry
years) and directly on adult females (which are less likely to produce clutches in
hot years independently of their food supply) appear to play an important role
in the population biology of this species.

Based on these and other studies the annual reproductive and social cycle of
this species includes the following features: (1) the annual nesting cycle is long
and lasts about 115 days (mid-April to early August near Las Cruces, New Mexico); in favorable years, females that produce a clutch early in the season may produce another clutch before the season ends; (2) by midsummer coveys of adults
of both sexes and young birds form that persist into late winter; (3) aggression
within coveys begins in late winter as adult males start to call and pair-bonds
between an adult male and female begin to form; (4) once formed, pairs of adults
become isolated from each other and the coveys break up; unmated adult males
are driven from the coveys and continue to call; and nesting begins followed
eventually by the reformation of coveys. Females are the nest builders and egg
incubators in this species. Nests are simply shallow depressions lined with grass,
leaves, and twigs. Clutch size is usually ten to twelve eggs, and incubation lasts
twenty-one to twenty-four days.

Gambel's quails, and gallinaceous birds in general, are well known for their
flocking behavior. But why form flocks? What are the pros and cons of this kind
of behavior? One of the major reasons for flocking in birds and formation of
herds in large mammalian herbivores clearly is predator defense: as the saying
goes, there is safety in numbers. Flocks or herds may be more visible to predators, but individual predation risk is often lower in the midst of a group than
it is for solitary individuals. Another benefit of flocking is that it provides both
males and females with easy access to mates. This is what happens in coveys of
Gambel's quails when mate selection begins in late winter. Hormones, particularly testosterone in males, are also involved in flock dynamics. Aggressiveness
among males increases in many bird species as testosterone levels increase prior
to breeding, and this can lead to the dissolution of flocks. Increased calling in
male quails at the beginning of the breeding season undoubtedly has a hormonal
basis. Conversely, flock formation begins as levels of reproductive hormones
diminish at the end of the breeding season.

An important negative aspect of flocking is that it potentially increases
competition for food. Competition for food is likely to depend on the nature

of the food itself. When food is scarce and/or is easily defendable, territoriality often occurs in many kinds of vertebrates as we will see in the discussion of hummingbirds. Territoriality is often, but not always, the antithesis of flocking or group formation. As an exception, both territoriality and group living are common in many species of primates; defense against predators is the usual explanation for their group living. In the case of Gambel's quails, their main food is green vegetation, which can be abundant and clumped in distribution, and seeds, which are widely scattered; together they are often not easy to defend. Hence competition for food is less likely to occur in these birds, and a seasonally gregarious lifestyle is not likely to be costly for individuals. In fact, given their size (not too large or small; 160–200 g) and highly terrestrial behavior, these birds are very attractive to many kinds of vertebrate predators. Thus, the benefits of group living outside the breeding season likely far outweigh its costs, hence the formation of coveys. Finally, it is important to note that the coherence of quail coveys ebbs and flows during the day. Coveys typically roost together in trees at night but then disperse somewhat when they're feeding. They reconvene when not feeding during the day and again at night.

How do female Gambel's quails choose their mates? Males in this species are highly ornamented, so we might expect that sexual selection based on female choice rather than male dominance as we've seen, for example, in diamondback rattlesnakes, occurs in this species. The doctoral research of Julie Hagelin at the University of New Mexico has addressed this question. She points out that sexual selection often involves intrasexual competition among males as well as mate choice by females. Regarding male-male competition, her behavioral observations and experiments indicate that males of this species are highly aggressive among themselves during the breeding season and that larger males and those with large plumes are usually dominant over smaller males with smaller plumes. Removal of their plumes creates subordinate males. Her experiments also indicate that when females are given a choice, they prefer to be courted by males that have high display rates. They're not as impressed with a male's body size or the size of its plume. Behavior, rather than size and ornamentation, seem to be most important to females when choosing their mates.

Display rates (as well as body size) are testosterone-based traits in these birds whereas male ornamentation is influenced by the absence of estrogen, which causes female plumage characteristics to develop in gallinaceous birds. Female mate choice thus appears to depend on testosterone levels in males. Since testosterone is costly to produce, high display rates in males seem to indicate high levels of circulating testosterone and hence a male's overall quality as a mate. If this is the case, then castration should have a strong effect on a male's attractiveness to females, right? When Hagelin did this experiment, she found that castration did indeed shut down a male's courtship behavior but had no effect on its plumage ornamentation or its aggressive behavior toward other males. Females always chose intact rather than castrated males as mates. So testosterone levels in males are clearly involved in mate choice in this species. Left unexplained in this research, however, is the evolution of gaudy ornamentation in male Gambel's quails (and in other gallinaceous birds). If female choice is not involved in this evolution, what is?

Julie Hagelin's experiments were conducted with captive-raised birds, and we need to know how her results compare with what is actually happening in wild populations of Gambel's quails. To this end, she also conducted a three-year study of color-banded birds in the field to document mate choice, reproduction, male-male interactions, and mating behavior at Bosque del Apache National Wildlife Refuge in central New Mexico. In this population, adult males were slightly more common than adult females, and both yearlings and adults were reproductively active. As in the captive studies, body size but not ornamentation in males played an important role in the timing of breeding and in male-male interactions. Heavier (older) males bred earlier and were dominant over lighter males both within and between age classes. Early breeding pairs produced larger clutches than later breeding pairs, and adult females but not yearlings sometimes produced a second brood.

Although we often are impressed by the tenacity with which adult males and females stay close together, it turns out that pair-bonds between males and females are not long lasting in this species. At Bosque, pairs rarely stayed together for more than one season, and some males and females even chose new mates within the same breeding season. While social monogamy (i.e., male-female pairs remain together for an entire breeding season) prevailed in two of the three years, especially among adults, polygamy (i.e., males and females have more than one mate during a breeding season) was not uncommon, especially among yearlings. Perhaps this is because mortality rates in these birds are relatively high, and many yearlings do not live long enough to breed as two-year-old adults. Give this mortality regime, it's important to reproduce as early and often as possible.

In summary, there's a lot going on in populations of Gambel's quails in the Sonoran Desert and other arid areas. First of all, they have to contend with a rather harsh and variable climate whose fluctuations have important effects on their breeding success. The availability of food and water strongly depend on year-year variations in weather, and this in turn affects nesting success. These birds mature rather quickly and are under pressure to reproduce before they succumb to predators. Mate selection, timing of breeding, and nesting success are strongly influenced by age and size in both males and females. If they live to become full adults, young quails will have greater reproductive success than they had as yearlings, but few of them live this long. The aggression that dominates male-male interactions largely disappears after the breeding season, and coveys containing a mixture of ages and both sexes form for the rest of the year. Finding adequate food and avoiding predators dominate the lives of these birds during this time.

What physiological tricks do Gambel's quails use to maintain a positive energy and water balance in their desert environment? Many studies of the energy metabolism and water economy of this species have been conducted in the laboratory and field since the 1970s. Results of these studies indicate that Gambel's quail is a conservative species regarding both its use of energy and water. For example, its field metabolic rate (FMR; see box 2), determined using the doubly labeled water method, is only about 40 percent of the FMR of other nonpasserine birds of the same size. Furthermore, its FMR is basically the same as its resting metabolic rate, which means that it expends relatively little energy to regulate its body temperature of 40°C while it's active. During the nonbreeding season, its low FMR results from a conservative daily activity schedule. While living in coveys, birds spend about six hours a day foraging—three hours in the morning and three hours in the late afternoon; they are inactive (loafing) during midday for an additional six hours; and they spend about eleven hours sleeping at night. When active, they usually walk or occasionally run and hardly ever fly. To cool themselves during very hot days (i.e., at T_as above 40°C), they open their mouths and undergo gular fluttering (i.e., rapid fluttering of their throat), which results in the evaporation of water from the moist surfaces of their mouths and throats.

Regarding their water economy, these birds need to ingest about 2.6 mL of water a day, which they usually obtain by eating succulent vegetation, seeds, and fruit in season as well as water-rich harvester ants. In the absence of free water and eating only dry food, however, they can tolerate dehydration and weight loss for several days before they become stressed and need to rehydrate. Compared with other birds of their size, these quails have rather small kidneys, the main organ of water conservation in birds and mammals. However, they can still change the concentration of their urine (the liquid portion of their uric acid waste product) to some extent in their kidneys in addition to absorbing water in the distal end of their gastrointestinal tract. As a result, this quail remains in positive water balance under most circumstances.

Finally, let's consider the evolutionary history of Gambel's quail. It's a member of the Galloanserae, the second of the three major monophyletic groups of modern birds (fig. 8). This group contains two taxonomic orders with worldwide distributions, the Anseriformes (ducks, geese, and their relatives) and the Galliformes (chickens, pheasants, quails, and their relatives). These two orders contain a total of eight families and about 452 species. The Galloanserae dates from the beginning of the Cenozoic Era (ca. 65 Ma), and its two orders split from their common ancestor in the Early Eocene (ca. 54 Ma). Recent molecular phylogenies place the Australasian family Megapodiidae (mound builders) at the base of order Galliformes and the Phasianidae (pheasants and partridges) as the most advanced family. Megapodes are turkey-like birds with unusual nesting habits in which forest-dwelling species bury their eggs in large mounds of decaying vegetation whose heat serves to incubate the eggs.

Members of the new-world quail family Odontophoridae are nonmigratory and have limited dispersal abilities. Therefore, it is surprising to know that these birds are most closely related to two species of *Ptilopachus* partridges from sub-Saharan Africa. These partridges and new-world quail diverged about thirty-six million years ago. Results of a recent phylogenetic and biogeographic analysis suggest that odontophorids were once widespread in the Old World and that they colonized the New World via the Beringia land bridge from Asia. New-world quails radiated, initially in Central America, in the Miocene (from ca. 21 Ma), and current species evolved relatively recently in the Pliocene and Pleistocene (i.e., within the last five million years). Gambel's quail and its close relatives (e.g., the California quail, *Callipepla californica*) likely evolved recently in arid parts of northern Mexico and the southwestern United States. Hence, this bird and its ancestors have made an immense journey in space and time: from somewhere in the Old World across the Bering Strait and into the New World sometime between thirty-six and twenty-one million years ago. From a Central American ancestry, our quail evolved in North America's arid southwest within the last five million years.

GREATER ROADRUNNER

Geococcyx californianus Lesson 1829, Cuculidae. *Meep, meep!* Who doesn't associate the greater roadrunner with the Sonoran Desert and the arid southwest? It's truly an iconic bird of this area, although it belongs to a family of about 136 species with a cosmopolitan distribution. New-world examples include "standard" cuckoos, anis, and squirrel cuckoos, to name a few. I've seen all of these species and more during my tropical fieldwork. European cuckoos and their calls were the inspiration for cuckoo clocks. I often heard their unmistakable calls during my sabbatical fieldwork with pied wagtails around Oxford in southern England.

I've really only had fleeting contact with roadrunners in my desert fieldwork and while living in Tucson. In the field I only got glimpses of them running through the vegetation. This was also my experience during most of my year of wandering around with cameras in our local nature park Tohono Chul. I knew roadrunners lived there, but I never saw them long enough to photograph them. That changed during the winter when I discovered where a male roadrunner basked and thermoregulated early on cold mornings. On several occasions, I found him standing on the top of a cholla cactus with his back feathers fluffed out and his black skin exposed to the sun. It was easy to photograph him then. Thermoregulating in this fashion is a common behavior in cuckoos. But my best photographic experience with this species at Tohono Chul came one spring morning when I heard one calling in dense vegetation. To get a better look at this bird, I turned on the roadrunner calls on my iBird West phone app and lured it out onto a gravel road. It stood there in a series of wonderful dappled shadows and posed briefly with a zebra-tailed lizard hanging from its beak before moving on. This photo is one of my all-time favorites (and it sells well in galleries).

To the best of my knowledge, roadrunners don't live in our neighborhood; it's too built up and lacks the open space that these bird need. But this wasn't the case when we lived on sabbatical in a house next to a wash in the foothills of the Tucson Mountains west of town. A pair of roadrunners lived on this property, and we eventually attempted to befriend them. To do this, I placed pieces of beef heart on the ground in our carport each morning. They quickly caught on to this and allowed me to sit and watch them as they fed (I wasn't a serious wildlife photographer at that time). It quickly got to the point where they expected to be fed every day. If I was a bit late in putting out the food, they would come to all the low windows looking for me as if to say, "C'mon buddy, where's the food? We're hungry!"

Greater roadrunners are slim, medium-sized birds with a strong beak, an erectable crest, long legs, and a long tail. Adult males are slightly larger than adult females (320 g vs. 290 g). Like Gambel's quails, they are much more comfortable running on the ground than flying, which is why they are called "ground cuckoos." Their toe arrangement with the first and fourth toes pointing backward and toes two and three pointing forward, a condition called zygodactyly, facilitates their running. They are shy and secretive and are fearsome vertebrate predators, eating lizards, snakes (including rattlesnakes), nestling and adult birds, and a variety of small mammals, including baby ground squirrels and baby rabbits. A Tucson friend recently sent me a series of photos of a roadrunner with a fluffy little bunny in its beak that it had captured on his driveway. As their name suggests, roadrunners usually run down their prey with impressive bursts of speed (up to 30 kph) and even jump high into the air to grab low-flying birds. Despite their important role as vertebrate predators, adults actually eat many more insects than vertebrates.

Despite being well-known birds, their ecology and behavior has not been extensively studied, particularly in the Sonoran Desert. Their home range behavior using radio-tagged birds has been studied in mesquite woodlands in northern and western Texas. These studies indicate that roadrunners have large overlapping home ranges and that male ranges are slightly larger than those of females. In north Texas, male home ranges averaged about 90 ha of which about 22 percent was used as their "core area" where they spent most of the time. Male ranges overlapped with those of females (especially when nesting) more than with other males. Although these birds are not strictly territorial, they will chase other birds of the same sex out of their core areas. In north Texas, annual mortality rates of adults were relatively high: 45 percent for females and 21 percent for males. These rates seem high for birds of this size. Perhaps their terrestrial lifestyle, like that of Gambel's quails, puts them at a higher mortality risk than similar-sized aerial species.

The breeding season of the greater roadrunner around Tucson and elsewhere is bimodal. Nesting occurs in mid-April to mid-June (before the summer monsoon) and again in late July to mid-September (during the monsoon). Not all mated pairs breed in both periods. This timing appears to coincide with peak numbers of insects (the main food for adults) and tiger whiptail lizards (the main food for nestlings). In our area, clutch size during the first period averages about 4.6 whereas it averages somewhat larger, 5.7, during the second period when lizard numbers are higher during the summer rains. Incubation is done by both adults and lasts seventeen to eighteen days. Nestlings fledge in another thirty to forty days at a weight of about 50 percent of their parent's weight of 300 g. Both parents continue to provision fledglings with food for a few days before they begin to feed for themselves.

Because both parents have to work hard to capture lizards for their babies, they need to spend significant amounts of time away from the nest during the day. Certain adaptations in the nestlings as well as nest placement allow them to do this. Around Tucson, for example, roadrunners usually place their nests in many-branched cholla cacti that provide shade and protection from predators, which include large snakes such as gopher snakes (and rat snakes in Texas). Adaptations in nestlings include a black skin that absorbs solar heat and keeps them warm before their feathers develop; nasal salt glands that excrete salt and help to conserve water, and an early onset of gular fluttering that helps them dissipate excess body heat. With these adaptations, which are unique to these birds, parents don't have to constantly brood their babies until they develop the metabolic machinery needed to elevate and maintain their high body temperatures.

Lab studies of adult physiology indicate that the metabolic rates of roadrunners and their ability to maintain a high body temperature are typical for many non-desert-dwelling birds of their size. But these birds do have one adaptation that is physiologically significant—the black skin of their shoulder and dorsal regions. As I witnessed while photographing an adult at Tohono Chul on cold winter mornings, birds bask by fluffing up their back feathers and exposing their black dorsal skin to the sun. In the winter when T_as drop below 10°C, these birds let their T_bs drop from their normal value of 38.4°C down to 34.3°C. Then when they bask, they passively gain heat from the sun and raise their T_bs back to their normal values. By basking (like ectotherms), they save about 41 percent of the metabolic energy they would normally spend to maintain a high, constant T_b on cold sunny mornings.

Finally, courtship behavior in roadrunners is quite elaborate and involves both acoustic and visual means of communication. Unlike Gambel's quails and many other birds, roadrunners are monomorphic, not sexually dimorphic. That is, males and females look alike, and biologists often have a hard time telling males from females during fieldwork. They often have to resort to genetic tests or behavioral differences that occur during courtship to do this. Roadrunners definitely are not songbirds, but they do produce a diverse array of sounds when they communicate over both long and short distances. Some of these sounds include coos (the most common long-distance call), barks, whines, and bill clacks (the most common call during courtship). In addition to acoustic signals, visual displays are important components of courtship, which is often a prolonged, many-day affair. Courtship has three basic phases: precopulation, copulation, and postcopulation. During the first phase, males coo from elevated perches early in the morning and spend a lot of time chasing females (they obviously are better at sorting out the sexes than we are) on the ground and during gliding flights while issuing coos and bill clacks; they also make popping sounds with their raised wings and raise and wag their tails and erect their crests; and they present nesting material (e.g., sticks and grass) and reptile prey to females. If a female is impressed by all of this, then they're on to phase two in which females raise their tails and present their cloaca to the male. This is an overt invitation for a male to hop aboard and initiate a "cloacal kiss" in which sperm is passed from the male's cloaca to the female's (most male birds do not have an intromittent organ as found in reptiles and mammals). An absolutely crucial part of this phase is that a male has to present a lizard to the female which she eats while they're copulating. After copulation, phase three begins and includes continued courtship moves by the male as well as further copulations by the pair. All of this is apparently necessary to cement a strong pair-bond between the birds that will last through the entire nesting cycle(s).

Nesting behavior in roadrunners is generally typical of many birds that have monogamous mating systems; both parents incubate the eggs and care for their nestlings. But they belong to a family (Cuculidae) that is notable among birds for the diversity of its nesting behavior. This includes cooperative nesting in neotropical anis, in which several females place their eggs in one nest and take turns incubating them, and brood parasitism, mostly in old-world cuckoos, in which females lay their eggs in the nests of other species and provide no parental care. Overall, about one-third of all cuckoo species, mostly in the old-world subfamily Cuculinae, are brood parasites. The European cuckoo, for example, is one of those species. Females of this species are territorial and keep watch on the nesting activity of much smaller songbirds in their territory. Actually, they spy on only one particular species whose egg color her egg will match. When a suitable nest becomes available early in its nesting cycle, she will swoop down when the songbird is away and grab the single egg and replace it with one of her own eggs; she then eats the host egg. Although European cuckoo eggs are larger than host eggs, their embryos develop very fast and hatch before most of the host eggs. The small cuckoo nestling then proceeds to eject host eggs and chicks from the nest so that it ends up being the only nestling begging for food from its hosts. Photographs of large European cuckoo chicks being fed by much smaller hosts make one wonder how can hosts be so easily duped.

There are many variations on this theme in other old-world parasitic cuckoos, and the evolution of host-nest parasite interactions is a fascinating story. My Cambridge behavioral ecologist friend Nick Davies has been a leading student of these interactions. His evolutionary analyses indicate that compared with cuckoos with parental care, which is the ancestral state in this family, species of parasitic cuckoos are smaller, lay smaller eggs, eat smaller prey, live in more open habitats (in the tropics), and are likely to be migratory rather than year-round residents in their breeding habitats.

Where do roadrunners fit in the evolutionary history of family Cuculidae? Like Gambel's quails, are they recently evolved members or older members of this family? Cuculidae is a member of the avian order Cuculiformes, which apparently diverged from two African bird orders Musophagiformes (arboreal fruit-eating turacos) and Otidiformes (large terrestrial bustards) just after the K/Pg boundary (ca. 63 Ma). As a result, cuckoos are likely to be an old bird family. MtDNA sequence divergences within this family are quite large, which also supports the idea that this family is old. Unfortunately, an age-dated phylogenetic analysis of this family that includes all or most of its species has not yet been done, so details of its evolutionary history remain poorly known. What is known, however, are the general relationships between its six subfamilies. The genus *Geococcyx* (roadrunners) belongs to subfamily Neomorphinae, a group of new-world ground cuckoos. This subfamily dates from at least the Early Oligocene (ca. 30 Ma) and is likely to be the oldest lineage in the family. In contrast, old-world brood parasitic cuckoos in subfamily Cuculinae are the youngest members of this family. It thus appears that the cuckoo family first evolved in the New World before dispersing throughout the rest of the world. *Geococcyx* roadrunners appear to be derived (not basal) members of their subfamily; basal members live in neotropical forests. I'm guessing that roadrunners likely evolved in the Miocene as arid habitats developed in northern Mexico and the southwestern United States. If this is true, its evolutionary history is likely to be similar to the histories of a number of other North American desert dwellers (e.g., spiny lizards, tiger whiptail lizards, diamondback rattlesnakes, etc.). Thus, it appears that its evolutionary journey has been relatively short in space (from the new-world tropics) but relatively long in time (from the Oligocene or older).

COOPER'S HAWK

Accipiter cooperii Bonaparte, 1828, Accipitridae. This is a medium-sized hawk characterized by reverse sexual size dimorphism. Males weigh about 260 g, and females weigh about 470 g. This hawk is primarily a forest dweller that uses stealth to capture its prey of small birds and mammals. It has relatively short, rounded wings and a long tail, which enable it to fly rapidly through a cluttered forest understory. Adult birds are elegant with their red eyes and gray headcaps, backs, and wings and cinnamon-tinted barring on their breasts. Nonadults are less elegant and are basically brown with many dark brown streaks on their breasts. Birds attain their adult plumage during their second summer.

I've had a lot of contact with this species since we moved to Tucson in 2008. It's likely that a pair has been nesting every year since then in a tall pine tree about 1.5 km south of us. In winter and early in the breeding season, the characteristic *keck-keck-keck* calls made by adults come from that direction. As a result, these hawks regularly pass over and through our yard all year. And they have occasionally eaten their prey—mostly mourning doves but also a desert cottontail rabbit and a northern cardinal—in one of our two large backyard mesquite trees. I also regularly saw them in the Tohono Chul nature park near us during my year-long photo wanderings in 2012–13. At that time, a pair was nesting in a large sycamore tree in the park's riparian area, and I photographed them mating near that nest in the spring of 2015.

But my most intimate contact with Cooper's hawks began on June 9, 2020, when a recently fledged hawk dropped the back half of a juvenile round-tailed ground squirrel at my feet while perched above me in one of our mesquite trees. From that point on, I started to pay close attention to the comings and goings of a trio of juvenile hawks that began to use our patio mesquites as their daytime activity center. To judge from their size, the trio consisted of two females and one male; females are larger than males (i.e., reverse sexual size dimorphism) in many species of hawks and owls. These birds began to hang out in our trees all day between June 18 and June 24 when they were being fed dove squabs by their father. Beginning early in the morning, an adult bringing food would fly low and silently into a tree, place the prey item on a branch, and quickly leave. As this happened, the juveniles would squeal excitedly before quieting down. Then one bird would approach the prey and begin to peck at it and feed. Meanwhile, the other two juvies would stand quietly on other branches and watch their sib feed. Their patience suggested to me that they knew their next meal would be coming soon. A second juvie would occasionally approach the feeding bird and try to grab a bite, but it was quickly repelled by the feeder. During this period, a parent delivered food at 1.5- to 2-hour intervals, beginning before 6:00 a.m. Between meals the juvies stood quietly and preened themselves. Between June 18 and 24, I saw a parent deliver thirteen dove squabs to the juvies during my casual observations. This adult was really hitting dove nests at this time.

Mourning doves (*Zenaida macroura*) are very common in Tucson, and they provide a steady food supply for Cooper's hawks. They have a long nesting season that begins in January or February. Although clutch size is usually two, a new clutch can be produced every thirty days, and multiple clutches (up to six in Texas) are produced each year. Thus, nestlings, subadults, and adults are available for consumption by these hawks nearly year-round.

Our mesquite trees, especially the north one which has a denser canopy, provided a shady place for the young hawks to hang out during the day. But our patio fountain with its running water also attracted these hawks to our yard. Over the years, we would occasionally see a hawk drinking at the fountain on hot summer days. In 2020, as air temperatures began in rise in late June, one or more of the juvies began spending long periods of time on the fountain, usually in the afternoon. It was also not unusual to see all three birds standing shoulder to shoulder on it. The size differences between these birds was especially obvious then. The two large females seemingly towered over the smaller male.

After June 23, the birds began to hunt for themselves and brought fully feathered birds (not squabs) into our trees to eat. They began spending less time simply hanging out in our trees and frequently left them only to return a little later; the juvies usually, but not always, came to and left the tree independently of one another. By this time, food deliveries by an adult had ceased. Our trees continued to be a central meeting place, but the juvies were now moving around our neighborhood searching for food. When in our trees, they were constantly scanning their environment, swinging their heads around, and crouching to get a better view of things. Their dark-feathered "eyebrows" supported by bony ridges at the top of their eye sockets gave them a menacing look. Sometimes they stared at me as I watched them with binoculars. At those times, I wondered what they were thinking. I doubt that they considered me to be a threat. Were they at all curious about this human being? All this time, the birds did not spend the night in our trees. They slept elsewhere, perhaps closer to the nest tree, and returned to our trees early in the morning.

During this period, I spent most of my time watching the hawks from behind my camera equipped with a 150–600 mm telephoto lens. The hawks quickly became accustomed to having me around and did not appear to be disturbed when I occasionally took a picture with an on-camera flash. They would continue to feed or stand quietly as I photographed them. Being quite close to the birds (and with frame-filling photos), I was able to observe them very closely. As a result, two things impressed me about this hawk: its small beak and its large feet tipped with large, very sharp claws. Its small beak suggests that it usually feeds on relatively small prey, and its sharp claws indicate that it will have a firm grip on its prey as it slams into it at about 40 kph. It also uses its sharp claws to hold prey down on a branch or the ground as it feeds. In fact, the hawk I watched often had a bit of trouble disengaging its claws from its prey when it wanted to shift positions while feeding.

The birds began feeding by tearing off small bits of flesh from its prey. When eating a squab, it didn't take long for a bird to remove most of the muscles and innards from the carcass. It then began to work on the less tender parts, including the wings and finally the legs and feet. By the time its feet were sticking out from the hawk's beak, the squab has been completely devoured. This is not the case with fully feathered birds or small furry mammals, however. Just the large muscles and innards are eaten from these larger prey; the feathers or fur (and the entire head in the case of a cottontail and a dove) are discarded, often ending up on our patio, much to my wife's disgust.

While watching these young birds day after day I became quite attached to them. I began to think of them as buddies that had started out life together as nestlings and that were probably on the verge of adopting independent lives when they finally dispersed from their natal territory. But before they separated, however, they seemed quite eager to stay in contact with each other when they were in or away from our yard. I could hear their high-pitched squeals from quite a distance away. And these squeals increased in intensity when they rejoined each other back in our trees or when an adult came by, even if it was no longer deliv-ering food. They seemed to be saying, "Boy, am I glad to see you!" Although they were now hunting on their own, one afternoon I watched a female juvie return to the tree carrying a young bird that it placed at the feet of her brother, who immediately began to eat it. I wondered whether she thought that he was hungry, perhaps because he hadn't hunted successfully for a while. I also wondered about how much concern these young birds generally have for each other. I'm guessing that they do in fact have concern for each other and are behaving like a close-knit group of friends before assuming a solitary life until they acquire a mate. I wit-nessed another case of deliberate food sharing between the two female juvies on the morning of July 7. Food sharing also supports the idea that they care for each other. I missed seeing them when they dispersed in early July. By the middle of July our yard was again full of small birds visiting our seed feeder and fountain. Somehow, they had gotten the word (I wonder how?) that the coast was now clear; the hawks had moved on.

We know a lot about the ecology and behavior of Cooper's hawks in and around Tucson as a result of several detailed field studies that were conducted by faculty and grad students in the School of Renewable Resources at the University of Arizona between 1994 and 2005. Several of these studies involved comparing the ecology of hawks living in an urban setting with those living in rural parts of southeastern Arizona. This comparison produced a number of striking results. In terms of general behavior, urban birds are much more "comfortable" around humans but will sometimes defend their nests against close approaches; rural birds are much shyer and will temporarily leave their nests without defending them if humans approach. Levels of potential food resources, especially doves, are much higher in urban areas, and this affects many aspects of Cooper's hawks' ecology. For example, the density of nests is much higher in Tucson than in rural Arizona (up to $1.5/km^2$ vs. $0.11/km^2$). The diets of urban birds are dominated by three species of doves (Inca, mourning, and white-winged doves) whereas the diets of rural birds are more diverse. The breeding season of hawks in Tucson begins almost two months earlier than in rural Arizona (mid-January vs. mid-March). Clutch sizes are larger in Tucson (3.6 vs. 3.2), and more food items are delivered to a nest each day (8.9 vs. 5.8). Finally, home range sizes of urban birds are much smaller (about 66 ha with a core area of 33 ha) than the ranges of rural birds throughout North America.

Although they live in a relatively food-rich environment full of doves, Cooper's hawks in Tucson pay a substantial price for concentrating on these prey species. Doves and other members of family Columbidae are often infected (e.g., up to 98 percent of white-winged doves tested in Tucson) with a nasty flagellated protozoan parasite, *Trichomonas gallinae*, which causes a fatal disease called trichomoniasis; infected birds suffer from lethargy and difficulty feeding. In Tucson 98 percent of nests examined had at least one infected nestling compared with only 13 percent in rural Arizona; 85 percent of urban nestlings were infected compared with only 9 percent in rural Arizona. As a result, 41 percent of urban nestlings died from this disease whereas the death rate in rural Arizona was much lower (< 10 percent). Interestingly, very few adult Cooper's hawks in both areas were infected with this disease. How adults avoid becoming infected by this parasite is currently unknown.

The high infection rate of trichomoniasis in nestling Cooper's hawks in Tucson raises an important question: Is this urban area an *ecological sink*, defined as an area in which population death rates are greater than birth rates, for this species? Based on many years of data on reproduction and mortality in the Tucson population, however, the answer to this question is no. Birth rates are greater than death rates, and this urban population is actually increasing. Despite the high death rate of nestlings, caused primarily by trichomoniasis, other demographic features, including relatively large clutch sizes and high fledgling and adult annual survival rates (up to 81 percent in adult females) more than compensate for the loss of some nestlings to this disease. High food densities in Tucson are probably responsible for the success of this urban population.

Details of mate selection and nesting biology in the Tucson area are also well known. Cooper's hawks attain sexual maturity in their second year, often before they have acquired their full adult plumage. So mated pairs can consist of different aged birds, for example, two full adults, two subadults, or a mixture of ages. It turns out that pairs of full adults, which represent about 83 percent of the southern Arizona population, have the highest reproductive success. They initiate nesting earlier, produce larger clutches, and have higher overall nesting success than other mate combinations. Pairs of subadults score lowest in each of these measures, which leads to the conclusion that experience matters when it comes to reproduction in this (and probably many other) long-lived species. Careful mate selection is a key to this success.

Like most birds, this species is monogamous, and mates often stay together for more than one breeding season. The division of labor between the sexes in Cooper's hawks shows why monogamy is the most common breeding system in birds. In this species, males are primarily responsible for nest building each year, and females do most of the incubation, which lasts thirty to thirty-six days. Males feed their mates during incubation, and after the eggs hatch, they deliver food to females which then feed the nestlings for up to twenty-one days; nestlings often ignore food brought to them directly by males. Young birds fledge about thirty-one days after hatching, which to me is an amazingly fast rate of development since young hummingbirds—orders of magnitude smaller than young hawks—fledge at about the same age (also see the Harris's hawk and hummingbird accounts). After they fledge, youngsters are fed by their fathers for several more weeks. This was what was occurring in our yard in mid-June in 2020. Once they've fledged, young birds are quite sedentary and stay within their natal home range for eleven to thirteen weeks before they begin to disperse and establish their own home ranges. As in most birds, female Cooper's hawks typically disperse farther from their birthplaces than males. In Tucson, the distance between their birth site and their first home range averaged 11 km in young radio-tagged females compared with only 6 km in radio-tagged males.

Hawks and owls are renowned for their amazing visual acuity. We've probably all seen red-tailed hawks soaring high above us looking for prey hundreds of meters below; they also typically perch on high structures such as power poles and tall trees when looking for prey. Cooper's hawks don't usually soar and instead hunt by stealth from low perches while scanning the environment for prey. Studies have shown that recently fledged youngsters like those in my yard have a success rate of about 56 percent when they first begin to hunt; with experience, their success rate will increase, especially when hunting by stealth. Extremely sharp eyesight is the key to this success.

Avian eyes differ in many ways from ours. For example, their retinas have two to ten times more cones, which are important for visual resolution, than our eyes. It's as though we're operating with 8-megapixel (MP) sensors for eyes whereas raptors are operating with 40 MP sensors. Also, the highest density of cones occurs in two visual fovea (depressions in the retina): a temporal fovea located on the side of the retina near the optic nerve, which enhances overall visual acuity, and a central fovea located in the center of the retina, which enhances peripheral acuity. Compared with red-tailed hawks, Cooper's hawks have wider fields of binocular vision in front of them, smaller blind spots behind them, and greater eye movement. These differences give Cooper's hawks more spatial information when attacking prey and enhance prey detection in visually cluttered environments. Wouldn't it be exciting to see the world as this hawk does? And then to accompany one as it scans for and detects prey and then pursues and captures it at about 40 kph? All the while flying through dense vegetation? I'm sure this would be much more exciting than Disneyland's Mr. Toad's Wild Ride.

As mentioned above, reverse sexual size dimorphism (RSD) in which females are larger than males is common in many species of raptors. Adult female Cooper's hawks are about one-third larger than adult males—a greater difference than occurs in most hawks. Reasons for this reversed size difference have been discussed by ornithologists for many years. It has been suggested, for example, that larger females—the incubators in raptors—can cover more eggs during incubation; this explanation has been rejected. In their review of relevant hypotheses to explain this phenomenon, Malte Andersson and Ake Norberg, two Swedish ecologists, suggested that three factors must be taken into account for an adequate explanation. These include (1) partitioning of sex roles—large females can effectively guard nests against predators while small males are effective at capturing small, agile prey; (2) direction of role partitioning and direction of size dimorphism—larger females can lay larger eggs but are less agile foragers than smaller, more agile males; and (3) degree of dimorphism—when birds (i.e., agile prey) are the main food type, smaller males should be more effective predators than larger males or larger females, hence their rate of prey delivery to females and their nestlings should be high. Furthermore, when both sexes begin hunting for food after nestlings are about half grown, then dimorphic males and females should compete less for the same prey than if they were monomorphic. An Australian ornithologist Jonny Schoenjahn and colleagues have recently reviewed hypotheses explaining the evolution of RSD in raptors and have concluded that only one hypothesis—larger females are favored because they can effectively defend nests—is needed to explain it. Whatever the ultimate reason, RSD must be a successful evolutionary strategy for avian predators that feed primarily on birds because it is common in these predators. It's what works for them.

A rigorous way to examine the evolution of reverse sexual size dimorphism in raptors (and other organisms) is to map this trait onto their phylogeny. The widespread availability of detailed phylogenies of all kinds of organisms in recent decades has revolutionized our understanding of how adaptations evolve. With a phylogeny in hand, we can ask, is the adaptation or trait of interest ancestral in our group or is it derived? If it is derived, how many times has it independently evolved in this group—only once or multiple times? Furthermore, have there been any evolutionary reversals or losses of this trait in this group? If so, under what conditions has this reversal occurred? In the case of RSD in raptors, this kind of study has apparently not yet been done, probably because a well-resolved phylogeny for these birds is not yet available. Nonetheless, the fact that this trait is widespread in raptors, whereas it is uncommon in most other groups of birds, suggests that it likely is the ancestral condition in this family. Supporting this, ospreys (Pandionidae) are the closest relatives of hawks, and they also exhibit RSD. Secretary birds (Sagittariidae) are ancestral to both ospreys and hawks, and they only exhibit a small degree of sexual size dimorphism. Therefore, it is likely that RSD evolved once in the ancestors of ospreys and hawks. It has apparently been lost in nonpredatory vultures.

Hawks and their relatives have recently been classified in the avian order Accipitriformes, which has been separated from order Falconiformes that contains a single family Falconidae (falcons and caracaras). Accipitriformes currently includes three families: Accipitridae (hawks and eagles, cosmopolitan with about 239 species informally divided into about eight subfamilies), Pandionidae (ospreys, cosmopolitan with one species), and Sagittariidae (secretary birds, Africa with one species). The order apparently evolved in the Early Eocene (about 50 Ma), probably in Africa; family Accipitridae evolved in the Late Eocene (about 35 Ma), and its modern genera date from the Early Oligocene (about 30 Ma). Early members of Accipitridae, including kites and vultures, were opportunistic feeders or scavengers. Species of *Accipiter* and *Buteo* that feed primarily on birds and mammals are relatively derived members of this family. We do not yet have a comprehensive, dated phylogeny of the cosmopolitan genus *Accipiter*, which contains about fifty-nine species, so details of its evolution are currently unavailable. *Accipiter cooperii* and its close relative *A. striatus* (sharp-shinned hawk) have a new-world distribution and presumably evolved there. Of these two species, *A. striatus* has the broadest geographic distribution; in addition to North and Central America, it also occurs in southeastern Brazil and northern Argentina. *Accipiter cooperii*, in contrast, occurs only in North America and northern Central America. Like many modern birds, evolution of species of *Accipiter* likely began in the Miocene, and if its new-world diversification was similar to that of *Buteo*, then it continued on into the Pliocene (i.e., within the last 5 Ma). If this is true, then the Cooper's hawk has probably had a relatively short evolutionary journey in space and time, although the evolutionary roots of its family obviously are much deeper.

HARRIS'S HAWK

Parabuteo unicinctus Audubon, 1837, Accipitridae. These handsome birds are substantially larger than the Cooper's hawk. Reverse sexual size dimorphism also occurs in this raptor. Males weigh about 700 g, and females weigh about 1,060 g. Besides being larger than Cooper's hawks, adults are dark brown overall with reddish wing coverts and a moderately long white-tipped tail with a large white base. As a result, adults are easily distinguished from other hawks in our area.

Like Cooper's hawks, this species is quite urbanized and can be seen throughout Tucson. This is a relatively new phenomenon dating from the late 1980s. It must nest close to our neighborhood because we sometimes see them perched on dead trees and power poles along Orange Grove Road, the major east-west road closest to us; we also see them perched on power poles along La Cañada Road, the major north-south road closest to us.

Compared with Cooper's hawks, I've had limited contact with this species. They've occasionally flown over our yard but have rarely landed in our large mesquite trees. I also seldom saw them during my desert fieldwork in Sonora (nor did I see Cooper's hawks there, either). I once caught a glimpse of a group of these hawks chasing a jackrabbit in Organ Pipe Cactus National Monument where we worked in the spring of 1997. My most extensive contact with them occurred in the summer of 2016 when I spent a month watching and photographing a nest containing two nestlings along Tangarine Road, which runs east-west between Oro Valley and the town of Marana about 16 km north of us. At that time, an extensive patch of undisturbed desert scrub containing a high density of saguaro cacti occurred south of Tangarine whereas a new housing development occurred north of it. That summer Tangarine was being widened, and the nest I was watching was located about 6 m up in a large saguaro on the southern edge of the road. Heavy truck traffic, including cement trucks, often passed by the nest tree, and extensive vegetation clearing was occurring near it along the roadway. After the young hawks fledged, the nest tree was destroyed.

I photographed at this nest from June 27 to July 28, a period when afternoon temperatures often were greater than 38°C. I spent from one to four hours observing and photographing at the nest on fourteen occasions for a total of about twenty-eight hours; these sessions occurred throughout the day because I wanted to know when adults were delivering food to the nestlings. This was likely a second nesting, according to Brian, a young apprentice falconer whom I met at the nest. He said the first nesting failed during a very hot spell in May.

The nesting cycle of this species includes the following major events. Both parents are involved in nest building, and the female does most of the incubation, occasionally aided by the father and at least one helper male; incubation lasts about thirty-five days. Nestlings gain their gray juvenile down at an age of about ten days; they begin to peck at food by themselves by seventeen days, having been fed by the female before then. Food is delivered to the nestlings for at least forty days after which they begin to "branch hop," which involves hopping and briefly flying among the branches of the nest tree. They fledge at an age of forty-five (males) or forty-eight (females) days. Fledglings remain within their nest home range for several months (in females) to up to several years (in males). Young birds begin to forage with their group two months after fledging.

On June 27 the nestlings were covered with gray juvenile down, which means that they were at least eight days old. By backdating, their eggs must have been laid about forty-seven days earlier (on about May 11), and they hatched on about June 19. Forward dating suggested that they should be ready to fledge on about July 27, which was exactly what happened. Between those dates, the nestlings were attended or watched by four adult birds: the female who brooded them and brought them food and three others, presumably the father and two helpers. The female was either at the nest (as I arrived) or perched on a nearby saguaro (after I arrived). The other three birds were either perched on distant power poles or saguaros or circling high above the nest area; they often called/screamed from the perches or on the wing.

During my visits, I only saw the nestlings eat three times—once on a rabbit that had previously been cached in the nest and once after the female delivered another partial cottontail rabbit to them one morning. On the third occasion, only one nestling was left in the nest, and it fed on a cached rabbit in the afternoon. In addition, I saw the female eating a rabbit while perched on a nearby saguaro late one afternoon. As I noted with young Cooper's hawks, the nestling Harris's hawks did not fight over food in the nest. One bird, probably the larger female, fed first before letting the smaller (male?) bird feed. Most of the time during my visits the nestlings were crouched low and asleep in the shade of the nest. After they began standing up, they remained in the shade of the cactus branches. They grew very fast and were approaching adult size and were well feathered by July 14 (at an age of only twenty-five days), when they began to occasionally issue "whistle" calls. I never saw an adult bird respond to these calls. Late in the afternoon of July 25, the nestlings began jumping up and down and flapping their wings; they then both hopped or flew to cactus branches in the nest tree. On July 27, one nestling (the larger one) was gone; it had probably fledged earlier that morning. Seeing the adult female fly across Tangarine heading northeast that afternoon, I guessed that's where the female nestling had gone. The remaining bird continued to branch hop late in the afternoon of that day and ate a cached rabbit. The next morning it fledged, and I found it in the desert flying clumsily from plant to plant 100 m south of the nest tree. The adult female and two other adults were watching it from nearby saguaros. I wished all these birds the best of luck as I left this site for the last time.

The social behavior of Harris's hawks, which often involves helpers at the nest and group foraging, differs strongly from that of the Cooper's hawk, which has a more typical avian social system involving only a mated pair of birds. Like the Cooper's hawk, the ecology and behavior of this species has been extensively studied in Arizona by faculty and students at the University of Arizona's School of Renewable Resources, mostly in the 1980s. At the same time they were also being studied in southeastern New Mexico by a graduate student at the University of New Mexico. Together, these studies provide us with detailed accounts of the fascinating social behavior of this hawk. For one thing, these and other studies show that there is a striking difference in the prevalence of cooperative breeding and group foraging in this species' broad geographic range, which includes parts of North, Central, and South America. In the United States, the frequency of group living is high in Arizona (53 percent) and New Mexico (51 percent) and low in Texas (9 percent). It is not present at all (or only very rarely) where this hawk occurs in arid parts of Central America and southern South America. This, of course, immediately raises the question, what's behind this geographic variation? Why is group living, which clearly is an evolutionarily derived condition, so high in the desert southwest? Before I address this question, we need to review the nesting cycle and the basic elements of social living in this hawk.

In southern Arizona, Harris's hawks are common and nest density is relatively high—up to 2.5 nests/km^2; nests are spaced about 1.8 km apart. Eggs are laid between mid-January and mid-August, and fledging occurs from April to October. Clutch size ranges from one to five with an average of 3.2 eggs per nest; about 50 percent of the eggs that hatch produce a surviving fledgling and about 74 percent of nests produce at least one fledgling each season. Sex ratio at hatching is slightly male biased (1.2 males:1 female). In years of high prey availability, about 22 percent of nests produce two clutches. Although the diets of Harris's hawks in this area are quite diverse and contain a variety of lizards, birds, and mammals, cottontail rabbits are the most common prey items; among birds, Gambel's quails are taken most frequently and among reptiles, desert spiny lizards are most common. Major nest predators here include ravens, great horned owls, and red-tailed hawks.

There is some disagreement about whether or not Harris's hawks defend their home ranges and hence are territorial. Researchers in Arizona claim that they are, mainly because adjacent home ranges do not overlap, but if it exists, aggressive territorial defense is not frequent. During the nesting season, Arizona birds remain within about 800 m of the nest except when they fly longer distances (up to 3 km) to water sources. In southeastern New Mexico, territorial behavior has not been reported and suitable habitat used by nesting birds is not completely occupied. Thus, suitable nesting habitat does not appear to be limited, and there probably is little reason for birds to defend their home ranges against conspecifics. In both areas, birds remain in their home ranges within and between years.

In Arizona, where cooperative breeding and group foraging occurs in about half of the nests, groups typically consist of a linear dominance hierarchy that includes a mated pair of alpha birds in which the female is dominant over the male, an adult beta male, and one or more young adult or subadult gamma males and females. Dominance in these birds is determined by how close individuals are allowed to the nest. In addition to defending nests, alpha males have access to their nest and are involved in incubation, brooding, and feeding the young; beta males can only bring food to an alpha bird which in turn feeds it to nestlings; gamma birds can only participate in group foraging and nest defense. Beta males are unrelated to the alpha birds whereas the gamma birds are offspring of the alpha pair that have not yet dispersed.

Cooperative breeding, in which three or more individuals participate in a single nesting event, is uncommon in birds; only an estimated 9 percent of all bird species exhibit this breeding system. In diurnal raptors, it is somewhat more common (e.g., in about 26 percent of genera and 13 percent of species in Accipitridae). Its evolution in birds has been widely discussed, but no single explanation appears to be adequate to account for its occurrence in Harris's hawk. One explanation involves nesting success: cooperative breeders raise more offspring per nesting attempt than pairs. But this is not the case in

Harris's hawks. Another explanation involves prey capture for feeding nest-lings: cooperative breeders should be able to deliver more food and perhaps larger prey to nestlings than pairs. Again, this is not true in Harris's hawks. A third explanation is that a particular habitat is saturated with territories, so it pays for young birds to remain with and help their parents until new space becomes available. This explanation seems to be true for Florida scrub jays, which have very restricted habitat requirements, but it probably isn't true for Harris's hawks.

In the cooperative breeders, group foraging occurs both during and after the nesting season. During the nesting season, hunting groups consist of birds associated with a particular nest. After the nesting season, aggregations of birds from several adjacent home ranges form. In Arizona, these units contain 4 to 11 birds (with an average of 5.9); they increase in size during the winter only to drop to zero when nesting begins. Interestingly, aggressive behavior, which is generally uncommon and very mild in this species, occurs only between birds in these hunting aggregations. The most intense form of aggression involves "foot grabbing" in which two birds stand on the ground next to each other and grab each other's feet for a few minutes; between bouts of foot grabbing, they may briefly strike each other with their wings and feet. Sounds pretty rough, right? As an indication of the highly social nature of these birds, foot grabbing and other milder forms of aggression (e.g., supplanting a bird from a nest or perch) in this species is quite stereotyped and understated. It's as though these birds are hardwired to think, "OK, I think I need to show some aggression here, but we're really just friends, so I don't need to beat the poop out of you. A little shove or foot grab will do."

Group hunting behavior in Harris's hawks is highly sophisticated, perhaps as sophisticated as that found in social mammalian carnivores such as lions and wolves. As described by James Bednarz in his New Mexico studies, these birds prey mostly on jackrabbits and cottontails in the nonbreeding season. Cotton-tails can be taken by solitary hunters, but jackrabbits are up to three times larger than Harris's hawks and cannot usually be captured by a solitary hawk. This spe-cies therefore uses a variety of techniques to capture jackrabbits. These include having the group perch on tall plants (usually saguaros in the Sonoran Desert) around a potential victim and then pouncing on it from different directions; hopscotching over each other in a prolonged chase that ultimately wears the prey down; and having a single bird flush prey out of dense vegetation or a pack rat nest into a group of waiting hawks. Whether they are hunting as a group or an aggregation, birds feed on all or most of their prey as soon as it is captured; nesting birds save some of it to take to their nestlings.

In the end, the jury is still out as to why cooperative breeding and foraging occurs in some, but certainly not all, populations of Harris's hawks. Bednarz and his collaborator, Dave Ligon, favor the "large prey" hypothesis: groups are needed for capturing hard-to-tackle animals such as jackrabbits. According to Bednarz's observations and calculations, it pays for individuals to hunt in groups of five or six when they concentrate on jackrabbits because their meal size is then large enough to meet an individual's daily energy needs. Group hunting thus allows this hawk to capture larger prey than if it hunted alone—a situation similar to that in lion prides. Two falconers with lots of experience working with Harris's hawks, Jennifer and Tom Coulson, favor another explanation: the "challenging habitats" hypothesis. This hypothesis states that group foraging is advantageous in habitats in which prey can easily take shelter and evade predators. Dense vegetation and/or a high density of pack rat nests, which often serve as shelters for mammals and lizards eaten by these hawks, in their view, represents a challenging habitat. Groups are more likely to be able to successfully capture prey in these places than solitary foragers. Whether or not this is true remains to be seen.

Ultimately, we need an explanation for the evolution of *both* cooperative breeding and group foraging in Harris's hawks. These two behaviors are not necessarily tightly linked. Florida scrub jays, for example, certainly are cooperative breeders with helpers at the nest, but they aren't group foragers when hunting for acorns, their main food. Harris's hawks are therefore unusual birds on two counts: they breed cooperatively and they forage in groups. As a result, they are highly social predators and exhibit ecological and behavioral traits that, when they occur together, are uncommon in birds.

Probably because they are social and accustomed to cooperative hunting, Harris's hawks have become a favorite species among falconers in recent years. Falconry, or the use of raptors to capture or harass prey, has been practiced in various countries for several thousand years. Birds used in this sport include species of eagles and a variety of accipitrids and falcons. Currently, most birds used for falconry in Europe are captive bred rather than harvested as juveniles from the wild and include peregrine falcons, goshawks, and Harris's hawks. In the United States, it is still legal to remove young birds from the wild at an estimated sustainable harvest rate of juveniles of 5 percent for northern goshawks (*Accipiter gentilis*), Harris's hawks, peregrine falcons (*Falco peregrinus*), and golden eagles (*Aquila chrysaetos*).

One afternoon in late October 2016, I accompanied Brian, the young falconer I had met at the nest I photographed in July, for two hours as he flew Indie, a second-year male Harris's hawk, which he had removed from the wild, in desert scrub south of the July nest site. Indie had made fifty kills last year, all of them cottontails, and had made a double rabbit kill just last week. At the beginning of the hunt, Brian carried Indie on a perch attached to a 2 m pole. From this perch, Indie, whose leather jess was equipped with a small metal bell and radio transmitter, would fly out ahead of us and land on various trees and saguaros looking for prey. He captured and killed a Harris's antelope squirrel (*Ammospermophilus harrisii*), but Brian didn't let him eat it (it's a protected species in Arizona). Instead, he gave him a white mouse to eat. Indie also explored two pack rat nests without flushing any prey. Brian and I flushed one black-tailed jackrabbit and a cottontail, which Indie chose not to pursue. At sunset, Brian gave Indie another mouse before we left the area. He told me that he hunts Indie at several different sites around Tucson every week or so during the fall and was hoping to gain his official falconer's license later that year.

Finally, where does the Harris's hawk fit in the evolution of accipitrid hawks? It's the only member of the genus *Parabuteo* ("near Buteo"), and as its name suggests, it is closely related to the cosmopolitan genus *Buteo*, which contains about twenty-eight species, including the familiar red-tailed and broad-winged hawks (*B. jamaicensis* and *B. platypterus*, respectively). *Parabuteo* and *Buteo* are derived members of this family and evolved in South America in the Late Miocene (about 8 Ma). They both eventually dispersed into North America; *Buteo* then dispersed into the Palearctic. So Harris's hawk's evolutionary journey has been rather extensive in space (through much of the New World's arid lands) but not particularly long in time. Along the way, it evolved an especially high degree of sociality at the northern end of its geographic range. This sociality is particularly well developed in and around the Sonoran Desert.

GREAT HORNED OWL

Bubo virginianus Gmelin, 1788, Strigidae. This regal and unmistakable bird is North America's largest raptor. Who doesn't recognize its distinctive calls? Their soft *hoo hoodoo hooo hoo* calls ring through our neighborhood during the nesting season. At other times of the year mourning dove calls also sound like this. Like many other raptors, it exhibits reverse sexual size dimorphism with adult females weighing about 31 percent more than adult males (1,710 g vs. 1,300 g, respectively). Its distribution includes nearly all of North America, Mexico, and southern South America, and it breeds successfully in many different kinds of environments, including the southwestern United States. Its feathery "horns," large facial disks that house large yellow eyes, and very soft feathers, which provide excellent insulation as well soft flight, are notable.

My first close contact with great horned owls (GHO) came in the summer of 1964 when I was a nature counselor at National Audubon's Wildwood Nature Camp in central Massachusetts. In addition to working with young campers, my job involved "wrangling" a small menagerie of local animals, including a young GHO, a tame red fox, and twenty-six species of amphibians and reptiles. Every day I supplied our owl (I can't remember its name) with a couple of dead baby chickens from a local chicken farm. I always enjoyed entering the owl's big pen and feeding it. I admired its large, heavily feathered feet with their large, sharp talons that I did not view as threatening. I was slightly intimidated, however, by its large beak, which it would *clack, clack, clack* at me as a kind of greeting every day. It was very friendly, however, and would hop onto my arm and shoulder after I fed it. All in all, I got along very well with this handsome bird.

Now fast-forward to October 2018 in Tucson when an adult owl showed up one morning in one of our backyard mesquite trees. It spent all day sleeping in the tree, occasionally preening and yawning, and showed no distress when I took flash photos of it. As sunset approached, it woke up and stretched its wings in obvious preparation for its night's activity. After the sun set, it hopped to a lower branch, stretched again, and then flew off over the small wash just north of us. I was pleased but not surprised to see an owl in our tree because we had occasionally seen and heard owls in or near our yard over the years.

In November 2019 this event repeated itself with a slight variation. This time, two adult owls perched in one of our mesquite trees for two days. I again photographed them and watched them prepare for a night of hunting. Close to sunset on the second day, the two owls began to hoot softly to each other, and they moved closer together on different branches. Suddenly, one of the owls turned to face me and crouched down while fluffing out all of its feathers. It looked really fierce. I couldn't initially figure out what was happening until I saw an adult bobcat walking right past me on our patio! As it approached the tree, both owls flushed and left the yard; one landed on the edge of our neighbor's roof. We both watched the bobcat jump up on our patio wall and then down into the small wash and slowly walk away. Although the owls did not return to our tree again, they remained in our neighborhood that month, calling to each other from tall trees south of us and occasionally calling from our roof. In both 2018 and 2019, we commonly heard and saw these owls near us only in the late fall. At other times of the year, they were either silent or somewhere else in their territory.

In the spring of 2018, I was told about an active GHO nest in Oro Valley about 12 km north of us. I first visited the nest early on the morning of March 26. There I photographed a female and her two fluffy gray chicks in a former red-tailed hawk's nest located about 6 m above ground in a large eucalyptus tree. The next day I visited the nest for about two hours in the late afternoon and took more photographs. Talking with neighbors, I learned that the adult male was roosting during the day in a mesquite tree two houses down the street and that these birds had nested last year in another hawk nest around the corner. The male began hooting just before sunset and then left his tree. At sunset the female and two chicks began eating a pack rat that had been cached in the nest. One of my photos shows the pack rat's tail sticking out of a chick's mouth. From then on I visited the nest two more times to check on the chicks' development. On April 4 the chicks now had visible "horns." Mom and the chicks again fed on another cached mammal, probably a rabbit, at sunset. This time, the chicks begged for food and were fed small pieces of flesh by mom before she left the nest. On April 13, the chicks were larger, and mom was roosting in the tree above the nest. One chick eventually left the nest and joined her. Dad began hooting from down the street and then flew into the nest tree where he continued to hoot after sunset. As before, mom and chicks began feeding on a young cached cottontail just after sunset.

Unfortunately, that was the last time I saw these owls. When I returned to the nest on April 24, it was empty! A neighbor told me that she had found a dead baby owl in her yard 30 m from the nest tree on April 16, the day after the parents abandoned the nest. No one knew what had happened, but I'm guessing that a predator, probably a red-tailed hawk, attacked the nest on April 14. Normally, adult female GHOs are very capable of defending their nests against hawks, but apparently not this time. I revisited the nest site a year later, on April 19, 2019, and noted that the nest was not active.

Because they are widely distributed and conspicuous, GHOs and their population biology and behavior have been studied in considerable detail in many places in North America. Unfortunately, none of those places appear to include Tucson and the Sonoran Desert. Unlike Cooper's and Harris's hawks, GHOs have not been the subjects of research studies at the University of Arizona. Thus, much of the following information comes from areas other than the desert southwest. Ecological studies generally report that GHOs are territorial and that mated pairs remain on their territories year-round. Many aspects of the ecology and behavior of these owls, including territory size, population density, breeding success, and diet breadth, depend on the availability of prey. In "good prey years," territories shrink in size and breeding success and survivorship, particularly of fledglings, is high; the opposite occurs in "bad prey years." As a result, population sizes of GHOs appear to be limited by and fluctuate with the availability of their prey.

These owls are visual perch hunters, which means that they scan habitats from elevated perches (e.g., saguaros in the Sonoran Desert) looking for prey movement. Hunting is concentrated in the hours just after sunset and again just before sunrise. Perches often occur on the edges of open areas or near water, giving owls a clear view of potential prey. Once a prey is spotted, an owl swiftly and silently drops on it and crushes it with its powerful feet and large talons. Death probably comes quickly. Although they have broad diets and can be opportunistic feeders, they mainly concentrate on mammals, including lagomorphs, pack rats, other rodents, and skunks in our area. Diets generally consist of about 90 percent mammals and 10 percent birds. Among birds, these owls often prey on Gambel's quails, other owls, and waterfowl. They also raid the nests of crows, ravens, and other raptors.

Unlike other raptors, owls have the distinctive habit of producing pellets containing the fur, feather, and some of the bones of their prey. Pellets are formed in the gizzard and are regurgitated at least ten hours after birds have fed. In 2018 I collected a few elliptical-shaped pellets from under the nest that I photographed. They were very dense and looked like the products of a trash compactor. They contained masses of gray fur in which a few broken bones, mostly leg bones and no skulls or teeth, were tightly embedded. I could see nothing of any nutritional value, except perhaps the calcium contained in the bone fragments, in them.

The breeding cycle of these owls often begins in winter, earlier than most other raptors. In our area, this means nesting starts in January or February while it's still relatively cold. As is well known, GHOs do not build their own nests. Instead, they use the stick platforms built by other raptors or crows and ravens as nests. Pairs produce one clutch of one to four eggs (two is usual) each year. As in Cooper's and Harris's hawks, females incubate the eggs for about thirty-three days; she is fed by her mate during this period. Nestlings usually grow very rapidly—from about 35 g at hatching to 800–1,000 g at twenty-five to twenty-nine days of age in males and females, respectively. They weigh about 75 percent of an adult's weight when they fledge, after a few days of branch-hopping, at forty-five to forty-nine days. As in other raptors, this rapid growth reflects a substantial hunting effort by the parents. To feed a family of four, parents must capture and deliver (parts of) several prey items to the nest every day. Most of this hunting is done by the male during the four-week period of nestling brooding; then both parents become the hunters.

Once they fledge, young GHOs stay within their natal territory for several months before dispersing. Although they attain sexual maturity by an age of two years, young birds are not able to breed until they gain their own territory. This means that they will be "floaters" (i.e., mobile birds that drift through but do not possess a territory) for several years. Adult pairs aggressively defend their territories, which are relatively small and average 70–150 ha in Utah, against intruders. Floaters thus lead a rather precarious life until they can acquire a mate and a territory.

Despite the vagaries of their social lives and fluctuations in their food supplies, GHOs are long-lived birds. This is because they are large, powerful predators. From the start, they experience low mortality rates; nestling mortality is less than 10 percent, thanks to strong nest defense by females. Once they fledge, these owls experience an annual survival rate of about 86 percent. And a few lucky individuals can expect to survive for twenty years or more. Since they are quite sedentary once they've attained a territory, adults have intimate knowledge of their real estate for many years. As a result, in some long-lived raptors, including GHOs, home ranges or territories often decrease in size the longer they are occupied. Experienced birds know where safe nest sites, good shelters from weather extremes, and good hunting areas are. Consequently, they don't have to move around much to stay safe and well fed.

Like those of other raptors, the lives of GHOs depend on their hunting skills. This is particularly critical during the nesting period when males are hunting for a family of four or more. Certain anatomical adaptations enhance their nocturnal hunting success. These include feathers with soft, rather than rigid, leading edges that give them the ability to fly silently. As important are their visual and auditory senses. Owls are notable among birds for having frontally placed eyes that give them excellent binocular vision. Their eyes are especially large and occupy about 50 percent of the volume of their skull compared with only 5 percent in humans. Their retina is dominated by rods rather than cones and has only a central fovea. For those of you with a photographic bent, the tubular eyes of barn owls have a focal length of 17.5 mm and a maximum aperture (f-stop) of 1.13; values for the larger eyes of GHOs are 38.7 mm and f1.42. These values indicate that owls' eyes are designed for wide-angle vision and high light-gathering ability—not surprising features in nocturnal predators.

Although owls are often thought to have exceptional vision and hearing compared with humans, this is usually not the case. Under low-light conditions as found in a forest understory, the visual acuity of many owls is comparable to that of humans and cats. Because it is an open, light-rich habitat, hunting for nocturnal prey in the desert, however, is likely to be a lot easier than hunting in closed canopy forests. The ability to hear prey movements under low-light conditions is also important, and the two kinds of owls—those with and without asymmetrically positioned ears—differ in this. Owls with asymmetrically positioned ears such as barn owls (*Tyto alba*), whose left ear is located a bit higher than its right ear, are able to hear prey in total darkness whereas those with symmetrically positioned ears such as GHOs cannot. Asymmetrically placed ears, which have evolved independently several times in owls, create tiny differences in the arrival of sound to the two ears. This difference produces greater acoustic acuity in these owls. Reflecting their greater ability to distinguish soft sounds coming from both the horizontal and vertical planes relative to their heads, the auditory regions of the brains of barn owls and other species with asymmetrically placed ears are several times larger than those of owls such as GHOs that lack this anatomical feature.

In the end, however, Graham Martin (1986) has argued that since the visual and auditory senses of most owls under low light conditions are not that much greater than those of humans, something else is needed to explain their evolutionary success. He suggests that a key factor behind this success is their territorial behavior, which, as discussed above, allows owls to become very familiar with the best perches from which to hunt.

Up to this point, I have not discussed the physiology of raptors—for example, their metabolism, temperature regulation, and water conservation—because I could not find any relevant studies. This may be because species such as Cooper's and Harris's hawks are not suitable for this kind of research. This is not the case with GHOs, however. In the 1990s, their metabolic characteristics were compared with those of the spotted owl (*Strix occidentalis*), a species of considerable conservation concern, in a lab in Flagstaff, Arizona. Though the geographic ranges of these owls overlap in the western United States, their habitat use is quite different. Spotted owls live in cool, dark forests whereas GHOs live in warmer, more open forests in the Flagstaff area and elsewhere. Not surprisingly, their physiological differences match the ambient conditions of their respective habitats: GHOs had a greater ability to tolerate higher ambient temperatures (T_as) under controlled conditions than the spotted owl; gular fluttering (the method birds use to cool themselves via evaporation) in GHOs began at a higher T_a than in spotted owls; GHOs experienced much lower evaporative water loss than spotted owls as T_as increased; and the mass-specific basal metabolic rate of GHOs was less than that of the spotted owl and lower than most other nonpasserine birds. Both species had a similar body temperature (T_b) of about 39.9°C at all T_as. In addition, the thermoneutral zone (TNZ) of the GHO was quite wide: 20.3°C–32.2°C; it was very narrow or nonexistent in the spotted owl (see box 2 for definitions of physiological terms). Finally, unlike Cooper's and Harris's hawks, GHOs don't need to drink freestanding water; they obtain all the water they require from their prey. These results give us important insights into why GHOs are geographically more widespread and can tolerate a much wider range of environmental conditions than the forest-dwelling spotted owl.

The evolution of owls is complex and is still being worked out with ever-increasing amounts of molecular data and species coverage. This totally distinctive group of birds is classified in its own order, Strigiformes, containing two families: Tytonidae, the barn owls with about twenty-five species, and Strigidae, typical owls with over two hundred species. Both families now have worldwide distributions. Within Strigidae, three subfamilies are often recognized: the basal Ninoxinae, Surniinae, and the most derived Striginae, which contains the genus *Bubo* (GHOs and relatives). Biogeographic analysis of owls and a variety of other land bird families from a phylogenetic perspective suggests that the ancestors of owls (both barn owls and typical owls) evolved in Africa and that the derived subfamily Striginae evolved in the Nearctic region after owls had dispersed from Africa through Europe to North America. To judge from the evolutionary history of barn owls, which are basal to typical owls, the timing of "out of Africa" dispersal by owls probably occurred during the Oligocene (ca. 30 Ma). GHOs are closely related to snowy owls (*Bubo scandiacus*), which suggests that these birds have had a relatively recent northern origin, perhaps within the Pliocene (ca. 5 Ma). So the evolutionary journey of GHOs apparently has been relatively short in space and time, despite the deep evolutionary history of owls having begun in Africa.

WHITE-WINGED DOVE

Zenaida asiatica Linnaeus, 1758, Columbidae. This rather large, handsome dove is a migrant in the Sonoran Desert from farther south in Mexico. Adults weigh about 150 g, and the sexes are similar in size. Along with another migrant, Bell's vireo (*Vireo bellii*), its ubiquitous song "who cooks for you" is a harbinger of spring in our area. Birds arrive here in late March and leave in September. Their songs can be heard from well before sunrise until after sunset on many days. Because it's a large and very strong flier, it sometimes resembles a falcon in flight to me. But its large white wing patches and white tail tip always give it away. It currently ranges from the southwestern United States through Mexico as far south as northwestern Costa Rica; it is also widespread in the West Indies.

As I discuss in detail below, my main interest in this bird has been its relationship as a pollinator of flowers of saguaro cacti. I've never gone out of my way to photograph them extensively, but I cannot resist photographing them when they're feeding at saguaro flowers and fruit because these two species have a very special mutualistic relationship that in many ways is quite undovelike. A lot of people have told me they don't like this dove because it acts like a bully toward other birds (and each other) around saguaro cacti. But once they learn how important this bird is for the reproductive success of the Sonoran Desert's most iconic plant, their attitudes soften somewhat.

Along with Gambel's quail, the white-winged dove (WWD) is an important game bird in the U.S. Southwest, so its population biology has been studied by several state game and fish departments, especially in Texas, for decades. Prior to its population expansion in the southern United States in the 1980s, its population density was highest in the lower Rio Grande valley in Texas. Its highest population density now occurs in San Antonio, Texas, which should be excellent hunting grounds for urban peregrine falcons!

Estimates of its population trends in Arizona and elsewhere have been based mostly on game bag counts during the hunting season (originally August 1–September 15 but now just September 1–15 in Arizona) when birds congregate in flocks to feed in agricultural fields after the nesting season. Population trends of doves nesting and feeding in saguaro-dominated habitats are less well known. Prior to the expansion of large-scale agriculture in Arizona in the twentieth century, populations of this dove occurred primarily in the mesquite bottomlands of the lower Colorado, Gila, San Pedro, and Santa Cruz Rivers, but they are now more widespread, though smaller overall. Game wardens in the 1930s reported population declines of 50–80 percent as mesquite bosques were being cleared. More recently, peak numbers based on standardized "call counts" (i.e., counts of calling birds made from automobiles along standard transects) occurred in 1968 and dropped to one-half this number from 2000 on. Bag counts from the hunting season totaled 740,000 in 1968 and declined to about 131,000 in 1980–2008. At least 50 percent of hunted birds have been juveniles in most years. In addition to habitat destruction, a change in agriculture from one based on seed and grain crops to one based on cotton and nut crops has greatly reduced the availability of nesting habitat and food for these birds in recent decades. Nonetheless, WWDs are still common in the Sonoran Desert and have exploded in cities such as Phoenix and Tucson. Interestingly, although urban WWDs are infected with *Trichomonas gallinae*, it does not kill their nestlings as it does for mourning doves.

Like most birds, WWDs are monogamous, and both males and females are involved in nest building, incubation, and feeding of nestlings. Nests are simple shallow piles of twigs collected by males and arranged by females. Courtship is literally quite flashy: in the presence of a female, a male jerkily flings its wings up and back, dramatically exposing its white wing bars, while raising and flaring out its tail feathers, dramatically exposing their white tail tips. This stationary act is sometimes followed by a spiraling ascent into the sky and direct plunge back down to the female. If a female is impressed by this (and why wouldn't she be?), she allows the male to mount her and give her a quick "cloacal kiss." During courtship, nesting, and brooding males defend a small territory of 0.1–4 ha around the nest against intrusions by other adults. Clutch size in WWDs is nearly always two eggs that hatch after an incubation period of fifteen to twenty days. Nestlings are fed "crop milk"—an aqueous suspension of protein- and fat-rich cells produced in a bird's crop that is regurgitated by the adult—for their first three days after which they are gradually fed normal adult food. Nestlings grow very rapidly: from about 10 g at hatching to about 90 g at twelve days when they can fly short distances. They fledge at thirteen to eighteen days but continue to be fed by adults for another two weeks. Young doves are strong fliers within a week after fledging. Parents living near agricultural fields often start a second nest shortly after the first nestlings have fledged; desert dwellers tend to produce one clutch per year. Though a number of birds such as cactus wrens, Gila wood-peckers, and GHOs as well as tree-climbing mammals and snakes prey on their eggs, nestlings, and fledglings, annual mortality rates of both young and adult WWDs are relatively low (about 23 percent), and some individuals can live over ten years. Young doves are sexually mature at one year of age.

Although most new-world doves and pigeons are granivores, this is not the case with WWDs in the Sonoran Desert where they rely heavily on the nectar and brilliant red fruits of saguaro cacti for their nutrients and water during the nesting season. We've all seen WWDs sticking their faces deep into saguaro flowers or feeding at ripe fruits that have split open (the "second flowering"), but how important are saguaro products in the energy and water budgets of these birds? A precise answer to this question is now available through the use of stable (i.e., nonradioactive) isotopes, a general technique that I first introduced in my discussion of the doubly labeled water technique for measuring field metabolic rates (FMRs) of Gila monsters (page 73). In dietary studies, stable isotopes of carbon (^{13}C) and nitrogen (^{15}N) are used to characterize the general food com-position and trophic (feeding) position of animals, respectively. Deuterium (^{2}H) is the stable isotope used to determine the source of water in an animal's body.

As I will discuss in more detail below in the saguaro species account, cacti and other arid-adapted plants such as agaves have a photosynthetic pathway that differs from most other plants. It's called crassulacean acid metabolism (CAM). For our purposes here, all we need to know is that the carbon-stable isotope signatures of CAM plants differ significantly from those of non-CAM plants: they are much more enriched in ^{13}C relative to ^{12}C compared with other plants in which the ^{13}C:^{12}C ratio is much lower. Thus, knowing this ratio in an animal's tissue tells us how much of an animal's carbon comes from CAM plants com-pared with non-CAM plants. It doesn't tell us exactly which CAM or non-CAM plants are being eaten, just the general composition of an animal's diet. Choice of tissue being analyzed is important because rates of carbon turnover differ strongly among tissues. Rates of carbon turnover in brain tissue and bone, for example, are much lower than they are in liver and muscle tissue. "Slow" tissues therefore provide us with a longer time frame (e.g., months) than "fast tissues" (e.g., weeks) for the accumulation of carbon. Believe it or not, exhaled breath is now being collected and analyzed to give us an almost instantaneous picture of the carbon that's being ingested and metabolized by an animal. In similar fashion, the amount of deuterium in an animal's tissue can be compared with values from potential sources of water in food items or from freestanding water in the environment to pinpoint their sources of dietary water.

When these techniques are applied to WWDs in the Sonoran Desert, we learn that they are indeed saguaro specialists on at least three counts. First, their nesting season coincides with the flowering and fruiting seasons of this one plant species. Second, their beaks are 8–10 percent longer than those in other non–Sonoran Desert populations of this species. Longer beaks allow doves to more easily drink the nectar found in large saguaro flowers. Third, and most important, the carbon in their bodies comes almost entirely from saguaro flowers and fruit. As Martinez del Rio, Wolf, and Haughey (2004) have written: "In isotopic terms, breeding white-winged doves are warm, feathered fragments of saguaro flying about in the desert." Overall, while these doves are resident in the Sonoran Desert, 60 percent of the carbon they ingest comes from the saguaro cactus. The same is true about the water in their bodies: most of it comes from saguaro flowers and fruit. Over the saguaro fruiting season, WWDs consume the contents of about 128 saguaro fruits to help meet their energy, nutrient, and water needs. No other plant comes close to meeting these needs.

White-winged doves and mourning doves (*Zenaida macroura*, MD) co-occur in the Sonoran Desert, and it is of interest to know whether both species are saguaro specialists. Again, stable isotope analysis has been used, in part, to answer this question, but there are also other clues about it. For instance, MDs have short bills, and they feed mostly by pecking at seeds on the ground. They don't routinely visit saguaro flowers or peck at saguaro fruit before it has fallen to the ground. Results from stable isotope analyses indicate that at the peak of the saguaro fruiting season, over 90 percent of the carbon in WWDs comes from saguaro fruit compared with about 50 percent in MDs but that overall, saguaro fruit represents 50 percent and 14 percent of the diets of WWDs and MDs, respectively. Also, stable isotope analysis indicates that saguaro fruits are important sources of water for WWDs but not for MDs. These results clearly support the idea that WWDs are saguaro specialists whereas MDs are not. Finally, in the section on saguaro cactus, I will describe the contribution of this species to the nutrients and water consumed by the wider Sonoran Desert animal community.

How do WWDs cope with the environmental conditions—particularly, high T_as (to 50°C or more) and low and variable water availability—they face during the summer in the Sonoran Desert? And how does their metabolism and water economy compare with Gambel's quail (GQ), a similar-sized bird with a very different lifestyle? As we've seen, quails are reluctant fliers and are very sedentary whereas doves are very strong fliers that sometimes travel long distances (e.g., up to 20 km) to feed and drink. Because of their sedentary lifestyles, quails are shade seekers during midday and are less exposed to the hot daytime sun than doves. Given these differences, we might expect to see significant differences in the basic physiology of these birds.

Measurements of body temperature (T_b), resting metabolic rate (RMR), and rates of evaporative water loss (EWL) under controlled ambient temperatures (T_as) provide answers to these questions and support the prediction that WWDs and MDs are more heat tolerant than GQs. Please see box 2 for definitions of these physiological terms. First, both quails and doves have stable T_bs of about 41°C within and below their thermoneutral zones (TNZs). The upper critical T_as of these TNZs, however, differ; that of the GQ is 41.4°C whereas that of the doves is 46.2°C. Above these T_as, T_bs (but not RMRs) begin to increase at a significantly faster rate in GQs than in doves. As in roadrunners, these increases result in some energy savings. Also, quails and doves differ in the way they cool themselves by evaporative water loss at high T_as. Quails resort to panting, which is metabolically costly because it involves muscular activity, whereas doves use cutaneous (skin) water evaporation, which is a passive (energetically cheaper) method, to keep cool. Therefore, doves can tolerate higher life-threatening T_as than quails (58°C–60°C vs. 52°C, respectively). The one advantage that quails have over doves is that their rate of EWL is lower at high T_as, which means that they don't need to drink as much as doves. As a result, in addition to the water they gain from their foods (e.g., saguaro fruits), doves need to drink freestanding water every day whereas quails can usually obtain the water they need from their food.

These physiological differences probably reflect differences in the evolutionary histories of quails and doves, which belong to different avian orders. They also emphasize the evolutionary maxim that there are different ways to cope with or adapt to similar environmental challenges (e.g., panting vs. cutaneous evaporative cooling). They also have important implications for the effects of global warming on quails and doves. Doves will probably be more tolerant than quails to increases in T_a, but they will be less tolerant than quails toward decreases in water availability. How this plays out in the Sonoran Desert remains to be seen.

Pigeons and doves (there is no phylogenetic reason to differentiate between these two groups; they simply differ in size) belong to the avian order Columbiformes that currently contains only a single family, Columbidae, with 344 species classified in forty-nine genera. This order previously included another family, Raphidae, containing the extinct Indian Ocean island-dwelling dodos and solitaires. The demise of these distinctive birds shows how vulnerable island birds, especially ones that can't fly, are to human overexploitation. At least a dozen species of island-dwelling (flighted) pigeons have gone extinct on Pacific Ocean islands once they were colonized by humans. The extinct passenger pigeon (*Ectopistes migratorius*), a close relative of *Zenaida* doves and once North America's most common bird, is another example of how there is no safety in numbers in the face of intense human hunting pressure. Pigeons and doves are particularly vulnerable to this pressure because many species are relatively large, they tend to occur in flocks, and they are good to eat.

The order Columbiformes is very distinctive, but its phylogenetic relationships with other orders of birds have not yet been completely clarified. It is an old group, probably first evolving in the Eocene (ca. 53 Ma), although a recent phylogenetic analysis based on the entire mtDNA genome suggests that the family dates only from the Late Oligocene (ca. 25 Ma) and radiated primarily in the Miocene (ca. 20 Ma). Worldwide in distribution, these strong-flying birds are notable for their occurrence on many isolated oceanic islands. Recent phylogenetic analyses indicate that the family first evolved in South America and that a neotropical clade containing *Geotrygon* (quail-doves; this genus is not monophyletic) and a sister group of two monophyletic genera—*Zenaida* (which includes WWDs and MDs) and *Leptotila* (white-tipped doves)—had evolved by about 18 Ma. Within *Zenaida*, which contains seven species, both *Z. asiatica* (WWD) and *Z. macroura* (MD) evolved in North America within the last 2 Ma. Thus, although it is a young species, *Z. asiatica* has deep roots in South America but evolved long after its ancestors had dispersed into Central and North America after the closure of the Panamanian land bridge about four million years ago. Its recent evolutionary journey, therefore, has been relatively short both in space and time.

HUMMINGBIRDS

Anna's Hummingbird (*Calypte anna* Lesson, 1829, Trochilidae)
Costa's Hummingbird (*Calypte costae* Bourcier, 1839, Trochilidae)
Broad-Billed Hummingbird (*Cynanthus latirostris* Swainson, 1827, Trochilidae)

I've chosen to include here the three species that live in our backyard because of the similarity of their life histories and their highly intertwined behavioral interactions centered on our hummingbird feeders and flowering plants. Hummingbirds (family Trochilidae, about 334 species) belong to another totally distinctive family that differs in many of its biological features from all other birds. To a large extent these differences stem from their tiny size, which ranges from about 3 g to 20 g. As a family, they are the smallest birds in the world. I list many of their unique biological features in box 3. As I've mentioned previously, many of an animal's biological features depend on its body size, and hummingbirds illustrate this truism in spectacular fashion. Almost any feature you're interested in is superlative in hummingbirds. Of these features, my favorite is their amazing ability to hover and fly forward and backward. Their hovering ability has no equal in vertebrates, including my favorite mammals, nectar-feeding bats.

Hummingbirds are by far my most favorite birds as exemplified by the name of our house here in Tucson: Casa Colibri (Hummingbird House). One of my bat researcher friends once asked me why I didn't name our house after the nectar bats that visit our hummingbird feeders in late summer and fall (i.e., Casa Murcielago or Bat House). But I had to tell him that I actually like

BOX 3 Some Fun Facts about Hummingbirds

+ Small species have the fastest wingbeat of all birds: at least 80/sec up to 200/sec.

+ They are among the fastest flying birds: 50–60 kph in forward flight, up to 95 kph in dives.

+ They have the largest relative heart size of all birds; heartbeats up to 1,260/min.

+ They have the largest breast muscles relative to their size (30 percent).

+ They are the only birds whose wing upstroke provides as much power as the downstroke.

+ Their brain size relative to body size (4.2 percent) is among the largest in birds.

+ The structure of their feathers is very specialized, and they have the fewest feathers of all birds.

+ Their flight mechanism is highly modified for hovering and backward flight.

+ They are among the only birds that can become torpid at night, dropping their T_bs up to 19°C.

+ Individuals consume more than half their weight in food and drink twice their weight in water per day.

Modified from Johnsgard (1997)

hummingbirds more than nectar bats. Besides, *colibri* rolls off the tongue more easily than *murcielago*, right?

In retirement, I've spent a lot of time photographing hummingbirds at feeders and flowers. In addition to shooting in our backyard and at Tohono Chul, our local nature park, I've photographed them using multiple flashes synced to my camera in the mountains of Ecuador, Panama, and southern Arizona (e.g., in Madera Canyon and around Portal in the Chiricahua Mountains). From south to north, these montane sites have included twenty, nine, and six to eight species. Notable species in these areas include booted racquet-tails, violet-tailed sylphs, Tyrian metaltails, and sword-billed hummers in Ecuador; violet sabrewings, green violetears, variable mountain gems, and scintillant hummers in Panama; and magnificents, blue-throateds, rufous, and violet-crowned hummers in southern Arizona. In most cases, the birds are as beautiful as their names suggest.

Many people in Tucson are enthralled with these tiny gems and provide food for them with feeders and plantings. At our house, we have three saucer-shaped hummingbird feeders: two in our inner patio spaced about 12 m apart (so that one bird cannot dominate both feeders) and one around the corner by our dining room window. In addition, we've planted a number of "hummingbird plants," including natives such as justicias, fairydusters, red yuccas, penstemons, salvias, and yellow bells, as well as attractive exotics such as several species of aloes and pomegranate, to attract and feed them. As a result, there is always something for hummingbirds to feed on throughout the year in our yard.

How many hummingbirds reside in and around my yard and how do they behave? I have no accurate way of answering the first question because none of "my" birds is banded. I do know that both sexes of the three species regularly visit our feeders. Sibley's *Field Guide to Birds* indicates that Anna's, which is a recent immigrant into Arizona from California, is a bit larger than the native Sonoran Desert's Costa's: 4.3 g vs. 3.1 g. To my eye, Anna's is a longer, more slender bird and Costa's is somewhat stockier. At 2.9 g, broad-bills are a bit smaller than the other two species. The males of these species are easy to identify. Anna's males have ruby-red crowns and throats, and their throat gorgets (elongated throat feathers) are relatively short. Costa's males have brilliant purple crowns and throats, and their throat gorgets are conspicuously longer. Broad-bill males are dark green with a bright orange bill, and they lack a gorget. Less spectacular than the males, adult females of these species are quite similar to each other except that Anna's have a few glittery red feathers on their throats and the bills of female broad-bills are orange at the base. I cannot confidently identify juveniles of these species, though I know that juvenile Anna's occur in my yard after they have fledged from their nests. Anna's is the only hummer that nests occasionally in our yard.

Answering the second question is somewhat easier because these birds are very conspicuous when feeding and resting. My feeders are either abuzz with birds or are quiet, but not for long. Each feeder usually appears to be "controlled" by one individual. Before broad-bills showed up, in the fall and winter Anna's males controlled the two patio feeders while a Costa's male usually controlled the side feeder. By *control* I mean that these birds vigorously chase other birds of the same or different species away from feeders. Once they've (temporarily) cleared the area, the dominant males feed and then perch nearby. Costa's males usually perch much closer to a feeder than Anna's males, who perch and chatter away from branches of oleanders and mesquite trees several feet from feeders. Both males chatter when other hummingbirds are in the area but will also rest quietly when the area is clear. While perched, all hummingbirds are constantly scanning their surroundings and looking for other hummers and predators.

The arrival of broad-bills in 2017 from farther east in Tucson upset the pecking order of hummers in our yard. Despite their smaller size, broad-bills are very aggressive, and they immediately began to take control of the two backyard feeders. For a while, there was much strife among all three species while the new order was being established. Things eventually calmed down, but it is clear that when they're in our yard, male broad-bills now control both patio feeders. They also feed occasionally at the side feeder. When not feeding, these males sit in nearby bushes or trees and chatter quite loudly. The other two hummers are left to sneak into feeders when the broad-bills are away.

I describe the calls of hummingbirds as "chatter" but this is unsatisfactory to most bird enthusiasts. Thus, Sibley describes the perch calls of Anna's as "a scratchy, thin and dry *sturee sturee sturee, scrrr, zveee, street street*" and its chase calls as "a rapid dry *zrrr jika jika jika jika jika*." (How does one come up with these phonetic translations of such weird bird calls?) In contrast, the perch calls of Costa's are "an extremely thin, high buzz *szeeeee-eeeeeeeeew*." And its chase call is "a very sharp, high twitter *stirrr stirrr*." And male broad-bills produce a rather loud *tek tek tek* when perched. As I've said, they all sound like chatter to me.

Females also perch and chatter conspicuously and often wait until a dominant male is chasing another bird before beginning to feed. Dominant males usually clear feeders of other birds when they return from a chase, causing females to retreat into vegetation to await another feeding opportunity. Feeding in all birds occurs all day—from dawn to dusk—so there is constant activity, including occasional frenetic high-speed chases, all day long in our yard.

Finally, in the spring when many native plants are blooming, hummers temporarily abandon our feeders to nest and feed elsewhere. But as soon as the nesting season ends, they are back at our feeders and are as feisty as ever. Although much of their diet is liquid, hummers also occasionally visit our patio fountain for a drink. They also hawk insects from their perches and hover in vegetation looking for insects.

As I've indicated, only Anna's hummer nests in our yard. As a result, I've been able to photograph its nesting cycle in some detail. In 2009 and 2010, the same female, which I called Annie, nested in our yard. I know it was the same female because of her choice of nest sites. Her first nest site in both years was on a low branch of the Texas ebony tree outside our bedroom window; her second one was in a thicket of oleander shrubs along our south patio wall. In both years she was able to fledge all four of her nestlings successfully, which is not always the case in these birds.

The breeding systems of hummingbirds are based on polygyny, not monogamy, the most common breeding system in birds. As is well known, male hummers are only sperm donors and have nothing to do with nest building, incubation, or raising the nestlings. They're always off looking for another female to impregnate while a mated female initiates and completes the nesting cycle alone. Here I will focus on Anna's hummingbird because this is the species whose nesting cycle I've photographed. During its breeding season, which usually lasts from December to May, Anna males defend and display on tiny (ca. 0.1 ha) breeding territories in an attempt to attract females. Courtship can be complex and involves horizontal flights around a female or, more spectacularly, one or more (up to forty) J-shaped dives from as high as 35 m above the female; he sings to her before beginning each dive. During the dive, he is flying at a speed of about 97 kph! Copulations may or may not occur after a dive; they are very brief and occur close to the ground. It is likely that females may copulate with several males before she lays her eggs.

Females build beautiful little cup-shaped nests that are just large enough for two eggs with mama sitting on them. They are about 4 cm in diameter and are composed of soft plant and animal material held together with spider webs. Once during nest construction in our yard, I placed a clump of my newly cut white hair under the nest tree; some of my hair was then incorporated into the nest. Hummingbirds invariably lay two eggs of jelly-bean size and shape in the nest. Incubation lasts about sixteen days during which females spend about 75 percent of each day on the nest. Hatchlings are altricial (helpless, not precocial), honeybee-sized, and black; their beaks are wedge-shaped at hatching. Once they've hatched, they're fed mixtures of nectar and tiny insects. Their eyes are open by five days of age, and they can thermoregulate by thirteen days; they sit on the edge of the nest and flutter their wings at twenty-one days. Young birds fledge at about twenty-three days and sit in nearby vegetation and beg for food from mom; she will feed them for an additional one or two weeks before they disperse. The entire nesting cycle from nest construction to fledgling takes about forty-three days, after which a female often initiates another nest. My photographs show that nestlings and their bills grow very rapidly. Within a couple of weeks after hatching, they have long, thin, adult-sized bills. They are about two-thirds the size of mom at fledging. Finally, most females breed when they are about one year old; a few from eggs laid early in the season will breed before that season is over.

Hummingbirds are renowned as the most specialized and important vertebrate pollinators of plants in the world. They are known to pollinate over three hundred *genera* (and likely thousands of *species*) of plants in ninety-five *families* of new-world plants. Major plant families containing hummingbird-pollinated plants (or simply called hummingbird plants) include Acanthaceae, Bromeli-aceae, Fabaceae, Heliconiaceae, Lamiaceae, and Rubiaceae. In Arizona, these families include Agavaceae, Bignoniaceae, Cactaceae, Convolvulaceae, Fouquie-riaceae, Polemoniaceae, and Scrophulariaceae as well as Fabaceae and Rubiaceae. Overall, about 60 percent of hummingbird plants are herbs or shrubs, and only about 10 percent are trees; epiphytes such as bromeliads are also important food plants in the tropics.

Hummingbirds have long had a coevolutionary relationship with their food plants in which plants provide energy-rich nectar to the birds and gain effective pollination and gene dispersal in return. As a result, it is quite easy to identify hummingbird plants by the characteristics of their flowers, which are often red in color and tubular in shape. Flowers from many plant families have acquired these kinds of flowers via convergent evolution. Many phylogenetic analyses have shown that hummingbird flowers have often evolved from insect-pollinated ancestors. Within the new-world pineapple family (Bromeliaceae), for instance, the ancestral condition is terrestrial plants like pineapples with bee pollination. Once they evolved an epiphytic habit, however, their flowers began to attract hummingbirds. As a result, species diversity in this family, especially in the Andes, has increased rapidly in the last five million years. Now most species in that family are epiphytic and hummingbird-pollinated; a few of them are even pollinated by nectar-feeding bats. Many bat flowers have evolved from hummingbird flowers within the past three to four million years.

A good example of a hummingbird plant in our yard is the firecracker plant (*Russelia equisetiformis*, Plantaginaceae) from Mexico and Guatemala. It is a small shrub with a large mound of long, thin branches that bear on their tips small, red, tubular flowers measuring 20 mm in length and 4–5 mm in width. Like many hummingbird flowers, they produce minute amounts of nectar (e.g., a couple of microliters). Both branches and flowers often sway in the wind, but this doesn't deter hummingbirds from visiting them. Hovering in front of a moving flower, a Costa's hummingbird inserts its 17–18 mm long bill into the narrow corolla tube with surgical precision for a few seconds before backing off and visiting another flower. This beautiful interaction never ceases to amaze me.

Hummingbirds invoke their elegant dance with flowers as a result of a suite of morphological adaptations that include their wings, tongues, and eyes. Unlike other birds whose wings have flexible wrist and forearm joints, hummingbird wings operate as a single oar-like unit during its upstrokes and downstrokes; their wings thus act like a variable-pitch rotor. During the downstroke the wing moves in a vertical oval whereas it moves in a horizontal figure-eight plane while hovering. During the upstroke, the wing feathers are rotated backward to provide thrust. A modified humerus and its articulation with the pectoral girdle, unique to hummingbirds, allows these complex wing movements.

Hummingbird tongues are forked and grooved, are about as long as their bills (e.g., usually 15–20 mm), and are thrust forward during feeding by the hyoid (throat) bones. They dip their tongues into flowers or feeders very rapidly, about ten to fifteen times a second. The groove-like tubular structure of their tongues allows them to obtain a small quantity of nectar rapidly with each dip. High-speed videography has shown that this occurs as the forks separate and the sides of the tube roll out to acquire nectar. The nectar-filled tongue is then retracted back into the mouth where the tube closes and squeezes out the nectar, all in less than one-tenth of a second.

Characteristics of a hummingbird's eyes are also intimately involved with its feeding. When they aren't feeding, courting, or nesting, hummingbirds spend a lot of time on perches looking around for food, competitors, and predators. From this, it is easy to infer that they have very keen vision. But this isn't necessarily the case. Under laboratory conditions, hummingbird visual acuity has been measured as the equivalent of about 20/100 (i.e., not even 20/20) compared with values of 20/4 to 20/9 for various raptors. I'm very jealous of these values because my visual acuity was once measured as 20/800! Their visual acuity is strongly limited by the small size of their eyes; hawks and owls, of course, are notable because of their very large eyes. Although they are not necessarily more sharp-eyed than most birds, more impressive is their ability to visually track other hummingbirds (or swaying flowers), often through environments that change rapidly in their extent of visual clutter (e.g., through vegetation and then through open spaces, etc.) during high-speed chases. How do they do this? The answer is quite technical, but it boils down to the unique ability of hummingbirds to focus visually on the rate of expansion of images in front of them rather than paying attention to images that are speeding by along their sides. I guess it's like the adage "Always keep your eye on the ball"; don't pay attention to other distractions. It's as though these birds are behaving like heat-seeking missiles that are locked onto a specific moving target. This kind of specialized visual system undoubtedly also helps hummingbirds locate and lock onto specific food sources in their environment.

Like other diurnal birds, hummingbirds have cone-dominated retinas and tetrachromatic vision. That is, they can see a wide range of colors, including those in the ultraviolet- or short-wavelength portion of the visible electromagnetic spectrum. Their color vision results from cones that contain visual pigments that respond to different wavelengths in this spectrum. For example, they have cones with visual pigments that respond to short (violet), medium (blue-green), and long (orange) visible wavelengths. In addition, many birds, including hummingbirds, have visual pigments that respond to very short (ultraviolet, UV) wavelengths. Since the petals and corollas of many flowers reflect in the ultraviolet, which we cannot see, it is thought that UV signals are aimed at pollinators. These signals often serve as nectar guides, literally visual paths to the nectar. Also, since many male hummingbirds have very iridescent plumages, it may be that females can discriminate subtle differences between males based on their UV luminescence. In addition to visual pigments, cones also contain three different kinds of oil droplets (red, yellow, and colorless) that further increase the spectral richness that birds can see. As a result, their visual worlds are much more colorful than ours, especially those of most nocturnal mammals that lack color vision altogether. Finally, although many of their flowers are red, their visual systems are not especially sensitive to that color. Experiments have shown that it is the nature of the floral reward, and not flower color, that is most important to these birds. They choose red flowers because they know from experience that they are likely to contain lots of (or at least some) nectar.

One sensory mode that is not available to hummingbirds and most other birds, unlike many reptiles and all mammals, is the sense of smell. As a result, with very few exceptions hummingbird flowers do not produce a scent, unlike flowers pollinated by most other animals. Hawkmoth flowers, which open at night, for example, produce a sweet scent whereas many bat-pollinated flowers that also open at night produce a "skunky" scent. When mango trees were in flower in my neighborhood in Miami, the air was heavy with a sickly-sweet (to me) scent that bees love. Interestingly, when bat flowers evolve from hummingbird flowers, they also evolve a scent.

In addition to their other fascinating biological characteristics (box 3), hummingbirds have an unusual diet dominated by sugary-rich liquid nectar. How do they deal with this unusual (for birds) diet that is rich in energy and water but poor in proteins and other nutrients? We know that in addition to nectar, hummingbirds eat a lot of small flying insects to the point that they are sometimes called avian insectivores that also visit flowers. Insects therefore supply the protein and most other nutrients that they don't get from nectar. In addition, hummingbirds have significantly lower daily nitrogen requirements than other birds, so they don't need to ingest particularly large amounts of protein to meet their daily nitrogen needs.

Their other major physiological challenge is getting rid of most of the water they ingest without losing the dissolved nutrients that it contains. Unlike other desert birds, Anna's hummingbirds and its relatives are not faced with a water shortage. Their problem is just the opposite—too much water. Most birds have kidneys that are designed to conserve electrolytes and concentrate their urinary wastes, but hummingbirds are an exception to this. Their kidneys do not have an exceptional ability to produce concentrated urine. As a result, they void rather copious amounts of urine along with uric acid; they are able to conserve some electrolytes in the cortex (the outer section) of their kidneys.

Putting it all together, how do hummingbirds manage their daily metabolic needs? For their size, hummingbirds have exceptionally high metabolic rates (MRs), primarily because of their high flight costs (i.e., hovering). On a mass-specific basis, their MRs are about 30 percent higher than that of a similar-sized mammal. But being very small, they don't actually need to ingest large amounts of energy every day to remain in positive energy balance. Furthermore, their main food—nectar that contains about 20 percent sugar—is nearly 100 percent digestible. So their feeding efficiency is also extremely high.

Researchers have used doubly labeled water and stable carbon isotopes to determine an Anna's hummer's daily cost of living. The former technique has been used to calculate its field metabolic rate (FMR; see above and box 2). Results indicate that in the nonbreeding season, a 4.5 g male hummer needs to ingest about 32 kCal of energy per day. This value is about 5.1 times its basal metabolic rate (BMR) and varies with time of day. During daylight hours, its FMR is about 6.8 times its BMR whereas it is only 2.1 times its BMR at night. A bird can meet this energetic goal by ingesting about 9.9 g of nectar containing 2.0 g of sugar each day.

How many flowers would this hummingbird need to visit to obtain 9.9 g of nectar? At an average of about 5.7 microliters (μL) of nectar per flower in a series of Arizona hummingbird plants, the answer is 1,737 flowers. Visiting this many flowers in a day translates into a whole lot of flying and hovering (and energy expenditure) per day by this hummingbird. And, from a plant's perspective, all this movement means a lot of pollen and gene movement, which is what the plant clearly wants. By producing a small nectar reward per flower, plants are therefore forcing their hummingbird pollinators to move around a lot to obtain the energy they need each day.

Carbon stable isotope analysis of samples of hummingbird *breath* has been used to determine the fate of this ingested sugar. Potential fates include (1) it is quickly oxidized and used to meet immediate energy needs, especially those associated with hovering, or (2) it is converted into fatty acids and stored as fat for future use. During the breeding season when energy needs are especially high, most of the ingested sugar is immediately oxidized by the bird's exceptionally large flight muscles; little of it is converted into fatty acids. But during the fall, when many hummingbirds are preparing to migrate, much of the sugar they ingest is converted into fat, which is their main fuel source for migration. Feeding rates are particularly high at this time of the year because birds need to meet both their daily energy needs as well as build up a fat reserve. Prior to migration, some small hummingbirds will add enough fat to increase their mass by almost 50 percent.

Finally, all of the energy expenditure associated with high levels of activity year-round has a cost in terms of evaporative water loss (EWL). In most birds and mammals, EWL begins to increase above baseline levels (i.e., we're always losing some water via insensible routes such as through our skin and when we breathe) when animals are active and environmental temperatures (T_as) increase beyond the high end of their thermoneutral zone (TNZ). Because of their small size, high activity levels, and high surface-to-volume ratio, even in their TNZs hummingbirds have especially high baseline rates of EWL. An increase in EWL above baseline levels is the usual way that endotherms maintain a stable body temperature (T_b) when T_as are high. Anna's hummingbird has a T_b of 42°C, one of the highest values in birds, and the upper critical T_a of its TNZ is about 37°C. When T_as are > 37°C, it has two potential means of maintaining a constant T_b (or at least minimizing how fast its MR increases): it can expend energy via evaporative cooling, resulting in an increase in its EWL and MR, or it can allow its T_b to increase to save energy and water. It turns out that Anna's hummingbird does a little bit of both: when T_as exceed 37°C, it allows its T_b to rise slowly and it also increases its rate of EWL by panting. However, compared with other birds, maintaining a constant T_b via evaporative cooling in hummingbirds is not very effective. So these birds are quite susceptible to overheating under hot conditions. And with overheating comes an increased risk of dehydration. When they're not feeding during the day, they lose about 2 percent of their body water per hour. So, ironically, despite their high daily rate of water ingestion, hummingbirds are sometimes in danger of dehydration.

In summary, a hummingbird's lifestyle, which features lots of flower visiting as well as insect hunting, places unusual physiological demands on these tiny birds. They need to expend a lot of energy to acquire the energy and nutrients that they need while maintaining their water balance. Living in a place like the Sonoran Desert with its seasonally high (or low) air temperatures, dry air, and limited freestanding water can be especially challenging. This is probably why relatively few kinds of hummingbirds live in the desert. Many more species of hummingbirds live in tropical forests where they can easily evade high temperatures (by shade seeking) and where humidity levels are higher and water is more available which help to reduce their rates of EWL.

Although we usually think of hummingbirds as quintessentially new-world birds, their meager fossil record suggests a far different evolutionary scenario. Hummingbirds are members of order Apodiformes and are most closely related to swifts (Apodidae), a family of about one hundred species of highly aerial insectivores whose greatest diversity occurs in Eurasia. Molecular evidence suggests that these two families last shared a common ancestor about 42 Ma, and fossil evidence suggests that this split likely occurred in the Old World, not the New World. Supporting this scenario, the German paleontologist Gerald Mayr (2004) reported in *Science* a fossil bird whose morphology, particularly several features of its wings (e.g., a very stout humerus and ulna) and long, thin beak, uniquely resembled that of hummingbirds. He named this specimen *Eurotrochilus inexpectatus*; its geological age was estimated to be Early Oligocene, about 30–32 Ma, some 8–10 Ma prior to the early radiation of true hummingbirds in the New World. Subsequent to Mayr's initial publication, fossil hummingbirds of similar age have been reported from France and Poland. The morphology of these fossils, including their long, thin bills and backward-rotating wings, suggests that they fed by hovering at flowers, just as their new-world relatives do today. It also implies that hummingbird-adapted flowers had evolved during the Early Oligocene in Eurasia, although these kinds of plants are missing from the fossil record and that flora today.

In the New World, hummingbirds began an extensive adaptive radiation that ultimately resulted in nearly 340 species (so far) in South America about 22 Ma. Jimmy McGuire and collaborators (2014) have suggested that these birds migrated from Eurasia over the Bering Straits land bridge into North America and continued south, island-hopping from Central America into South America prior to that time. Unfortunately, we currently lack fossils to corroborate this scenario. Also, this or any other evolutionary scenario implies that there were appropriate food plants along the way. Since it can sometimes take a million years or so for plants to evolve hummingbird-adapted flowers from insect-pollinated flowers—the usual evolutionary pathway—dispersal from Eurasia ultimately into South America must have been a slow process. But again, fossils of hummingbird-adapted flowers from the Late Oligocene or Miocene in North America have not yet been found.

Once in South America, hummingbirds radiated rapidly, especially in the last 10 Ma with uplift of the northern Andes where at least 140 species have evolved. They colonized Caribbean islands and underwent a modest radiation there beginning about 5 Ma. At about the same time, they began to (re) colonize Central and North America with the closing of the Panamanian land bridge. Overall, this radiation has produced nine monophyletic clades of hummingbirds, of which the three youngest clades—mountain gems, bees, and emeralds—are the ones that contain species that currently occur in North America. Of our three common Tucson hummingbirds, for example, Anna's and Costa's are bees, and broad-bills are emeralds. Each of these species is a derived member of its clade and is less than five million years old. Interestingly, most of their major food plants both here in southern Arizona and farther north in western North America for species such as rufous, broad-tailed, and calliope hummers that pass through Arizona on their way to their northern breeding grounds, have temperate North American, not tropical Central or South American, origins. Exceptions to this include cacti, agaves, and ocotillos whose origins lie farther south in the New World. Most of the north temperate hummingbird plants are also less than five million years old.

The hummingbirds in our yard have recently evolved from species whose ancestry lies deeper within the new-world tropics. They have resided in North America for less than five million years, and in the case of the two closely related species of *Calypte*, they are recent additions to the fauna of the desert southwest. Of these species, Costa's hummingbird is truly a Sonoran Desert specialist; Anna's hummingbird is an urban opportunist that has immigrated here very recently from the chaparral of Southern California; and broad-bills are immigrants from arid lands in central Mexico. Their recent evolutionary journeys have been relatively short in both space and time, though their deeper evolutionary history likely began in Eurasia.

GILA WOODPECKER

Melanerpes uropygialis Baird 1854, Picidae. This is another easily recognized species based on its appearance, flight characteristics, and ubiquitous loud vocalizations. Medium-sized in its family, males are about 14 percent larger than females in mass and bill length (mass: males = 70 g, females = 62 g); only males have a red patch of feathers on the top of their heads. With flapping flight alternating with short glides, a woodpecker's undulating flight is distinctive. The Gila woodpecker's white wing patches are also distinctive. Its geographic distribution is restricted to the arid deserts of the southwestern United States and northwestern Mexico where it is common in cactus-rich desert scrub; it also nests in the broken branches of large cottonwood trees along rivers and streams. Although it eats many adult and larval insects captured either by pecking, probing, or by gleaning, it is quite omnivorous and eats cactus fruit and mistletoe berries in season. It's also the largest species that visits our hummingbird feeders for a sip of sugar water.

Gila woodpeckers were my constant companions during desert fieldwork in Sonora where they frequently visited the flowers and ate the fruit of saguaro and cardón (*Pachycereus pringlei*) cacti. In Tucson a pair that nests in a saguaro across the street from us often forages for insects in the large mesquites in our backyard. I've rarely been outside of the calling range of this species in the desert, cities, and towns of southern Arizona. In the "sky island mountains" here, however, Gila's are replaced by the very handsome and interesting black, white, and red acorn woodpecker (*Melanerpes formicivorus*), which lives in groups and stores acorns in communal granaries that they construct. Differences in their sociality and diet indicate that these two species are not closely related.

Gila woodpeckers are very common in southern Arizona where their population densities can be as high as fifty-eight birds/km² in desert scrub and from sixteen to twenty-nine birds/km² in urban areas, depending on the availability of suitable nest sites. Pairs of individuals remain together year-round and live in relatively small territories of up to about 10 ha. As we all know, their preferred nest sites are located in the trunks and branches of large columnar cacti, mostly saguaros around Tucson but also in cardóns in Sonora. Both males and females are involved in nest excavation, which usually begins in February. Nest cavities are about 30 cm deep and 5 cm in diameter. They cannot be occupied immediately because cacti need to form callus (wound) tissue around the cavity before it is suitable for use; this callus tissue persists as an "Apache boot" long after the nest plant has died. Since callus formation can take several months to complete, these birds are "building for the future" when they begin a new excavation. Once it is ready to be occupied, a nest will often be used for several years by a pair.

Gila woodpeckers have a typical monogamous social system. Their annual nesting cycle begins in April and ends in August in Arizona during which they may produce up to three clutches of three to five eggs. Although details of nesting and brooding of young are incompletely known, owing to the well-concealed nature of their nests, it is known that both parents incubate the eggs and both feed the nestlings several times an hour in the morning. Males and females tend to forage in different places—females are more likely to be gleaners of insects and males are more likely to excavate substrates for insect larvae—and hence they often bring different kinds of food to their nestlings. At the nest that I've photographed in May and June, both parents were bringing large insects and lots of saguaro fruit pulp and seeds to their nestlings. While out foraging, both birds are in constant contact by issuing their loud *quirr, quirr, quirr* calls. Young are fledged at about four weeks of age and often stay with their parents as they begin another nesting cycle. Gila woodpeckers are highly aggressive and territorial toward their own and other species, so, like young owls, recently fledged young woodpeckers likely become "floaters" in their population until they can acquire a territory.

As we all know, many saguaro plants are riddled with holes created by generations of Gila woodpeckers, and these plants become condominiums for other nesting birds once the woodpeckers have moved on. In my desert fieldwork, I saw elf owls, ash-throated flycatchers, violet-green swallows, house finches, and a colony of big brown bats nesting or roosting in them. Kestrels also nest in woodpecker holes, and ospreys and red-tailed hawks place their large stick nests in the crotches of saguaro branches near the Sea of Cortez. As we've seen, Harris's hawks also place their nests on saguaro cacti and use them as lookout posts. By creating nest sites for a variety of birds and mammals, Gila woodpeckers are playing an important role in the ecology of the Sonoran Desert: they have created a web of *commensal interactions* between saguaro cacti and nesting birds. Ecologists define commensal interactions as ones in which one or more species (e.g., the birds) benefit from interacting with another species (e.g., saguaro cacti) that is not necessarily affected by the interactions. Because many other animals use their burrows or dens for shelter, desert tortoises are also an important commensal species in this desert.

We've all seen woodpeckers foraging on trees, moving up trunks or along branches using their stiff inner tail feathers and zygodactylous toes (i.e., the first and fourth toes face backward or laterally, as in cuckoos and parrots) as props. But have you ever wondered about the challenges and mechanics of how, exactly, they feed when they're drilling for insects or their larvae? How do they avoid injuring their brains, for example, when they're pounding away? How do they avoid constantly being plagued by migraine headaches? As you can guess, these birds have important morphological adaptations for dealing with their unique feeding style. These adaptations involve their skulls, brains, and tongues. In recent years, material scientists and mechanical engineers have studied some of these adaptations using such techniques as micro-CT scanning, computer-produced 3-D models of skulls to measure various stresses, and mathematical modeling. Somehow, I doubt that the results of these sophisticated studies are of great interest to woodpeckers, who undoubtedly take their hard-won adaptations for granted and have done so for millions of years. But they are of considerable interest to structural engineers who are keen to apply lessons learned from biodiversity to building safer, stronger, and more efficient human devices.

When a woodpecker drills for food, its head is moving about twenty times a second at a speed of about 6–7.5 m/sec; it decelerates in about one millisecond (ms) at a force of 600–1,500 g. And it does this without incurring a concussion! For comparison, humans experience a concussion from a blow to their head lasting only 1 ms at a force of only 300 g, about one-fifth to one-half the force a woodpecker's head experiences. If the duration of impact is longer (typically 15 ms in NFL players), then the concussion threshold is even lower in humans. So woodpeckers must be doing something special to be able to do this. One thing in their favor is their relatively small size: they don't have particularly large brains, and the distances their heads travel is short. This means that their brains don't accelerate for very long, and they can potentially tolerate high forces associated with quick deceleration. Furthermore, their brain is more vertically oriented in the skull than in other birds, which spreads out its area of impact, and it is tightly packed in the braincase and surrounded by very little cerebrospinal fluid. Thus, the brain doesn't move much inside the skull during drilling, which also reduces its chances of suffering a concussion. In addition, the hinge-like joint between the upper beak and skull is particularly large in woodpeckers, which helps to decrease the compressional force between these bony elements, further reducing forces on the brain during pecking.

Finally, two other skull features help to reduce stress on the brain during drilling. These include the bar-like jugal bone that connects the upper beak to the braincase and differences in the resonance frequencies of the skull bones and brain during pecking. The jugal deflects stress from the skull's braincase toward the neck to reduce the impact of pecking. Also, the resonance frequency of the skull during impact is higher than that of the brain, meaning that forces generated during pecking resonate more strongly in the skull bones than in the brain.

Woodpecker tongues and their support by the hyoid apparatus are also special. Their tongues are nonfleshy, as in other birds, and are lanceolate in shape with barbs at the tip; they are very long and extendable (as in hummingbirds). In addition to spearing insects in woody tissue, their long tongues enable them to extract nectar from large cactus flowers as well as from hummingbird feeders, although their precarious perching on feeders is hardly very elegant compared with hovering hummingbirds. Their tongues are attached to a highly modified hyoid apparatus consisting of a Y-shaped, hornlike chain of four thin bones emerging from the throat region. The distal two bones in this chain are very long and wrap around the top of skull together; they sometimes end up inserting into a nasal cavity in the beak or around an eye, depending on the species. Muscles that extend and retract the tongue are attached to these "horns." Contraction of the extension muscles quickly shoots the tongue forward, well past the end of the beak. The flexible tongue tip then quickly searches for prey in the excavation and adjacent insect tunnels. Not all woodpeckers feed primarily by pecking, and their skulls and tongues therefore differ somewhat from those of the excavators.

When feeding their nestlings on hot days, adult woodpeckers sometimes slow down and seek shade on the trunks of saguaros and other trees. Their rate of food delivery to their babies is therefore constrained somewhat by their ability to tolerate high temperatures. How does the physiology of Gila woodpeckers compare with that of other Sonoran Desert birds? Results of a thorough analysis of the metabolism and water balance of Gila woodpeckers and gilded flickers (*Colaptes chrysoides*) conducted by Eldon Braun (1969) for his doctoral dissertation at the University of Arizona revealed that these two birds are not exceptional in their physiology. Both respond metabolically to changes in ambient temperatures (T_as) in typical endothermic fashion: they have thermoneutral zones (of about 30°C–38°C in the winter in Gila woodpeckers) below and above which their metabolic rates increase as they expend energy to either warm up or cool down, respectively. Their rate of evaporative water loss (EWL) increases at T_as above their TNZs. And their body temperature remains constant (at 39.4°C in Gilas) until T_as exceed 35°C above which it begins to increase slightly with an increase in T_a. At high T_as, these woodpeckers pant to lose heat via EWL. Nonetheless, they don't appear to be particularly water stressed and apparently obtain all the water they need from their food. I've never seen Gilas drinking at our patio fountain, unlike many other birds.

The one behavioral feature of these birds that helps them ameliorate the need for special metabolic responses to the T_as they face throughout the year is their regular use of their nest cavities in saguaros as shelters both day and night. The orientation of these cavities might be expected to be nonrandom in two ways: they should face north in the summer to remain cool, and they should face south in the winter to gain heat. Is the orientation of these cavities nonrandom? A study in Organ Pipe Cactus National Monument showed that cavities faced north more often than expected by chance but with considerable variation; many cavities faced southeast or west. Another study closer to Tucson reported that woodpecker cavities in saguaros were randomly oriented. Since many saguaros have many cavities in them, together these results suggest that woodpeckers always have a choice of where to shelter. On hot days, they should choose north-facing cavities and on cold days, just the opposite. I wonder which direction they choose when they're starting a new nest cavity. Does it depend on where the cavities that are already present in a saguaro are facing?

Woodpeckers are classified in family Picidae, which contains about 217 species in thirty-three genera with a nearly worldwide distribution, in the avian order Piciformes; they do not occur on Madagascar or in Australasia. In northeastern Australia, for example, their woodpecking ecological analogs are riflebirds (genus *Ptiloris*) in the bird of paradise family (Paradisaeidae), which represents a striking example of ecological convergence. In addition to woodpeckers, this order contains eight more families, all of them tropical in distribution; toucans (Ramphastidae) would be the most familiar one to most people. This is another old order, probably first evolving in Europe in the Late Paleocene or Early Eocene (ca. 55 Ma); modern families in this order likely date from the Late Oligocene or Early Miocene (from 30 to 23 Ma). The family Picidae dates from at least 22.5 Ma (Early Miocene) and first evolved in the old-world tropics. It is divided into three subfamilies of which Picinae, typical woodpeckers, is most advanced and contains most of the family's genera and species. This subfamily probably first evolved in Southeast Asia, also in the Early Miocene (ca. 20 Ma). Within Picinae, the Gila woodpecker belongs to tribe Melanerpini, a clade found only in the New World; it is an advanced member in this tribe. Like a number of other

Sonoran Desert vertebrates, it evolved in the arid lands of northern Mexico and the southwestern United States about four million years ago. Its closest relatives, *M. aurifrons* (golden-fronted woodpecker) and *M. carolinus* (red-bellied woodpecker) are Mexican or eastern United States, respectively, in distribution. The immediate ancestors of these birds occur in Central America. Therefore the Gila woodpecker's recent evolutionary history has likely involved a relatively short journey from Central America to the arid lands of North America where speciation has occurred within the past few million years.

CACTUS WREN

Campylorhynchus brunneicapillus Lafresnaye, 1835, Troglodytidae. Along with the greater roadrunner, the cactus wren clearly deserves to be considered an icon of the Sonoran Desert. Anywhere you find stands of teddy bear or jumping cholla cacti (*Cylindropuntia bigelovii* and *C. fulgida*), you're likely to find this species. Their preferred habitat is open desert rich in chollas and saguaros. Unlike other Arizona wrens, this is a large bird: adults of both sexes weigh about 39 g compared with about 11 g in the canyon wren (*Catherpes mexicanus*). With its long, slightly curved bill, rufous cap, white eyebrow, brown-streaked breast, and black-and-white-striped wings and tail, this species is visually distinctive. Even more distinctive are the constant loud vocalizations that males make to proclaim their territories year-round. Sibley describes their songs as low-pitched unmusical growls: *krrr, krrr, krrr*. They also issue low, knocking *kot, kot, kot* calls in long series. Whenever they're singing, often from high perches such as saguaros, male cactus wrens can be heard from long distances.

Cactus wrens do not occur in our yard because it lacks cholla cacti. But these plants occur around the periphery of our walled community, and so do cactus wrens. I have not made a special effort to photograph them but always do so when I encounter them. In my year of photo-wandering around Tohono Chul, for example, I took lots of pictures of them (when they let me). Although they are usually aggressive birds, they also can be quite shy, running or flying away from an approaching person. I found that I had to slow up and let them settle down before I could watch and photograph them. Once they seemed to be behaving normally, I was always impressed by their curiosity as they searched high and low for insects. They literally left no stone or leaf unturned during their searches. As a result, they certainly were much more fun to watch than robotic mourning doves pecking at the ground for small seeds.

A large amount of information is available about the biology and ecology of cactus wrens, much of it coming from a thirty-year study conducted by Anders and Anne Anderson (1973) in southeastern Arizona. Here I will summarize some of the basic features of its population biology. These birds have a basic passerine (songbird) life history, taking into account that they are nonmigratory and sedentary. Most Temperate Zone passerines (and many other birds) establish and defend territories prior to the breeding season, only to abandon them before migrating. Being sedentary, pairs of cactus wrens defend and remain on their territories year-round. Here in Arizona their territories are quite small: 1–3 ha during the nesting season and 4–6 ha in the winter when food availability—mostly insects year-round—is lower. To help visualize how small (or large) a 3 ha area is, remember that the formula for area is $A = \pi r^2$. A 3 ha area includes 30,000 m^2, so its radius is about 98 m—an area of about the size of six football fields (appendix 1). The nesting season here begins in February and lasts for several months during which pairs produce up to three clutches of two to four eggs each year. Females incubate the eggs for sixteen days and then brood the nestlings for another few days. Both parents deliver food—usually small insects—to their young. Nestlings are fully feathered by sixteen to seventeen days posthatching and fledge a few days after that. Young from the first nest usually stay in their natal territory for the rest of the year. They help their parents feed subsequent broods and help defend the territory. Like Gila woodpeckers and many other birds, once they disperse, young cactus wrens become floaters until they acquire a territory and a mate. They attain sexual maturity at one year of age. Annual survivorship for both fledglings and adults is around 50 percent, which is typical for many Temperate Zone passerines.

The nesting biology of cactus wrens differs significantly from that of many Temperate Zone passerines, however, because they build and use several nests in their territory each year. Some nests are used for egg laying while others are used for shelter. Nests are often placed in cholla cacti and other spiny plants, including saguaros. These spiny nest sites reduce the threat of avian and mammalian predation but don't necessarily protect them from snakes (e.g., gopher snakes). Nest building begins each year in February and is initiated by the female prior to egg laying; males are responsible for building additional nests while the female is incubating and brooding. The globular nests are composed of long-stemmed grasses carefully woven together to form a compact ball and are lined with feathers. They have a landing "porch" and measure about 18 cm in diameter and 30 cm long. It takes a pair of birds up to six days to build one, beginning with the floor, then the sides and roof, and finally the porch. Like other birds, they use only their beaks and feet to build these exquisite structures.

Weighing 39 g, cactus wrens are relatively small passerine birds, which means that their metabolic physiology is strongly influenced both by their size and their evolutionary history. This point has been emphasized by a recent comparative study of the metabolic physiology of seven species of Sonoran Desert passerines. These birds ranged in size from lesser goldfinches (*Spinus psaltria*, 9.7 g) to curve-billed thrashers (*Toxostoma curvirostre*, 70.1 g). Like many other passerines, the cactus wren's normal body temperature is 41°C, and the upper end of its TNZ is 37°C, above which it begins to pant to cool itself by EWL (box 2) Panting as a means of cooling to maintain a constant T_b is characteristic of passerine birds; it is an energetically expensive way to cool compared with cutaneous water loss used by doves (Columbidae). This study found that at T_as above each of the seven species' TNZs, metabolic rates (MRs), rates of EWL, and T_bs increased in a mass-dependent fashion: rates of increase were highest in the smallest species and lowest in the largest species. This means that small Sonoran Desert passerines, including cactus wrens, are especially vulnerable to suffering from high rates of heat gain and water loss during hot summers. This study also compared the passerine results with those of three previously studied Sonoran Desert nonpasserines: the much larger mourning and white-winged doves and Gambel's quails (see above). Compared with the passerines, these nonpasserines are physiologically much more tolerant of high T_as. Their TNZs extended to higher T_as, their MRs were slow to rise at T_as above their TNZs, and their rates of EWL were much lower above their TNZs. Large body size and a nonpasserine ancestry therefore can be physiologically advantageous for Sonoran Desert birds. As a result, if you are a small Sonoran Desert passerine, you need to take special care to avoid overheating and becoming dehydrated in the summer.

Observations of the foraging behavior of Cactus wrens in the summer indicate that, as expected, they move from exposed substrates (e.g., bare soil) to shady substrates as daily temperatures increase; differences in black-bulb (i.e., absorbing) temperatures in open versus shady substrates can exceed 10°C. That they are very sensitive to slight differences in ambient temperature is further indicated by their moving into open microhabitats, their preferred foraging microhabitat, when the sun is cloud covered and quickly moving back into shady microhabitats when the sun is exposed. Feeding visits to nests are also temperature dependent: they visit nests more frequently when T_as are < 35°C than when it exceeds this T_a. A controlled experiment showed that the reduced activity at high temperatures in these birds reflected an avoidance of heat stress rather than a decrease in prey availability.

An additional way that the cactus wren reduces its exposure to high temperatures is by building and using alternate domed nests as shelters. Another Sonoran Desert passerine, the tiny 7 g verdin (*Auriparus flaviceps*, Remizidae) builds and uses even more complex alternate nests as shelters year-round. Their nests are compact balls composed of an outer layer of small, spiny twigs and an inner layer of softer plant material with an outside diameter of about 18 cm. For years, a pair of verdins nested in the hopbush in our front yard, and they still frequently feed on small insects in our backyard vegetation.

Unlike verdins, which place their nests in shady trees, nests of cactus wrens in cholla cacti are totally exposed to the sun. As a result, during the nesting season, the interiors of breeding nests tend to be warmer than the outside air. This is advantageous to nestlings which don't begin to thermoregulate until they are seven to eight days old; they don't need to expend energy to maintain a high T_b before they can thermoregulate, especially in nests early in the breeding season. Later in the breeding season when T_as are higher, nestlings produce water-rich fecal sacs that help to reduce temperatures inside nests by evaporation. Nest orientation also affects their interior temperatures. Early season nests are built facing away from prevailing winds to avoid cooling whereas those built later in the season face into the wind and cool the nest's interior by convectional cooling. Nonbreeding nests are thermally advantageous to adults for two reasons: they protect birds from the direct rays of the sun during hot days and they reduce exposure of birds to radiative cooling at night.

Above I briefly compared the foraging behavior of cactus wrens and mourning doves, saying that wrens were more curious foragers than doves. As a result, to my mind, these wrens appear to be more intelligent than doves. In my rather limited work with birds, I've seen another dramatic example of differences in the curiosity of foraging birds. This occurred when I was on sabbatical at the Edward Grey Institute for Field Ornithology at Oxford University, where I studied the roosting and foraging behavior of pied wagtails (*Motacilla alba*, Moticillidae). This handsome black-and-white passerine somewhat resembles our northern mockingbird (*Mimus polyglottos*). It feeds by picking very small insects off the ground and grassy vegetation (and cow pats in pastures). At night in the nonbreeding season, it roosts communally with several hundred other wagtails in reed beds and departs in the morning and returns at night in groups. What I wanted to know was whether the communal roost was an "information center" in which birds shared information about the locations of good feeding areas.

One way to test this hypothesis is to put out rich patches of food (fishing maggots) in the feeding areas of individually recognizable birds to see whether they would bring conspecifics with them the next morning. Did they somehow tell their roost mates, either directly or indirectly, that they had found a rich feeding area? On mild winter mornings, I had to put the maggots in large plastic trays on the ground to keep them from crawling away. Whereas the wagtails readily ate maggots when they were on bare frozen ground, they completely ignored them in trays. Instead, small European robins (*Erithacus rubecula*, Muscicapidae), which like cactus wrens are opportunistic and curious foragers for insects, eagerly ate the maggots in the trays. In their stereotyped foraging, wagtails never even noticed that the robins were eating maggots near them. Incidentally, wagtails seemed to be tight beaked about the maggot patches. They never recruited new individuals to their enriched feeding grounds.

So how intelligent are birds, and does behavior that I've labeled "curiosity" denote intelligence? Are cactus wrens and European robins more intelligent than other passerines? We know that various species of ravens, crows, and parrots appear to be very intelligent, but what about the rest of birds; how bright are they? How can we measure intelligence in birds and compare it with other kinds of animals? One way to do this is to compare the relative brain sizes (or parts of brains) within and between groups of animals (e.g., crows or parrots vs. primates). Another way is to subject animals to various kinds of discriminatory tests to measure, for example, ability or speed of learning. The twentieth-century psychological and animal behavior literature is full of these kinds of studies. They tell us that corvids and parrots, like primates, have large brains relative to their body size and that in some cases their cognitive abilities are comparable (or even superior) to those of some primates. But what about other kinds of birds? A recent statistical analysis examined correlations between degree of habitat breadth, diet breadth and innovation (i.e., the addition of novel food items to a diet), degree of technical feeding innovation (i.e., the use of tools or food caching), and relative brain size (compared with body mass) in 765 species of birds. Results indicated that diet breadth, feeding innovation, and technical innovation, but not habitat breadth, were significantly correlated with relative brain size. The implication here is that bird intelligence, as measured by relative brain size, is correlated with feeding diversity. I'm not sure how curiosity relates to feeding diversity but would be surprised if it wasn't related. Therefore, it is possible that birds like cactus wrens and European robins with flexible feeding behavior are "brighter" than birds like mourning doves with stereotyped feeding behavior.

Cactus wrens (family Troglodytidae) are members of the advanced suborder Oscines (true songbirds) of the order Passeriformes, the largest order of birds and one that contains about 140 families and 60 percent of all bird species. This grand radiation began in the Australian region in mid-Eocene (47 Ma) with its two major suborders (Suboscines and Oscines) diverging at about 44 Ma. Oscines reached Eurasia at about 27 Ma. From there they dispersed to Europe and Africa and began diversifying in the New World at the Oligocene/Miocene boundary (25 Ma). Troglodytidae, the wren family, dates from about 17 Ma and contains about seventy-five species with a center of diversity in Central America, although the family probably originated in North America. The fifteen species of *Campylorhynchus* wrens are nested within this family (i.e., they are not basal). They likely began to evolve in the Early Pliocene (ca. 5 Ma), and close relatives of the cactus wren (e.g., *C. yucatanicus*) occur in Mexico. The cactus wren apparently evolved in the mid-Pliocene (ca. 3 Ma). Its recent evolutionary journey, therefore, has been relatively short in both space and time despite its ancestral roots in Eurasia.

PHAINOPEPLA

Phainopepla nitens Swainson, 1838, Ptilogonatidae. Three species of cardinals or cardinal-like birds live in the Sonoran Desert: the northern cardinal (*Cardinalis cardinalis*), the desert cardinal or pyrrhuloxia (*Cardinalis sinuatus*), and the phainopepla. Each of these passerines is strongly crested. The phainopepla can be easily distinguished from true cardinals (Cardinalidae), however, because adult males are shiny black with large white wing patches whereas females are dull gray; also, both sexes have rather short and slender bills. Sexes are similar in size and weigh about 22.1 g. Like cactus wrens, the phainopepla is a bird of southwestern U.S. deserts and arid lands of northern and central Mexico in areas where mistletoes are common.

Whereas the calls and songs of certain birds (e.g., white-winged doves and Bell's vireo), signify that spring is here in the desert, the soft but distinctive single-note calls of the phainopepla (they sound like *wurp*) always signify the beginning of fall to me. Fall and winter are the times when these birds are most common and conspicuous in Tucson. At this time of the year, they can be easily spotted singing from exposed perches and individually guarding clumps of mistletoes, whose fruit is its major food then. During my spring desert fieldwork, I also enjoyed watching males during their courtship displays. At these times, males flew high in the air in swirling flight while issuing melodious, flutelike songs and flashing their black-and-white wings.

Phainopeplas have perhaps the most unique lifestyle of any Sonoran Desert songbird: they have two distinct breeding grounds and they live in two different social configurations. One of their breeding grounds is in the Sonoran Desert where they live from late September until they finish raising a brood in May. During this time they are strongly territorial. Prior to the breeding season, males and females defend separate territories centered on one or more clumps of fruiting desert mistletoes (*Phoradendron californicum*). When the nesting season begins in February, males and females pair up to defend a single mistletoe-based territory. After nesting, they leave the desert and migrate up to a few hundred kilometers to a completely different habitat: oak and sycamore canyons located in Arizona and California. There, new pairs initiate nesting and raise a brood, but they do so in the midst of a loose colony of up to fifteen other pairs of phainopeplas that live in undefended and overlapping home ranges. In this habitat they again feed heavily on fruit (e.g., hollyleaf redberry [*Rhamnus ilicifolia*] and blue elderberry [*Sambucus mexicana*]) but do so in groups, not as territorial pairs. When this nesting is done, they return to the Sonoran Desert, sometimes close to their previous territories, and the annual cycle begins again. Nesting success is often related to food availability. Many nests fail during years of low fruit production in both habitats, probably as a result of low rainfall. Another source of nest failure is predation. Important predators of eggs and/or chicks in phainopepla nests include western scrub jays, cactus wrens, loggerhead shrikes, ravens, pack rats, and gopher snakes.

Other than their shifts in breeding locations and social structure, phainopeplas have reproductive life histories that are typical of many passerines. A recent detailed genetic analysis has revealed that this is a socially monogamous species in which extra-pair liaisons and copulations do not occur. All the chicks in a nest have the same father, their mother's mate. This differs somewhat from many other Temperate Zone socially monogamous passerines in which clutches can sometimes contain chicks whose father is not the female's mate. The distinction between social versus genetic monogamy did not become apparent until the rise of paternity analyses using DNA microsatellites in the early 1990s (see page 83). When these kinds of analyses were applied to birds, it was discovered that many songbirds (e.g., blackbirds, buntings, chickadees, orioles, sparrows, and warblers) have 'leaky' social systems in which females sometimes briefly leave their territories to mate with other males.

Reasons for extra-pair paternity have been debated among behavioral ecologists for many years. Adaptive possibilities for females include gaining fertility assurance, genetic diversity in their clutches, "good genes" from other males, and increased genetic compatibility with other males. Ecological (potentially non-adaptive) reasons for this include low survival rates so that males cannot retaliate against their mates for being cuckolded and highly synchronous breeding and high population densities so that females can compare the quality of other males with that of their mates. However, to my knowledge, no general explanation for its adaptive significance has yet to appear. Finally, although it is socially and genetically monogamous, the phainopepla does not mate for life. Observations made during the genetic study mentioned above indicate that birds change partners in each habitat, usually because pairs do not travel together when they change habitats.

The Sonoran Desert nesting cycle of phainopeplas usually begins in February when males begin to build one or more nests to attract a mate. Courtship involves flight displays, chases, and males feeding insects and berries to a potential mate; groups of males and females often participate in these displays. Once a pair-bond has formed, the nest, which is a rather small compact cup of twigs and plant fibers lined with feathers, is completed. Nests are usually placed in the shady canopies of common desert trees such as mesquites and palo verdes or in clumps of mistletoes. Clutches contain two to four eggs which females incubate for about two weeks. Both parents feed the altricial (i.e., naked and helpless) nestlings insects and crushed fruit for another seventeen to nineteen days; young birds usually have attained adult weight by the time they fledge. After this nesting cycle is finished, the adults migrate from the desert to tree-filled canyons elsewhere in Arizona and Southern California to begin another nesting cycle.

For many years it was not known whether the birds nesting in the Sonoran Desert also nested in the canyons later in the year. One possibility was that the desert and canyon populations contained different sets of birds. But a recent study employing two high-tech techniques—tracking individual birds using tiny (1 g) GPS-based data loggers and DNA markers—have confirmed that desert birds do migrate to canyon habitats and that the genetic composition of populations of birds in the two habitats is basically the same. Individual phainopeplas actually do nest twice a year.

In addition to its unusual annual cycle, phainopeplas are also unusual because of their heavy reliance on fruit throughout the year. Like many other desert birds, they eat insects that they capture by aerial hawking, but fruit provides the bulk of their diet year-round. Only the northern mockingbird is as frugivorous in the desert as the phainopepla. As a result, these two species sometimes undergo brief conflicts when they try to feed together at the same mistletoe plant. To deal with its frugivorous diet, the phainopepla has a modified digestive system compared with most other passerines. Its digestive system lacks a crop and has a very small gizzard (the second chamber of a bird's two-chambered stomach) when it feeds on mistletoe fruits. Its gizzard increases 2.2 times in weight during the summer when it feeds on nonmistletoe fruits in riparian canyons. Feeding involves quickly eating a series of mistletoe berries that are stored temporarily in the esophagus. These fruits are then passed into the small, thin-walled gizzard where their skins (exocarps) are removed and stored briefly while the seed and its pulp is passed into the intestine where digestion of the pulp occurs. Groups of eight to sixteen seeds are consumed and defecated in about twenty-nine minutes; packets of their skins are then excreted after the seeds have passed. Captive birds eat about 264 mistletoe fruits per day, and their digestive efficiency of its fruit pulp is about 49 percent, a value that is relatively low for birds. In the wild, these birds can ingest 1,000 or more mistletoe fruits in a day, which presumably meets their daily nutritional and water needs.

Mistletoe berries provide nutrients, mainly carbohydrates, lipids, and protein, plus water for phainopeplas while making sure that their seeds will be excreted in a viable condition. They are small (3–5 mm in diameter) and easily swallowed whole. The pulp surrounding the seed is viscous and adhesive, unusual characteristics for most bird fruits. Its viscosity serves two purposes: it facilitates easy removal of the fruit's skin in the gizzard and it enables many defecated seeds to stick together on the branches of potential host plants. Piles of seeds up to 3 cm tall can sometimes be found beneath phainopepla perches on the branches of desert trees. The rough bark of mesquite trees is an especially good site for establishment of these parasitic plants. Many fruits eaten by Temperate Zone birds contain mainly water and carbohydrates but are poor in lipids and proteins. Mistletoe fruits are somewhat different; their pulp contains about 15 percent lipids and 1.2 percent protein—values that are similar to many species of new-world tropical fruits. Phainopeplas presumably increase the protein content of their diets by eating insects.

Two other groups of birds have become mistletoe berry specialists. These include finches of the genus *Euphonia* (Fringillidae) in the new-world tropics and flower-peckers of the genus *Dicaeum* (Dicaeidae) in the old-world tropics. Like phainopeplas, these birds have simplified digestive tracts with very small gizzards. Ingested seeds and pulp are passed directly into the small intestine while bypassing the gizzard. But unlike phainopeplas, they remove the skins of mistletoe fruits in their mouths before swallowing the pulp and seed. Only phainopeplas seem to have evolved a specialized way of dealing with the skins of mistletoe fruits.

Finally, we can ask, what is a black bird such as a male phainopepla doing in a solar-intense desert environment? Except for ravens, most desert birds are basically earth colored. But male phainopeplas aren't. As a result, do they pay a physiological price for being dark colored and if so, how much of a price? At the outset, it is naïve to think that white or light plumage reflects all incoming solar radiation whereas black plumage absorbs all of it. It turns out that while white feathers do reflect most solar radiation, the amount that isn't reflected penetrates the plumage and heats the skin. In contrast, while black feathers do absorb shortwave radiation, this radiation doesn't necessarily penetrate deeply to the skin and is often lost by reradiation or convection from feather surfaces. So what does a black plumage "cost" a male?

As expected in this sexually dimorphic species (i.e., males are black and females are gray), male plumage is less reflective than female plumage: 6–10 percent compared with 17–23 percent, respectively. But does this difference have an effect on the radiative heat gain experienced by males and females? This kind of heat gain is a function of the difference between a bird's body temperature T_b and its effective thermal environmental T_e (i.e., the sum of all sources of heat in the environment); the greater this difference, the greater the heat gain that a small passerine bird must counter either by increasing its evaporative water loss by panting, which increases its metabolic rate, or by letting its T_b increase as occurs in different desert birds (e.g., cactus wrens). To determine how much a male heats up compared with a female when exposed to solar radiation under field conditions, the ecologist Glenn Walsberg placed lifelike taxidermic mounts of phainopeplas whose skin and plumage were glued to a hollow copper model in places where these birds normally perch. Using this technique, he found that male T_bs were 0.9°C–2.3°C higher than those of females depending on time of day and wind conditions. Since real birds can adjust their exposure to the sun and seek shade when it's really hot, he concluded that this difference was unlikely to have a significant physiological cost to males compared with the benefits gained from being very conspicuous to mates and territory intruders (and to predators!). To be sure, a rate of thermal gain of 1°C–2°C above a male's thermoneutral zone will have some metabolic cost, but it can be easily overridden by changes in posture, plumage adjustments, and/or microhabitat. Hence, males are not likely to be paying a metabolic cost by being black. Nor are other black birds in the desert. According to Walsberg's calculations, white birds in the desert are more likely to experience thermal stress than black birds. Perhaps that's why desert birds aren't white, except for water birds such as egrets that don't really live under true desert conditions (i.e., in the absence of standing water).

Like cactus wrens, phainopeplas are advanced oscine passerines (i.e, true songbirds). Their family, Ptilogonatidae, is a small one; it contains only four species in three genera and occurs only in the new-world subtropics (phainopeplas) and tropics in Central America (silky-flycatchers, *Ptilogonys*, and the black-and-yellow phainoptila, *Phainoptila*). As their name implies, silky-flycatchers are as elegant as phainopeplas. The gray silky-flycatcher (*Pt. cinereus*), for example, which I've photographed in Oaxaca, Mexico, has a blunt gray crown, a bright white eye-ring, lemon-yellow flanks, and a relatively long black tail with a white band across its base. Like phainopeplas, they perch in conspicuous places and eat lots of fruit.

A recent phylogenetic analysis based on mtDNA and nucDNA sequences indicates that the immediate ancestor of Ptilogonatidae is the cedar waxwing family Bombycillidae. Waxwings are a north-temperate family of birds containing only three species (two new-world and one old-world species) in one genus (*Bombycilla*). Like silky-flycatchers, they are heavily frugivorous, eating fruits such as raspberries, blackberries, cherries, and juniper berries in the summer. Some populations of cedar waxwings (*B. cedrorum*) are long-distance migrants and spend their winters in south Florida, where I often heard their soft twittering calls as flocks passed through our neighborhood in Miami.

Precise ages of Bombycillidae and Ptilogonatidae are not yet available, but it appears that the former family dates from the mid-Eocene (ca. 45 Ma) and the latter somewhat more recently (Late Eocene, 37 Ma?). Likewise, the biogeographic origins of these families are currently unknown. Being strictly New World in distribution, silky flycatchers probably evolved there, perhaps in Central America. This implies that it cannot be older than about 25 Ma. I'm guessing that phainopeplas are younger than this and that they evolved in the Late Miocene (ca. 6 Ma) as northern Mexico and the southwestern United States became increasingly drier. One way to test this hypothesis is to look at the evolutionary history of its major food, *Phoradendron* mistletoes. How old are these mistletoes and what's their history? We'll do this in the plant section below. If this scenario is correct, then the evolutionary history of phainopeplas has likely involved a journey of relatively short distances in space and but perhaps longer in time.

HOW MANY EGGS ARE IN YOUR BASKET?

Before moving on to species of Sonoran Desert mammals, I wish to discuss a topic of considerable importance in the life histories of all organisms—that is, the evolution of "clutch size." In vertebrates, the term *clutch size* is usually used to describe the number of eggs a female lizard, snake, or bird produces per reproductive event; its mammalian equivalent is "litter size." But the number of embryo-containing eggs or seeds a female produces per reproduction and per lifetime is a general life history feature of all life on Earth. And discussions of its evolution in birds have occurred numerous times over the past century.

To begin this discussion, consider the range of variation in clutch size that we see in birds. Much, but not all, of this variation has an important taxonomic or phylogenetic component. Thus, one-egg clutches occur in various seabirds, including petrels, albatrosses, and shearwaters. Two-egg clutches are standard in doves, vultures, and hummingbirds. Clutches of two to three eggs occur in gulls and terns. Hawks and many songbirds produce clutches of two to five eggs. And pheasants and partridges lay clutches of eight to eighteen eggs. In the Sonoran Desert birds I have discussed, clutch sizes range from two in doves and hummingbirds, two to four in many species, and up to twelve in Gambel's quails.

What factors account for this variation in birds? One factor that *doesn't* predict clutch size in birds is body size. This is interesting because many other avian life history features (e.g., average life span, size of chicks at hatching, age at first reproduction, etc.) are generally positively correlated with body size. One obvious feature that *does* affect clutch size is condition of chicks at hatching— are they altricial or precocial? Altricial young need to be fed by their parents at a considerable energetic cost whereas precocial young do not. Hence, it's not surprising that precocial species such as most gallinaceous birds invariably produce much larger clutches than altricial species such as most passerines. Another factor, and probably the most important one, is the availability of food resources relative to population sizes of consumers. The ratio of supply to demand in both the breeding and nonbreeding seasons can be important. Thus, whenever bird population densities are high relative to their food supply during the breeding season, natural selection will favor individuals that produce smaller clutches than those produced in populations characterized by low densities relative to their food supply. That resource availability has an important effect on clutch size can be seen in year-year variation in clutch sizes in birds such as Gambel's quails in which clutch sizes are much smaller in years of low winter rainfall followed by low spring plant productivity than in wetter and more productive winters. Another factor that affects clutch size in birds is average life expectancy. Long-lived species, which are often large, can afford to produce fewer eggs per reproductive event than species with high mortality rates and short life expectancies. Long-lived species clearly have more breeding opportunities per lifetime than short-lived species.

Clutch size in birds (and its analog in other organisms) is an important adaptation in all species and is clearly the result of natural selection, as Darwin would have predicted. This is because the production of surviving, reproducing offspring in individuals is the basic currency of organic evolution. It is our measure of an organism's fitness. It is important to note here that adaptations such as

clutch size must be viewed from the perspective of individuals and their reproductive success rather than from the perspective of their effect on populations.
Early discussions about the evolution of clutch size in birds emphasized its effect
on compensating for mortality and maintaining a stable population size. But
David Lack, whom we first met in his work with Darwin's finches, was perhaps
the first modern evolutionary biologist to shift the discussion of clutch size evolution in birds away from its population consequences to its consequences for
individuals. According to his most famous hypothesis (i.e., Lack's hypothesis),
"the clutch size in birds is adjusted by natural selection to the maximum number
of nestlings the parents can feed and nourish" (Gill 1990, 419). This hypothesis,
which clearly applies to altricial species, was published in the late 1940s. And
although it has been tweaked over the years, it is still relevant in current discussions of this topic. An important tweak, for example, is that the "best" or "optimal" clutch size is the one that maximizes lifetime, not just the current season's,
fitness. Egg supplementation experiments have shown that some birds produce
a smaller clutch than the one they could raise but that smaller, unsupplemented
clutches result in higher adult survival and a greater potential for reproducing
in the next season. The evolution of clutch size in birds can therefore be viewed
as involving a tradeoff in adults between maximizing current production and
maximizing future survival and reproduction.

Up to this point we've only considered the effect of clutch size on the fitness
of adult birds. But what about its effect on the fitness of offspring? When we
consider the fitness of offspring, we encounter an example of "parent-offspring
conflict" in which individual offspring in altricial species will usually benefit from
more parental investment than parents are willing to give. This should sound
familiar to human parents, too. Thus, offspring in one-egg clutches are in an ideal
situation in which they will receive more food and will grow faster than those in
multiple-egg clutches. Selection favors fast growth rates whenever nest predation
pressure is high in altricial species. Beyond single-egg clutches, per capita feeding
and growth rates of chicks will inevitably decline because parents cannot usually
supply enough food to guarantee that all chicks in multiple-egg clutches will
grow at the same high rate as those in single-egg clutches. The end result of this
is that "optimal" clutch sizes are those that balance the fitness concerns of parents
with those of their offspring. They will always be a compromise between what
is best for parents (i.e., more eggs per clutch, up to a point) and their offspring
(i.e., fewer eggs per clutch and more food per chick).

SONORAN DESERT MAMMALS

ROUND-TAILED GROUND SQUIRREL

Xerospermophilus (formerly *Spermophilus*) *tereticaudus* Baird, 1858, Sciuridae. Two species of ground squirrels live in the Sonoran Desert around Tucson: the 126 g colonial *X. tereticaudus* and the 130 g solitary Harris's antelope squirrel (*Ammospermophilus harrisii*). Both species are common in open sandy areas where round-tails, but not antelopes, match the substrate in color. With large, bright eyes and small ears, round-tails (RTs) resemble in appearance and behavior small prairie dogs (Sciuridae, *Cynomys*).

I did not encounter RTs very often during my desert fieldwork in Sonora but did so as soon as we moved to Tucson. Their burrows pockmarked the ground everywhere in open areas. But I did not pay any attention to them until June 2013, when I stopped to watch a mom and two of her pups playing at Tohono Chul Park where I had just spent a year photographing plants and animals. Prior to June, these delightful rodents had been spending most of their time underground. I decided then that I needed to spend time photographing them next spring. So I spent many mornings in March–June 2014 and again in April–June 2015 doing so. My "study area" turned out to be a relatively large open sandy area in a power line right-of-way and the adjacent yard of a friend. A small colony of several adult females and their young lived there. Because my friends John and Barbie love to garden, they were not pleased to have these omnivorous vegetarians as neighbors and eating their plants, but they tolerated them—barely. John kept asking me to shoot the creatures with something other than a camera.

So what did I learn by sitting quietly day after day behind my camera and watching them? RTs were scarce and shy when I first began my work. In March I quickly noted that only adult males, easily identified because of their large testes, were active. They fought fiercely, rolling around the ground, when they encountered each other. From early April on, adult females began to appear above ground to feed on plant material and clean out their burrows. I concentrated on one female who didn't mind my presence and whom I called Shirley. I knew she was nursing a litter underground because her three pair of nipples were swollen. I also knew that her pups were growing because her nipples kept getting larger in April and May. When she wasn't searching for food, she would stretch out in the shade and rest. Her foraging area covered an area of about 0.5 ha. While she did most of her foraging on the ground, she also climbed into palo verde and mesquite trees plus cholla cacti to feed. She ate palo verde, mesquite, and cactus flowers as they became available and then switched to their fruits in late May and June. When she was foraging in trees, I was impressed by how agile she was. She easily climbed out to the ends of thin branches to harvest flowers and fruit.

In 2014, I did not know when Shirley's young were going to appear above ground, but finally on May 19 her six pups emerged; they were about half her size with relatively large heads and big feet. And then the show began. For about the next three weeks I concentrated on the antics of the pups. Young RTs are very feisty and spend a lot of time play fighting. They leaped at and on each other and briefly wrestled before scampering away. Then one pup would sneak up and attack a sib again. Frontal attacks, sneak attacks, and all of this were repeated endlessly. Between bouts of fighting, they spent time exploring their world either individually or with their mom. Early on they began to leap into the lower branches of trees and quickly became adept at clambering around on thin branches. By early June, pups, probably females, began to dig new burrows within sight of their natal burrow. I saw basically the same routine with another family in 2015. The litter of five pups that I watched that year emerged on May 20.

As I sat quietly watching and taking pictures, other wildlife made occasional appearances. These included two solitary and shy coyotes that quickly left the area when they spotted me. Less perturbed was a javelina that walked slowly through the area after stopping briefly to stare at me. Cooper's hawks sometimes perched on the power pole above the colony and scanned the area, but I never saw them attempt to capture ground squirrels (though they do; see page 105). Antelope ground squirrels and desert cottontails also occasionally passed by me without appearing to be disturbed.

What I witnessed those two springs were some of the major events in the lives of these rodents. The annual cycle of RTs includes adults emerging from hibernation in January and February; copulations occurring in March; litters appearing above ground in May and beginning to disperse in June; all individuals entering into hibernation in August and September. Adult males are present in an area in January through March and then leave; a different set of adult males arrives in this area the next January. Young females establish new burrows near their natal burrow in June; many young males leave their natal area then. In sum, adult females and their daughters live near each other all year; juvenile and adult males are ephemeral members of a local population. Where males go when they leave an area is not well known.

The extent of social tolerance and territorial behavior in RTs varies during their active season. Prior to copulations in March, social tolerance among adults is high and sharing of burrows is common. Once females become pregnant, however, they become territorial and defend the area around their burrows against conspecifics, mostly adult females, for the rest of the active season. One important reason for doing this is to prevent infanticide in which females kill the litters of other females. Infanticide appears to be common in some species of ground squirrels, including prairie dogs, but its frequency in RTs apparently has not been documented. Once they disperse, juveniles are also territorial. This behavior helps to limit population density, since territoriality by definition divides an area into noninvadable plots of land; territory size then limits population density. Another factor limiting population size is an apparent innate tendency for both juvenile and adult males to disperse from populations. Unfortunately, where these individuals go once they disperse is unknown. In the case of adult males, which disperse in March after mating has occurred, they do not appear to immigrate into other populations of nursing females. This is also true of juvenile males; they do not show up in other populations of adult and juvenile females. This implies that males and females live separately from each other for most of the year.

Like many colonial ground squirrels, including prairie dogs, RTs occasionally issue "warning calls." These are rather high-pitched, birdlike, single-tone whistles. These calls are made by females either as single notes when a predator is spotted, or in groups during intraspecific social interactions. I rarely saw the RTs I was watching give these calls. The few that I saw were single-note calls, but I was not aware that a predator was nearby. Like the occurrence of extra-pair copulations in socially monogamous birds, the evolutionary significance of these calls has been debated in the behavioral ecology literature for decades. The basic question here is, Are these calls "selfish" or are they "altruistic?" Selfish calls benefit only the caller and its genes whereas altruistic calls benefit the caller and close genetic relatives (e.g., recent offspring) at some cost (e.g., increased risk of predation) to the caller. Altruistic behavior thus benefits an individual's genes as well as that fraction of its genes (e.g., 50 percent in offspring) that it shares with close relatives.

Actually, the most selfish thing a ground squirrel can do after spotting a predator would be to retreat silently into its burrow. In that way it would avoid risking its own life while putting other individuals at risk. This would be the ultimate "selfish gene" behavioral strategy. The second most selfish thing it could do would be to call and warn only its close relatives about the predator. By calling, it might attract a predator's attention, but saving the lives of close relatives might be worth the risk. The social structure of RTs with daughters (but not sons) living close to moms is conducive to this kind of behavior. As the British evolutionary biologist William D. Hamilton taught us with his theory of *kin selection* in the mid-1960s, an altruistic act in which the actor (i.e., mom) incurs some risk while attempting to save the lives of close relatives (i.e., daughters) should only occur when the receivers share a high proportion of the actor's genes. Otherwise the risk is probably not worth taking. Since RT warning calls are loud and carry some distance, however, it is difficult to imagine that they are detected only by close relatives. Surely other unrelated individuals are able to hear and respond to these calls. So these calls are likely to benefit many individuals in a population, not just moms and their daughters.

Another explanation for the evolution of warning calls is that they are "aimed" at predators and not necessarily at other ground squirrels. That is, they might be saying to a predator, "I see you so it's unlikely that you will be able to catch me. You might as well give up this time." This tactic might be especially effective from a "selfish gene" perspective if the call causes conspecifics to increase their exposure to a predator, for example, by running for cover. RTs typically give their alarm calls from the mouth of their burrows after they spot a distant predator, not one that is an imminent threat to them. They don't continue to call as the predator approaches. This suggests that warning calls are "safe" and pose no immediate danger to the caller. They appear to be more selfish than altruistic in this species. In the end, however, no single explanation is likely to hold for the evolution of warning calls in all species of colonial ground squirrels. These calls can benefit just the caller, the caller and its close kin if they reside close by, or they might simply be warnings to predators.

Round-tailed ground squirrels spend much of their lives underground in their burrows. Burrows can be up to 4 m long and slant downward to about 0.5 m below the soil surface. A grassy nest is located near the bottom of the burrow. During their active season, ground squirrels spend a lot of time working on their burrows, as my photographs show. Adults and juveniles are constantly digging and scraping dirt with their front feet and kicking it backward with their hind feet. From about September to January they remain underground in "hibernation." Actually, RTs are not true hibernators like some of their northern relatives (e.g., golden-mantled ground squirrels, *Callospermophilus lateralis*) and marmots. Instead, they go into extended torpor in which their T_bs and MRs are reduced somewhat but not profoundly. When RTs are active their T_b is 36°C; in torpor it's 23°C–28°C. During hot periods in the summer, they also retreat to their burrows and undergo shallow torpor, often called *estivation*. In this respect, they resemble certain nonmammalian desert vertebrates (e.g., desert tortoises and Gila monsters).

Round-tailed ground squirrels are members of the largest mammalian order Rodentia (with thirty-three families, 481 genera, and about 2,277 species). This order dates from the Paleocene (ca. 66 Ma) and first evolved in the northern supercontinent of Laurasia. Its sister order is Lagomorpha (rabbits, hares, and pikas). The squirrel family Sciuridae is relatively large, containing six subfamilies, about 58 genera, and 285 species, and occurs on all continents except Australia. Fossil evidence suggests that it first evolved in North America in the Late Eocene (ca. 36 Ma). North American ground squirrels (i.e., colonial prairie dogs *Cynomys* and its relatives, including the RT *Xerospermophilus tereticaudus*) are classified in subfamily Xerinae and date from about 8 Ma. This subfamily is an advanced member of Sciuridae; noncolonial antelope squirrels (*Ammospermophilus*) are basal members of this subfamily. Four species of *Xerospermophilus* are currently recognized. Except for *X. perotensis*, which is restricted to coastal Puebla and Veracruz in Mexico, these species occur in grasslands or arid lands in the central United States (*X. spilosoma*) or the southwestern United States and central Mexico (*X. tereticaudus* and *X. mohavensis*). It therefore appears that *X. tereticaudus* likely evolved relatively recently in the arid southwestern United States. If this is true, then its evolutionary journey has been short in space and time.

MERRIAM'S KANGAROO RAT

Dipodomys merriami Mearns, 1890, Heteromyidae. With their large heads and bright eyes, long tails often ending with a feathery plume, and bipedal locomotion, kangaroo rats (genus *Dipodomys*) are among the most charismatic mammals of deserts in the southwestern United States and Mexico. Weighing about 36 g, *D. merriami* is a medium-sized kangaroo rat (k-rat). Its geographic range is similar to that of a number of other desert-associated vertebrates (e.g., Gila woodpecker, cactus wren, and phainopepla) and includes the Sonoran and Mojave Deserts and arid parts of north-central Mexico. It is most common in sandy, creosote-dominated desert scrubland.

I've had limited personal experience with these rodents, mainly because they are nocturnal. I was partially nocturnal during my desert fieldwork, but I was working with bats, not rodents. I spent many hours watching nectar-feeding bats visiting the flowers of columnar cacti but seldom had a chance to watch anything else. I can probably count on one hand the times I was aware that kangaroo rats were foraging around me. Nonetheless, I've long admired this animal, starting with the famous Disney film *The Living Desert* of the early 1950s. It was then that I fell in love with these adorable rodents. In graduate school in Ann Arbor I babysat a Merriam's k-rat (MKR) one summer for my officemate while he was away doing fieldwork. But what can you learn by watching an animal in a terrarium stuffing seeds into its cheek pouches or sandbathing? Much later a friend gave my sixteen-year-old daughter an MKR while we were on sabbatical in Tucson. The most notable thing about this animal was its unexpected acrobatic ability. When we released it to hop (not run) around in our carpeted spare bedroom, it immediately climbed to the top of a floor-to-ceiling sheer window curtain and launched itself into space, landing safely on the carpet below. It must have gotten a big thrill from this because it immediately repeated this trick. Who knew that these animals were adept climbers and daredevil jumpers?

Because they are common desert inhabitants, Merriam's k-rats have been studied by many biologists over the years. As a result, we know a lot about its basic biology and ecology. Here I will review major results of these studies from several different perspectives, including population and community ecology, metabolic physiology, and predator avoidance. Study of MKRs has contributed significantly to each of these fields.

Population studies tell us that these are solitary rodents that live in their own shallow burrow systems in the middle of territories that they defend against other MKRs. Both males and females defend their territories year-round. Unlike some heteromyid rodents, MKRs do not hibernate or estivate but forage actively for food all year. Although their diets sometimes include green vegetation, especially during rainy times of the year, and insects, these animals are primarily seedeaters, harvesting a diversity of kinds as they become available seasonally. Probably using a keen sense of smell, they locate buried seeds and collect them in their fur-lined cheek pouches. They don't store these seeds in their burrows, however. Instead they bury them in small shallow caches around their territories and retrieve them later for eating.

A twelve-year study of MKRs in the creosote-dominated flatlands south of Tucson provides us with an excellent overview of their population ecology. This species was most common in areas of loose sandy soil where it could easily burrow. Unlike round-tailed ground squirrels, MKRs have small, delicate front legs and are not strong diggers. As a result, they create simple and shallow burrows, usually at the base of mesquite trees, in which they spend about 75 percent of the time; their grassy nest is located about 30 cm below the soil surface. In sandy habitats, its population density averaged about 15 animals per ha and fluctuated from year to year depending on the seed production of annual and perennial plants. In this area, the home ranges of males and females were quite similar and averaged 1.16 and 0.91 ha, respectively. Male ranges overlapped with those of other males and females whereas those of females were defended territories that did not overlap with those of other females. Most females produced two litters averaging two pups each year, one in May and another in September. Pups grew rapidly and were weaned at two weeks of age. Some females first bred before they had attained full adult size. Individuals spent several hours each night all year searching for and caching seeds in small holes. Based on the contents of their cheek pouches, MKRs collected seeds of about sixty species in twenty-seven plant families; their preferred seeds were produced by annual grasses. Finally, experimental work using rodent exclosures indicated that MKRs failed to recover all the seeds they cached. This resulted in the dispersal and successful establishment of certain desert plants, particularly large-seeded perennials and mesquites. In this way, this granivore acts as both a predator and a disperser of the seeds of certain desert plants.

Being nocturnal and burrow dwellers, MKRs are not exposed to the extreme heat of summer, but they must endure cold winter nights as they search for seeds. Laboratory studies indicate that its range of tolerable environmental temperatures T_a is 7.2°C–38.0°C. It cannot survive at T_as lower or higher than these. Other physiological studies have indicated this species' body temperature T_b is 36°C–37°C and that its TNZ is quite narrow: 31°C–34°C. This means that at T_as outside this range, they must expend energy to maintain a constant T_b; they do this either by shivering (at T_as below its TNZ) or panting and evaporating water (at T_as above its TNZ). Actually, like certain other desert vertebrates, it allows its T_b to increase slightly at high T_as to save energy and water.

The water economy of MKRs is very impressive. In fact, the physiologist Ken Nagy calls it the "world's champion" among desert mammals for its stingy water economy. It never drinks free water and instead obtains all of its water from the seeds and other plant material that it eats. As a result, an important factor in its choice of which of the many kinds of seeds that it collects it actually eats is the seed's water content. It also gains water metabolically by oxidation of the carbohydrates in its food. Water loss is also important and occurs via two routes in heteromyid rodents: via evaporation from the lungs and in urine and feces. Since they produce very dry feces, their main routes of water loss are via evaporation and urine. It turns out that MKRs and other desert heteromyids produce very small amounts of highly concentrated urine. Compared with humans, urine produced by heteromyids is 3.2 times higher in electrolytes (e.g., salts) and 3.8 times higher in urea. Compared with lab rats, heteromyids can excrete electrolytes and urea using only half as much water. Their ability to produce concentrated urine results from their highly specialized kidneys that have much longer loops of Henle in the medulla (the inner part of the kidney) than found in most other mammals. These loops are involved in concentrating the amount of urea and electrolytes that is voided in urine.

The other major route of water loss in MKRs is via evaporation of water from the lungs. Again, k-rats expire about half the amount of water as lab rats. One reason for this is that they have long nasal passages in which expired air is cooled and its water is condensed and reabsorbed (fig. 10). They also spend a lot of time in their burrows which tend to be cooler and more humid than outside air. For example, on hot summer days air temperatures can be 20°C–45°C compared with 25°C–30°C in the burrow; nighttime outside air temperatures can be 15°C–25°C. Humidity inside burrows is 30–50 percent compared with outside humidities of 1–15 percent during the day and 15–40 percent at night.

How did Ken Nagy come to conclude that the water economy of MKRs is exceptional, even among desert birds and mammals? He did this by reviewing data on the field metabolic rates (FMRs) and water turnover rates of many species of terrestrial vertebrates as determined by the doubly labeled water technique (see page 73). This technique has been used by ecologists and physiologists to measure energy and water use in free-ranging animals since the 1980s, and Nagy is a pioneer in this research area. In his review, he made all the data directly comparable by computing for each species a water economy index (WEI) by dividing the mL of water "turned over" per day by the kJ of energy used per day (i.e., mL/kJ per day, a measure of water use efficiency relative to overall energy use). His results generally indicated that desert-dwelling mammals and birds had WEI values only 55 percent and 77 percent of their nondesert relatives. So, not surprisingly, desert living selects for economical water use in these animals.

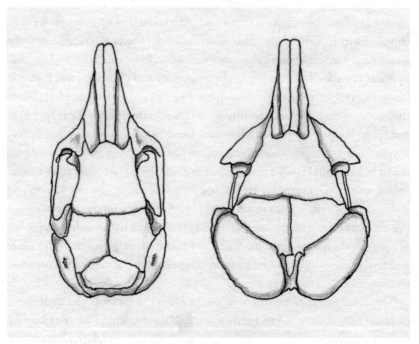

FIGURE 10 Dorsal views of the skulls of two kinds of desert heteromyid rodents: the qua-drupedal *Chaetodipus penicillatus* (left) and the bipedal *Dipodomys merriami* (right). Please note the greatly enlarged auditory bullae of the biped. Redrawn from illustrations in Hoff-meister (1986).

But among desert mammals, the WEI of MKRs was about 0.04 mL/kJ com-pared with the average value for this group of 0.11mL/kJ; nondesert mammals had an average WEI value of 0.20 mL/kJ.

Merriam's kangaroo rats live in a Sonoran Desert mammal community that includes six species of nocturnal seed-eating rodents and two species of diurnal granivores (the ground squirrels *Ammospermophilus harrisii* [130 g] and *Xeros-permophilus tereticaudus* [126 g]). In addition to the 45 g MKRs, the nocturnal rodents include three other heteromyids—*Dipodomys spectabilis* (120 g), *Perog-nathus flavus* (7.2 g), and *Chaetodipus penicillatus* (17.1 g)—and two species of typ-ical mice in family Cricetidae (*Reithrodontomys megalotis* [11.4 g] and *Peromyscus maniculatus* [24.3 g]). Do these species compete for food, and if not, why not? Many studies have addressed this question for rodent communities in both the Sonoran and Chihuahuan Deserts and it appears that in some years and some places, competition does occur between the nocturnal species, particularly the heteromyids which tend to be much more common than the cricetids. Exclusion experiments show this most clearly. For example, when three species of *Dipodomys* were excluded from exclosures at a site in the Chihuahuan Desert, densities of *Perognathus flavus, Chaetodipus penicillatus*, and two less common granivores increased by a factor of 3.5.

But rather than reviewing all of these studies, I will simply focus on the big picture here, especially on how body size, microhabitat use, and predation affect the coexistence of these animals. First consider body size. Classical ecological theory predicts that similar-sized species that eat the same things are most likely to compete if food availability is limited. But note that the four Sonoran Desert heteromyids differ in body size with MKR being intermediate in size; it also tends to be more common than the other three species. This size spacing is not random but is more uniform than expected by chance, given the pool of heteromyid species that occur in the deserts of the southwestern United States. So size differences alone might be important in reducing competition, especially if the kinds and sizes of the seeds collected by these rodents depend on their body size. A common finding in vertebrate communities is that average food size is positively correlated with a consumer's body size. There is evidence that this is also true in heteromyids and the size of the seeds they collect; they appear to be searching for and eating different sets of seeds. To be sure there is overlap in the kinds of seeds found in heteromyid cheek pouches, but on average, small species are collecting smaller seeds than larger species.

A second way these species can avoid competition is by foraging in different microhabitats. The classic way of viewing this is that these deserts have two broadly defined kinds of microhabitats for seed-seeking rodents: open space and under and around shrubs and other vegetation. Bipedal species of *Dipodomys* are usually associated with open sandy areas whereas the smaller species of *Perognathus* and *Chaetodipus*, which are quadrupedal rather than bipedal, are associated with shrubby habitats. Again, these microhabitat distinctions are not absolute, and bipeds can sometimes be seen foraging under shrubs and other vegetation where seeds tend to be more common than in the open. But it is certainly true that bipedal kangaroo rats can travel in open areas much faster and more agilely than quadrupedal spiny pocket mice. As a result, they are much less vulnerable to predators, including rattlesnakes and owls, in the open than are the quadrupeds.

In addition to being fast bipeds, kangaroo rats also have another morphological feature that reduces their vulnerability to predators. As you can see in figure 10, the part of their skull that is associated with hearing—the auditory bullae—is greatly enlarged and thin walled compared with that of quadrupedal heteromyids and other rodents. Bipedalism and enlarged auditory bullae also characterize certain other rodents (e.g., jerboas and gerbils) that live in sandy deserts in other parts of the world, a classic example of convergent evolution in totally unrelated species. Inflated auditory bullae allow species of *Dipodomys* to hear the low frequency sounds made by swooping owls and striking rattlesnakes. Their hearing curves range from 5 Hz to about 30 kHz with peak sensitivity at about 20 Hz, a very low value. For comparison, our hearing curve ranges from 20 Hz to 20 kHz with peak sensitivity at 2–5 kHz. Thus, k-rats are sensitive to much lower sounds than we are.

Laboratory tests have shown that kangaroo rats have the most sensitive hearing in their family. Their inner ears respond to much softer sounds than their relatives. In addition to their inflated auditory bullae, they accomplish this by having an enlarged tympanic membrane and a chain of three thin middle ear bones that efficiently transmit airborne sounds, especially those of low frequencies, to the inner ear whose cochlea is also specialized for responding to these sounds. As a result, species of *Dipodomys* are adept at evading rattlesnakes and owls in open areas even in total darkness. Experimentally blinded animals with intact ears can also do this whereas sighted animals with plugged ears cannot. Quadrupedal species of *Perognathus* and *Chaetodipus* with less specialized ears cannot hear soft, low frequency sounds as easily and are therefore more vulnerable to predation by rattlesnakes and owls, which explains why they mostly avoid open spaces in the desert.

To see just how nimble and athletic kangaroo rats are when they are being struck at by rattlesnakes, please visit https://www.ninjarat.org and watch their video clips. After seeing these rodents in action, I can understand how our pet MKR could survive leaping from our bedroom curtain to the floor and why this was such great fun for it.

Classified in suborder Sciuromorpha (squirrels and their allies) of order Rodentia, the family Heteromyidae is strictly New World in distribution. It contains about fifty-nine species in six genera. Its sister family is Geomyidae (the highly subterranean pocket gophers), also distributed only in the New World. Three subfamilies each with two genera have traditionally been recognized in Heteromyidae: Heteromyinae (*Heteromys* and *Liomys*), Perognathinae (*Perognathus* and *Chaetodipus*), and Dipodomyinae (*Dipodomys* and *Microdipodops*); modern molecular studies support this classification. Members of the former two subfamilies are quadrupedal whereas the latter, as we've seen, are bipedal. As an aside, although I have not studied desert heteromyids (the neatest members of this family, in my opinion), I worked extensively on the population ecology and behavior of species of *Heteromys* and *Liomys* in tropical rain forests and dry forests in Panama and Costa Rica early in my research career. My interest in this family is therefore longstanding and dates from those studies in the 1960s and early 1970s.

Fossil evidence indicates that the modern genera in this family date from the Early Miocene (ca. 22 Ma). Species of Dipodomyinae first evolved about 15.4 Ma, and at an age of about 4 Ma, *D. merriami* is among the youngest of the twenty species of *Dipodomys*. Members of Heteromyinae and Perognathinae are sister lineages and diverged about 22 Ma. Heteromyids diverged from the Geomyidae at about 30 Ma (Early Oligocene) and subsequent divergence of heteromyid subfamilies in the Miocene was probably centered in Mexico and Central America. It occurred as this area, particularly central and northern Mexico, became drier and with the emergence of mountain ranges and plateaus. Adaptation to more arid habitats from the Middle Miocene on (ca. 15–12 Ma) occurred in perognathines and dipodomyines but not in heteromyines. The former two clades likely dispersed north into the southwestern United States in the Pliocene (from ca. 5 Ma to the present). The evolutionary journey of *D. merriami* has thus been relatively short in space (from Mexico) and time (from ca. 4 Ma).

WHITE-THROATED WOODRAT

Neotoma albigula Hartley, 1894, Cricetidae. Although its scientific common name is "woodrat," most people call these animals "pack rats," and that's what I'll do here. This medium-sized rodent (males weigh about 220 g, females weigh about 188 g) with large ears, bright eyes, and a long, well-furred tail is familiar to most people living in the desert Southwest and northern Mexico. Not necessarily for positive reasons, however, because of its destructive tendencies. As we all know, they love to chew on electrical wires (and sometimes build nests) in cars and recreational vehicles, sometimes causing hundreds of dollars in damage. But because they are common and build rather large, conspicuous nests, pack rats certainly have an upside: they are very important in the ecology of deserts in the southwestern United States and Mexico as seed dispersers, as food for predators, and as shelter providers for many animals. And as we've already seen, the middens associated with their nests have provided us with an important window into the vegetational history of the Sonoran Desert and other southwestern U.S. and Mexican habitats dating back tens of thousands of years.

I've had little personal experience with these handsome animals with one exception. When we moved into our house in northwestern Tucson in 2008, our back patio housed an old redwood-covered spa that served as an admirable shelter for a hive of Africanized honeybees and a pack rat nest. This was obviously an important hunting ground for gopher snakes because their shed skins littered the undergrowth surrounding the spa. We had the spa removed the next year and replaced it with a pleasant sitting area shaded by one of our two large mesquite trees. At least one pack rat moved behind a patio planter where it proceeded to chew into thick plastic conduit housing electrical wires. I reluctantly trapped this rat and dispatched it, unlike my good friend and former biologist Roger Carpenter. He has always trapped and relocated the pack rats that continually chewed on the electrical system of his truck. He then releases them into new housing developments—kind of like a housewarming present, I imagine.

Like Merriams's kangaroo rat, *N. albigula* (symbolized here as WTWR) has been studied by many kinds of biologists over many decades, so we know a lot about its ecology, behavior, and physiology. After describing its basic ecology, I'll concentrate on its diet, which includes some chemically very nasty plants, and the evolution of its body size, which provides us with a window into the possible effects of global warming on it (and by inference, on other desert vertebrates). These rodents are basically solitary and nonsocial except during the breeding season, which lasts from January to July in Southern California. During this season, females produce two litters of two to three pups. Gestation lasts about thirty-seven days, and females nurse their young for twenty to twenty-five days. By the time they are weaned, pups are adept at handling spiny cholla cactus joints, which is an important food for them in the desert. Prickly pear (*Opuntia spp.*) and cholla (*Cylindropuntia spp.*) pads or joints and fruit represent about 44 percent of the diet of desert pack rats.

WTWRs are active at night throughout the year and spend their days in their lodges or dens. In the desert, the outsides of these dens are constructed of piles of branches and cholla joints and can be 2 m in diameter and 60 cm high. Away from rocky sites, they often include shallow but extensive burrows under them. The nest is located inside the den and is lined with twigs, leaves, and cactus material; it also often contains a diverse array of human artifacts such as spent ammunition shells, keys, jewelry, and bottle caps in addition to charcoal, cactus fruit, and many other items. Male WTWRs have ventral scent glands which they use, along with urine, to mark the area outside their dens. These scents convey information about an individual's identity, sex, and reproductive condition. Density of dens varies with habitat and ranges from about 1/ha to over 12/ha. In the desert, home ranges of WTWRs are small (ca. 0.05 ha) and overlap. Only the area around a den is defended against other pack rats. As mentioned previously, these dens are often inhabited by a large variety of invertebrates and vertebrates, including frogs, lizards, other species of rodents, shrews, rabbits, and skunks. Predators of pack rats include rattlesnakes, gopher snakes, owls, foxes, coyotes, weasels, skunks, badgers, and bobcats.

Packrat middens are justly famous for the information that they contain about past climates and vegetation. They are debris piles made by pack rats that are located in or near their dens. They contain feces, seeds, pollen, and other plant materials in addition to "trinkets" that the rats have collected. Packrats routinely urinate on these piles, and their sticky urine sometimes crystallizes as it dries to form a hard substance called *amberat*. Items in the middens are thus cemented together and preserved for millennia. Middens created in sheltered areas such as caves and rockslides are the most long-lasting and can sometimes contain material in amberat that has been carbon-dated as being up to 50,000 years old.

Compared with kangaroo rats, pack rats do not have special physiological adaptations for coping with the desert environment. Their kidneys, for example, are similar to those of most other rodents and cannot create highly concentrated urine for water conservation. As a result, they need to include succulent plant material in their diets. In addition, they are not particularly well adapted for dealing with high summer temperatures, which they avoid by being nocturnal and remaining in their dens or burrows during the day. Ambient temperatures greater than 36°C can be fatal to them. When faced with high T_as, they do not resort to evaporative cooling to maintain a constant T_b. Their nasal cavities are not capable of recovering water from expired air as kangaroo rats can. Instead, they rely on adjustments of their pelage and metabolism to reduce environmental heat load; they allow their stable T_bs of 38.5°C to slowly increase at T_as >

32°C. In the summer their pelage is thinner than it is during winter to facilitate heat loss.

As we've seen, an animal's body size has myriad biological consequences, including important metabolic consequences. Mass-specific metabolic rates, for instance, are negatively correlated with body size. Also, surface-to-volume ratios, which are important for determining rates of heat loss in endotherms, decrease with increasing body size. Larger mammals can also support a thicker, more insulative pelage than smaller ones. Because of its biological importance, contemporary and historical trends in the body sizes of pack rats, including WTWRs, have been the focus of several studies. A study of four species of western North American pack rats, for example, has shown that body size in current populations, both within and between species, is negatively correlated with mean annual temperature of their environments; northern species are larger than southern species such as WTWR. This trend reflects Bergmann's rule, which we met in the discussion of the evolution of English sparrows in North America (page 15).

A novel approach has been used to study changes in body size (i.e., its mass) in western North America's bushy-tailed woodrat *Neotoma cinerea* over the last 14,000 years, a period ranging from the cold last glacial maximum to the much warmer present. Fecal samples were removed from radiocarbon-dated pack rat middens and used to estimate pack rat body size because the width of fecal pellets is positively correlated with an animal's body size (i.e., its mass). As expected if Bergmann's rule is operating via directional selection over time in this (and other) species, this pack rat was significantly larger 14,000 years ago than it is today. This trend, of course, has important implications concerning the effects of climate change on pack rats and other arid land vertebrates in western North America. Increasing annual temperatures will certainly lead to increased thermal stress on these animals and selection for smaller body sizes; it will also likely affect their ability to persist in habitats where they currently occur. For example, during the last glacial maximum (i.e., prior to the last 14,000 years), Death Valley, which is currently one of the hottest places on Earth, was cooler and wetter; two species of pack rats, *N. cinerea* and the desert pack rat *N. lepida*, both lived there. As temperatures rose and water sources evaporated after the glacial maximum, however, *N. cinerea*, the larger of the two species, disappeared from areas it had previously occupied as recorded in pack rat middens. Relatively long-term climate fluctuations (primarily mean annual temperatures) have thus had at least two important effects on these rodents: they have led to in situ evolutionary changes in body size, and they have changed the habitat distributions of a thermally sensitive species. The fact that pack rats produce long-lasting middens chock full of biological information has given us a unique window into the past biological history of western North America.

Because they need to eat succulent vegetation to acquire sufficient water to maintain their water balance, desert-dwelling pack rats such as *N. albigula* eat a lot of cactus pads, cholla joints, and fruit. This material is notable for its oxalate content. In the cooler Great Basin Desert, they eat substantial amounts of juniper foliage (*Juniperus monosperma*) in the winter. Other pack rats (e.g., *N. lepida*) routinely eat the foliage and stems of creosote bushes (*Larrea tridentata*), particularly in the winter. These dietary choices are interesting because they involve plants whose tissues have evolved to reduce their palatability to herbivores. Natural selection has placed a premium on chemical tissue defense as well as on spines and thorns to protect plants against herbivores in water-limited environments such as deserts. How these herbivores deal with these plant toxins or otherwise unpalatable substances in their food is therefore of considerable interest.

Consider cactus tissue, for example, which contains about 1.5 percent dry-weight oxalate. This secondary plant substance (i.e., secondary because it is not directly involved in plant metabolism) can be toxic to some mammals and is water soluble (which is why it is recommended to boil *nopales* pads [*Opuntia ficus-indica*] before eating them); it is insoluble when it binds with calcium to form calcium oxalate. Ingestion of large amounts of oxalate, therefore, can lead to calcium deficiency; it can also lead to the formation of kidney stones in humans. *Neotoma* pack rats, however, have a special ability to digest oxalates compared with other rodents, even those that ingest substantial amounts of it. The question thus becomes, Do these rodents have special digestive adaptations in their gut to deal with this substance or do the microorganisms in their guts do this job for them? The answer is that composition of the food-digesting bacteria in the gut of these rodents is especially rich in oxalate-digesting microbes such as *Oxalobacter* that enable pack rats to digest oxalate-rich plant material. Experimental manipulation of the amount of oxalate eaten by WTWRs and monitoring the species composition of their gut microflora using DNA sequencing techniques has shown that the abundance of these specialized bacteria increases with an increase in the oxalate concentration in the rodent's diet. As a result, *Neotoma* pack rats (and not just *N. albigula*) have a unique ability to deal with this potentially toxic substance.

Two other potentially toxic plant foods that are especially common in the diets of pack rats include juniper foliage and the leaves and stems of creosote bushes. Juniper foliage is especially rich in polyphenolics and terpenes, which are secondary plant substances that are generally successful at repelling most herbivores. It turns out that juniper consumption by pack rats such as the WTWR is much more common in winter than in summer. There seems to be a physiological basis for this. Consumption of juniper foliage results in an increase in the metabolic rate and body temperature of pack rats. An increase in its T_b in the winter is probably beneficial but it isn't in the summer in these thermally very sensitive animals. Hence, consumption of this potentially toxic foliage varies seasonally. Interestingly, the pack rat *Neotoma stephensi*, unlike the WTWR, is a specialist on juniper foliage which it eats year-round. Its gut must be loaded with a microflora that deals with juniper toxins.

Creosote bushes cover vast areas of the arid southwest, and most native as well as domestic herbivores do not eat it. An exception to this is the desert pack rat, *Neotoma lepida*, whose diet in the Mojave Desert can contain 75 percent creosote stems and foliage. Creosote protects its tissues by coating them with 10–25 percent dry-weight polyphenolic resins, the material that is used by humans along with wood or coal tar to protect wood from insect damage. These chemicals reduce protein digestion in animals and can be toxic if eaten in large amounts. Feeding trials with these pack rats indicate that they are very selective feeders when eating creosote stems and leaves. They avoid resin-rich new foliage and concentrate on older foliage whose resin coating is smaller. Nonselective feeding of creosote foliage by these rodents causes them to lose weight and die. If the new foliage is chemically washed to remove its resins, however, it is perfectly acceptable to them. By being selective feeders, desert pack rats have a nearly unlimited food supply and few herbivore competitors for it.

Packrats of the genus *Neotoma* are members of the large family of typical mice, Cricetidae. This family includes hamsters, lemmings, voles, and new-world rats and mice and is distributed throughout Europe, Asia, and the New World. It first evolved in the Old World during the Early Oligocene (ca. 30 Ma) and quickly dispersed throughout the world. It currently contains five subfamilies, 112 genera, and 580 species. North American rats and mice, including pack rats, occur in subfamly Neotominae, which is an advanced member of the broad group of rats and mice called "muroid" (i.e., mouse-like) rodents. Fossil evidence suggests that neotomines first evolved in western North America, probably in Mexico, in the Late Miocene (ca. 8 Ma) and that *Neotoma albigula* evolved in the

Late Pliocene and Pleistocene (i.e., within the last 3 Ma). Its closest relative is the southern plains pack rat, *N. micropus*, which occurs in northwestern Mexico and the plains of the southern United States; together they are sister species to the eastern pack rat, *N. floridana*, which separated from its western relatives in the Late Pleistocene. Like a number of western arid-adapted vertebrates that currently inhabit the Sonoran Desert, the evolutionary journey of *N. albigula* and its recent ancestors likely has been relatively short (from Mexico) in time and space.

LESSER LONG-NOSED BAT

Leptonycteris yerbabuenae Martinez and Villa, 1940, Phyllostomidae. Characterized by fawn-colored adults with slightly elongated snouts and large, bright eyes, this 23–32 g nectar-feeding bat is one of the largest members of subfamily Glossophaginae of the new-world leaf-nosed bat family Phyllostomidae. This family gains its name from the presence of a triangular flap of skin—a nose leaf—above its nostrils. In some members of this family, this nose leaf is long and spear shaped whereas in others, including all of the flower visitors, it is small; it is especially rudimentary in the family's three species of true blood-feeding vampire bats. The nose leaf is thought to help direct the echolocation calls that in this family are emitted through the nose rather than through the mouth as in most other echolocating bats. Distributed throughout the American tropics and subtropics from the southwestern United States to northern Argentina, including the West Indies, phyllostomid bats, particularly the fruit eaters, are among the most common mammals in lowland neotropical forests. I spent nearly two decades studying the ecology and behavior of one of those fruit eaters—Seba's short-tailed bat, *Carollia perspicillata*—in Panama and Costa Rica.

Of all the animals I treat in this book, the lesser long-nosed bat (which I'll call "Lepto" for short) is the animal I know best because it has been the focus of much of my desert research beginning in the spring of 1989. I've described many of the results of this research in two books that I've written for a general audience: *A Batman in the Tropics* and *No Species Is an Island*. Here I will describe some of the highlights of this research, most of which took place in Sonora, Mexico. But before that, I need to describe my experiences with Leptos closer to home.

When I formally retired from academia and moved from Miami, Florida, to Tucson in the summer of 2008, I figured that my research days were basically over. We moved here because I had fallen in love with the Sonoran Desert and many of its animals and plants during my desert research. I certainly knew we were moving into Lepto country and its main spring and summer food plants, the flowers and fruit of columnar cacti, including the saguaro. But I didn't really think that Leptos would actually end up visiting our backyard each night for over two months every year. But that's what happened. And the reason for this is simply because I put up one hummingbird feeder on our patio in front of our family room window so that we could watch hummingbirds doing their thing. But one evening in early September 2008, Marcia came in from the patio and told me that a large bat had just flown past her. I knew immediately what she had just seen: a Lepto. From then until the end of October, a pair of young Leptos (I could tell their ages from photos that I took) visited our feeder almost every night. Before they migrated south into Mexico, I put up a second feeder on our patio, mostly to keep our hummingbirds from squabbling too much. The Leptos also appreciated having two feeders to visit.

Despite the economic collapse that was occurring worldwide, the year 2008 was ultimately propitious for me. This is because shortly after we moved here, I learned of a new citizen-science (or community-science) project that was being organized by the Town of Marana in cooperation with bat biologists from the U.S. Fish and Wildlife Service (USFWS), the Arizona Game and Fish Department (AZGFD), and Bat Conservation International. Its aim was to study the seasonal use of hummingbird feeders by two species of nectar bats in the Tucson area. These bats included Lepto and its distant cousin, the Mexican long-tongued bat, *Choeronycteris mexicana*.

It turns out that beginning in 2007 something new was happening with these bats in Tucson. Whereas people living on the east side of Tucson and in the foothills of the Santa Catalina and Rincon Mountains were used to seeing a few nectar bats visiting their hummingbird feeders at night, mainly in late summer and early fall, people living in central and western Tucson suddenly began to see bats at their feeders during this time, too. Many of these people began reporting this to the USFWS; it was something they had never experienced before. These reports were enough to initiate a citizen-science project in which people were asked to visit a website hosted by the Town of Marana to report their bat observations. When I heard about this project, I contacted Scott Richardson of the USFWS and indicated that I would be happy to participate in it. I officially came on board in 2009. My job was to correspond with and answer questions about bats from volunteers. I also encouraged them to send me digital photos so that I could identify the bats visiting their feeders. And I occasionally helped Scott capture bats in mist nets in volunteers' yards.

As I write, this citizen-science project is now in its thirteenth year and has involved more than five hundred volunteers; some of them have participated in it for more than ten years. Their observations and reports have provided us with a wealth of new information about the abundance and behavior of these nectar bats in an urban setting in and around Tucson. In addition to helping to document the spread of Lepto, which is much more common than the Mexican long-tongued bat in our area, throughout Tucson and its suburbs, our volunteers helped us to precisely define the time period when these bats are visiting feeders, how many bats are visiting these feeders, and the age and sex composition of Leptos visiting feeders.

What we call the "Lepto feeder season" in Tucson generally runs from about August 21 to October 21 with little year-to-year variation. It's almost like clockwork the way these bats show up in our yards each year. In my yard in 2020, Leptos first arrived on August 27 and were here until early November. In 2019, they arrived on September 2 and left on November 7. In most years, only a handful of Leptos visit my two feeders, but each year some volunteers report that dozens of bats are visiting their feeders. The usual number is six to ten bats visiting feeders per household in mid-September, which is the peak of the season. This allows us to conclude that many Leptos—certainly hundreds if not thousands—are visiting feeders in and around Tucson in late summer and early fall each year. Finally, we have captured bats at a couple dozen sites over the years and have found that most sites are being visited by young female Leptos—both young of the year and one-year-olds—and not by adults. This raises the fascinating question, how do these young bats find feeders? We know from a radio-tracking study conducted by biologists from the AZGFD in 2007–8, that bats radio-tagged at feeders in Tucson are spending their days resting in caves or mines in the Santa Catalina and Rincon Mountains at least 25 km from their feeding sites. Each night groups of young bats head into urban areas to search for "free" food; they are not being led to feeders by knowledgeable adults.

So where are the adult Leptos feeding during this season? From historic records and current roost censuses conducted by the AZGFD, we know that most Leptos are roosting and feeding in upland grasslands and oak-juniper forests in southeastern Arizona in late summer and early fall. Their only food plants during this time are flowering *Agaves* (century plants). None of their spring foods—flowers and fruits of columnar cacti found in the Sonoran Desert—are available then. So at face value, it appears that different age classes of Leptos are feeding in different areas during the *Agave* flowering season. We have no idea why this is. Unlike hummingbirds, lesser long-nosed bats are not territorial around food plants. Groups that can sometimes contain a dozen or more individuals feed without conflict at flowering plants (or at feeders) by taking turns visiting flowers. So it is unlikely that adults are preventing young Leptos from feeding at *Agave* plants.

Adding to this mystery, the predominance of young Leptos at feeders in the Tucson area appears to be a very recent phenomenon. For example, when personnel from the AZGFD were capturing bats at feeders in Tucson for their radio-tracking study in 2007–8, they caught nearly all adults. Similarly, when we captured bats at a few sites in 2010, we caught mostly adults. But the next year when we again sampled these sites, we caught only young bats at three of five of them. In other words, the switch from adults to young bats being most common at some feeders apparently occurred in 2011. This wasn't the case in our yard, however. Based on photos and bat captures, only young bats have been visiting our hummingbird feeders every year since 2008.

Results from our citizen-science program emphasize how much we still have to learn about the biology of the lesser long-nosed bat. Or, conversely, how much we still don't know about its biology. I've been working with this species since 1989, so I have a pretty good understanding about many aspects of its biology, including its annual cycle in western Mexico and southern Arizona. This cycle begins in October and November when literally tens of thousands of males and females congregate in one or more caves in southwestern Mexico. I'll let you guess what they're doing there. After all that jazz is over, most of these bats disperse to other parts of Mexico. A large number of the females are now pregnant and begin to head north toward a series of maternity roosts located in the Sonoran Desert of northwestern Mexico and southwestern Arizona. Some females fly 1,200 km to reach these roosts. Like migrant hummingbirds, they probably do this in stages, refueling at each stop for some time, before moving on. They arrive at them beginning in late March, just as several species of Sonoran Desert columnar cacti are starting to flower. After a gestation period lasting about six months, which is much longer than that of their relatives, they give birth to a single pup beginning in mid-May. In late summer after crops of cactus fruits have been depleted, females and their recently weaned young leave the maternity roosts for parts unknown. It is likely that some of them travel farther north into southeastern Arizona to feed at *Agave* flowers (and hummingbird feeders) before migrating back into Mexico.

We have used stable carbon isotope techniques (see page 73), to gain insights into the diet and migratory pathways used by this bat. As you'll remember, cacti (and *Agaves*) are CAM plants whose ratio of $^{13}C:^{12}C$ differs strongly from that of the so-called C3 plants, which includes most plants in the Sonoran Desert. By sampling small pieces of tissue from either living animals (e.g., from a bit of wing membrane) or from long-dead museum specimens, it is possible to determine how much CAM versus C3 carbon occurs in an animal's diet. When we did this using muscle tissue from museum specimens collected throughout Mexico and southwestern Arizona, we learned that bats migrating either north in the spring or south in the fall contained much more ^{13}C than ^{12}C whereas bats that remained in southern Mexico all year contained more ^{12}C than ^{13}C year-round. These results told us that migrating bats were using CAM plants—columnar cacti in the spring and *Agaves* in the fall—to provide most of the fuel for their migration. Knowing this, we could then identify "nectar corridors" consisting of columnar cacti in the spring and paniculate *Agaves* in the fall that these bats use to migrate to and from their maternity and mating caves. The spring corridor occurs along the lowlands of coastal western Mexico where spring-blooming columnar cacti are most common; the fall corridor occurs farther inland along the Sierra Madre mountains where fall-blooming *Agaves* are most common. Because Leptos are important pollinators of the flowers of both columnar cacti and *Agaves*, our carbon stable isotope data also highlights the codependence that exists between these bats and their major food plants. And, incidentally, how columnar cacti and agaves are indirectly codependent upon each other for providing the fuel that these bats use to complete their annual migratory cycle.

Two features of the biology of Leptos set them apart from most other glossophagine phyllostomid bats: they are highly gregarious and they are strong long-distance fliers both daily and seasonally. This species roosts in caves and mines, and colonies can contain a few thousand to over one hundred thousand individuals. Colonies of their tropical forest-dwelling relatives are usually small and contain a few hundred individuals at most. The Mexican long-tongued bat, for example, roosts seasonally in small colonies of up to a dozen individuals in the mountains of southern Arizona. In their day roosts, the large Lepto colonies generate a lot of body heat that helps them save energy. Their body heat can maintain cave temperatures at 33°C–34°C, which is within its thermoneutral zone. It also increases the developmental rate of their babies in maternity roosts.

But living in the midst of large numbers of hungry confreres has its downside. At night these bats have to spread out over a large area and sometimes travel long distances to find food. Radio-tracking studies have shown that it is not unusual for these bats to fly over 30 km one way (and sometimes much more) from their day roosts to their feeding grounds. As you might guess, this bat is morphologically and physiologically equipped to do this. Being relatively large with long narrow wings, these bats are efficient fliers and can easily fly at speeds of 40 kph or more. They also lack a tail membrane between their hind legs which reduces the drag they experience during fast flight. I've calculated that a female Lepto needs to make only eight cactus flower visits, removing 0.1 mL of nectar per visit, to recoup the cost of flying nearly 30 km from its day roost to its cactus-rich feeding area in coastal Sonora. Thus, when the cost of flight is this cheap, this bat can afford to live in large colonies during the day.

Like hummingbirds, lesser long-nosed bats and their flower-visiting relatives have an unusual diet among mammals; it is rich in water and carbohydrates but poor in protein. But unlike hummingbirds, Lepto does not usually eat insects to obtain its protein. Instead, it does something that hummingbirds cannot do: after grooming its pollen-covered fur with its long flexible tongue, it ingests pollen grains and extracts the amino acids they contain in its stomach. It then uses these amino acids to build the proteins and other nitrogen-rich compounds that it needs. Like hummingbirds, it also quickly digests and converts the sugar-rich nectar that it ingests into energy-rich compounds that are carried directly to its flight muscles. Given its water-rich diet, these bats are not particularly water stressed (but they do sometimes drink free water), and they excrete very dilute urine to reduce their water load. Their kidneys are also designed to maximize the resorption of salt and other electrolytes back into the bloodstream before it is lost by excretion.

What senses do Leptos use to interact with their world? They have large eyes and a keen sense of smell, so these senses must be important to them. In addition, and in contrast to most other mammals, they share another important sense with most other bats. They can echolocate, which means that they produce and detect high frequency sounds (above our upper hearing range of about 20 kHz) that they use for communication, navigation, and food gathering. Insectivorous bats rely exclusively on echolocation to capture their flying prey. And they are extremely adept at doing this. When I walk around my neighborhood just after sunset during the summer, I am amazed to see tiny canyon bats (*Parastrellus hesperus*, Vespertilionidae), which weigh 3–6 g, darting back and forth, zigging and zagging, about 2–3 m above the street chasing tiny insects. Lepto is a much larger and less maneuverable bat, and it doesn't have to chase flying insects. Instead, its food, at least in the Sonoran Desert, consists of flowers and fruit produced by large columnar cacti that are 2–10 m tall; flowers and fruit occur at or near the tops of these plants. Cactus flowers produced by saguaro, cardón (*Pachycereus pringlei*), and organ pipe (*Stenocereus thurberi*) are fist-sized, white, and emit a faint musky odor. They are highly visible in the open desert and clearly want to be found.

So what senses does Lepto use to find them—all three or just one or two? It's likely that they use all three senses, which clearly operate at different distances from the food source. In the open desert, vision must be important for navigating across the landscape and for spotting light-colored flowers on the tops of tall cacti at a distance. These flowers are probably visible from a distance even on the darkest nights of the month. The senses of smell and echolocation operate at much shorter distances than vision, so we might expect them to be important for selecting flowers and orienting correctly to them before they plunge their face into their large corollas. These bats approach flowers (and the hummingbird feeders in my yard) in a rather stereotyped fashion: they always approach flowers from below and stall in midair briefly above them before plunging their faces into the flower. Their actual visits are very fast, lasting about 0.4 sec on average. In this interval, they must extend their 53 mm long tongue, mop up about 0.1 mL of nectar, and then retract their tongue. My photos show that they don't always retract their tongue completely as they leave a flower or feeder. They sometimes leave with their tongue hanging out and dripping with nectar.

High-speed video recordings coupled with ultrasound microphone recordings have shown that these bats use echolocation while approaching and positioning their faces before entering a cactus flower. Their echolocation calls begin at a frequency of about 80 kHz and drop to about 57 kHz when bats are within 0.5 m of the flower; call repetition rates also speed up during this approach. So it's clear that echolocation information is important to these bats as they approach flowers. But what about scent? Is the pungent smell of cardón flowers also important in this orientation? Food choice experiments have shown that both flower scent *and* echolocation cues provided by bell-shaped cactus flowers are important in flower visitation. Individuals are more likely to visit cactus flowers that provide both auditory (echo) and olfactory cues than they are to visit flowers (or their models) that lack one of these cues. Thus, Leptos are using all three major senses to find and acquire their nectar and pollen food.

In sum, lesser long-nosed bats have evolved to become very efficient foragers in desert habitats. They are very mobile and have large foraging areas that can measure 0.25–0.50 km^2. Unlike hummingbirds, which are highly territorial and don't usually move pollen outside their small feeding territories, Leptos are long-distance pollen movers; our radio-tracking studies show that they can fly and move pollen a kilometer or more between plants. These kinds of movements can have evolutionary consequences for their food plants. Long-distance pollen movement, as provided by mobile nectar-feeding bats such as *L. yerbabuenae*, can increase the size of the genetic neighborhood (i.e., the size of a population whose members potentially or actually share genes via pollination) of their food plants and can reduce the rate at which a species' populations diverge genetically because of reduced gene flow. As we've seen, reduced gene flow between populations is one of the prerequisites leading to speciation. As a result, over time plants that are pollinated by mobile pollinators such as Lepto might be expected to have lower rates of speciation than those pollinated by short-distance pollen dispersers such as hummingbirds. We'll revisit this topic in the discussion of saguaro cacti below.

The evolutionary history of new-world leaf-nosed bats (Phyllostomidae) and their flower-visiting species is well known as a result of recent DNA-based phylogenetic studies. The order Chiroptera, which contains twenty families and over 1,600 species, evolved in Laurasia in the Late Paleocene or Early Eocene (ca. 56 Ma). Its ancestors belonged to order Eulipotyphia, which includes shrews, moles, and hedgehogs (fig. 9). Surprisingly, its relatives also include carnivores and odd- and even-toed ungulates (horses, cows, etc.) and not Primates and Rodentia. Family Phyllostomidae is strictly New World in distribution and is about thirty million years old. Although it may have evolved in North and Central America, its greatest diversity currently resides in tropical South America. Its 216 species are classified in eleven subfamilies, including two independently evolved subfamilies of nectar-feeding bats: Glossophaginae (which includes *Leptonycteris* and *Choeronycteris*) and Lonchophyllinae. Glossophagine bats (with

36 species) date from the Early Miocene (ca. 20 Ma), but the three species of *Leptonycteris* are much younger (ca. 2 Ma); their most recent common ancestor may have first evolved in the Greater Antilles before colonizing Central America and Mexico. *Leptonycteris curasoae* from Venezuela, Colombia, and adjacent Caribbean islands and *L. yerbabuenae* are sister species that separated during the Pleistocene about 0.5 Ma as the cactus-filled arid corridor between the arid west coast of Central America and northern South America disappeared. Like many other desert-adapted animals and plants, bats of the genus *Leptonycteris* likely evolved in Mexico, so the evolutionary journey of *L. yerbabuenae* appears to have been short both in space and time.

COYOTE

Canis latrans Say, 1823, Canidae. "God's dog" is familiar to everyone here in the desert, by sound if not by sight. Weighing 8–20 kg, males are somewhat larger than females (7–18 kg). These handsome medium-sized canids are distributed throughout North America, except on the tundra, as well as in Mexico and Central America as far south as Nicaragua. In recent decades they have become increasingly urbanized throughout the United States, especially in the East.

Coyotes occur in our neighborhood and can sometimes be heard vocalizing at night, often in response to police sirens. We occasionally see one to four of them on our main residential street or passing between houses. Marcia and her walking buddy Pam once saw a group of eight crossing a residential street south of our neighborhood. As is the case throughout Tucson, they sometimes prey on cats and small dogs. Our daughter and at least one of our neighbors has lost an outdoor cat to them. Although our backyards are walled, this is no deterrent to coyotes and bobcats, and pets in yards are fair game for these predators.

I've had little personal experience with coyotes. My best coyote photos come from Yellowstone National Park in the winter. There we saw a pair at a dead male elk killed by wolves. They were sharing leftovers with magpies. On one memorable afternoon we followed and photographed a beautiful female coyote, resplendent with a coat of thick winter fur and a bushy tail, as she walked and trotted along the snowy southern bank of the Madison River hunting for her next meal. We followed her from across the river for nearly 8 km, stopping to photograph her as she passed by. At our third and final stop, we saw her approaching, and then she spotted a male Barrow's goldeneye duck next to the bank. In a flash she launched herself at the duck in the water, grabbing it by the neck amid a cascade of water. She then climbed up the bank and finished killing it. She picked up her dead prey and stared at us before bounding off through the deep snow toward the distant forest. We photographers were thrilled with the fleeting images we had just captured.

Like other North American predators, coyotes have been studied by wildlife biologists for decades, and we know a lot about their ecology and behavior, although they are shy and not easily studied. Because they sometimes prey on livestock, particularly sheep and goats, reduction of predation by coyotes has been a long-standing concern. Nonetheless, here I will focus on the biology of these fascinating carnivores with particular emphasis on their historical range expansion, their population ecology and social behavior, and their use of urban areas as newly acquired habitat.

Historically, the coyote is an open country animal; grasslands, prairies, and deserts are its natural habitats. For the past 10,000 years, its geographic range has included much of North America west of the Mississippi and Ohio River valleys, Mexico, and the Pacific coast of Central America as far south as Nicaragua. Since 1900, however, its range has expanded so that it now includes much of the eastern United States. In addition, it now ranges far north into much of Alaska and far south into Panama. About 40 percent of this expansion has occurred since 1950. Overall, this expansion has been attributed to the demise of its larger predators (e.g., wolves and mountain lions) and deforestation associated with agriculture. Although it was not originally a forest dweller, in the East it now occurs in deep forests. Along with this geographic expansion, it is now living and thriving in many urban areas throughout its range. During this expansion, it has also hybridized with its close canine relatives, including gray and red wolves (*Canis lupus* and *C. rufus*, respectively) and domestic dogs. This hybridization was evident when I was conducting field work in Sonora, Mexico. One afternoon while we were having a picnic at my field site, an obvious "coydog" wandered up to us, looking for a handout. Most of its body resembled a coyote except for its long, German Shepard–like legs and its floppy ears. Its demeanor was certainly doglike and not furtive like the coyotes living in the area.

The dramatic increase in its geographic range in less than 150 years emphasizes the opportunistic and generalized nature of this carnivore. Whereas Mark Bekoff (1977), a major researcher of coyotes, described it as being nonterritorial (except possibly for females) and less social than wolves, much recent research describes it as being a pack-living, highly territorial species. Packs include a socially dominant alpha pair of long-term mates, a couple of beta individuals (both males and females), and young of the year; packs can contain up to ten individuals. In most years, only the alpha female produces a litter within a pack. Given its large geographic range and habitat diversity, it is not surprising to learn that coyote population densities are quite variable. Densities generally range from 0.2 to 2.3 individuals/km^2 and vary with latitude; southern densities, which generally have a larger prey base, are higher than northern densities. Territory sizes can be as large as 40 km^2, so these animals can be very wide ranging.

Most researchers divide the coyote's year into four distinct seasons. In our area, these seasons are *breeding* (January 1–March 15), *gestation* (March 16–April 30), *pup rearing* (May 1–August 31), and *dispersal* (September 1–December 31). During the breeding season, males begin to court their mates a couple of months before copulation actually occurs. Females come into heat only once a year, and copulation ends with a brief male-female "tie," just like in dogs. Females give birth and nurse their young in a den which they usually excavate (as opposed to using, for example, a badger's den); the same den can be used for several years. Gestation lasts about sixty-three days, and average litter size is about five to six pups. Litter size and proportion of females, including beta females, breeding in any year varies with food availability, which sets the overall limit on coyote population density. Baby coyotes are blind and helpless at birth but grow quickly, being provisioned with solid food mostly by their fathers, and are weaned at five to seven weeks—a rapid rate of development for animals their size (e.g., compare with round-tailed ground squirrels, page 163). Pups generally leave their pack and begin to disperse at ages of six to nine months. Many youngsters choose to remain in their natal pack whereas others choose to strike out on their own. Like many birds and mammals, dispersers will become floaters or transients until they find another pack that will accept them. As a result, transients tend to have lower survival rates than territory holders, a common situation in many territorial species. Overall, most coyotes live only six to eight years, a relatively short life span for animals of their size.

As in most mammalian carnivores, the sensory world of the coyote includes visual, auditory, and olfactory components. They are very visual animals, especially during social interactions, when, like dogs, they are very aware of each other's postures and facial expressions. They also rely heavily on vision for navigating at night and for hunting. Although coyotes can be active during the day, they are most active at night. Not surprisingly, they have rod-dominated retinas characteristic of nocturnal mammals. But their retinas also contain two kinds of cones—one that is sensitive to relatively short visible wavelengths (blues) and another that is sensitive to middle-to-long visible wavelengths (reds). This means that they have dichromatic color diurnal vision in addition to monochromatic nocturnal vision. Visually, they are adapted to operate well during both day and night and hence are visual generalists.

As we all know, coyotes are very vocal, although their vocal repertoire is less varied than that of gray wolves. Single individuals produce lengthy long-distance howls, perhaps to communicate with other members of their group, and groups produce both howls and cacophonous yips to advertise their territories. Folklore suggests that coyotes vocalize more frequently during the bright parts of the lunar month. But a study conducted during the summer in Saskatchewan, Canada, found that howling by solitary individuals was unrelated to lunar conditions and that vocalizations by groups actually decreased, rather than increased, on moon-bright nights. So folklore appears to be wrong about this.

As dog owners know, olfaction is also a very important sense in canids. Urine, feces, and glandular secretions all convey important sensory information about an individual's identity, reproductive condition, and general health to other individuals. Scents are also widely used by carnivores to mark their territories. Anal glands are the major source of these scents in canids. Although they are most successful using visual cues when hunting, coyotes also use odors produced by prey to detect them. Observations and experiments have shown that coyotes often approach their prey from downwind, using their sense of smell to help locate them.

Except when they're resting, coyotes are often on the move, usually covering several kilometers in a day. Much of this movement is directed toward finding prey both day and night. Though they often live in packs, they do not hunt large prey cooperatively as a group as wolves (or Harris's hawks in Arizona) do. Instead, they hunt for food individually. The advantage of pack living in coyotes appears to come from defense of large carrion such as elk killed by wolves. Unlike certain other sympatric carnivores such as bobcats, coyotes are dietary generalists. Much of their diet, however, consists of mammalian flesh. In central Arizona, for example, they prey more on lagomorphs (rabbits and jackrabbits) and larger mammals such as peccaries and deer and less on rodents than bobcats. They also eat lots of saguaro and opuntia fruit (important water sources) in season. During the late spring and summer, it is not uncommon to find coyote scats full of cactus seeds on the desert floor. As a result, it is likely that this species is an important disperser of cactus and other seeds. Birds, reptiles, and insects are minor dietary items for them in our area.

Coyotes use a variety of strategies when hunting for food. All of them involve active hunting rather than sitting and waiting. One of these is long-distance searching in which an individual covers a lot of ground while constantly searching for prey. Another is area-restricted searching in which an animal thoroughly searches a small area where it suspects a prey is hiding. Yet another involves pouncing on a prey by rearing up on its hind legs and dropping down on its victim. This behavior is often used in the winter when a coyote hears a rodent active in a tunnel under the snow, as we witnessed and photographed in Yosemite National Park. Finally, coyotes will quickly dash 100 m or more to chase down an animal. Its success rate in this method is only 50 percent or less.

How do these well-furred, medium-sized carnivores deal with the physiological challenges they face in the desert, particularly during the summer? One way is via their annual molt in which they replace their thick insulative winter pelage with a thinner, less insulative summer pelage. Although coyotes give birth in a den, they do not use dens to escape high summer temperatures as do many small mammals, including kit foxes in the Sonoran Desert. Instead, they seek shade from vegetation or rocks during the hottest parts of the day and are more active at night in the summer. They also allow their T_bs, which are normally 36.5°C, to rise as T_as increase above 34°C as a means of saving water and reducing metabolic costs. At T_as > 34°C, they begin to pant, and they become very heat-stressed at T_as > 40°C. To remain hydrated, they actively seek natural or man-made water sources and consume water-rich cactus fruits in the summer; they also rely on their vertebrate prey to supply them with water year-round. All in all, although they have lived in hot and arid environments in western North America and Mexico for millennia, their physiology tells us that they are not truly desert-adapted animals regarding their tolerance of high T_as. With the expected further increases in average T_a associated with climate change, desert populations of coyotes will likely be thermally stressed for many months of the year. How they respond to this challenge remains to be seen.

In Tucson, coyotes are urban dwellers, and several studies have compared their diets and movements in urban (or suburban) and rural areas. For example, movements of eight animals (six in one pack) equipped with satellite radio transmitters (a technical advance over traditional radio tracking) living in central Tucson were followed for one year. These animals lived in home ranges or territories that averaged 23 km²—a large area of about 870 city blocks. Most of their activity was centered in medium density residential areas (2–7 houses/ha), dry washes, and golf courses; they avoided high density residential areas (>

7 residences/ha) and commercial areas. An important food source in residential areas apparently was domestic cats! City life turned out to be rather hazardous for these animals, however; several were killed by traffic or died during this study.

Two other studies were focused on the movements and diets of coyotes living in or near Saguaro National Park East and in a rural area away from the suburbs southeast of Tucson. A total of thirteen animals was radio-tagged (nine in or near the park and four in the rural area) and tracked for one year. Animals in both areas had home ranges or territories averaging about 16 km² (i.e., smaller than in Tucson), and their movements were greatest during the pup-rearing season when males were provisioning their litters. The nonrural animals often entered the suburbs for food; some households routinely fed coyotes, which is against Arizona law. Based on these results, it is not surprising that a study of the diets of coyotes living in or near Saguaro National Park East and in a rural area reported that suburban animals ate more human-produced food and fewer rodents and plant parts (i.e., mesquite pods and cactus fruits) than their rural cousins. Diets in this and many other studies of vertebrate carnivores were determined by the analysis of fecal scats, which are often easy to find in dry, open habitats such as deserts. Wildlife biologists also often use scat counts from transects or study plots to determine the relative abundance of mammalian carnivores.

Results of these studies emphasize the opportunistic and adaptable nature of coyotes. Although city life can be hazardous, the advantages of this lifestyle probably outweigh the disadvantages for at least two reasons: the food base may be larger and more dependable in cities (as is the case in Cooper's hawks) and the threat from predators (other than cars and trucks) may be less. It would be interesting to know whether reproductive success is higher in urban compared with rural coyotes. As in the case of Cooper's hawks, we can ask, Are cities ecological "sinks" (i.e., with birth rates < death rates) or "sources" (i.e., with birth rates > death rates) for population growth? I suspect that the answer in both species is that cities are sources rather than sinks.

Finally, what is the evolutionary history of coyotes? When and where did they evolve? Coyotes are members of the mammalian order Carnivora and family Canidae that currently contains thirty-four species with a worldwide distribution. All modern canids belong to subfamily Caninae. The order evolved in Laurasia about fifty million years ago (i.e., in the Early Eocene). Doglike carnivores separated from catlike carnivores about forty-five to forty-two million years ago (i.e., in the Middle Eocene). Canids belonging to extinct subfamilies first appeared in North America in Late Eocene (ca. 38–34 Ma). Within this family, the North American clade containing foxes (*Vulpes*) dates from about 16 Ma and is basal to the clade containing wolves and their relatives (*Canis*), which dates from about 10 Ma. The closest relatives of *Canis latans* (coyotes) are gray wolves (*C. lupus*) with a Holarctic (north temperate) distribution and golden jackal (*C. aureus*) found only in Africa; this group dates from about 2.5 Ma. The estimated age of *C. latrans* is about 0.4 Ma. Of these three taxa, it is the only one found strictly in the New World. In summary, genetic data, including entire genome analyses, indicate that the coyote likely evolved in western North America very recently, certainly within the Pleistocene epoch, from ancestral stock also found in this region. The evolutionary journey of the coyote has therefore been relatively short in both time and space.

BOBCAT

Lynx rufus Schreber, 1777, Felidae. Bobcats are the smallest native felids in North America. They are about twice the size of large domestic cats, and adult males (9.6 kg) are significantly larger than adult females (6.8 kg). Their distinctive features include broad facial ruffs, dark ears with prominent white spots, soft tawny and spotted fur, relatively long legs, and a short, striped tail. Their geographic range covers much of North America from the midlatitudes of Canada (to 50° north) to central Mexico; it has been exterminated in parts of the U.S. Midwest. Like the coyote, it appears to be well suited for life in urban areas.

I have to admit that I am a cat person and am drawn to cats of all kinds. Marcia and I have had one or two domestic cats for nearly all of our married lives. We did have a yellow lab dog when our kids were young but didn't replace it when it died. I've often lived in "cat country" during my tropical and desert fieldwork but have rarely seen them. My luck at spotting mountain lions and jaguars living in my Costa Rican field site was so bad that I just missed seeing a puma bounding across a road behind me one morning. It wasn't until much later that I finally saw and photographed an old male jaguar and two ocelots in the Pantanal, the giant swamp found in southern Brazil, Paraguay, and Bolivia.

But I've had much better luck seeing bobcats in Arizona. For one thing, they occasionally pass through our yard, and at least two have stopped for a long drink at our patio fountain. One afternoon in December 2019 a youngster sunned itself and slept for a while on a low horizontal branch of one of our patio mesquite trees. On at least two occasions, bobcats have spent the night on our flat roof, climbing up one of our large mesquites to get there. Female bobcats sometimes give birth and raise their kits on people's roofs in Tucson. Most of my encounters with bobcats have been very short lived, but three are particularly memorable. The first one occurred in our daughter's cholla-filled and undeveloped backyard in northwest Tucson. One winter afternoon I was bird-watching there when I spotted an animal walking along a brushy wash in front of me. At first I thought it was a coyote, but it turned out to be an adult bobcat. I simply sat down (without a camera!) to watch it, and it did the same: it lay down in the open about 5 m from me and began to watch me. Just then a second adult bobcat came along the same wash from the opposite direction, and it too lay down about 5 m from me and the other bobcat. The three of us just sat in a triangle and looked at each other for several minutes before they moved off together.

The second memorable occurrence happened one morning at home. When I raised a bedroom window shade and looked out into the large patio planter just below the window, I saw a bobcat sleeping there under a large cycad. It woke up and was probably as surprised to see me as I was to see her. But no matter, she simply lay down and went back to sleep. She stayed there all morning and into midafternoon, adjusting her position occasionally, and didn't mind me taking pictures of her through the window. She eventually woke up and walked off through our yard later that afternoon.

Finally, in December 2019 I was wandering around Tucson's Sweetwater wetlands, a water treatment plant that attracts lots of waterfowl in the winter, with a camera buddy when we spotted an adult male bobcat walking along the path ahead of us. As we slowly approached it, the bobcat ignored us and went into serious hunting mode. It had apparently heard something in the cattails next to the path. It crouched down and slowly slinked closer and closer to the wall of cattails at the water's edge. After several minutes of intense concentration, it leaped into the water and disappeared in the cattails only to come back out empty mouthed. It had apparently missed its prey. It then proceeded to shake itself off, sending sprays of water everywhere, and began grooming itself. It did this for several minutes as we maneuvered around with our cameras to get better shots. All the while it paid us no mind. It then stopped grooming and walked past me so close that I could have touched it on its way to somewhere else. It stopped to spray a shrub with urine before disappearing.

In his excellent book *Bobcat*, Kevin Hansen writes: "The paradox of *Lynx rufus* is that it is the most exploited and most studied wild felid in the world, yet it endures throughout most of its historic range in North America and in some places actually seems to be expanding its range" (2007, 159). Sound familiar? The same can be said about coyotes, which have been persecuted extensively since the early nineteenth century. Both of these species demonstrate admirable adaptability in the face of human domination of all places on Earth, including the Sonoran Desert.

Unlike coyotes, bobcats are basically solitary animals except when females are accompanied by their kits before they disperse. Although litters can be born in most months, the main breeding season is December to July. During this period, females produce one or two litters averaging two to three kits each. Females give birth and nurse their young in a main den that she uses every year as well as one or more auxiliary dens. Gestation lasts about two months, and females nurse their young for an additional two months. Like male hummingbirds, male bobcats are only sperm donors and do not provide any parental care. Unlike coyotes, no long-term pair-bonds form in this species.

Like most carnivores (e.g., hawks and owls), bobcats have a land tenure system in which adults live in well-established home ranges. Female ranges tend not to overlap whereas male ranges overlap with those of females and other males. Although they frequently mark the boundaries of their home ranges with visual scrapes and scent deposits produced by urine, feces, and anal gland secretions, their home ranges are usually not actively patrolled or defended as if they were inviolate territories. Living in established home ranges is absolutely essential for bobcats because it assures them of a predictable food supply, allows them to breed, and increases their survival rates.

But life is not as salubrious for young bobcats. Once they leave their mothers, young bobcats, like young coyotes, become transients in search of an unoccupied area where they can establish their own home range. Some youngsters, usually males, travel substantial distances (e.g., 20–40 km) from their natal areas before establishing their own home ranges. During this transient period, they are subject to starvation and other sources of mortality and cannot breed until they become settled. As a result, survival rates of young bobcats are usually significantly lower than those of adults living in home ranges.

Population density of bobcats in rural central Arizona is relatively high and ranges from 3.6 to 4.1 animals per km². Bobcats there and elsewhere live in separate home ranges with male ranges being larger than female ranges (i.e., 9.1 km² vs. 4.8 km² in central Arizona). Even when their home ranges overlap, bobcats of both sexes avoid each other except during the breeding season. A study of radio-tagged bobcats in central Arizona reported that average distance between individuals tracked simultaneously was 2–3 km.

Unlike coyotes, bobcats are strictly carnivorous, and they tend to specialize on cottontails and jackrabbits. Depending on location, their diets also include a variety of small and large rodents (up to porcupines in size), small foxes, javelinas, and deer that they usually attack while they're sleeping. A variety of birds (mostly quails) and reptiles are also included in their diets. Their usual method of hunting involves stealth and quick pounces (as I've seen both at the Sweetwater wetlands [see above] and also in Yellowstone National Park). They also sometimes wait in concealment until a potential prey passes by and then make a quick pounce or brief chase.

How do bobcats (and other felids) perceive their world? From watching housecats, it's obvious that they use visual, auditory, olfactory, and tactile (whiskers) senses at different times and places. Like coyotes (and other canids), bobcats live in a visual world, but their visual acuity is not particularly sharp. They have relatively large eyes and elliptical pupils which allows them to emit large amounts of light at night while protecting their eyes from bright light during the day. As in many nocturnal mammals, behind their retina is a reflective layer of cells called a *tapetum lucidum*. This layer reflects incoming light back through the rods of the retina, thus enhancing their low light vision. The visual acuity of domestic cats is not particularly high and has been reported to be 20/100 to 20/200 (i.e., like me, they're pretty nearsighted). Since they are primarily nocturnal hunters, their retinas are rod dominated, but like coyotes, they do have cones with visual pigments that provide some color vision. These pigments are especially sensitive in the shorter (bluer) end of the visible electromagnetic spectrum. Overall, however, their visual world contains more muted and less saturated colors than, say, primates like us with trichromatic vision. Their lenses are also known to transmit UV light, which we cannot perceive and which suggests that they can perceive short wave lengths. Whether this aids them in hunting is currently unknown. Finally, like those of owls, cat's eyes are forward facing, giving them binocular vision. This vision enhances their depth perception, another key adaptation for a nocturnal predator.

Cats in general have a highly developed auditory sense. With their very mobile ears, cats have a wider auditory field than that of canids. The lower end of their auditory spectrum is similar to ours, but the upper end of this spectrum is about 64 kHz, which is much higher than ours and canids. With their ability to detect motion under very low light conditions and their ability to hear soft and high frequency sounds, cats are very effective nocturnal hunters, especially of small rodents that can produce high frequency sounds (ultrasound) for communication. Like all other felids, bobcats are highly vocal and "meow" when communicating at close or far distances. They also purr, especially when females are with their young. Females in heat also caterwaul, a high-intensity form of meowing.

Cats also have a very keen sense of smell, some nine to sixteen times more sensitive than ours. This is because their nasal passages contain forty-five to two hundred million epithelial cells compared with only five million in our noses. It is likely that they use this sense more during social activities than while hunting. As we know all too well, scent marking as a means of communication is common in cats, and scents are produced by anal glands as well as by glands located on the cheeks and paws. With their longer muzzles, canids such as coyotes have many more scent-sensitive epithelial cells in their noses than felids, and they use scent for hunting much more than felids.

Finally, cats are well-equipped with vibrissae—stout hairs around their faces that convey tactile information to an animal. Our Maine coon cat Django is a "whisker champ"; its facial whiskers are up to 10 cm long. Vibrissae around the mouth are located in four rows; whiskers in the upper and lower two rows can move independently. They also occur above the eyes, under the chin, and on the front and hind limbs. These vibrissae are very sensitive to movement, whether it's movement of air or animals. The region of the brain that receives information from the vibrissae is located near the visual region. Together, these two regions provide cats with 3-D information about their world. When a bobcat hunts, it spreads its whiskers out like a fan and then extends them forward like a net during prey capture and transport.

Although bobcats appear to be common in Tucson, their urban ecology has not yet been well studied here. One such study was conducted for four years in an area containing a mixture of natural habitats, modified natural habitats (e.g., golf courses), and residential and commercial developments in Southern California west of Los Angeles. In that study fifty bobcats and eighty-six coyotes were equipped with radio collars that transmitted information about whether an animal was active (moving), inactive (resting), or dead. This study aimed to determine the extent to which animals incorporated urban versus nonurban habitat into their home ranges and how this affected their home range sizes and activity patterns. Results for bobcats indicated that adult females were much more likely to avoid human association than adult males and young females. As in purely natural areas, male bobcats had larger home ranges than females (3.0 vs. 1.7 km^2). Annual survival rates in bobcats were generally high (ca. 75 percent) and were not affected by extent of human association. Overall, the home ranges of all bobcats contained much more natural habitat than developed habitat. Results of this study provide us with two important conservation messages: (1) bobcats living in close proximity to humans still need undeveloped habitat to prosper, most likely because of their larger prey base (rabbits and rodents), and (2) adult female bobcats are especially sensitive to urban development. In contrast, coyotes in that study were more human associated than bobcats, most likely because of their more generalized diets.

Now that we've reviewed the ecology of the two common Sonoran Desert mammalian carnivores, we can put this information into a community context just as we did for Merriam's kangaroo rat. The parallels between the community structures of these two groups of mammals are striking, probably because competition for food is a major factor in determining the ecological relationships between these species. Abundant evidence indicates that food availability influences many features of the population and community ecology of mammalian carnivores. For example, food availability is known to determine their population densities, patterns of habitat use, and reproductive activity. Population densities are positively correlated with food availability (usually rodent densities for both coyotes and bobcats); densities tend to be highest in food-rich habitats; and more females breed (and sometimes breed a second time) during years of high rodent populations than in low years.

Given that they live in a food-limited world, it is not surprising that these carnivores compete for food. How does this competition affect the community structure—i.e., the number of co-occurring species—of Sonoran Desert canids and felids? This structure includes four species of canids (kit foxes, gray foxes, coyotes, and gray or Mexican wolves) but only two species of felids (bobcats and mountain lions). We've already seen that the distribution of body sizes in co-occurring species of Sonoran Desert seed-eating rodents is not random. Instead, their body sizes are more uniformly spaced apart than expected by chance. The same pattern is clearly evident in the Sonoran Desert canids. Maximum body masses of these species are kit fox (2.7 kg), gray fox (7 kg), coyote (20 kg), and gray wolf (40 kg); ratios of body masses between adjacent species in this size spectrum are 2.6, 2.9. and 2.0, respectively. These ratios imply that desert canids must differ in body mass by a factor of at least two in order to coexist. Since average prey size is known to be positively correlated with a predator's body size in these canids, their size differences assure that the diets of sympatric canids are likely to differ significantly. The size difference between bobcats (maximum mass = 9.6 kg) and mountain lions (100 kg) is even more striking; this ratio is about ten. Differences in the diets of bobcats (mostly rodents and rabbits) and mountain lions (mostly deer and other large ungulates) clearly are extreme. Not considered here are size differences between males and females within these species. These differences can be considerable (females are smaller than males in most of these species), and they likely also result in dietary differences.

But what about the diets of similar-sized canids and felids (e.g., between coyotes and bobcats and mountain lions and gray wolves)? How do these pairs of species avoid competition for food? Bobcats and coyotes co-occur in many places, but dietary comparisons usually show that their diets differ significantly. Bobcats are more specialized on eating rodents whereas coyotes have broader, less specialized diets that also include significant amounts of plant material seasonally. As a result, these two species probably are not serious food competitors in most places. Dietary comparisons also show that sympatric coyotes and wolves have significantly different diets and are not serious competitors. Coyotes eat much smaller prey, on average, than wolves, which are large prey specialists. Regarding competitive relationships between wolves and mountain lions, any conclusions that we may reach are marred by the extirpation of wolves in many parts of their range. They had been eliminated in the eastern United States by the end of the nineteenth century and from most of the west by the mid-twentieth century. As a result, along with the extirpation of grizzly bears in most of the western United States plus increases in populations of deer and elk, populations of mountain lions in the west have been increasing in recent decades. They certainly are relatively common in the mountains of Arizona, including the Tucsons and Santa Catalinas around Tucson, where no wolves occur. Historically, though, wolves, mountain lions, and grizzly bears co-occurred in many places in North America and likely competed for ungulates, including deer, elk, and bighorn sheep. Being solitary and with very cryptic behavior, mountain lions likely were able to coexist with these predators by avoidance behavior. Like bobcats and coyotes, mountain lions are also quite adaptable to the presence of humans and occur on the edges of our urban developments today. They have prospered in the absence of their mammalian competitors (and predators).

Bobcats are members of family Felidae in the mammalian order Carnivora. This family is currently classified in two extant subfamilies: Pantherinae (the big cats) with two genera and seven species and Felinae (the small cats) with ten genera and thirty-four species. Catlike (i.e., feliform) and doglike (i.e., caniform) mammalian carnivores last shared a common ancestor about 45–42 Ma (i.e., in the Late Eocene or Early Oligocene). First evolving in tropical Asia, early felids arrived in North America by about 25 Ma (i.e., in the Late Oligocene), about ten million years after canids were here. Based on molecular evidence, modern felids date from about 10 Ma (i.e., Middle Miocene) and radiated into different lineages quickly. Members of the genus *Lynx*, for example, date from about 7.2 Ma (i.e., Late Miocene) with *L. rufus* (the bobcat) being basal to the Canadian and Eurasian lynxes. Our domestic cats (*Felis catus*) and other small European cats of the genus *Felis* are the youngest members of this family and evolved in Eurasia about 6.2 Ma (i.e., in the Late Miocene). Bobcats thus appeared in the middle of the evolutionary radiation of modern felines and are native to North America. Their evolutionary journey has been relatively long in time but short in space.

JAVELINA

Pecari tajacu Reicherbach, 1835, Tayassuidae. This new-world pig that we call collared peccary or javelina appears to be a very recent immigrant into the Sonoran Desert. Its size (20–40 kg) and appearance—pink pig snout, dark bristly hairs along its back, rather short legs, gregarious, and so forth—make it unmistakable. Unlike many other ungulates, including true pigs (Suidae), javelinas are sexually monomorphic; males and females are similar in size and appearance. It's basically a tropical species whose geographic range includes all of South and Central America, Mexico, and the desert Southwest. It was not known to occur in Arizona until about 1700 but is now a familiar resident in our two major cities.

I've only had passing acquaintance with these animals in my tropical and desert fieldwork. When I worked in the tropical dry forest of northwestern Costa Rica, small groups of javelinas were always around, but I basically ignored them. I spent a lot of time there sitting quietly watching birds and monkeys feeding in fruiting trees during the day, and I frequently heard javelinas shuffling around in the forest understory near me. But they never came over to visit me. When we spent two sabbatical years living in the foothills of the Tucson Mountains, they were often in our yard, especially if I had put a seed block out for quails, but they never stayed very long. They also occur in our current neighborhood, but I've rarely seen them on my walks. Neighbors tell me they are more likely to smell them than see them. They like to upend garbage containers but rarely do so on our street. I've seen coyotes and bobcats much more frequently in our neighborhood. Our backyards are walled, which prevents javelinas from feasting on most of our plants. This is probably why they are scarce here.

There seems to be some confusion about what javelinas really are. For example, once when I was taking the tram ride in Sabino Canyon in northeastern Tucson, I heard the driver, whose job included telling passengers about the plants and animals they were seeing, exclaim as a javelina crossed the road: "Oh look, there's a big rodent called a javelina just ahead of us." Needless to say, javelinas are not rodents; they are even-toed ungulates related to cows, goats, and old-world pigs. When the tram stopped, I quietly told the driver that javelinas are not rodents, hoping that he would remember this the next time he saw one. This incident makes me wonder just how many people think that javelinas are rodents.

Biologically and ecologically, javelinas are notable for many reasons. For one thing, they are highly social animals that live in cohesive groups of up to about nineteen animals; some males are solitary. Groups contain both sexes and a mix of age classes (e.g., adults, subadults, and juveniles). A study of radio-collared javelinas in southern Texas reported their population density to be about two to nine animals per km^2 and home range sizes of groups of about 1.8 km^2. Home ranges of groups did not overlap and were defended against other groups, indicating that they were territories. Reports of javelina population densities in Arizona are similar. In the Tucson area, group home range sizes are about 1.8 km^2. Overall, javelina population densities and home range sizes tend to be similar in the northern arid portions of their geographic range to those in tropical forests of Central and South America.

Group life in these animals is rather low-key because of the absence of strife among individuals. Individuals communicate with each other with low grunts and frequently rub each other's musk glands located on the back just ahead of the tail and on the face. They tend to excrete their very pungent musk either as a means of maintaining group cohesion or as a warning when danger is sensed. When they aren't feeding, groups bed down in the shade under trees or in caves to avoid high temperatures or snow. When bedding down, animals are either scattered away from each other in summer or huddled together to keep warm in the winter. Feeding is restricted to cooler parts of the day (early morning and early evening) during the summer, but it occurs all day during the winter. Groups travel from bedding areas to feeding areas in single file with juveniles trotting along to keep up with their mothers.

Second, their breeding season usually lasts all year long. Unlike other ungulates such as deer and bighorn sheep, female javelinas are polyestrous (i.e., they go into estrus and mate again soon after the birth of a litter) and can produce two litters of one to three young per year. Mating takes place within the group, whose individuals usually pay no attention to mating pairs. As in bobcats, males are simply sperm donors and take no interest in their offspring. Genetic analyses indicate multiple males and females breed within a group (i.e., there is no dominant mated pair); that a litter can have multiple fathers (i.e., that the mating system is promiscuous); and that males from adjacent groups can sometimes sire babies within a group (i.e., that extragroup copulations occur). Although newborns can be seen in most months, in Arizona they are most common in June through August. Female reproductive activity is strongly influenced by annual changes in food availability as determined by rainfall. In drought years, less than 25 percent of adult females breed whereas over 70 percent breed in years of good rainfall. As a result, javelina numbers decline during drought years, but they can quickly bounce back in wet years as females produce more and larger litters.

As in other ungulates, after a gestation period of about five months, newborn javelinas are precocial at birth (like baby quails) and figuratively hit the ground running. Their long gestation period is in strong contrast to the two-month gestation periods of similar-sized coyotes and bobcats, whose newborns are altricial (i.e., their eyes are closed and they are helpless at birth). The precocial young of ungulates undergo a much longer gestation period in which much more development occurs in utero than is the case in mammalian carnivores. Among North American mammals, the babies of marsupials (i.e., pouched mammals that lack a placenta) such as the common opossum (*Didelphis virginiana*) hold the record for minimizing the time that their offspring remain in utero—thirteen days. Virtually all of the development of marsupial babies occurs in their mother's pouch rather than in utero. Although they nurse from their mothers for two to three months, baby javelinas begin sampling solid food shortly after birth. They are born with bright reddish pelage that is replaced by darker adult pelage at three to four months of age. After they are weaned, they continue to stay close to their moms for several months and often do not disperse; instead, they remain in their natal group. When young javelinas do leave their natal groups, it is usu-ally males that disperse (the usual situation in mammals), and they only move into neighboring groups. Whether sedentary or dispersing, young javelinas are particularly vulnerable to predation by coyotes and bobcats.

A third distinctive feature is that they are omnivores, which means that their diets contain a broad mixture of plant and animal material. In the desert, however, their diet is heavily skewed toward the pads of opuntia or prickly pear cacti. Over 75 percent of their diet comes from these plants in many places. As we've seen with pack rats, not many vertebrates consume the succulent and relatively nonwoody pads of opuntias because their tissues are laced with oxalic acid, a substance that forms insoluble crystals in water and is toxic to most vertebrates. But javelinas eat these pads and their short spines with impunity. How they deal with these crystals is currently unknown, but their kidneys are known to excrete them. Javelinas are known to feed selectively on different *Opuntia* species and different morphs within species. They select cactus pads that are higher in water and lower in calcium oxa-late than occurs in other *Opuntia* species and their intraspecific morphs. Other important food items in the Sonoran Desert include fruits of saguaro, prickly pear, and barrel cacti and the pods of mesquite and palo verde trees. At higher elevations, they consume large amounts of the tannin-rich acorns of oak trees, another gen-erally unpalatable kind of food. They also spend time everywhere digging in the ground for roots, stems, and rhizomes that they locate by smell.

Javelinas are well known for their weak eyesight, so their visual world is rel-atively restricted compared with that of many other ungulates. Smell, rather than vision, is their most important sensory mode. I witnessed this once while I was photographing round-tailed ground squirrels in a power line clearing in my neighborhood. One morning a large solitary male javelina approached the clearing from along a shady trail. It stopped at the clearing's edge and looked my way while obviously sniffing the air. It must have decided that I posed no threat to it and proceeded to calmly cross the clearing and continue on its way. Javelinas use smell and scent to keep track of each other within their group, to find food, to mark their territories, and to detect predators. As already mentioned, they have pungent musk glands for individual and group recognition and communication; they deposit musk on vegetation and create scat stations—small areas that serve as communal latrines—to mark their territories; and they often travel upwind while looking for food. They are more likely to detect predators by smell rather than by vision and respond to them by excreting musk before fleeing. If they stand their ground, they use their long incisors as formidable defensive weapons.

Unlike their major predators, bobcats and coyotes, which have highly insulative pelages, javelinas are covered with a pelage of relatively poor insulative quality. As a result, they are in danger of overheating in summer and losing substantial body heat during the winter. Therefore, they must carefully choose their activity periods and bedding sites throughout the year to avoid excessive heat gain or heat loss. High summer temperatures in the desert pose an especially significant physiological challenge to these animals. One way in which they meet this challenge is via a labile body temperature, which varies from 37.5°C to 40.9°C depending on air temperatures. As in other endotherms with labile T_bs, this flexibility saves metabolic energy and reduces evaporative water loss. Nonetheless, javelinas still lose considerable water via panting when T_as exceed 39.5°C. If they become dehydrated, they can reduce their evaporative water loss by up to 68 percent by seeking cool microhabitats such as caves or rock shelters while reducing their urinary output by up to 91 percent. By consuming succulent prickly pear pads that typically contain 78 percent water, however, javelinas can usually maintain a positive water balance; eating succulent cactus fruits in the summer also helps. To maintain both energy and water balance, individual javelinas need to eat about 1.6 kg of opuntia tissue every day during the summer and 1.9 kg of cactus tissue daily in the winter. At these consumption rates, large javelina herds can potentially consume about 20 percent of opuntia tissue production in an area each year. This species can thus be a major consumer of annual prickly pear tissue production in some areas.

Collared peccaries belong to the mammalian order Artiodactyla, the even-toed ungulates. Given the recently discovered evolutionary connection between hippopotamuses and whales, this order is now often called Cetartiodactyla. This order first evolved in the Early Eocene (ca. 53 Ma) in Laurasia. Excluding whales, it currently contains about 239 species in ten terrestrial families, including camelids, pigs, hippos, pronghorns, giraffes, deer, cows, and antelopes. Artiodactyls are usually classified into two major groups based on the anatomy of their stomachs: nonruminants and ruminants. Nonruminants have simple, nonchambered stomachs and are basal members of this order. Piglike artiodactyls are technically nonruminants because they lack four-chambered stomachs. But peccaries have three-chambered stomachs and so are different from the rest of the older artiodactyls, including true pigs (Suidae). True ruminants include pronghorns through cows and antelopes. With the aid of a diverse bacterial microflora, their four-chambered stomachs serve as fermentation chambers for the digestion of cellulose-rich foodstuffs.

Although the peccary family Tayassuidae is currently restricted in distribution to the New World, its evolution actually began in Europe about 25 Ma in the Late Oligocene. The family has a good fossil record that tells us that these piglike mammals once occurred on all continents except Australia and Antarctica. It disappeared from the Old World at the end of the Miocene (ca. 6 Ma), possibly as a result of competition with true pigs (Suidae), its sister family. Wild hogs (*Sus scrofa*) are invasive species in North America, among many other places around the world, and are known to negatively affect the population ecology of javelinas when they occur together in places such as central Texas. There, population densities of javelinas in hog-free habitat are five to eight times higher than in places where hogs are present. Group sizes are also larger, and home ranges are smaller when hogs are absent; their reproductive rates and patterns of habitat use, however, do not differ in the two areas. Tayassuids invaded South America from North America with the closure of the Panamanian water gap in the Pliocene about 3–4 Ma. Three or four species in three genera evolved in South America with collared peccaries moving back north into Central America and Mexico later in the Pliocene. It has been suggested that their colonization of arid areas in northern Mexico and the southwestern United States resulted from their dietary association with prickly pear cacti. Data from human archaeological sites in the Sonoran Desert indicate that javelinas, an important food species for indigenous humans elsewhere in the Americas, didn't live as far north as Arizona until the seventeenth century. It thus appears that the evolutionary history of this species probably began in South America less than 5 Ma, and its presence in the Sonoran Desert is very recent. Compared with many other Sonoran Desert animals, collared peccaries have undergone a rather long journey in space and time.

SONORAN DESERT PLANTS

The Sonoran Desert contains over 2,000 species of flowering plants, including many succulents, trees, and shrubs, and a few other growth forms (e.g., a host of small annual plants). Given my background as a zoologist, however, I have chosen to highlight only three of these species that play special roles in the lives of animals in this desert. In-depth accounts of many species of Sonoran Desert plants, especially of saguaro, are readily available in other publications.

SAGUARO CACTUS

Carnegiea gigantea (Engelmann) Britton and Rose, 1908, Cactaceae. This stately cactus is synonymous with the Sonoran Desert, although it doesn't occur everywhere in this biome. Primarily because of low summer rainfall, for example, it is missing from Baja California where its status as the largest columnar cactus is taken by cardón. Saguaro's geographic range includes most of south-central Arizona south through western Sonora nearly to the Sinaloan border. Throughout this area, it is now rather patchily distributed as a result of human agriculture. It still occurs in extensive stands, however, in Tucson Mountain Park, Saguaro National Park, and Organ Pipe Cactus National Monument, or as small patches or widely scattered individuals in many parts of Sonora.

Saguaros in the sunset—tall, stately, and many branched—are perhaps the most iconic images of Arizona just as images of the multihued October hardwood forests are for Vermont. But I think we'd all agree that saguaros with their ribbed stems and branches covered with clusters of very sharp spines are much weirder, or at least less familiar, plants than maple or beech trees. For one thing, large adults have a candelabra-like appearance. Up to 16 m tall and weighing many tons, they tower over the rest of the Sonoran Desert landscape. They have two highly conspicuous "flowering" seasons: once when the tips of their branches are covered with large white flowers and a second "season" when their ripe fruits split open to reveal their bright red pulp. They have a very slow life cycle in which only a minuscule fraction of their prodigious seed production ever reaches adulthood. And finally, a few lucky adults can live for centuries.

I have had rather extensive experience with saguaro as a result of our study of its pollination biology in Sonora and southwestern Arizona. We also included cardón (only in Sonora) and organ pipe (*Stenocereus thurberi*) in these studies. Of these three species, saguaro has the most straightforward pollination biology, and as a result it was my least favorite columnar cactus in this multiyear study. Another strike against saguaro from my perspective was its height and spininess. Saguaros can sometimes be over 15 m tall, and they produce their flowers in clusters on the tops of their branches. As a result, we always had to use long extension ladders to reach them. Their flowers are also surrounded by large numbers of very sharp, 3 cm long spines, so leather gloves and pliers were essential gear for tagging flowers. Although cardón is at least as large in height and overall mass as saguaro, its flowers are usually produced on the sides of branches (an adaptation for bat pollination), and its branches are far less spiny, which made conducting pollinator exclusion experiments with its flowers far less painful while working on a 6 m ladder in the dark.

Cactus spines are modified leaves that help to characterize this family. Like thorns, barbs, and other sharp plant parts, they are often considered to be defensive adaptations against herbivores, but they can also have an important physiological function. That is, in the summer they can produce a significant amount of shade that helps to reduce the surface temperature of plants, and in the winter they can trap heat radiating from the plant's surface to ameliorate somewhat the effect of cold winter nights.

In terms of its reproductive biology, saguaro is a typical so-called bat-pollinated columnar cactus based on its nocturnal flower opening and prodigious nectar production. It is a spring bloomer—May and June around Tucson—and produces large, showy flowers that are about 10 cm long and 2.4 cm wide; its tepals (similar to petals) are white and waxy. Because it has evolved to attract bats and birds as its major pollinators, its flowers produce copious amounts of nectar and pollen (about 1.5 mL and 0.5 g, respectively). They open and begin secreting nectar a couple hours after sunset and do not close until well into the next afternoon, significantly later than cardón and organ pipe. Results of our pollinator exclusion experiments indicated that diurnal flower visitors, primarily white-winged doves and honeybees, are more important pollinators of saguaro flowers than are nocturnal lesser long-nosed bats. Finally, like most columnar cacti, saguaro has a self-incompatible breeding system in which its flowers must receive pollen from other individuals for successful fertilization of its ovules; its flowers cannot self-pollinate. Its reproductive success is thus in the hands (wings) of its vertebrate and invertebrate pollinators.

Results of a ten-year study of saguaro phenology at a site east of Tucson indicate that most but not all adults, which are at least fifty years old, flower every year and that timing of flower production and intensity of flowering depends on weather conditions and plant size, respectively. In general, flowering begins earlier, lasts longer, and is more intense in warm years whereas it is delayed and less intense in wet years. Larger plants begin flowering earlier and longer and hence produce more flowers than smaller (younger) adults. It was suggested that global warming may increase flower production in saguaro with significant implications for its reproductive mutualists and its population dynamics.

Successful pollination results in the production of mature fruits containing nearly 1,400 small black seeds weighing about 1.5 mg each and surrounded by sweet red pulp about a month after flowers close. A typical saguaro at our study site in Sonora produced about 330,000 seeds in a season. At this rate, over a period of one hundred years, individuals have the potential to produce about 33 million seeds in their lifetime! Mature fruits split open, revealing their red pulp, in what has been called saguaro's "second flowering." Many birds, from house finches to ravens, as well as lesser long-nosed bats consume saguaros' fruit pulp and disperse their seeds. Fruits that fall to the ground are avidly eaten by many other kinds of birds and mammals, including coyotes and javelinas. Mature saguaro plants, which usually reach reproductive age when they are fifty to seventy-five years old, produce crops of flowers, fruits, and seeds every year and can do this for the rest of their lives (i.e., sometimes for one hundred years), Their reliable annual fruit production despite significant year-to-year variation in rainfall makes saguaro fruits important food resources for animals and humans.

Despite their prodigious seed production, saguaro populations are not usually overrun with baby saguaros. Instead, the overwhelming fate of their seeds is to die without germinating and producing a new plant. Many seeds are eaten by a diverse array of seed-eating ants, birds (e.g., Gambel's quails), and mammals (e.g., Merriam's kangaroo rat). Those avoiding predation usually die because of insufficient rainfall in the year that they are dispersed. Unlike many annual desert plants, saguaro seeds are not long lived and cannot accumulate in the soil waiting for a rainy year. Lab experiments indicate that saguaro seed germination requires soaking in water, exposure to daylight, and temperatures around 25°C; under these conditions, germination success is about 49 percent. Seeds do not germinate in the absence of water, at night, and at temperatures of 15°C or 35°C. These results tell us that in the field, saguaro seeds need sufficient rainfall and relatively mild temperatures (at ground level) to germinate. These conditions occur most frequently during the summer monsoon (July–September) when most saguaro seed germination occurs.

Even under optimal abiotic conditions for seed germination, however, additional factors are involved in the production of new saguaro seedlings. As is well known, seedlings of saguaro and other cactus species can often be found under "nurse plants," that is, shrubs (e.g., *Ambrosia* species) and mesquite, ironwood, and palo verde trees where soil moisture conditions and soil temperatures are somewhat higher and lower, respectively, than those in the unshaded desert. Observations and experiments at our study site in Sonora indicated that three processes are involved in the successful production of new saguaro seedlings. First is the nonrandom dispersal of saguaro seeds by birds and bats. After grabbing a beakful or mouthful of fruit pulp and seeds, these animals typically fly to a shady tree to ingest this food. Since seed passage rates through these animals are usually fast, many of the seeds they ingest are deposited under these nurse plants. Second, the litter that accumulates under these plants provides a refuge from predation for some seeds and seedlings. Finally, the somewhat less harsh abiotic conditions and soil nutrients under nurse plants allow more seedlings to survive than in the open.

Since most plants, unlike animals, are immobile (except for their pollen and seeds), their population dynamics are relatively easy to study, at least in theory. Counts of tagged individuals in permanent plots over time provide these kinds of data. For long-lived plants such as saguaros, plant ecologists often use a two-step procedure to study population trends over long periods of time. The first step involves measuring the height of all marked individuals in a plot to determine the population's size structure—that is, the frequency distribution of different size classes. This size structure alone provides a qualitative picture of a population's dynamics. Thus, a population dominated by small size classes indicates that it is recruiting many individuals and is growing whereas a population dominated by large size classes indicates the opposite. But a more refined indication of a population's dynamics can be obtained by converting the size structure into an age structure. This is done by measuring the growth rates of tagged individuals over particular time intervals (e.g., every ten years or more in the case of saguaros) and creating an age-specific growth curve for individuals in a population. This growth curve can then be used to estimate the approximate ages of different-sized individuals and to convert the size structure into an age structure. Regular recensusing of a population for determination of individual growth rates also provides data on the mortality rates of marked individuals. These data can then be used to create an age-specific mortality rate curve, which is also useful for understanding a population's dynamics. Estimates of the ages of individuals can also be used to determine when they were recruited into the population.

The general growth rate curve for the Tumamoc Hill saguaro population indicates that individuals that are about 2 m, 4 m, 6 m, and 10 m tall are about 40, 52, 65, and 140 years old, respectively. Branching indicates the onset of sexual maturity and usually occurs when plants are 2–4 m tall (50–60 years old). Using these techniques, long-term studies of saguaro populations in Arizona indicate that their dynamics are controlled primarily by climate and that seedling recruitment is episodic and occurs only during years of sufficient summer rains and the absence of cold winter temperatures. For example, the saguaro population growing on Tumamoc Hill west of Tucson has been under study since 1908 but general observations on its demography are available from the middle of the nineteenth century. During this period, a population decline owing to mortality and a lack of seedling recruitment occurred beginning in the 1860s until well into the twentieth century; a population upswing resulting from increased recruitment occurred between 1920 and 1970; and another decline has ensued since then. During the periods of decline, recruitment was low despite some years of good moisture, suggesting that factors other than annual rainfall were in play; these factors include intensity and seasonality of rainfall (i.e., low recruitment occurs in years of especially high rainfall) and low winter temperatures.

A broader survey of ten saguaro populations throughout the northern Sonoran Desert in Arizona and Sonora, Mexico, over a period of nearly fifty years supports the results from Tumamoc Hill. Again, recruitment in this region has been very episodic, and saguaro populations regularly undergo long periods of decline punctuated by periods of elevated recruitment under favorable environmental conditions. Although living under the same general climatic regimes, detailed comparisons of temporal changes in age structure of these populations indicate that their dynamics are not broadly synchronous. Periods of recruitment and decline have not been strongly correlated geographically. In general, however, mortality rates in these populations are highest among young (small) and old (large) age classes, a typical pattern in many species of plants and animals. The largest (oldest) individual in these populations was estimated to have been recruited in 1790! Average life span of successful recruits in these populations is about 100–175 years. Finally, plant densities in these populations range from 26 plants/ha (= 2,600 plants/km^2) to 426 plants/ha (= 42,600 plants/km^2) and are highest on rocky slopes and lowest in flatlands.

As we have seen in the accounts of Sonoran Desert vertebrates, the combination of high summer and low winter temperatures and low annual rainfall poses significant physiological challenges to desert organisms. In plants, adaptations to these challenges are perhaps most dramatic in the Cactaceae, a distinctive group of stem succulent species that have converted their leaves into spines and their stems and branches into water storage and photosynthetic organs. The water storage capacity of large saguaros is enormous. When fully hydrated, its accordion-like stems swell in diameter and contain over 70 percent water. During prolonged dry spells, the water content of these stems shrinks to less than 40 percent, and stems shrink in diameter.

Energy capture in saguaros occurs in their photosynthetic stems while capture of water and nutrients occurs underground in their root systems. These root systems are extensive and shallow. Long lateral roots radiate out from plants for distances of up to 30 m. They occur 5–15 cm below the soil surface and quickly capture surface and soil water whenever it is available. A single taproot of only 1 m in length also helps to anchor the plant. In addition to the unbranched main lateral roots, small so-called rain roots quickly emerge from the laterals whenever it rains. They are responsible for acquiring much of the water that plants capture during rain events. These roots are shed as the soil dries up.

Given its dependence on soil surface water because of its shallow root system, we might expect the distributions of young saguaros under nurse plants to be highest in areas where water availability is highest (e.g., in water runoff areas [runnels] where soil moisture is high after rains). But this does not seem to be the case, at least at one site in the western (driest) part of its range in Arizona. In the Kofa National Wildlife Area, palo verde trees serve as common nurse plants for young saguaros, and their densities are highest near runnels. In contrast, the occurrence of young saguaros was highest under palo verdes that were not associated with runnels. One possible explanation for this is that seeds and young seedlings are washed away from their nurse plants in areas of heavy water runoff. In any case, the relationship between the distribution of young saguaro plants and soil moisture is likely to be complex. Not all saguaros become established where soil water availability is highest, as least in desert flatlands.

Energy capture in saguaros and other cacti occurs via a specialized photosynthetic system called crassulacean acid metabolism (CAM). This system differs from typical C3 photosynthetic systems found in most flowering plants in that CO_2 capture occurs at night rather than during the day. To conserve water, which is lost via transpiration whenever stomates (i.e., small pores located on leaf and stem surfaces) open in all plants, cactus stomates open to obtain atmospheric CO_2 only at night at a substantial savings of water. This CO_2 is then converted into four-carbon acids in chlorophyll-filled cells at night. Photosynthesis requires light to proceed, hence the CO_2 captured at night is removed from the organic acids during the day and combined with other simple organic compounds to ultimately create sugars containing six carbon atoms. As we all learned in elementary biology, the simple formula for the conversion of CO_2 into this sugar is CO_2 plus water (in the presence of sunlight and chlorophyll) yields glucose plus oxygen. In college biology, however, we learned just how complex this "simple" conversion really is. For example, it involves a series of cyclic "light" and "dark" reactions during photosynthesis.

As mentioned in the account of white-winged doves, CAM photosynthesis has a unique carbon-stable isotope ratio because the enzyme in this system that captures CO_2 captures more atmospheric ^{13}C than the one in C3 photosynthesis. As a result, carbon stable isotope analysis has become an important tool for determining the diets of animals (also see the account of lesser long-nosed bats), including humans.

Because they serve as important nest sites for many birds and their nectar, fruits, and seeds are eaten by many desert animals, the saguaro cactus is usually described as a "keystone" species in the Sonoran Desert. One definition of a keystone species is that its ecological importance is greater than simply its relative abundance. An implication of this concept is that the disappearance of a keystone species would have a significant negative effect on many co-occurring species. In 2014 Taly Drezner reviewed the number of animals associated with the saguaro. Her list included the number of species of birds and mammals by specific use as follows: nesting—twelve species of birds plus one bat (not listed by her); flower nectar—eleven birds and five mammals; and fruits and seeds— nineteen birds and eighteen mammals. She also listed the species of reptiles (only two) and the invertebrates (many) associated with this plant. These data support the idea that the saguaro can have a positive effect on the lives of many Sonoran Desert animals, hence its keystone status. In addition, resources provided by saguaro, including fruits, seeds, and skeletal materials, have also played important roles in the lives of Native Americans living in this desert. But not all of the saguaro-animal associations are positive. Many of the birds and mammals associated with saguaros consume its seeds and sometimes its seedlings and thus can have a negative effect on it. Because certain birds and mammals are involved in saguaro's reproductive success via pollination and seed dispersal, however, my guess is that the number of positive plant-animal interactions in this system outweighs the number of negative ones so that the net effect of these interactions is positive. As a result, birds and mammals play important roles in the reproductive success and population dynamics of these plants.

As a member of the Cactaceae, saguaro belongs to one of the most distinctive plant families in the New World. Although the amount of fossil material from this family is limited, recent DNA-based studies have provided us with a detailed picture of its evolution and phylogeny, whose current composition includes four subfamilies and a total of about 1,750 species. Two of these subfamilies—Opuntioideae (chollas and prickly pears) and Cactoideae (many "typical" cacti, including columnars)—contain a majority of cactus species. This family is endemic to the New World, and its evolution began in the central Andes of northern Chile, Bolivia, and Peru in the Early Oligocene about 32 Ma. From there, different lineages have migrated south and east in South America and north into the Caribbean and Central America and North America, particularly in the last 10–15 Ma. Radiation of this and other arid-adapted plant families correlates with the worldwide increase in Earth's aridity in the mid-Miocene. Saguaro belongs to the advanced tribe Pachyceereae, a clade containing about seventy mostly bat-pollinated species of columnar cacti that live mainly in the arid lands of Mexico and whose age is about 7 Ma. It is the northernmost member of this clade, and its evolutionary age is about 2 Ma, making it one of the youngest members of its clade. There has been some disagreement about its ancestry—whether its sister species belongs to *Neobuxbaumia*, whose nine species occur in central and southern Mexico, or *Pachycereus*, with about twelve species (including cardón) and whose southern distribution is similar to that of *Neobuxbaumia*. Saguaro currently does not co-occur with any species of *Neobuxbaumia* but does so with at least two species of *Pachycereus* in the Sonoran Desert. In summary, whereas saguaro's ancestral roots lie deep in South America beginning in the Oligocene, its immediate ancestors come from Mexico within the past few million years. Its specific evolutionary journey, therefore, has been relatively short in both space and time.

FOOTHILLS PALO VERDE

Parkinsonia microphylla Torrey, 1857, Fabaceae. Along with mesquites (*Prosopis* species) and ironwoods (*Olneya tesota*), this handsome plant is one of the most common legume trees in upland parts of the Sonoran Desert. The common occurrence of these legumes in the Sonoran Desert reflects the overall dominance of this family in many tropical and subtropical forests worldwide, especially in the Neotropics. Only in Southeast Asia and Australia are legumes not common members of forest communities.

Palo verde trees are unmistakable because, as their Spanish name indicates, their stems and branches are green. Their branches contain many small leaflets, hence the specific epithet *microphyllum*. The biomass of these leaves represents about 0.5

percent of total plant biomass. As a result, unlike mesquites and ironwoods, palo verde trees have a more open canopy. Like other desert legumes, however, this palo verde sheds its leaves during periods of drought. As in columnar cacti, the major photosynthetic surface of this plant is its stems and large branches. Palo verde thus differs from mesquites and ironwoods that lack photosynthetic stems and branches and whose only photosynthetic surfaces are their leaves.

Like the saguaro, palo verde's geographic distribution is restricted to the Sonoran Desert where it commonly grows in bajadas, flatlands, and hillsides throughout most of its range. Low winter temperatures and low summer rains limit its northern and western distribution, respectively.

Flowering in *P. microphyllum* occurs in the spring, usually April and May in the Tucson area. At this time of the year Tucson is awash with its yellow flowers, which dominate the visual landscape much as the red flowers of Royal Poinciana (*Delonix regia*) and lavender flowers of Jacaranda (*Jacaranda mimosifolia*) dominate the springtime color palettes of Miami, Florida, and Brisbane, Queensland, Australia, respectively, among many other tropical localities. Flowers of *P. microphyllum* contain five petals (four yellow and one white) that are 0.5 cm wide and occur in clusters. They are pollinated mostly by large native bees and the introduced honeybee; hence its pollen is not very mobile by itself compared with the pollen of wind-dispersed and allergy-producing species such as triangle bursage (*Ambrosia deltoidea*). Seed pods develop about six weeks after flowering; they are about 7.5 cm long and contain one to three seeds that are eaten by larvae of bruchid beetles and rodents.

Palo verde seedling emergence is stimulated by the summer monsoon rains. A six-year study of the emergence of seedlings of fifteen species of Sonoran Desert plants, including *P. microphyllum*, in a plot on Tumamoc Hill (see the saguaro account of this site near Tucson) revealed that palo verde differed from most other species in that many of its seedlings emerged each year despite annual differences in summer rainfall. The fate of most of these seedlings, however, was to be destroyed, mostly by rodents and rabbits. Only about 1.2 percent were still alive after one year, and none survived for four years. If they survive until they reach sexual maturity, however, palo verde is very long lived, and life spans can exceed one hundred years or more. As a result, over its lifetime, it is highly likely that individual trees will replace themselves by at least one surviving seedling owing to its strategy of producing a new crop of seedlings every year. This strategy appears to be common in other long-lived desert plants such as saguaro. It differs from the seedling strategy of many short-lived plants such as desert annuals and shrubs, which only produce seedlings in years of high monsoon rainfall. Perhaps because of its prolific production of seedlings and resistance to drought, *P. microphyllum* is often the most common woody plant growing on Sonoran Desert hillsides. Its density on the hillsides at Tumamoc, for example, is about five individuals/ha. In desert flatlands it is usually replaced by another long-lived species—creosote (*Larrea tridentata*)—as the dominant woody plant. Despite their long life spans, however, foothills palo verde trees do not live forever. A careful review of long-term survival and mortality data for these plants at Tumamoc Hill has revealed that two factors—prolonged drought and size (age) of plants—are associated with high mortality rates. In the case of very large plants with a diameter of $\geq$ 50 cm, perhaps drought accelerates senescence and death. At any rate, mortality does eventually catch up with old plants but not until they've lived for one hundred years or more.

Parkinsonia microphyllum is a deep-rooted tree that undergoes C3 photosynthesis, the method used by most plants. In this process, leaf or stem stomata open during the day to obtain atmospheric CO_2 at some loss of water via transpiration. Unlike most nondesert plants, however, most of the photosynthesis in *P. microphyllum* occurs in its green stems and branches rather than in its tiny leaves. Gas exchange studies using ^{14}C radioisotopes indicate that about 72 percent of its photosynthesis occurs in its stems and 24 percent in its leaves. Highest photosynthetic rates occur in the fall after the monsoon season and as ambient temperatures begin to decline. Environmental factors that affect photosynthetic rates in this species include the availability of soil water and ambient temperature. Photosynthesis declines as soils dry out and as daily temperatures increase (e.g., in June before the monsoon begins). Even under cool conditions and adequate soil moisture, daily rates of photosynthesis are highest around 8:00 a.m. and decline thereafter during the day. This daily rhythm is reminiscent of the daily activity patterns of certain desert vertebrates, including both ectotherms and endotherms that are most active during the coolest parts of the day. Finally, although it has deep roots that give this plant access to more soil moisture than shallow-rooted plants (e.g., saguaros), prolonged periods of drought are physiologically challenging for this species. To reduce water loss via transpiration during strong droughts, palo verde trees shed their leaves and also drop some of their branches. Once rains begin again, they are quick to flush a new crop of leaves and to undergo branch elongation.

Finally, it is well known that *P. microphyllum* has an important role as a nurse plant for Sonoran Desert plants, including saguaros. That is, it is important for facilitating the establishment of seedlings of saguaro and other desert plants. Ecologists have given this process the formal name of *facilitation*, defined as an ecological relationship in which one species provides a beneficial service to another species without necessarily benefiting itself from the interaction. In symbolic form, facilitation is often depicted as a +/0 relationship in which one (or more) species benefits (a + relationship) while another (the facilitator) does not (a 0 or neutral relationship). It is easy to see how this is true when small seedlings are becoming established under the canopy of a palo verde tree. But as the seedlings grow, the relationship can become far from benign for the nurse plant: one or more seedlings can grow into large plants that eventually compete with the nurse plant for resources such as water and soil nutrients. When this occurs the +/0 relationship becomes a +/− relationship in which the − sign denotes a negative effect based on competition. In extreme cases, nurse plants can be replaced by their former nurslings. This appears to be a common occurrence in the foothills palo verde/saguaro association. In a survey conducted at Organ Pipe Cactus National Monument, for example, 64 percent of large palo verde trees associated with one or more large saguaro cacti were dead compared with only 15 percent of large palo verde trees that lacked associated saguaros. This particular nurse plant association, therefore, can definitely be fatal to the facilitator.

If this negative effect were to commonly occur for a species, one wonders why nurse plants tolerate the presence of seedlings of potential competitors under their canopies. Darwinian logic would suggest that nurse plants should evolve some method for preventing seeds from germinating under their canopies. One way of doing this is for mature plants to produce and release toxic, inhibitory substances, either from their leaves or from their roots, into the soil beneath their canopy. In fact, some desert plants (and other kinds of nondesert plants) are known to do this via a process known as *allelopathy*, which can be defined as the chemical inhibition of the germination or growth of one plant by another plant through the release of toxic substances. For example, it is known that the very common shrub, creosote, which is often spaced in a regular, nonrandom pattern in desert flatlands, exudes diffusible toxic compounds from its roots that inhibit the growth of other plants under its canopy. Despite this, saguaros do sometimes become established under creosote bushes, suggesting that saguaros are not necessarily affected by creosote toxins. In contrast, foothills palo verde does not appear to be an allelopathic plant, but one wonders why not if nurslings such as saguaros cause significant mortality in their nurse plants.

The foothills palo verde is a member of the highly successful plant family Fabaceae, which contains six subfamilies, about 730 genera, and 19,400 species and has a worldwide distribution. As previously mentioned, this family is often dominant, at least in terms of species richness and abundance, in many tropical habitats. Its ability to acquire atmospheric nitrogen directly with the aid of its root-inhabiting, nitrogen-fixing rhizobia bacteria is often cited as a major reason for its ecological dominance, especially in many tropical habitats with nitrogen-poor soils.

Fabaceae is a member of the advanced eudicot rosid clade of angiosperms (see fig. 4). The early evolution of its specific clade (order Fabales) occurred in the Late Cretaceous, about 75 Ma. Fossil evidence suggests that evolution of Fabaceae (sensu stricto) began in the Paleocene, about 65 Ma. Modern groups of this family likely date from the Eocene (56–34 Ma). It has been suggested that the family first evolved in West Gondwanaland (i.e., Africa/South America), but this is currently in dispute.

Of the three traditionally recognized subfamilies of Fabaceae (Caesalpiniodeae, Mimosiodeae, and Faboideae), foothills palo verde with its radially symmetrical, five-petaled flowers, belongs to the Caesalpiniodeae lineage. Both this subfamily, which now contains the former subfamily Mimosiodeae, and Faboideae are advanced members of family Fabaceae. The genus *Parkinsonia* is an advanced member of its subfamily. *Parkinsonia* contains eleven or twelve species that inhabit arid regions of Africa (at least four species) and the New World (at least seven species). A DNA-based phylogenetic analysis indicates that African species of *Parkinsonia* are basal in the genus. It is likely that *P. microphyllum*'s closest relative (perhaps *P. praecox* of South America and northwest Mexico or *P. florida* of northwestern Mexico and southwestern Arizona) evolved in Mexico during the Late Miocene based on the evolutionary history of many other Sonoran Desert organisms. Fossil evidence from pack rat middens suggests that foothills palo verde is a very recent member of the Sonoran Desert plant community. It is known from middens in Sonora from 9,400 BP (before present) and from middens in Arizona from 5,400 BP. Its close ecological associate—the saguaro cactus—appears to have arrived in the northern Sonoran Desert several thousand years before its major nurse plant *P. microphyllum*. Although the foothills palo verde's deep evolutionary history may lie in Africa, its recent history probably dates from about 5 Ma and involves relatives from northwestern Mexico. Thus, its evolutionary journey has been relatively short in both time and space.

DESERT MISTLETOE

Phoradendron californicum Nuttall, 1848, Santalaceae, formerly Loranthaceae. Unlike most Sonoran Desert plants that are firmly rooted in the soil, the desert mistletoe, which occurs in the Sonoran and Mojave Deserts, is firmly rooted on the branches of a variety of trees, including palo verdes, mesquites, ironwoods, and catclaws (*Acacia greggii*). It thus resembles an epiphyte, a growth habit found in at least eighty-four families of flowering plants containing over 23,000 species, most notably in orchids, bromeliads, and aroids of tropical habitats, but it is not an epiphyte. Whereas epiphytes are nutritionally independent of their host plants, mistletoes are technically known as *hemiparasites*—epiphytes that obtain some, but not all, of their nutrients from their host plants. In contrast to epiphytes, this parasitic lifestyle is not particularly common. It has evolved in only twelve families of flowering plants containing about 2,100 species; most hemiparasites belong to the order Santalales, which includes mistletoes. Nearly all hemiparasites, including desert mistletoes, have chlorophyll in their leaves and stems and can undergo photosynthesis and make sugars independently of their host plants from which they obtain water, additional carbon, and nitrogen. They obtain host nutrients by producing haustoria, rootlike structures that penetrate the host's bark and cambium layer and that obtain nutrients from its xylem and, in some species but not *P. californicum*, its phloem.

Mature desert mistletoes are long lived, essentially nearly leafless woody shrubs consisting of a ball-like cluster of jointed, photosynthetic stems that start to droop as they age; large individuals can be 1–2 m in diameter or length. Because of their dense ball-like growth form, mistletoes are highly visible in the crowns of their hosts, especially when hosts are leafless. Several individuals sometimes colonize a single host plant, and they can sometimes kill their host, especially during periods of extended drought. In the Mojave Desert of Southern California, for instance, 97 percent of large individuals of blue palo verde (*Parkinsonia florida*) infested with desert mistletoe died during a drought compared with only 39 percent of similar-sized plants that lacked mistletoes.

The desert mistletoe is a dioecious plant with separate male and female individuals. Flowering and fruiting occur in the winter, and both sexes produce small, inconspicuous but fragrant flowers that lack petals and that are visited by native and non-native bees and other insects. When successfully pollinated, female flowers develop into small (i.e., several millimeters in diameter) red or pink berries containing one or a few seeds. Large plants can literally be covered by a cascade of colorful fruits, which makes them a highly defendable resource by fruit-eating birds such as phainopeplas and mockingbirds. The pulp around the seeds is highly viscous which aids in their dispersal. Whenever birds defecate, regurgitate, or wipe the sticky seeds from their bills on branches, seed dispersal is likely to be successful. After seeds have been deposited on plants, they germinate and produce a rootlike radicle that firmly anchors them to a branch or other plant part. After the seed is attached, it produces a rootlike haustorium that penetrates the host tissue in search of nutrients. Male plants begin to flower in their second year after seed germination. Female plants first flower in their third year and begin producing fruit in their fourth year.

Infestation of host plants by *P. californicum* is not likely to be random. A study of the infestation of catclaw (*A. gregii*) in the Mojave Desert near Las Vegas, Nevada, for example, indicated that frequency of infestation was positively correlated with the size and age of the host plant as well as its water status; large catclaws living near washes were more likely to be infested than similar-sized plants living away from washes. Desert mistletoes living on hosts near washes also were larger and had larger fruit crops than those living on hosts away from washes. I have seen a similar situation in my neighborhood. Mesquites and catclaws living near a wash are heavily infested with large mistletoes whereas infestations are light or nonexistent in these species away from the wash.

The overall geographic distribution of *P. californicum* in the Mojave and Sonoran Deserts is dependent on three or four interacting factors, including one set of abiotic factors and three biological factors. The abiotic factors include the set of temperature and rainfall conditions under which this mistletoe can survive; cold winter temperatures and low annual rainfall are known to limit the distribution of this plant. The three biotic factors include the distributions of suitable host species, which are mainly species of desert legume trees; the distribution of its most common seed disperser, namely the phainopepla; and the distributions of its insect pollinators. The relative importance of three of these factors (climate, host species, and phainopepla) in determining *P. californicum's* distribution has been determined in a study involving *ecological niche modeling*, a computer-based technique in which the distributions (geographic niches) of host species and the seed disperser are compared with that of the mistletoe, which primarily reflects suitable climatic conditions. Since none of the insect pollinators is specialized on mistletoe flowers, they were not considered further in this study. Results indicated that the geographic range of this mistletoe is a nonrandom subset of the ranges of its host plants and main avian disperser. It co-occurs with these species only where climate conditions are favorable. Its ecological niche, and hence its geographic distribution, is only a subset of the niches of its host and disperser species.

Effective seed dispersal is a crucial aspect of *P. californicum's* life history. Its dispersal ecology is well known, in part based on the doctoral research of Julia Aukema at the University of Arizona. In one study, she and her colleagues worked at the Santa Rita Experimental Range south of Tucson and concentrated on the distribution of mistletoes and its seed deposition by phainopeplas on velvet mesquite trees (*Prosopis velutina*), a common legume tree at this site. Here the number of mistletoe plants in a tree was correlated with host plant height (as in *Acacia greggii* in Nevada) and ranged from a few to over twenty mistletoe plants per tree. This pattern undoubtedly reflects the fact that phainopeplas choose to perch and display on high trees when defending their territories. As a result, they deposit many mistletoe seeds on branches of their perch trees, which produces a highly clumped distribution of these hemiparasites. These clumps are also the result of mistletoe seeds being brought in from other parasitized trees as well as from mistletoe plants in the perch tree. This deposition pattern is an example of *directed dispersal* in which seeds are removed from plants and deposited directly (although incidentally) on appropriate germination sites. Directed dispersal differs from other more common kinds of dispersal in which seeds are often deposited in a variety of sites, only some of which are favorable for seed germination.

In a second study, Aukema and colleagues studied mistletoe dispersal and colonization at a site northwest of Tucson that contained a greater variety of legume tree species. At this site ironwood (*O. tesota*) was the most common legume and was heavily parasitized by *P. californicum*. As with *Prosopis velutina* at the Santa Rita site, large individuals of ironwood were more heavily parasitized than small individuals. In addition to plant size, this study found that canopy architecture also influenced the likelihood that a tree would be parasitized. That is, two species with very dense or spiny canopies (*Acacia constricta* and *Parkinsonia microphyllum*, respectively) were parasitized less frequently than species with more open and less spiny canopies (*O. tesota* and *Prosopis velutina*). At this site phainopeplas definitely had preferences about where to perch, and these preferences resulted in the nonrandom distribution of mistletoe clumps among species.

Finally, large individuals of desert mistletoe sometimes serve as nest sites for a variety of desert birds, including verdins, desert cardinals, phainopeplas, and Cooper's hawks. This association is another example of the ecological interaction known as *commensalism* in which one species (the bird) benefits with no (apparent) effect on the other species (the nest plant); it is another example of a +/o kind of relationship. Overall, this mistletoe is involved in three kinds of ecological relationships: (1) a potentially +/− relationship with its hosts, (2) a +/+ relationship with its pollinators and seed dispersers, and (3) a +/o relationship with certain nesting birds. As a result, its life history is certainly full of interesting ecological interactions.

Many species of mistletoes have large green leaves and are fully photosynthetic in addition to being parasites of their hosts. Their photosynthesis occurs via the common C3 pathway in which stomata open during the day and close at night. This is not true, however, in *P. californicum* which lacks large leaves. Although it does photosynthesize via its green stems, this mistletoe obtains most of its carbon, along with water, nitrogen, and minerals, from its host plants. Its haustorium connects with the host's xylem system to accomplish this; host carbon is acquired via phloem leakage into the xylem. Mistletoes generally are known to have higher transpiration rates than their hosts (sometimes by a factor of two to five), and this has been hypothesized to be an adaptation for actively obtaining nitrogen from hosts; other nutrients are passively acquired during this process. Support for this hypothesis comes from a comparison of transpiration rates of species of *Phorodendron* parasitizing nitrogen-fixing versus non-nitrogen-fixing hosts. The transpiration rate of *P. californicum* was similar to that of its host, *Acacia greggii*, a nitrogen-fixing plant. In contrast, the transpiration rate of *P. juniperum* was much higher than its non-nitrogen-fixing host, *Juniperus osteosperma*. This difference reflects the fact that the nitrogen concentration in the xylem of *A. greggii* is much higher than that of *J. osteosperma*. It also reflects the importance of *water use efficiency*, defined as the ratio of net photosynthesis to transpiration, in arid land mistletoes. High transpiration rates may be needed to acquire sufficient nitrogen in *P. juniperum* but at the cost of lower water use efficiency. Water conservation, as well as the easy acquisition of nitrogen, a critical growth-promoting element, is likely to be an important reason why *P. californicum* commonly parasitizes desert legume trees, although not all of these trees (e.g., *Parkinsonia microphyllum*) are nitrogen-fixers.

Many species of mistletoes have host-specific relationships, implying that these hemiparasites have greater evolutionary fitness on certain host species than on others. In the extreme case, certain Australian mistletoes, including species of *Amyema*, and dwarf mistletoes (species of *Arceuthobium*) can only grow on a single host species. This raises the question, does host specificity exist in *P.*

californicum, which as we've seen parasitizes several species of plants throughout its geographic range? A study in which the survival of seeds from desert mistletoes growing on one host that were placed on another potential host was monitored in Baja California to address this question. Thus, seeds from mistletoes growing on *Prosopis articulata*, *Parkinsonia microphyllum*, and *Acacia greggii* were cross-dispersed to another species. Results revealed that two host-specific types of *Phorodendron* exist in that area: one that is specific to *P. articulata* and one that is specific to *Parkinsonia* and *Acacia*. Furthermore, it was found that these two types differ in the timing of their flowering; the *Prosopis* host type flowered later in the winter than the *Parkinsonia-Acacia* host type, suggesting that some degree of reproductive isolation likely exists between these two host types. Recent studies in Arizona have also confirmed the existence of host races and genetic differences between them in *P. californicum*. Reproductive isolation, of course, is one of the prerequisites for speciation, so it is possible that these different host types are on the road to speciation.

What is the basis for host specificity in mistletoes? It likely depends on characteristics of both the mistletoe seeds (e.g., their genotypes) and the host plant (e.g., its chemical response to mistletoe seeds and their haustoria based on their genotypes). As a result, some seeds of *P. californicum* will be accepted more readily than others on a particular host. In the Baja study, it was also found that the four potential host species differed significantly in their susceptibility to infection by desert mistletoes. The order of susceptibility was *Acacia* > *Prosopis* > *Parkinsonia-Olneya*. Since infestation by desert mistletoes is known to sometimes kill host plants, these results seem to suggest that the mistletoe/host interaction can truly be viewed as an antagonistic relationship (i.e., a +/− interaction) in which different host species have evolved different susceptibilities to mistletoe infection as a result of selection caused by the parasite.

Although twelve families spread across angiosperm phylogeny contain hemiparasites, a majority of these species occur in order Santalales, which includes family Santalaceae (with its many mistletoes). This order is allied with the asterids, a lineage of advanced eudicot angiosperms (fig. 4). Fossil evidence suggests that this order dates from the Late Cretaceous (ca. 70 Ma) whereas DNA-based evidence suggests a somewhat older age (i.e., 123 Ma). Family Santalaceae is an advanced member of the Santalales, and its evolutionary age (based on DNA evidence) dates from ca. 82 Ma. Mistletoes of the genus *Phorodendron* occur only in the new-world tropics and subtropics and include about 240 species. This high species number probably reflects the importance of selection for host plant specificity, which can result in reproductive isolation and (eventually) speciation. *Phorodendron californicum* occurs in the Sonoran and (barely) Mojave Deserts and hence is one of the northernmost and presumably one of the youngest species in the genus. Morphological evidence suggests that it is closely related to *P. olae* of southern Mexico, which suggests that it has migrated north from that region. Based on chloroplast DNA data, its age has been estimated to be 3.8 Ma (i.e., mid-Pliocene), somewhat younger than the phainopepla. During the last glacial maximum of 11,000 years ago, *P. californicum*'s distribution likely included the Lower Colorado River Valley, coastal Sonora, and the Eastern Cape region of Baja California. Based on fossil evidence from pack rat middens, its presence in the current Sonoran Desert dates from about 6,400 years ago, several thousand years more recently than some of its current host species. Therefore, like many other Sonoran Desert organisms, it is a recent immigrant into this area, and its evolutionary journey has likely been relatively short in space (from southern Mexico) and time (from the Pliocene).

A REVIEW OF SONORAN DESERT ECOSYSTEM PROCESSES AND THE EVOLUTION OF SOME OF ITS ANIMALS AND PLANTS

Before reviewing the history of our species (*Homo sapiens*) in this desert, let's revisit the ecology of the Sonoran Desert from two different perspectives, in part based on information we've gained about some of its iconic animals and plants. To do this, first picture again in your mind's eye what this desert looks like in springtime, for example, west of Tucson as you're driving over Gate's Pass down toward Kinney Road, perhaps heading to the Arizona-Sonora Desert Museum or Saguaro National Park West. As you descend the western slope of the Tucson Mountains and enter its bajada, you're seeing a magnificent landscape replete with many saguaros and palo verdes as well as a myriad of other plants, many of which are now in flower. From the car you probably can't see any of the animals that live in this habitat, but they are there. If you were to stop the car and get out, you might see a few lizards and birds, but you're not likely to see the larger mammals—the javelinas, mule deer, coyotes, gray foxes, bobcats, and mountain lions—that live here. Nevertheless, it's fun to imagine what it would be like to actually see all of the plants and animals that call this habitat home together at the same time.

My first and most abstract view of this system deals with the movement of energy and nutrients through it. Though it is invisible to us as we gaze at this Sonoran Desert scene, we know that all of species living here are ultimately tied together by the movement of energy and nutrients from one species to another. In the species accounts, for instance, we've seen desert tortoises and other herbivores munching on foliage, fruits, and seeds and carnivores eating insects, doves, and cottontail rabbits. The energy contained in these food items moves from plants to herbivores and then to carnivores in a unidirectional process that begins with the capture of solar energy by plants and ends with the decomposition of dead organic matter. The second law of thermodynamics states that no energy transformation (e.g., from plant tissue to herbivore tissue) is ever 100 percent efficient; some of it is lost from the system during these transformations. Herbivores such as jackrabbits and mule deer, for example, usually convert only about 40–50 percent of the plant material (i.e., plant energy) they ingest into new tissue for their maintenance, growth, and reproduction. Likewise, carnivores such as hawks and bobcats assimilate only about 60–80 percent of the energy they consume for their life processes. Nectar feeders such as hummingbirds and nectar bats, in contrast, are able to assimilate an amazing 95 percent or more of the nectar energy they ingest.

The upshot of all of this is that the biomass of each trophic or feeding level in terrestrial ecosystems is always smaller than the one preceding it. Thus, plant biomass is always greater than herbivore biomass and so on. A variety of decomposers, including bacteria, fungi, and detritus eaters such as millipedes and termites, are the "mop up" species in this desert. Because of the limited availability of water, however, rates of decomposition of dead organic matter here are quite slow. Finally, unlike the flow of energy, the chemical elements such as carbon, nitrogen, and phosphorus found in the bodies of organisms move through ecosystems in cyclical, not unidirectional, fashion. Thus, animal waste products and the nutrients in their bodies that are released during decomposition can become available for reuse by plants and other organisms.

Owing to the limited availability of water and soil nutrients, particularly nitrogen and phosphorus, in deserts, annual plant productivity in them is very low—only about 70 g of new plant tissue per m^2 per year. Plant productivity in temperate forests, for comparison, is much higher, about 1,250 g of new plant tissue per m^2 per year. Low plant productivity sets the stage for the low population densities of most desert animals, with ectotherms such as insects and reptiles with their much "cheaper" physiologies often having higher population densities and biomass in some trophic levels than their energy extravagant endothermic counterparts.

As an example of this, I once visited a ranch owned by Ted Turner in the grasslands of central New Mexico with a group of ecologists. This ranch housed a herd of bison as well as a small group of wolves that were being kept for release into the wild. The ranch manager who gave us a tour of the ranch told us that Ted Turner was very proud to be raising a herd of bison whereupon we told him that this was not correct. Instead, Turner should be proud of raising lots of grasshoppers, whose biomass was much greater on the ranch than that of mammalian herbivores such as bison.

My second perspective on the Sonoran Desert is based on the actual lives and adaptations of all of the species I've just described. The suite of animals and plants that currently live together in this ecosystem have been doing so for a relatively short period of time, geologically speaking. Major elements of the plant community such as saguaros and palo verdes, for example, have only been living together in southern Arizona for a few thousand years. Likewise, some of the animals, including white-winged doves, lesser long-nosed bats, and javelinas, are also recent immigrants to this area. Many of these species, however, have evolutionary histories that have long been associated with arid lands in Mexico and Central and South America. Others—mostly larger habitat generalists such as hawks, owls, and certain mammalian carnivores—have large geographic ranges and are adapted to live under a wide variety of environmental conditions, including deserts. I have summarized the geographic origins and evolutionary ages of some of the species I have discussed in this book in figure 11. As we've learned, the bulk of small vertebrate species evolved close to the Sonoran Desert whereas certain larger species come from farther away, either in North or Central and South America. Regardless of their geographic area of origin, some of these species are surprisingly young (e.g., diamondback rattlesnakes and coyotes) whereas others are much older (e.g., desert tortoises and desert spiny lizards).

To survive and reproduce in this habitat, all of its inhabitants are faced with the duel climatic challenges of low and variable rainfall and very high diurnal air temperatures during the summer. Because frost is uncommon in this desert, low winter temperatures are not as physically challenging as high summer temperatures, but they do still help to determine the geographic range limits of many plants (e.g., saguaros and mistletoes). Likewise, low water availability associated with seasonal rainfall patterns also limits the geographic ranges of certain species (e.g., saguaros). Aside from limits to their geographic ranges, seasonal changes

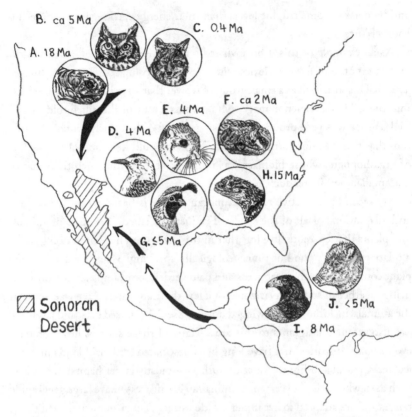

FIGURE 11 A summary of the evolutionary journeys taken by some of the Sonoran Desert's iconic higher vertebrates. Information for each species includes general area of geographic origin and approximate age in millions of years (Ma). Species include (A) desert tortoise; (B) great horned owl; (C) coyote; (D) Gila woodpecker; (E) Merriam's kangaroo rat; (F) diamondback rattlesnake; (G) Gambel's quail; (H) desert spiny lizard; (I) Harris's hawk; and (J) javelina. Artwork by Kim Duffek.

in temperatures and rainfall also have profound effects on the daily activities of many Sonoran Desert species. In plants, both daily and seasonal patterns of photosynthesis are temperature dependent; rates of photosynthesis slow down during hot times of the day and year. Plant growth patterns are generally correlated with seasonal changes in rainfall and the availability of soil water. For example, mature saguaros don't usually produce new branches until after the summer monsoon season when they are maximally hydrated.

The lives of many Sonoran Desert vertebrates are also affected by daily and seasonal changes in temperatures. Diurnal species, for example, are usually most active during the coolest parts of the day, and many reptiles and certain heteromyid rodents and ground squirrels avoid low winter temperatures by hibernating underground. By remaining underground for large periods of the year, desert tortoises and Gila monsters are extreme examples of this kind of behavior.

Now let's return to the sweeping landscape on the western slope of the Tucson Mountains and try to picture the flow of energy and nutrients through this Sonoran Desert location. Some of its details are easy to visualize: for example, round-tailed ground squirrels eating *Opuntia* cactus flowers and fruit and then being eaten by red-tailed hawks or coyotes. But the actual food web here is obviously much more complex than this. It quickly becomes a "tangled bank," to quote Charles Darwin, of connections between the many species of flowering plants, animals, and microorganisms that live here, all of which are attempting to maximize their maintenance, growth, and reproduction in the face of many abiotic and biotic challenges. The wide variety of life histories and adaptations that we've seen above reflect in part the diverse ways by which plants and animals have met these challenges and have evolved to survive and reproduce successfully in this desert. To be sure, most of these adaptations did not evolve de novo in this desert. Instead, they represent the results of millions of years of prior evolution in the lineages to which Sonoran Desert species belong. The green stems and branches of the Sonoran Desert endemic tree, foothills palo verde, for instance, have evolved to reduce rates of water loss via transpiration but are not unique to this species. All twelve species of *Parkinsonia*, which occur widely in arid lands in Africa and the Americas, also have green stems and branches.

One example of a suite of adaptations that is unique to the Sonoran Desert, however, involves white-winged doves and their major food source, saguaro cacti. The Sonoran Desert subspecies of this dove, *Zenaida asiatica mearnsi*, has a longer bill than its other two subspecies (*Z. a. asiatica* and *Z. a. australis*). A long bill, which is a derived condition in this genus, gives it greater access to saguaro nectar than would a short bill as seen in the mourning dove. Reflecting the close mutualistic association between this dove and saguaro cacti, the cactus also has a derived condition in the timing of its flower opening and closing and its nectar production schedule. All of its relatives are bat pollinated with flowers that open shortly after sunset, have a single nectar production peak that occurs before midnight, and close shortly after sunrise. In contrast, saguaro flowers open well after sunset, have two nectar production peaks—one that occurs at about 2:00 a.m. and another that occurs after sunrise—and they close the next afternoon. Saguaro's flowers are clearly aimed primarily at diurnal pollinators rather than at bats. And our pollinator exclusion experiments have confirmed this.

Other examples of derived anatomical, physiological, and behavioral adaptations in Sonoran Desert organisms will undoubtedly be found in the future. This is because we now have the tools—e.g., species-level phylogenies upon which various character states can be mapped—for doing this. As we've seen, these phylogenies allow us to identify basal (i.e., ancestral) versus derived character states in species. For example, green stems are basal in *Parkinsonia* trees whereas inflated auditory bullae and their specialized kidneys are derived in *Dipodomys* kangaroo rats. Regardless of whether or not derived characters are common in Sonoran Desert species, the range of their adaptations is impressive and calls to mind another of Darwin's well-known quotes, "There is grandeur in this view of life," whenever we consider the diverse array of adaptations that are found in species that live and thrive in this physically challenging environment. Despite searing summer temperatures and highly variable water supplies, the Sonoran Desert is full of life.

HUMANS IN THE SONORAN DESERT

Like many other Sonoran Desert plants and animals, our species (*Homo sapiens* L., 1758, Hominidae) is a recent arrival here. Based on rather meager physical evidence, archaeologists infer that humans have lived in this part of the world for about 11,500 years—even before many of the current desert plants and animals lived here. In her book *A Desert Feast*, Carolyn Niethammer (2020) gives us an overview of the history of humans from that point on in the northern Sonoran Desert in the Santa Cruz River/Tucson valley area. Early Paleo-Indians in this region were hunter-gatherers, living off whatever the land and, more distantly, the sea (i.e., the Sea of Cortez) could give them. Their terrestrial foodstuffs included whatever fruits were available; the seeds of wild grasses and trees; and whatever wildlife they could kill with their spears and clubs. To obtain this food, their small groups moved frequently, following seasonal changes in plant production and the availability of water and wildlife. By 9,500 years ago, the climate in this area was becoming warmer and drier, and these changes brought new, more arid-adapted plants into what was becoming the Sonoran Desert. New food sources (e.g., fruits of columnar cacti and pods and seeds of legume trees and shrubs) were now available for humans.

The Seri Indians or Comcáac ("the People") of coastal Sonora, Mexico, are modern-day hunter-gatherers that provide us with a view of what that lifestyle must have been like for Paleo-Indians. Our ecological research in Mexico was based at Bahia de Kino (Kino Bay), a small Mexican fishing village on the Sea of Cortez, about 25 km south of Punta Chueca, one of two major Seri villages; the other is El Desemboque farther north up the coast. I had occasional contact with the Seris, who are fiercely independent and have been very resistant to assimilation with Mexicans, and worked with them looking for bat caves along the Sonoran coast and Isla Tiburon, the largest island in the northern Sea of Cortez and, historically, the seasonal home of the Seris. Modern Seris are renowned for the exquisite basketmaking skills of the women and the beautiful ironwood carvings made by the men.

Living close to the sea, the Seris harvested both marine and terrestrial resources. Access to fresh water, and not food, was the most important limiting factor in their lives. Tracking seasonal sources of water as well as plants and wildlife resulted in a mobile lifestyle, in which small groups, likely extended families, moved from camp to camp consisting of brush shelters. Population density of these people was very low. From the sea they used reed boats (balsas) to harvest sea grass (*Zostera*) and a bounty of fish and sea turtles (e.g., *Chelonia*) as well as oysters, clams, and crabs from estuaries. On land, several species of columnar cacti became important sources of food, especially the fruits and seeds of saguaro, and building materials. Other plants from desert scrub that were important foods include *Agave* species, cholla and barrel cacti, and legume pods and seeds. Important species of wildlife included desert tortoise, various sea birds (e.g., pelicans), mule deer, desert bighorn sheep, black-tailed jackrabbits, and California sea lions.

Paleo-Indians living in the northern Sonoran Desert began to develop agriculture based on edible weedy plants growing in damp alluvial soils about 5,000 years ago. It took another 1,000 years for corn (maize) that had been domesticated by Indians farther south in Mexico to become an important food for Sonoran Desert people. The arrival of corn led to the development of true agriculture and a more sedentary lifestyle resulting in the development of small settlements that were often located along important water sources such as the Santa Cruz River that passes through Tucson. Irrigation of corn crops in this area began about 3,500 years ago, and corn was a dietary staple, still supplemented by seeds of native grasses and perennials such as lamb's-quarters and amaranth, by 3,000 years ago. Beans, including tepary beans (*Phaseolus acutifolius*), did not become an important dietary item until about 1,500 years ago after clay cooking pots became common. Eventually, jack and lima beans as well as a couple variet-ies of squash were added to the cultivated crops.

Beginning in about AD 450, the Hohokam people were present in the desert in Arizona; they apparently arose in this area from hunter-gatherer ancestors. In addition to harvesting mesquite pods and saguaro fruit from the desert, they initiated more sophisticated agriculture with better, more extensive irrigation systems, sometimes many kilometers long that included dams for growing corn and other crops. They would become the dominant farmers in southern Arizona until about AD 1500 when they completely disappeared for reasons that are cur-rently under vigorous debate by archaeologists and anthropologists. One recent hypothesis, based on many lines of evidence centered on events in the lower Salt River valley near Phoenix, proposes that Hohokam collapse resulted from multiple factors, including overpopulation, degradation of agriculture through-out their extensive irrigation system, and social conflict. Migration north and south away from this major population center also likely occurred. As a result, the Tohono O'odham Indians that currently live in southern Arizona consider the Hohokam to be their ancestors, although this has been disputed. They may have simply developed from Paleo-Indians that had been living along the north-eastern coast of the Sea of Cortez for at least 6,000 years.

The Spanish first arrived in Mexico in 1519, but it wasn't until the arrival of the Italian Jesuit priest Father Eusebio Francisco Kino south of Tucson in 1692 that European culture and food crops came to the Sonoran Desert. After establishing the mission of San Xavier del Bac near a Tohono O'odham farming village of about eight hundred people, Kino began to introduce to them new plant foods, including chickpeas, lentils, cabbage, lettuce, onions, leeks, garlic, cilantro, anise and, as cuttings, fruits such as figs, quinces, oranges, pomegran-ates, peaches, apricots, pears, grapes, and apples. In addition, he brought two important grains—wheat and barley—as well as horses and cattle to this area. For the first time in their history, the Tohono O'odham finally had reliable, year-round food security.

The Spanish established a presidio—a military outpost to protect settlers in the area from attacks by Apache Indians—in 1776 on the banks of the Santa Cruz River in southern Arizona. Originally manned by about one hundred Spanish soldiers, the population in the Presidio eventually increased to several hundred people. Because they lived a long distance from supplies from Mexico City, people turned to subsistence farming for a living, like their nearby Tohono O'odham neighbors. In addition to crops of winter wheat and summer corn, presidio residents also had large herds of cattle, sheep, and horses to care for. After Mexico won its independence from Spain in 1821, the presidio was manned by Mexican soldiers with many retired Spanish soldiers remaining in the area. It wasn't until 1856, two years after the signing of the Gadsden Purchase that ceded southern Arizona from Mexico to the United States, that U.S. soldiers assumed command of the Presidio, which officially became the city of Tucson shortly thereafter.

3

CONSERVATION CONCERNS IN THE NORTHERN SONORAN DESERT

I WILL FINISH this book with a brief discussion of the current and future status of this fascinating desert. Because I live in the northern region of this desert and am most familiar with its local fauna and flora, I will restrict most of my discussion here to the U.S. portion of the Sonoran Desert, even though over half of it occurs in Mexico. To be sure, Mexican scientists and conservation biologists are just as concerned about the current and future status of this desert and its inhabitants as their U.S. colleagues. Reflecting their common interest, a new consortium of U.S. and Mexican researchers called N-Gen was formed in 2012 with the aim of publishing papers focused more broadly on this region.

THE CONSERVATION STATUS OF SOME SONORAN DESERT VERTEBRATES

Our current understanding of the conservation status of many Sonoran Desert reptiles, birds, and mammals is summarized in appendix 2, which is based on the Red List of the International Union for Conservation of Nature (IUCN). This list is usually considered to be the gold standard for reporting species' conservation status. For species that have been evaluated, their status occurs in one of the following categories: LC = least concern, NT = near threatened, VU = vulnerable, EN = endangered, CR = critically endangered, and EW = extinct in the wild. Category LC usually includes widespread and abundant species that are not currently threatened with extinction. Category NT includes species judged to be at some extinction risk because of low population numbers, at least in parts of their geographic range. Category VU includes species judged to be at high risk for becoming endangered because of very low population numbers (e.g., < 250 mature individuals) and/or small geographic range sizes.

The good news is that most (95 percent) of the 111 Sonoran Desert species listed in appendix 2 are currently categorized as LC. As far as we know, most populations of Sonoran Desert reptiles, birds, and mammals are in reasonably good shape. However, based on many breeding bird censuses, we cannot be complacent about this. Populations of many North American birds, including formerly abundant local species such as cactus wrens, black-throated sparrows, black-tailed gnatcatchers, and the gilded flicker, have been declining since the 1960s. None of these species is in imminent danger of disappearing, but significant population declines are always worrisome. The combination of habitat fragmentation—a common occurrence throughout the world today—and low population numbers in these fragments can lead to *demographic stochasticity*— the further loss of numbers (and genetic diversity) simply due to random events.

Four species—Gila monster, loggerhead shrike, lesser long-nosed bat, and Mexican long-tongued bat—listed in appendix 2 are categorized as NT, presumably because their population numbers are low. This is certainly true of the Gila monster, which is often killed by people thinking that because they are venomous, they are dangerous. In truth, they pose no threat to us. It is a protected species in most of its geographic range. In recent decades, the loggerhead shrike, which is still widely distributed in North America, has seen population declines for several reasons, including the negative effects of pesticides and loss of their grassland nesting habitats. The lesser long-nosed bat was listed as endangered in the United States and Mexico in the late 1980s because of apparent historic declines in its numbers. But much field work since then has revealed that this species is common throughout its range. Tens of thousands, for example, reside temporarily in southern Arizona in the late summer and early fall before migrating back to central and southern Mexico. As a result, it has recently been removed from the endangered species lists in both countries. Because of its highly gregarious roosting habits in caves and mines, however, it is still considered to be vulnerable to significant population losses. Little is known about the population status of the Mexican long-tongued bat, which is known to roost in very small colonies, making it vulnerable to population loss. Finally, the desert tortoise is the only species in appendix 2 that is officially listed as vulnerable by the IUCN. Its conservation status throughout its range has been of concern for many decades. Multiple factors, including habitat loss, human activities, predation, and disease, are known to have had negative effects on this species. As a result, it is officially protected and is being actively managed, sometimes by rather controversial geographic translocations, by governmental agencies throughout its range.

MAJOR THREATS TO THIS DESERT

Many governmental and nongovernmental agencies are currently involved in the protection of Sonoran Desert animals and plants in the United States and Mexico. As my friend Scott Richardson of the U.S. Fish and Wildlife Service tells me, "Nearly every Federal agency in existence has a role in or affects conservation in the Sonoran Desert." These agencies in the United States include the Bureau of Land Management, the Fish and Wildlife Service, the Department of Agriculture, the Forest Service, and the National Park System. State agencies such as the Arizona Game and Fish Department are also involved. In Mexico these agencies include CONANP (the Commission of Protected Areas), CONABIO (the Scientific Authority), INECC (National Institute of Ecology and Climate Change), DGVS (the General Directorate of Wildlife), and PROFEPA (the Office of the Attorney General for the Environment). At the state level in Mexico, CEDES (Commission of Ecology and Sustainable Development) is involved in conservation in Sonora. In addition to the federal and state agencies, many nongovernmental organizations (NGOs) in both countries are actively involved in desert conservation. In the Tucson area, these agencies include the Arizona-Sonora Desert Museum, the Center for Biological Diversity, the Coalition for the Protection of the Sonoran Desert, the Native Plant Society of Southern Arizona, the Tucson Audubon Society, and the Tucson Cactus and Succulent Society. Despite all of these important efforts, however, this biome and its inhabitants still face serious threats, primarily from pressure from human development and climate change.

In 2015, Brigette Marazzi and colleagues reviewed these threats in the context of biological interactions (e.g., plant-plant, plant-animal, and plant-soil microbe) in the Sonoran Desert and described the various threats posed by humans and climate change on these interactions. A summary of these threats follows.

EFFECTS OF HUMAN IMPACTS

For most of its history, the population density of humans in the Sonoran Desert was low, and human impact was correspondingly low. This began to change, however, with the arrival of Europeans and their farming practices and livestock in the late sixteenth century. For the past 150 years ranching has been widespread in this desert with a strong negative impact on its soils and vegetation. By the late twentieth century, about 70 percent of land in the southwestern United States had been grazed (overgrazed?) by livestock. As a result, many areas of this desert have been "cowed out" by trampling of the soil, consumption of vegetation, including many seedlings, alteration of the quality and quantity of water in streams (where cattle always congregate), and disruption of nutrient cycles. Where cattle range, the density of woody shrubs decreases, and the density of cholla and prickly pear cacti increases. Perhaps most insidiously, buffel grass (*Pennisetum ciliare*), a fire-resistant grass native to Africa and the Middle East, was introduced to ranches in the United States in the 1940s and in Mexico in the 1970s as a means of "range improvement." Now much of central Sonora, Mexico, for example, is a sea of this plant, which escapes from pastures to roadsides and then into washes and up onto hillsides everywhere. The harmful ecological effects of buffel grass are many, but the bottom line is that it has the potential to convert cactus deserts in which the occurrence of fire is very infrequent into fire-prone savannas. Unless this plant is eliminated from the Sonoran Desert, the future of its iconic plants, including saguaro cacti, is in serious jeopardy as are the lives of all of the animals that depend on it for food and shelter. Control of this invasive species is often labor intensive and involves removal by hand. Application of herbicides such as glyphosate can also be effective hopefully without harming native plants.

Other obvious human impacts in the Sonoran Desert include habitat fragmentation resulting from agriculture and its abandonment, urbanization, massive alteration of above and below ground water availability (e.g., over 90 percent of Arizona's formerly free-flowing watercourses are now dry), and habitat damage caused by mining, road and railroad construction, irrigation canals, solar and wind energy development, and off-road vehicles. As an example of urbanization in this area, consider the following data. The three major human population centers in the Sonoran Desert include Tucson and Phoenix in Arizona and Hermosillo in Sonora, Mexico. The population of Tucson in 1900, 1950, and 2000 was 7,531, 77,000, and 723,000, respectively; of Phoenix in these years, it was 5,554, 221,000, and 2,923,000, respectively; of Hermosillo in these years, it was 14,000, 44,000, and 552,000, respectively. And, of course, population growth and economic development in and around these cities will continue into the foreseeable future, probably until water supplies run out.

The effect of agriculture and its abandonment on Sonoran Desert vegetation has been carefully studied near Hermosillo, Mexico. Beginning in the 1950s, large-scale industrial farming began in this and other parts of the desert. Planting of easily grown cultivars of corn and wheat that required a large input of water and nutrients initially produced substantial yields, but these quickly declined as groundwater and soil became salinated. As a result, large agricultural fields west of Hermosillo (as well as in southern Arizona) were abandoned, beginning in the 1980s, and became wastelands. Although colonization and succession (i.e., systematic natural replacement) of native plants occurred in both saline-rich and nonsaline-contaminated abandoned fields, plant diversity and density were generally lower in these fields than in nearby nonagricultural areas for at least eighteen years postabandonment. By thirty years postabandonment, however, abandoned fields once again resembled nonfarmed areas in their plant composition. Results of this study indicate that, in contrast to common understanding, plant succession does occur in this desert and that, if given a chance, abandoned fields will not remain barren wastelands for very long.

The effects of urbanization on Sonoran Desert vertebrates, especially birds, have also been studied by many ecologists. One study in the Phoenix area compared bird communities in urban and nonurban areas. Not surprisingly, the species richness of birds, be they permanent desert residents, winter residents, or tropical residents, decreased as the density of housing, roads, and exotic plants increased. The most common species in upland rural sites were black-throated sparrows, cactus wrens, house finches, and mourning doves. In upland urban sites, the most common species were house sparrows, Inca and mourning doves, and house finches. This decrease was mitigated to some extent in some urban areas by the density of their native vegetation. Similarly, a study of bird communities in Tucson found that the best predictor of the species richness and density of native birds was the volume of native vegetation in an area; housing density was not a good predictor of these trends. Results of these surveys convey an important and obvious message concerning the conservation of vertebrate diversity: **native species thrive when native vegetation is preserved during development; when lands are scraped clean and replanted with exotic vegetation, the diversity of native animals declines.** A brief survey of the abundance of nocturnal rodents at low (< 0.5 houses/ha) and moderate (7.5 houses/ha) sites in developed and nearby undeveloped areas in central and northern Tucson, respectively, reinforces this idea. This study reported finding four species of native rodents (three heteromyids, including *Dipodomys merriami*, and the pack rat *Neotoma albigula*) and one exotic species (*Mus musculus*). Rodent densities were higher in the low-housing-density sites than in the moderate-density sites.

Species richness and density of reptiles also exhibit differences between urban and rural areas. In urban Phoenix, for instance, researchers have found fifteen species of snakes with two species (the rattlesnake *Crotalus atrox* [!] and coachwhip *Masticophis flagellum*) being by far most common. In nearby rural Florence, in contrast, nineteen species of snakes were found with no single species dominating this assemblage. A transect running from undeveloped desert outside of Tucson to high-development inside Tucson revealed a similar trend: lizard species richness, abundance, and evenness (i.e., the extent to which one or a few species dominate the counts) declined as residential density increased. In this transect, whiptail lizards (*Aspidoscelis* species) were most commonly observed followed by the ornate tree lizard (*Urosaurus ornatus*) and desert spiny lizard (*Sceloporus magister*). All three of these species plus the zebra-tailed lizard (*Callisaurus draconoides*; the fourth most common species) have occurred in our yard, but their numbers are now very low. In contrast to many reptiles, one uncommon but fascinating lizard, the Gila monster, has responded differently to urbanization in the Phoenix area. A study of the home range and movement behavior of radio-tagged individuals found that degree of urbanization did not dramatically change their behavior. Home range size and movement patterns did not differ between urban and rural individuals. Surprisingly, city life apparently agrees with this species.

EFFECTS OF CLIMATE CHANGE

All climate models predict that the U.S. desert southwest is going to become warmer and drier as a result of global warming. An average temperature increase of about 4.5°C and an average annual precipitation decrease of about 3.7 cm (= -11 percent) have been predicted to occur in the arid U.S. southwest by the end of the twenty-first century. How will these changes affect the flora and fauna of the Sonoran Desert? How many of the lives of its current inhabitants are threatened by this degree of climate change? Answering these questions has motivated much research in the past two decades. What follows is a brief summary of the results of some of these studies.

One trend that has emerged has been an increase in minimum winter T_as and longer frost-free periods in much of the Sonoran Desert during the twentieth century and beyond. Since low winter T_as limit the distribution of many Sonoran Desert and Sinaloan thornscrub plants, milder winters could allow these plants to move northward and eastward as well as higher up in elevation. With continued winter warming, the geographic boundaries of these (and other) biomes are likely to change through time, as it has in the past. For the Sonoran Desert's iconic saguaro cactus, it is not clear how these temperature (and precipitation) changes will affect its distribution, at least in the short term. As we've seen, seedling recruitment in this species is episodic and depends on rainfall patterns rather than winter temperatures. Nonetheless, the historic record indicates that saguaros have moved northward in northern Mexico and southern Arizona with warming temperatures in the past few thousand years. It just takes time for this long-lived and slow-moving species to move across the landscape. It may be the "desert tortoise" of the plant world.

The effect of increases in winter T_as and declines in winter precipitation are also known to have a significant effect on the demography of certain Sonoran Desert winter annual plants near Tucson. Results of a twenty-five-year study of the demography of nine species of winter-flowering annuals in the desert flatlands near Tumamoc Hill showed that germination has occurred later in winter owing to a shift in the first occurrence of winter rains from October in the 1980s to December in the early twenty-first century. As a result, seedlings are now germinating at colder minimum T_as with this shift in rainfall, and populations of all nine species have declined through time owing to reduced recruitment. But reductions in population densities have been greater in species adapted for germinating early in winter than in species adapted for germinating later in winter. Plant physiology thus has a significant effect on how populations of desert annuals respond to changes in temperature and precipitation during climate change. This community of desert annuals is likely to become dominated by more cold-tolerant species than less cold-tolerant species through time.

In addition to long-term "on the ground" empirical studies of the responses of desert plants (and animals as described below) to climate change, models of global climate change created using supercomputers are now being used to predict large-scale changes in the abundance and distribution of many species of southwestern U.S. trees, shrubs, and grasses as climate changes. The basic (greatly oversimplified) approach here is to determine the current climate niches of these plants, as I described for the desert mistletoe, and to predict, based on climate change models, how the locations and sizes of these niches will change through time. Results of one major study using this approach indicate that, over-all, vegetation cover in the southwestern United States will decrease by about 39 percent by the end of this century; cover of evergreen trees will decrease more than that of deciduous trees. For many species, vegetation changes in Arizona and elsewhere will be driven primarily by changes in cold season temperatures rather than by precipitation. At the species level, a majority of the 170 trees and shrubs included in this study will move north; 76 of these species will exhibit an increase in the size of their geographic ranges whereas 70 species, particularly those at high elevations, will exhibit a decrease. Because of its increased geographic area, overall species richness in the Sonoran Desert could actually increase rather than decrease. Finally, it should be noted that these predicted changes only occur over a short period of time (until the end of the twenty-first century). Predictions about longer term changes will undoubtedly be forth-coming with longer-term vegetation changes continuing to depend on further changes in temperatures and precipitation, at least in most current models. To be more realistic, however, researchers say that predictions about vegetation changes will also need to take into account the effects of biotic interactions such as competition, mutualism, and predation (including herbivory). The fate of desert and other vegetation will ultimately be determined by a complex interaction involving abiotic and biotic factors, including human impact.

Because their maintenance, growth, and reproductive characteristics are often temperature dependent, ectotherms such as lizards are excellent vertebrates for assessing the effects of climate changes occurring in the Sonoran Desert. To this end, University of Arizona researchers conducted a twenty-five-year study of population trends in five common lizards (tiger whiptail, zebra-tail, side-blotched [*Uta stansburiana*], ornate tree, and desert spiny) at Organ Pipe Cactus National Monument in southwestern Arizona. Results indicated that populations of the one winter-spring breeder (side-blotched) that inhabits rocky areas increased substantially through time whereas those of two spring-summer breeders (whiptails and zebra-tails) that forage in open habitats decreased through time. The two species that are arboreal (ornate tree) or semiarboreal (desert spiny) and hence live in shady environments showed no systematic population trends through time. Precipitation during the study period (1989–2013) decreased, especially during the winter; maximum T_as increased through time, but minimum T_as showed no change. Statistical analyses showed that although these population trends were more closely associated with changes in annual precipitation than temperature, population dynamics were also likely influenced by short-term food availability (mostly insects) and predation. In general, however, populations of these and other diurnal arid-zone lizards are predicted to decline with increasing T_as as animals reduce their foraging times to avoid lethally high temperatures.

What about the fate of endothermic birds and mammals? How are they coping with climate change in the Sonoran Desert? Many species of desert birds (e.g., white-winged doves and cactus wrens) currently exist near the limits of their thermal tolerances. How vulnerable are they to the temperature increases predicted by climate change models? One way to assess this is to compare desert bird communities that were surveyed at sixty-one sites in the Mojave Desert early in the twentieth century by biologists from the University of California, Berkeley, with birds at those same sites today. Such a comparison found that 39 of the 135 original species (29 percent) declined in the frequency of occurrence at survey sites and only one species (the common raven, *Corvus corax*) increased in site occupancy. Species exhibiting occupancy declines included hawks, turkey vultures, and many passerines; carnivorous birds showed especially large decreases in site occupancy. Species loss in surveyed sites averaged 42 percent, resulting in avian communities that now have significantly reduced biodiversity. Loss of bird diversity at these sites was associated more strongly with a decrease in precipitation through time than with changes in average temperatures, net primary productivity, or fire history (for grasslands). Interestingly, no desert-hardy Sonoran Desert bird species have moved into the survey sites yet.

A follow-up study of these Mojave Desert birds revealed that species with the greatest mass-specific water requirements (typically large species such as hawks and vultures) exhibited the greatest decrease in site occupancy through time. This study provides a physiological explanation for how decreasing rainfall affects the fitness of certain species of desert birds. Increasing T_as, especially during and after the spring-summer breeding season, require a greater intake of water, either from surface water sources or from food, for thermoregulation and the maintenance of a constant body temperature in birds. Decreases in seasonal and annual precipitation will reduce plant net primary productivity with a subsequent decline in water-rich plant products such as leaves, fruits, and seeds as well as insect prey. As a result, birds with the highest water needs—typically large species—will be strongly stressed during periods of increasingly warmer and drier years.

Over the one-hundred-year period of the Mojave Desert bird community study, average annual air temperature has increased by 18 percent, which means that these birds now need to acquire more water to thermoregulate. This requirement increases with body size, which helps to explain why large species have experienced greater decreases in site occupancy than small species. A major implication here is that climate change will have a stronger negative effect on large birds, both intra- and interspecifically, than on small birds. Selection pressure in accordance with Bergmann's rule will be at play here (see page 15). This effect is likely to be stronger in carnivorous and insectivorous species than in herbivorous species which often hydrate from surface water sources. As a result, we might expect the composition of Mojave and Sonoran Desert bird communities to increase in the proportional representation of small species and to decrease in large species through time with global warming. If true, these changes will have a profound effect on the trophic structure and ecosystem functioning of these biomes.

In addition to negative community-level and physiological effects, climate change can also have a negative effect on the reproductive success of desert birds. For example, results of a six-year study of the nesting success of thirteen species of Sonoran Desert birds (greater roadrunner and twelve passerines) indicated that nest initiation was delayed by up to three weeks in years of reduced winter rainfall. This delay, in turn, resulted in increased loss of nests and nestlings to nest parasitism by brown-headed cowbirds (*Molothrus ater*) and predators such as snakes and cactus wrens. These results suggest that further decreases and increased annual variability of winter rains through time will have a profound negative effect on the breeding success and fitness of certain common Sonoran Desert birds.

How have Sonoran Desert mammals responded to climate change? Unfortunately, I could find no studies of long-term community or population trends of Sonoran Desert mammals similar to the one-hundred-year Mojave Desert bird study. However, a very similar one-hundred-year study of changes in small mammal communities along a 3,000 m elevational transect west of and within Yosemite National Park conducted by University of California, Berkeley, researchers is available. Increase in the minimum monthly temperature over this period in this area has averaged 3.7°C. Along the western (and major) section of this transect, which includes the Mojave Desert, the ranges of ten of twenty-eight species (all desert-adapted lowland species) expanded upward whereas the ranges of seven high elevation species contracted, as expected in response to climate change. One of the consequences of this is that new assemblages of rodents now live together in places along this elevational gradient. Unlike the results of the Mojave Desert bird survey, though, no species of small mammals have disappeared from these sites, most of which are protected by the U.S. National Park Service.

The results of these two historic surveys have provided researchers with a unique opportunity to compare the response of arid land birds and small mammals to climate change. Results of this comparison have revealed a dramatic difference between these two groups of endotherms. Whereas site occupancy for birds has decreased significantly, leading to a 'collapse' of Mojave Desert bird communities, no such change has occurred for small mammals. In birds, species richness per site declined at fifty-five of sixty-one resurveyed sites (90 percent) compared with only three of ninety sites (3 percent) in mammals. These dramatic differences reflect a critical difference between the biology of birds and mammals. Most birds are active during the day and seek shelter from high temperatures by moving into shady aboveground microhabitats. Most small mammals, in contrast, are active at night and spend their days in cool, moist underground burrows. Unlike small mammals, birds are thus more exposed to high daytime temperatures and are more likely to experience heat stress and dehydration. Detailed modeling of the physiology of birds and mammals indicates that cooling costs, which depend heavily on evaporation of water, are substantially higher in these desert birds than their mammalian counterparts. It should be no surprise, therefore, that climate change involving increasing T_as and decreasing precipitation are having a stronger negative effect on desert birds than on small mammals. Desert mammals appear to be more strongly buffered against these changes than birds.

As a point of historic interest, the bird and mammal surveys in California in the early twentieth century were conducted by Dr. Joseph Grinnell (1877–1939), who was the first director of the Museum of Vertebrate Zoology at the University of California, Berkeley, which was established in 1908. When Grinnell was hired, the museum's founder, Annie Alexander, encouraged him to conduct research documenting California's bird and mammal faunas. And did he ever take this to heart! Over a period of about twenty years, he and his field crews conducted the two monumental faunal surveys described above in which they collected tens of thousands of specimens and took thousands of photos of their survey sites. This material was supplemented by thousands of pages of detailed field notes and maps done meticulously by a method devised by Grinnell. Since then, the "Grinnell method" of recording field observations has become the standard modus operandi used by field researchers conducting biological surveys throughout the world. All of the material and detailed information that Grinnell and his colleagues collected during these surveys were clearly critical for enabling researchers to resurvey these same sites nearly one hundred years later.

In addition to being an inveterate collector, Grinnell was an influential ecologist and was the doctoral adviser of a generation of excellent vertebrate biologists, including two members of my doctoral committee at the University of Michigan—Emmett T. Hooper (my adviser) and William H. Burt. Thus, I'm an academic grandchild of Joseph Grinnell. I was able to see Grinnell's continuing influence in action early in my retirement in Tucson when I participated in the University of Arizona's mammalogy course that was given every fall by Dr. Michael Nachmann. Over Labor Day weekend, Nachmann always took this class to the Southwestern Research Station in southeastern Arizona to livetrap and study Chihuahuan Desert rodents; I went along on several trips to introduce students to some of the many species of bats living in the area. During these trips, Michael taught his students how to use the Grinnell method to record their field and lab observations. Sadly for me but good news for Michael, after seventeen years at the University of Arizona, he was chosen to become director of Berkeley's Museum of Vertebrate Zoology. I'm sure that Michael Nachmann was an excellent choice to follow in the footsteps of the museum's famous first director, Joseph Grinnell.

Although results of the comparison of the historic response of Mojave Desert birds and mammals indicate that birds may be more susceptible to climate change than mammals, at least one study indicates that survival in a common Chihuahuan Desert kangaroo rat, *Dipodomys spectabilis*, is also sensitive to summer daytime soil surface temperatures; burrow temperatures and nighttime soil surface temperatures are significantly correlated with diurnal soil temperatures. Adult survival in a four-year study was lowest in the year (2005) in which daytime summer soil temperatures were highest. These temperatures exceeded the upper critical temperature of this rodent's thermoneutral zone and sometimes even approached its lethal temperature. A combination of physiological stress, reduced plant productivity, and increased activity of ectothermic rodent predators such as gopher snakes and rattlesnakes during especially warm years likely all interact to reduce survivorship in this and probably other rodents.

CONSERVATION OF THE SONORAN DESERT

I wish to begin the final section of this book by asking you to recall the song "This Land Is Your Land," which was written in 1940 by the beloved American folk singer Woody Guthrie (1912–67). In an age of increasing environmental (and cultural) awareness, doesn't this song and its message that America belongs to you and me seem anachronistic? Who made this land (sensu lato) for you and me? Does this land really belong to only one species, *Homo sapiens*? What about the other ten million or so species that inhabit this planet—the only place in the universe where we currently know that diverse multicellular life-forms exist? Doesn't this land belong to all of them, too? What gives us the right to think that we can convert at least 40 percent of the Earth's surface (and increasing) to meet the needs of an ever-expanding and consuming human population? What are we doing to prevent Earth's sixth extinction from happening? What will it take to safely preserve 30–50 percent of Earth's land for all of Earth's biodiversity, as recommended by some conservation activists? These are tough questions, I know. As an ecologist who has studied certain aspects of Earth's biodiversity for most of my life, it is easy to ask them. Answering them, however, is entirely another matter.

As Aldo Leopold wrote in "Round River": "One of the penalties of an ecological education is that one lives alone in a world of wounds. Much of the damage inflicted on land is quite invisible to laymen. An ecologist must either harden his shell and make believe that the consequences of science are none of his business, or he must be the doctor who sees the marks of death in a community that believes itself well and does not want to be told otherwise" (1949, 165). Ever since Aldo Leopold, ecologists and environmental biologists have been trying to educate the world about the importance of preserving as much of life on Earth as possible. And increasing numbers of laypeople have taken up this cause. But like Sisyphus, are we pushing our cause uphill against tremendous resistance? As a technologically superior species, are we destined to consume and destroy our planet (i.e., making it unlivable for us) without realizing how selfish and foolish that is? What is our ultimate Manifest Destiny? Hopefully, it's not "Abandon a ruined Earth and move elsewhere" as some futurists believe.

EXTENT OF PROTECTED LANDS

This book, of course, is not about preserving all of life's biodiversity. It's obviously focused on one rather small portion of our land—the Sonoran Desert, an area straddling the U.S. and Mexican border that encompasses about 260,000 km^2 with about half located in the United States and half in Mexico. How much of this land is actually under the protection by the U.S. and Mexican governments and other conservation agencies? In the United States, the Sonoran Desert is protected from exploitation by one national park (Saguaro National Park East and West) and three national monuments (Ironwood Forest National Monument, Organ Pipe Cactus National Monument, and Sonoran Desert National Monument). The total area of these units is about 4,241 km^2 out of a total area in the U.S. portion of this biome of about 130,000 km^2 (ca. 3.3 percent) (table 2). In addition, seven national wildlife refuges and at least eighteen other mostly small protected areas occur in the U.S. portion of this desert. The major piece of federally protected land in Mexico currently occurs in the Alto Golfo de California (or Pinacate) Biosphere Reserve located at the northern end of the Sea of Cortez; its area is 16,520 km^2 (ca. 12.7 percent of 130,000 km^2). Several other protected areas occur in the Baja California peninsula and islands in the Sea of Cortez (table 2). In total, therefore, at least 15 percent of this desert is currently under federal protection by the U.S. and Mexican governments. But in the United States, at least, large areas of the Sonoran Desert also occur on national forest land that is protected and managed by the U.S. Forest Service. Coronado National Forest, for instance, includes the Santa Catalina, Rincon, and Santa Rita Mountains that surround the Tucson valley. Since their inception in 1891, however, our national forests have been under constant threat from the logging, mining, and livestock industries whose influence ebbs and flows with different federal administrations. Unlike U.S. national parks and monuments, resource extraction such as logging, mining, and, increasingly, energy extraction is permitted (and often encouraged) in national forests. Countering this pressure, the Endangered Species Act of 1973 has played an important role in protecting wildlife in these forests.

Two additional significant landholders within Arizona's Sonoran Desert include Native Americans and the U.S. military. For example, most of southwestern Arizona south of Interstate 8, which runs from Casa Grande through Yuma to San Diego, is occupied by the Tohono O'odham Nation Indian Reservation and the Barry M. Goldwater Air Force Range, in addition to Organ Pipe Cactus National Monument and the Cabeza Prieta National Wildlife Refuge.

Altogether, conservation of much of the U.S. portion of the Sonoran Desert is currently under the management of a variety of agencies, including federal, state, county, local, U.S. military, and tribal entities at various levels. These agencies often differ in their management approaches and goals, their strategies for

TABLE 2 Examples of Federally Protected Areas of the Sonoran Desert in the United States and Mexico

COUNTRY	PROTECTED AREA	AREA (KM²)
United States	Organ Pipe Cactus National Monument	1,340
	Saguaro National Park (E and W)	370
	Ironwood Forest National Monument	522
	Sonoran Desert National Monument	2,009
Mexico	Alto Golfo de California Biosphere Reserve	16,520
	Sierra de San Pedro Mártir National Park	729

Note: In addition, the following protected areas occur in the United States: national wildlife refuges, n = 7, and other protected areas, n = 18. In Mexico, several additional protected areas occur in Baja California, Baja California Sur, and the Sea of Cortez. The total area of the Sonoran Desert is about 260,000 km².

meeting these goals, and the resources they have to implement management strategies. Climate change and the spread of invasive species such as buffel grass are two of the most important threats to this desert that challenge the ability of all of these agencies to preserve this desert and its fauna and flora. Results of a recent survey of about thirty-five nonmilitary land managers representing twenty-five jurisdictions indicated that their three most important concerns were environmental conservation, fire suppression, and recreation; for military managers, protection of humans and infrastructure and recreation were most important. While attaining objectives related to fire suppression can occur as a result of interagency cooperation and collaboration, this survey found that current goals concerning environmental and cultural conservation may not be attainable under a new fire regime in the Sonoran Desert. Therefore, adaptive shifts in management objectives and implementation will be needed to prevent environmental and cultural loss in this region.

It is widely appreciated that climate change will have a significant effect on the threats posed by fire in the arid southwest United States. These threats include the spread of invasive plant species, especially fire-adapted grasses, increased flammability of vegetation, and reduced recruitment in native species. This raises a question: How widespread is the threat of fire in the Sonoran Desert? One way to answer this question is to conduct a statistical analysis of the relationship between the occurrence of fire at a site and an estimate of its vegetative productivity that can be obtained from satellite-based remote sensing (how high-tech can you get?). Such an analysis of the occurrence of large-scale wildfires (i.e., fires

> 50 ha in area) over a twenty-two-year period (1988–2010) in southwestern Arizona found that vegetative growth resulting from infrequent heavy rainfall events was the best predictor of the locations of these fires; low elevation and low density of roads were also important predictors. Greater-than-normal rainfall stimulates plant growth that results in more fuel for fires when vegetation dries out. We normally think that those infrequent years with high rainfall should be good for Sonoran Desert plants (and animals), and, historically, it usually has been. But in the presence of invasive, fire-prone grasses and other non-native plants, this isn't necessarily true. This is because these plants have altered the vegetative and fire potential environment in their favor at the long-term expense of native vegetation. The worry here, as I've mentioned before, is that a desert whose upland areas are dominated by columnar cacti and legume trees will be changed into a grassy savanna lacking some of the Sonoran Desert's dominant plants. If this happens, the Sonoran Desert as we currently know it will be a thing of the past, primarily as a result of man's propensity to tinker with nature for his own benefit (e.g., range "improvement" for his livestock). Unfortunately, I can hear Aldo Leopold muttering, "I told you so. Why didn't you listen to me?" Indeed, that's the 64-dollar question (or in today's dollars, the 587-dollar question), isn't it?

THE SONORAN DESERT CONSERVATION PLAN

Conservation of an area as large and geologically, biologically, and culturally diverse as the Sonoran Desert is a tall order. But many people and agencies in both countries are working on this. One notable effort is the Sonoran Desert Conservation Plan (SDCP), a multiagency attempt to develop a science-based land use plan for Pima County, Arizona, where Tucson is located. This effort began in 1998 with the discovery of very low population numbers of an endangered species of owl: the cactus ferruginous pygmy owl (*Glaucidium brasilianum cactorum*) in Pima County. At the northern edge of its geographic range, this species is a rare inhabitant of mesquite thickets, saguaro forests, and riparian woodlands—areas slated for development at the time of its discovery. Planning involved discussions among many stakeholders, including land use planners, developers, environmentalists, ranchers, and Native Americans, who ultimately agreed that the plan should be science based rather than politically based. To this end, biologists conducted surveys for this owl and many other species of concern in the county and ended up creating maps indicating the distributions of fifty-six species of plants and animals. These maps were then used to indicate important conservation areas—areas in which future development was to be limited—and wildlife corridors connecting them. An important provision of the plan was to protect the 22,400 ha of open (but still cowed-out) land on private ranches from being sold to developers. In addition, a new county ordinance stipulated that builders must leave 80 percent of new developments as open land in biologically sensitive areas. As a result of this planning, two areas of high conservation value—the 51,600 ha Ironwood Forest National Monument northwest of Tucson and the 16,800 ha Las Cienegas National Conservation Area southeast of Tucson—were created. In summary, according to Roseann Hanson, at the time the executive director of the Sky Island Alliance, an NGO whose aim is to protect the unique biodiversity found in the mountains of southern Arizona, with the SDCP, "We are not talking about creating a new refuge or national park, nor are we talking about taking over private lands. [Instead] we are talking about creating healthy, balanced wildlands that would include parks and monuments and private lands that are still largely undeveloped." With this kind of thinking, protection of biologically important portions of the northern Sonoran Desert in Arizona would seem to be possible.

The Coalition for the Protection of the Sonoran Desert was founded in 1998 to oversee the implementation of the SDCP. According to its website (https://www.sonorandesert.org), "The Coalition brings together and earns the trust of a wide variety of stakeholders and divergent interests and uses sound science and grassroots organizing to conserve the Sonoran Desert through effective land-use planning. I [its founder and executive director Carolyn Campbell] am proud that the Coalition has created a legacy in Pima County that includes ongoing implementation of the nationally-recognized Sonoran Desert Conservation Plan; preservation of hundreds of thousands of acres of wildlife habitat and open space in Pima County; protection of critical wildlife linkages that connect the Sky Islands and desert seas; and, perhaps most importantly, a regional conservation ethic born from true collaboration and coalition-building."

Over the years, the coalition has worked closely with Pima County's Board of Supervisors in its support for the SDCP. For example, this includes the Conservation Lands System, which uses a science-based system to advocate that development be limited to less biologically sensitive areas of the county, and the county's Multi-Species Habitat Conservation Plan, which includes endangered species protection through monitoring and management. As a final example, in 2009 the coalition was able to convince the Arizona Department of

Transportation to begin planning the construction of a wildlife bridge across busy SR 77, which runs north from Tucson through Globe and Showlow to the Utah border, to connect wildlife populations living in protected areas in the Santa Catalina Mountains, the Tortolita Mountains, the Tucson Mountains, and the Ironwood Forest National Monument. A wildlife highway underpass was also built near the overpass. Construction of the bridge and underpass and its associated fencing was completed in 2016. An array of camera traps confirms that it is now being used by many vertebrate species, including javelinas, mule deer, coyotes, bobcats, and at least one mountain lion. All in all, the SDCP with its tremendous support from the coalition represents an impressive model of how to begin to preserve biodiversity in this biome.

SOME FINAL WORDS FROM THE THREE AUTHORS THAT INSPIRED ME TO WRITE THIS BOOK

It only seems fitting to conclude this book by providing a few choice quotes from Loren Eiseley, Aldo Leopold, and George Gaylord Simpson.

In his quixotic search for the secret of how life on Earth began, Loren Eiseley writes: "Once even on a memorable autumn afternoon I discovered a sunning blacksnake brooding among the leaves like the very simulacrum of old night. He slid unhurriedly away, carrying his version of the secret with him in such a glittering menace of scales that I was abashed and could only follow admiringly from a little distance. I observed him well, however, and am sure he carried his share of the common mystery into the stones of my neighbor's wall, and is sleeping endlessly on in the winter darkness with one great coil locked around that glistening head" (1957, 204). A poetic way, indeed, of pondering one of the great mysteries of life on Earth.

Of his version of a land ethic, Aldo Leopold writes: "It is inconceivable to me that an ethical relation to land can exist without love, respect, and admiration for land, and a high regard for its value. By value, I of course mean something far broader than mere economic value; I mean value in the philosophical sense. . . . Perhaps the most serious obstacle impeding the evolution of a land ethic is the fact that our educational and economic system is headed away from, rather than toward, an intense consciousness of land. Your true modern is separated from the land by many middlemen, and by innumerable gadgets. He has no vital relation to it; to him it is the space between cities on which crops grow. Turn him loose for a day on the land, and if the spot does not happen to be a golf links or a 'scenic' area, he is bored stiff" (1949, 223–24). This seems to be as true today, if not more so because of the tremendous proliferation of electronic gadgets, as it was in the middle of the twentieth century.

And G. G. Simpson writes: "Evolution appears to be not only a mixture of random and of oriented changes but also highly opportunistic, in a purely impersonal sense. Most, although not all, of the possible ways of life in any given period of earth history have usually been followed by one group or another. Among possible different solutions of a given functional problem, . . . many or all are commonly followed by various groups. There is no effect of over-all plan ending toward the same solution of such a problem" (1949, 342). I would agree with this and note that this conclusion is supported by the many different ways Sonoran Desert animals and plants have evolved to deal with the abiotic and biotic challenges they face in this seemingly hostile environment.

As I mentioned early in this book, living in the Sonoran Desert is essentially an aesthetic experience for me. Desert spiny lizards doing push-ups, hummingbirds hovering at *Penstemon* flowers, Cooper's hawks eating mourning doves in our mesquite trees, and bobcats drinking from our fountain are wonderful to behold. These and many other pleasures are a few of the reasons why many people choose to live here, especially in retirement. But the Big Question still remains: Are we in danger of loving this place to death—a danger that all of Earth's beautiful places face?

I'm afraid that the jury is still out on this. On the one hand, as seen by the success of our local Sonoran Desert Conservation Plan, we have the will to consider more than our own well-being in an effort to preserve significant portions of this desert. But, as Yuval Harari has written in *Sapiens*: "Despite the astonishing things that humans are capable of doing, we remain unsure of our goals and we seem to be as discontented as ever. . . . We are more powerful than ever before, but have very little idea what to do with all that power. Worse still, humans seem to be more irresponsible than ever [e.g., our refusal get vaccinated and to wear face masks during the COVID-19 pandemic of 2020–21]. Self-made gods with only the laws of physics [and nature] to keep us company, we are accountable to no one. We are consequently wreaking havoc on our fellow animals and on the surrounding ecosystem, seeking little more than our own comfort and amusement, yet never finding satisfaction" (2018, 416–17). If this is universally true, it is a very sad commentary indeed on the present state of *Homo sapiens*. A continued emphasis on human population growth in the Sonoran Desert because it's needed to fuel our capitalistic economic system does not bode well for the future of this (and many other) biome(s).

In closing, I'd like to recommend that you check out the lyrics of the song "Evolution," written by Ivan Lins and Brock Walsh. A lovely version of this song was performed in 1994 by jazz vocalist Kitty Margolis with a beautiful guitar solo by Joyce Cooling. Its YouTube URL can be found in the notes. The gist of this song is that, as also suggested by Yuval Harari, we have set ourselves apart from nature but could likely suffer the same fate as that of all the extinct creatures that once lived on Earth unless we change our behavior. I'm sure this song would resonate with Eiseley, Leopold, and Simpson. I hope it does with you, too.

ACKNOWLEDGMENTS

I WROTE MOST of this book while in semi-isolation during the coronavirus pandemic. During that period I had no access to brick-and-mortar libraries or interlibrary loans and therefore had to rely on material in my own library and the internet. I certainly could not have written it without access to the enormous resources available on the internet. In particular, I appreciate resources provided by Wikipedia, Google Scholar, and Web of Science. Remote access to online resources available through the University of Miami Library is also greatly appreciated. Kudos, too, belong to all of the scientific societies that have put their publications online. Young scholars cannot appreciate how valuable online resources are to someone like me who over five decades ago started his professional career spending endless hours working in college and university libraries and having to actually handle books and journals and take handwritten notes. Modern scholarship, at least in the sciences, is now far different (and much easier) from the way it was in the 1960s and 1970s. But the discipline enforced on me and many others by the "bad old days" before the birth of the internet and electronic libraries, I think, was very beneficial. Look at what Charles Darwin and David Lack and my other intellectual heroes were able to accomplish without the aid of electronics or computers! But conversely, this book is a testament to what an army of organismal and evolutionary biologists have been able to accomplish in the age of electronics and molecular biology.

I thank the following people for helping me by providing information, materials, and encouragement: Doug Altschuler, Peter Boyle, Judie Bronstein, James Brown, Bill Broyles, Rick Brusca, Carolyn Campbell, Roger Carpenter, Mark Dimmitt, Kim Duffek, Brock Fenton, Curt Freese, David Inouye, Julian Lee, Bill Lofquist, Michael Nachmann, Sharon Pairman, Courtney Patel, Scott Richardson, Chuck Sterling, Tom Van Devender, Wayne Van Devender, and Ben Wilder. Two outside reviewers provided many comments and suggestions that improved the final version of this book. I thank Kerry Smith for his careful copyediting of this book. In addition I thank my wife Marcia and the staff at the Northwest Medical Center in Tucson for comforting and caring for me during a two-month hospitalization (non-covid related) during the COVID-19 pandemic. Finally, as always I thank Marcia for her love, encouragement, and tolerance of my writing obsession.

APPENDIX 1

Conversion Factors for Changing Metric Units into English Units

VARIABLE	METRIC	ENGLISH
Length	1 meter (m)	39.4 inches (in)
	1 kilometer (km)	3281 feet (ft) or 0.62 miles (mi)
	1 centimeter (cm)	2.54 in
Area	1 square meter (m^2)	10.76 square ft (ft^2)
	1 hectare (ha) (= ca. 2 football fields)	2.47 acres (A)
	1 square km (km^2)	0.39 square miles (mi^2)
Mass	1 gram (g)	15.4 grains
	28.35 g	1 ounce
	1 kilogram (kg)	35.3 ounces or 2.21 pounds (lb)
	1 metric ton	2,204.6 lb
Volume	1 cubic centimeter (cc or cm^3)	0.061 cubic inches (in^3)
	1 liter	1.057 U.S. quarts (qt) or 0.264 U.S. gallons (gal)
Velocity	1 m per second (m s^{-1})	2.24 mi per hr (mi h^{-1})
	1 km per hr (kph)	0.62 mi per hr (mph)
Energy	1 joule (j)	0.239 calories (cal)
	1 kilojoule (kj)	0.239 kilocalories (kcal)

APPENDIX 2

List of Representative Species of Reptiles, Birds, and Mammals
That Reside in the Sonoran Desert at Least Seasonally

VERTEBRATE CLASS	FAMILY	COMMON NAME	SCIENTIFIC NAME	MIGRATORY?	GENERAL DISTRIBUTION	CONSERVA-TION STATUS
Reptiles	Testudinidae	Desert tortoise	Gopherus agassizii	N	AL	Vu
	Iguanidae	Desert iguana	Dipsosaurus dorsalis	N	AL	LC
		Sonoran collared lizard	Crotaphytus nebrius	N	AL	
		Zebra-tailed lizard	Callisaurus draconoides	N	AL	LC
		Yuma desert fringe-toed lizard	Yuma rufopunctata	N	AL	
		Long-tailed brush lizard	Urosaurus graciosus	N	AL	LC
		Desert spiny lizard	Sceloporus magister	N	AL	LC
		Common chuckwalla	Sauromalus ater	N	AL	LC
	Phrynosomatidae	Desert horned lizard	Phrynosoma platyrhinos	N	AL	LC
		Regal horned lizard	Phrynosoma solare	N	AL	LC
	Teiidae	Tiger whiptail lizard	Aspidoscelis (Cnemidophorus) tigris	N	WS	LC
	Eublepharidae	Western banded gecko	Coleonyx variegatus	N	AL	LC
	Helodermatidae	Gila monster	Heloderma suspectum	N	AL	NT
	Boidae	Rosy boa	Lichanura trivirgata	N	AL	LC
	Elapidae	Sonoran coral snake	Micruroides euryxanthus	N	AL	LC
	Colubridae	Sonoran shovel-nosed snake	Chionactis palarostris	N	AL	LC
		Western shovel-nosed snake	Chionactis occipitalis	N	AL	LC
		Variable sand snake	Chilomeniscus stramineus	N	AL	LC
		Ground snake	Sonora semiannulata	N	AL	LC
		Western lyre snake	Trimorphodon biscutatus	N	WS	LC

VERTEBRATE CLASS	FAMILY	COMMON NAME	SCIENTIFIC NAME	MIGRATORY?	GENERAL DISTRIBUTION	CONSERVATION STATUS
		Gopher snake	Pituophis cantifer	N	WS	LC
		Glossy snake	Arizona elegans	N	WS	LC
		Spotted leaf-nosed snake	Phyllorhynchus decurtatus	N	AL	LC
		Saddled leaf-nosed snake	Phyllorhynchus browni	N	AL	LC
		Western patch-nosed snake	Salvadora hexalepis	N	AL	LC
		Sonoran whipsnake	Masticophis bilineatus	N	AL	LC
		Coachwhip	Masticophis flagellum	N	AL	LC
		Long-nosed snake	Rhinocheilus lecontei	N	WS	LC
		Common king snake	Lampropeltis getula	N	WS	LC
	Viperidae	Western diamondback	Crotalus atrox	N	AL	LC
		Mohave rattlesnake	Crotalus scutulatus	N	AL	LC
		Sidewinder	Crotalus cerastes	N	AL	LC
		Tiger rattlesnake	Crotalus tigris	N	AL	LC
Birds	Accipitridae	Cooper's hawk	Accipiter cooperii	N	WS	LC
		Harris's hawk	Parabuteo unicinctus	N	WS	LC
		Red-tailed hawk	Buteo jamaicensis	N	WS	LC
	Falconidae	Crested caracara	Caracara plancus	N	WS	LC
	Phasianidae	Gambel's quail	Callipepla gambelii	N	AL	LC
	Columbidae	White-winged dove	Zenaida asiatica	Y	WS	LC
		Mourning dove	Zenaida macroura	N	WS	LC

VERTEBRATE CLASS	FAMILY	COMMON NAME	SCIENTIFIC NAME	MIGRATORY?	GENERAL DISTRIBUTION	CONSERVATION STATUS
	Cuculidae	Common ground dove	Columbina passerina	N	WS	LC
		Greater roadrunner	Geococcyx californianus	N	WS	LC
	Strigidae	Western screech owl	Otus kennicottii	N	WS	LC
		Great horned owl	Bubo virginianus	N	WS	LC
		Ferruginous pygmy owl	Glaucidium brasilianum	Y?	AL	LC
		Elf owl	Micrathene whitneyi	Y	AL	LC
		Burrowing owl	Speotyto cunicularia	N	WS	LC
	Trochilidae	Broad-billed hummingbird	Cynanthus latirostris	N	AL	LC
		Black-chinned hummingbird	Archilochus alexandri	Y	AL	LC
		Anna's hummingbird	Calypte anna	N	AL	LC
		Costa's hummingbird	Calypte costae	N?	AL	LC
	Picidae	Gila woodpecker	Melanerpes uropygialis	N	AL	LC
		Ladder-backed woodpecker	Picoides scalaris	N	WS	LC
		Gilded flicker	Colaptes chrysoides	N	WS	LC
	Tyrannidae	Black phoebe	Sayornis nigricans	N	AL	LC
		Say's phoebe	Sayornis saya	Y	WS	LC
		Vermilion flycatcher	Pyrocephalus rubinus	N	WS	LC
		Ash-throated flycatcher	Myiarchus cinerascens	Y	WS	LC
		Brown-crested flycatcher	Myiarchus tyrannulus	Y	AL	LC
	Remizidae	Verdin	Auriparus flaviceps	N	AL	LC

VERTEBRATE CLASS	FAMILY	COMMON NAME	SCIENTIFIC NAME	MIGRATORY?	GENERAL DISTRIBUTION	CONSERVATION STATUS
	Troglodytidae	Cactus wren	Campylorhynchus brunneicapillus	N	AL	LC
		Rock wren	Salpinctes obsoletus	Y	AL	LC
		Canyon wren	Catherpes mexicanus	N	WS	LC
	Polioptilidae	Black-tailed gnatcatcher	Polioptila melanura	N	AL	LC
	Mimidae	Northern mockingbird	Mimus polyglottos	N	WS	LC
		Curve-billed thrasher	Toxostoma curvirostre	N	AL	LC
		Crissal thrasher	Toxostoma crissale	N	AL	LC
	Ptilogonatidae	Phainopepla	Phainopepla nitens	N?	AL	LC
	Laniidae	Loggerhead shrike	Lanius ludovicianus	Y	WS	NT
	Vireonidae	Bell's vireo	Vireo bellii	Y	WS	LC
	Emberizidae, Parulinae	Lucy's warbler	Vermivora luciae	Y	AL	LC
	Emberizidae, Cardinalinae	Northern cardinal	Cardinalis cardinalis	N	WS	LC
		Pyrrhuloxia	Cardinalis sinuatus	N	AL	LC
	Emberizidae, Emberizinae	Abert's towhee	Melozone aberti	N	AL	LC
		Rufous-winged sparrow	Aimophila carpalis	N	AL	LC
		Black-throated sparrow	Amphispiza bilineata	N	AL	LC
	Emberizidae, Icterinae	Bronzed cowbird	Molothrus aeneus	Y	AL	LC

VERTEBRATE CLASS	FAMILY	COMMON NAME	SCIENTIFIC NAME	MIGRATORY?	GENERAL DISTRIBUTION	CONSERVATION STATUS
		Hooded oriole	Icterus cucullatus	Y	AL	LC
		Scott's oriole	Icterus parisorum	Y	AL	LC
	Fringillidae	House finch	Carpodacus mexicanus	N	WS	LC
		Lesser goldfinch	Carduelis psaltria	N	WS	LC
Mammals	Phyllostomidae	California leaf-nosed bat	Macrotus californicus	N	AL	LC
		Lesser long-nosed bat	Leptonycteris yerbabuenae	Y	AL	NT
		Mexican long-tongued bat	Choeronycteris mexicana	Y	AL	NT
	Vespertilionidae	Cave myotis	Myotis velifer	Y?	AL	LC
		California myotis	Myotis californicus	Y	WS	LC
		Big brown bat	Eptesicus fuscus	Y	WS	LC
		Canyon bat	Parastrellus hesperus	N	WS	LC
		Western yellow bat	Lasiurus ega	Y?	AL	LC
		Pallid bat	Antrozous pallidus	N	WS	LC
	Molossidae	Brazilian freetail bat	Tadarida brasiliensis	Y	WS	LC
		Pocketed freetail bat	Tadarida femorosacca	Y?	AL	LC
		Western mastiff bat	Eumops perotis		AL	LC
	Heteromyidae	Desert pocket mouse	Chaetodipus penicillatus	N	AL	LC
		Rock pocket mouse	Perognathus intermedius	N	AL	LC
		Bailey pocket mouse	Perognathus baileyi	N	AL	LC
		Desert kangaroo rat	Dipodomys deserti	N	AL	LC

VERTEBRATE CLASS	FAMILY	COMMON NAME	SCIENTIFIC NAME	MIGRATORY?	GENERAL DISTRIBUTION	CONSERVATION STATUS
		Merriam's kangaroo rat	Dipodomys merriami	N	AL	LC
	Cricetidae	Cactus mouse	Peromyscus eremicus	N	AL	LC
		Whitethroat woodrat	Neotoma albigula	N	AL	LC
	Leporidae	Antelope jackrabbit	Lepus alleni	N	AL	LC
		Desert cottontail	Sylvilagus audubonii	N	AL	LC
	Canidae	Gray fox	Urocyon cinereoargenteus	N	WS	LC
		Coyote	Canis latrans	N	WS	LC
	Felidae	Bobcat	Lynx rufus	N	WS	LC
		Mountain lion	Puma concolor	N	WS	LC
	Tayassuidae	Javelina	Tayassu pecari	N	WS	LC
	Cervidae	Mule deer	Odocoileus hemionus	N	WS	LC
	Bovidae	Desert bighorn sheep	Ovis canadensis	N	WS	LC

Conservation status based on IUCN Red List

Abbreviations: N = No, Y = Yes; AL = Arid lands, WS = Widespread

IUCN status: LC = Least concern, NT = Near threatened, VU = Vulnerable

NOTES

Note: Full citations of books and articles that I cite here can be found in the bibliography.

PREFACE AND INTRODUCTION

The books by Loren Eiseley (*The Immense Journey*), Aldo Leopold (*A Sand County Almanac*), and George Gaylord Simpson (*The Meaning of Evolution*) served as the inspiration and introduction for this book. I used Wikipedia accounts for overviews of the lives of these three men.

1. OUR IMMENSE JOURNEY TO CLASSIFY AND DETERMINE THE HISTORY OF LIFE ON EARTH

WHAT'S IN A NAME?

I used many Wikipedia accounts as background and material for many topics in this part of the book. Historical overviews of taxonomy and classification came from chapters in Mayr (1982, chaps. 3 and 4) and Futuyma (1986, chap. 10). Richard Conniff (2009) describes mankind's frenzied attempts to find new species. The response of the King of Spain to seeing specimens of birds of paradise is described in Frith and Beehler (1998, 30) and Laman and Scholes (2012, 36–38). Modern views of the kingdoms of life include Robert Whittaker (1969), Carl Woese and George Fox (1977), and Michael Ruggiero and colleagues (2015).

AND THEN CAME CHARLES DARWIN

I used Wikipedia accounts of historical figures mentioned in this section to supplement much of the information found in Eiseley's (1958) book (*Darwin's Century*). In addition to describing the intellectual antecedents of Darwin and Darwin's experiences on the *Beagle* (also recounted in Darwin's [1839] *The Voyage of the* Beagle), this information includes discussions of the evolution of historical geology, the concept of the scala naturae, contributions to Darwin's thoughts from the geologist Charles Lyell, the Darwin-Wallace discovery of natural selection, and the publication of Darwin's (1859) *The Origin of Species*.

HOW FAR OFF WAS THE BISHOP OF USSHER'S CALCULATION OF THE AGE OF EARTH?

I used Eiseley's (1958) *Darwin's Century*, supplemented with Wikipedia accounts (e.g., the Bishop of Ussher), to describe early attempts to estimate the age of Earth and the rise of the science of stratigraphy. Descriptions of modern methods for dating rocks using radioactive isotopes come from Zimmer (2001, chap. 3).

NATURAL SELECTION IN ACTION

Futuyma (1986, chap. 6) and Zimmer (2001, chap. 4), among many others, describe the basic features of natural selection. The evolution of English or house sparrows in North America is described by Richard Johnston and Robert Selander (e.g., 1964, 1971) in several publications. Description of the evolution of the bacterium *Staphylococcus aureus* and its emergence as MRSA is based on its Wikipedia account. Finally, an article by Mauro Galleti (2013) describes changes in the seed size of a common palm tree over the past one hundred years as a result of deforestation in the Brazilian Atlantic Forest.

BUT WHAT ABOUT THE ORIGIN OF SPECIES, DARWIN'S "MYSTERY OF MYSTERIES"?

Ernst Mayr's (1942) biological species concept first appeared in his book *Systematics and the Origin of Species*. This concept and discussions of different modes of speciation can be found in many books on evolution, including Futuyma (1986, chap. 8) and Mayr (1982, chap. 6). Darwin (1839) discusses species of Galapagos finches in *The Voyage of the* Beagle. Peter Grant's (1998b) description of possible evolutionary scenarios in Darwin's finches appears in a book chapter (Grant 1998a).

ANCESTRY 101

Simpson (1953, chap. 7) discusses adaptive radiation in depth in his book. Darwin's (1859, 118–19) hypothetical history of several lineages appears in *The Origin of Species*. Standard ornithology and mammalogy texts (e.g., Gill [1990]; Vaughan, Ryan, and Czaplewski [2000]) describe morphological traits used in classification. Wetterer, Rockman, and Simmons (2000) use many morphological characters to estimate the phylogenetic history of American leaf-nosed bats. A more recent phylogeny of these bats based on DNA data has been published by Dany Rojas, Warsi, and Davalos (2016). The modern taxonomy and classification of birds is being updated regularly by the American Ornithologist's Union. I used the following Wikipedia accounts for most of the section on modern molecular methods: history of molecular evolution, phylogenetics and molecular evolution, DNA, RNA, mtDNA, PCR, DNA sequencing, genomics and phylogenies, the molecular clock, and Kary Mullis. Convergent evolution and the logic of phylogenetic analysis are discussed by Futuyma (1986, chap. 10), among many others. Avise (2004, chap. 3), among others, describes the PCR reaction. David Lack (1947a) provides the first modern accounts of Darwin's finches as well as describing their taxonomic history. Other more recent studies of the evolution of these birds include Grant (1986); Sato et al. (1999); Burns, Hackett, and Klein (2002); and Lamichhaney et al. (2015).

2. IMMENSE JOURNEYS: AN EXPLORATION OF THE NATURAL HISTORY AND EVOLUTION OF SOME OF MY FAVORITE SONORAN DESERT ANIMALS AND PLANTS

A SENSE OF PLACE: EVOLUTION OF THE SONORAN DESERT

The map of the Sonoran Desert comes from Dimmitt (2015). Tom Van Devender (2002) and Van Devender and Richard Brusca (2015) describe the evolutionary history of the Sonoran Desert, and Robert Scarborough and Richard Brusca (2015) describe its geological history. Details about the climate of this desert and many of its biological features can be found in these two volumes (Phillips and Comus [2000] and Dimmitt, Comus, and Brewer [2015]). My treatment of the history of plate tectonics comes from the Wikipedia account (plate tectonics) plus a brief section in Kolbert (2014, 197–98). Research on pack rat middens began with Tom Van Devender's doctoral dissertation (1973). The use of pack rat middens for vegetation reconstruction is also described by the Wikipedia account (pack rat). They can also be used to identify and date vertebrate remains (e.g., Mead, Van Devender, and Cole 1983).

THE BIG PICTURE, BOTANICALLY AND ZOOLOGICALLY SPEAKING

This section is based on Wikipedia accounts of the evolution of angiosperms, reptiles, birds, and mammals for general overviews and many specific articles. Loren Eiseley (1957, chap. 5) introduces us to the evolution of flowering plants. A review of the history of evolutionary studies of these plants can be found in Soltis et al. (2018). The latest version of APG (APG IV) is Chase et al. (2016). Darwin's "abominable mystery" is discussed in Friedman (2009). Figure 4 and the dates of evolution of 106 angiosperm families come from Fleming and Kress (2013, table 1.3 and fig. 6.3). Chapter 6 of that book also discusses the historical biogeography and evolution of the angiosperms. Magallon et al. (2015) present a detailed dated phylogeny of angiosperms that indicates that much of the early evolution of these plants took place in the Late Cretaceous.

An overview of the phylogeny of vertebrates based on molecular data comes from Meyer and Zardoya (2003). To pique your imagination about the former diversity of reptiles and amphibians, it's worthwhile to peruse one of the many encyclopedias of dinosaurs (e.g., Malam and Parker's [2002] *Encyclopedia of Dinosaurs*). For an overview of reptile evolution and the source of figure 6, see Pough et al. (2016, chaps. 2–4). A reconsideration of the relationship of turtles to other reptiles is discussed by Hedges and Poling (1999) and Hedges (2012). Brusatte (2018) presents a very readable account of the evolutionary history of dinosaurs. Their demise and that of many other forms of life as a result of the asteroid impact at the end of the Cretaceous and the discovery of this impact is described in detail in Elizabeth Kolbert's book (2014, chap. 4). A key paper hypothesizing the reality of this profound event is by Alvarez et al. (1980).

Brusatte, O'Connor, and Jarvis (2015) discuss the evolution of key avian morphological features from archosaurian reptiles (see fig. 7). The mass extinction of archaic birds in the Late Cretaceous is described by Longrich, Tokarykb, and Fielda (2011) and Brusatte (2016). Attempts to classify and determine the evolutionary relationships of birds date from the nineteenth century. The evolution of birds using modern phylogenetic techniques began in the late 1970s. Recent detailed avian phylogenies based on a combination of molecular and fossil data can be found in Jarvis et al. (2014) and Prum et al. (2015). The biogeographic history of passerine birds, the largest avian order, is described by Oliveros et al. (2019).

The evolutionary history of mammals is reviewed in standard mammalogy texts, for example, Vaughan, Ryan, and Czaplewski (2000) as well as Kemp (2005). George Gaylord Simpson (1945) authored a long-held modern classification of mammals which has now been replaced by molecular-based phylogenies, as seen in figure 9. Recent molecular mammalian phylogenies include those of Bininda-Emonds et al. (2007); O'Leary et al. (2013); and Upham, Esselstyn, and Jetz (2019).

In my overview of the higher vertebrates of the Sonoran Desert, I consulted the following sources: for reptiles, Brennen and Holycross (2006); for birds, Russell and Monson (1998); and for mammals, Burt and Grossenheider (1964) and Hoffmeister (1986). Hoffmeister (1986) also provides a list of fossil vertebrates that have been found in Arizona.

Data for my comparison of the physical conditions on Earth and Mars come from the website https://www.lpl.arizona.edu/missions/phoenixmarsiii.php. Data on specifications of the Airbus 320 come from the website https://www.globalair.com/aircraft-for-sale/specifications?specid=639. Calculations of the wingspan of birds on Mars were provided by Douglas Altschuler (pers. comm.).

Major websites for details about the biology of particular species of reptiles, birds, and mammals include the Reptile Database (http://www.reptile-database.org); Birds of the World (https://www.birdsoftheworld.org); and Mammalian Species (http://www.mammalsociety.org/publications/mammalian-species). Pianka (1989) reviews the species richness of lizards in different deserts.

SONORAN DESERT REPTILES

DESERT TORTOISE: The scientific literature on *Gopherus agassizi* is extensive. Accounts of its population ecology and behavior include Berry (1986); Bjurlin and Bissonette (2004); Doake, Kareiva, and Klepetka (1994); Gienger (2009); Niblick, Rostal, and Classen (1994); Turner et al. (1986); and Woodbury and Hardy (1948). Papers dealing with sex determination in reptiles and the desert tortoise include Bull (1980), Janzen (1991), and Spotila et al. (1994). Its physiology is described in Nagy and Medica (1986), Peterson (1996), and Zimmerman et al. (1994). Papers dealing with its conservation include Averill-Murray et al. (2012, 2013), Barrows et al. (2016), and Esque et al. (2010). The evolution of turtles, including the Galapagos tortoise, is discussed in Caccone et al. (1999, 2002), Hedges (2012), Krenz et al. (2005), Pereira et al. (2017), and Rieppel and Reisz (1999). Finally, an introduction to Archie Carr's conservation work with sea turtles can be found in Carr (1980) and Bjorndal and Carr (1989).

DESERT SPINY LIZARD: Accounts of its ecology and behavior can be found in Cooper (2009); Mendez-de la Cruz, Villagran-Santa Cruz, and Andrews (1998); Ruby (1978); and Smith and John-Alder (1999). Its physiology and senses are treated in Cooper and Burns (1987), Duvall (1979), Munsey (1972), Nagy (2004), Simon et al. (1981), and Sinervo (1990). Its evolution and that of its relatives are discussed in Leache et al. (2015); Townsend et al. (2004); Vidal and Hedges (2005); Wiens et al. (2010); and Wiens, Kozak, and Silva (2012).

TIGER WHIPTAIL LIZARD: The ecology and behavior of whiptail lizards can be found in Crews, Grassman, and Lindzey (1987); Eifler and Eifler (1998); Lueck (1985); and Winne and Keck (2004). Whiptail physiology is discussed by Diaz de la Vega-Perez et al. (2013). The evolution of parthenogenesis and parthenogenesis in whiptails is discussed by Avise (2015); Crews and Fitzgerald (1980); Cuellar (1977); Manriquez-Moran, Villagran-Santa Cruz, and Mendez-de la Cruz (2000); Parker (1979a, 1979b); and Parker and Selander (1976). Phylogeny of whiptail lizards is treated by Giugliano, Collevatti, and Colli (2007); Harvey, Ugueto, and Gutberlet (2012); and Reeder, Cole, and Dessauer (2002).

GILA MONSTER: The ecology and behavior of this iconic lizard are covered in Beck (1990); Beck and Jennings (2003); Cooper, Deperno, and Arnett (1994); Gienger (2009); Jones (1983); Kwiatkowski et al. (2008); and Pianka and Vitt (2003). Its physiology is discussed by Davis and DeNardo (2009, 2010) and Gienger, Tracy, and Nagy (2014). Its evolution is described by Bhullar and Smith (2008), Townsend et al. (2004), and Vidal and Hedges (2005).

GOPHER SNAKE: This wide-ranging snake has been studied by many biologists. Discussions of its ecology and behavior include Cunningham (1959); Diller and Wallace (1996); Eichholz and Koenig (1992); Fitch (1949); Greenwald (1974); Rodriguez-Robles (2002, 2003); and Williams, Hodges, and Bishop

(2012). Its physiology has been studied by Greenwald (1971) and Licht and Bennett (1972). Studies of its evolution include Dahn et al. (2018); Figueroa et al. (2016); Lee et al. (2007); Lele, Rand, and Zweifel (2016); Pyron, Burbrink, and Wiens (2013); Rodriguez-Robles and De Jesus-Escobar (2000); and Utiger et al. (2002). Sweet (1985) reports on its mimicry and convergence with the appearance of rattlesnakes.

WESTERN DIAMONDBACK RATTLESNAKE: This large pit viper has been studied by many biologists. Greene (1997) describes some of its basic biology. Darwin (1871) discusses sexual selection in animals and humans. Its ecology and behavior, including sexual selection, are discussed by Beck (1995); Clark et al. (2014); Gillingham, Carpenter, and Murphy (1983); Kardong and Smith (2002); and Taylor and DeNardo (2005). McCue (2007) reports on its physiology. The evolution of vipers has been described by Castoe and Parkinson (2006); Castoe, Spencer, and Parkinson (2007); Douglas et al. (2006); Lee et al. (2007); Murphy et al. (2002); Pyron, Burbrink, and Wiens (2013); and Wuster et al. (2008).

ECTOTHERMY VERSUS ENDOTHERMY

This topic has been of great interest to biologists for over a century and has a vast literature. Standard "ology" books for herps, birds, and mammals have chapters devoted to this subject. I have been selective in the use of this literature and have only touched on some of the major issues on this topic. For starters, Calder (1984) provides an extensive discussion of the effect of body size on many biological features of animals. Physiology is one of the major areas in which body size is very important. The classic studies of Scholander et al. (1950a, 1950b) introduce us to thermoneutral zones and how they differ between arctic and tropical birds and mammals. Metabolic rates and the actual cost of living of ectotherms and endotherms are discussed by Ken Nagy (1987, 2004, and 2018), who pioneered the use of the doubly labeled water technique to measure these rates. Ricklefs, Konarzewski, and Daan (1996) also provide background information about vertebrate metabolic rates and their daily costs of living. Gillooly, Gomez, and Mavrodiev (2017) provide an overview of differences in the aerobic scope of vertebrate ectotherms and endotherms. General overviews of the evolution of vertebrate endothermy include Bennett and Ruben (1986); Grigg, Beard, and Augee (2004); Kotaka (2004); Koteja (2000); Lovegrove (2012, 2017); McNab (1978); and Ruben (1995). Parental care as a driver behind the evolution of endothermy is discussed by Angilletta and

Sears (2003). Brain size evolution as another driver of endothermy is covered by Benoit et al. (2017), Gillooly and McCoy (2014), Isler and van Schaik (2006), Jarvis et al. (2005), and Milner and Walsh (2009). The size of dinosaur brains is discussed by Hopson (1977), Jerison (2004), and van Dongen (1998). The evolution of feathers in birds is discussed in Pana et al. (2019), and the evolution of fur in mammals is covered by Martin et al. (2017).

SONORAN DESERT BIRDS

GAMBEL'S QUAIL: The scientific literature for this important game bird is extensive. The account for this species in Birds of the World (Gee et al. 2020) provides a detailed summary of the biology of this species. Population ecology and general behavior are treated by Gullion (1960), Hagelin (2002), Heffelfinger et al. (1999), and Rait and Ohmart (1966). Mate selection is discussed by Hagelin (2001, 2002, 2003) and Hagelin and Ligon (2001). The physiology of these birds is summarized in Carey and Morton (1971); Goldstein and Nagy (1985); Henderson (1961); Weathers (1981); and Williams, Pacelli, and Braun (1991). The evolution of quails and their relatives is reviewed in Hosner, Braun, and Kimball (2015); Kimball et al. (2013); and Wang et al. (2013).

GREATER ROADRUNNER: Hughes (2020) provides a detailed summary of the biology of this species in Birds of the World. Its ecology and behavior are described in Audsley et al. (2006); Davis et al. (2018); Kelley et al. (2011); Montalvo, Ransome, and Lopez (2014); and Whitson (1971). Its physiology has been studied by Calder and Schmidt-Nielsen (1967); Dunson, Dunson, and Ohmart (1976); Ohmart (1972, 1973); and Ohmart and Lasiewski (1971). The evolution of cuckoos, including the greater roadrunner, is discussed by Jarvis et al. (2014); Johnson, Goodman, and Lanyon (2000); Kruger, Sorenson, and Davies (2009); and Kruger and Davies (2001).

COOPER'S HAWK: The biology of this species is described by Rosenfield et al. (2020). Details on the ecology and behavior of this hawk come from Boal (2001); Boal and Mannan (1998); Boal and Mannan (1999); Estes and Mannan (2003); Mannan and Boal (2000); Mannan, Steidl, and Boal (2008); and Mannan et al. (2007). Its visual acuity is discussed by O'Rourke et al. (2010). Size dimorphism and its evolution in hawks are discussed by Andersson and Norberg (1981); Friedman and Remes (2015); Kruger (2005); Schoenjahn, Pavey, and Walter (2020); and Sonerud et al. (2012). The evolutionary history of hawks, including both the Cooper's hawk and Harris's hawk, comes from Griffiths et al. (2007); Kimball, Parker, and Bednarz (2003); Lerner and Mindell (2005); Lerner, Klaver, and Mindell (2008); and Raposo do Amaral et al. (2009).

HARRIS'S HAWK: The biology of this interesting hawk is summarized by Dwyer and Bednarz (2020). Its ecology and behavior are described by Bednarz (1987, 1988), Bednarz and Ligon (1988), Dawson and Mannan (1991), Coulson and Coulson (2013), and Whaley (1979). Its cooperative breeding is described by Kimball, Parker, and Bednarz (2003). The use of this hawk in falconry can be found in Erickson, Marsh, and Salmon (1990) and Kenward (2009). See the Cooper's hawk account for papers dealing with the evolution of hawks.

GREAT HORNED OWL: The biology of this large, geographically wide-ranging raptor has been studied extensively, but apparently not in detail in the Sonoran Desert. As a result, I have relied on its Wikipedia account and Artuso et al. (2020) for information about its general ecology and behavior. Its physiology has been studied by Ganey, Balda, and King (1993), and its vision and hearing have been described by Fite (1973); Gutierrez-Ibanez, Iwaniuk, and Wylie (2011); Martin (1986); Orlowski, Harmening, and Wagner (2012); and Wylie, Gutierrez-Ibanez, and Iwaniuk (2015). The evolution of owls is described by Ericson (2012), Kang et al. (2018), Ksepka (2017), Salter et al. (2020), Uvaa et al. (2018), and Wink et al. (2009).

WHITE-WINGED DOVE: The basic biology of these large, handsome doves is summarized in Schwertner et al. (2020). Its ecology and behavior are described in Neff (1940); Rabe and Sanders (2010); and Small, Baccus, and Schwertner (2010). Its diet and physiology have been studied extensively, and these studies include Gerson et al. (2018); Martinez del Rio, Wolf, and Haughey (2004); Smith et al. (2015); Smit et al. (2018); Wolf and Martinez del Rio (2000, 2003); and Wolf, Martinez del Rio, and Babson (2002). The evolution of doves is described by Johnson and Weckstein (2011) and Soares et al. (2016).

HUMMINGBIRDS: Detailed accounts of the biology of the three species I discuss here occur in the following Birds of the World articles: Clark and Russell (2020), Baltosser and Scott (2020), and Powers and Wethington (2021). Field guides by Sibley (2000) and Williamson (2001) provide additional general information about these birds. Hummingbird vision is discussed by Altshuler and Wiley (2020), Bergamo (2016), Bergamo et al. (2016, 2019), Goller et al. (2019), and Chitka et al. (2001). Physiology of these birds is described by Bakken and Sabat (2008); Dawson (1982); Powers (1991, 1992); Powers and Nagy (1988); and Welch, Altshuler, and Suarez (2007). Fleming and Kress (2013, chaps. 6 and 7) discuss the evolution and coevolution of hummingbirds and their food plants. Abrahamczyk and Renner (2015) discuss the evolution of North American hummingbirds and their food plants. Brown and Kodric-Brown (1979) describe the features of Arizona hummingbird plants. Mayr (2004) reports on the occurrence of fossil hummingbirds in Europe. McGuire et al. (2014) present a molecular phylogeny of extant hummingbirds.

GILA WOODPECKER: This cavity-nesting specialist and saguaro cacti are both iconic residents of the Sonoran Desert. Its basic ecology and behavior are described by Edwards and Schnell (2020). Placement of its nests is discussed by Inouye, Huntley, and Inouye (1982) and Kerpez and Smith (1990). Woodpecker pecking behavior and tongues are described by Bock (1999); Gibson (2006); Jung et al. (2019); Spring (1965); and Wu, Zhu, and Zhang (2015). Its physiology is discussed by Braun (1969) and Martindale (1983). The biogeography and evolution of woodpeckers has been studied by Garcia-Trejo et al. (2009), Ilsoe et al. (2017), Navarro-Siguenza et al. (2017), and Shakya et al. (2017).

CACTUS WREN: This large wren has been well studied in the Sonoran Desert. A review of its biology occurs in Birds of the World (Hamilton et al. 2020). Anders Anderson and his wife published a book summarizing the results of a thirty-year study in southeastern Arizona (Anderson and Anderson 1973). The cactus wren's social behavior is described by Arnold and Owens (1999) and Fisler (1977). Its nesting behavior and physiology are described by Austin (1974); Facemire, Facemire, and Facemire (1990); Ricklefs and Hainsworth (1968, 1969); Simmons and Martin (1990); and Smith et al. (2017). Discussions of bird intelligence can be found in Boucherie et al. (2019); Ducatez, Clave, and Lefebvre (2015); and Emery (2006). The evolution of wrens and other passerines is described by Barker et al. (2013), Oliveros et al. (2019), and Salvatti et al. (2015).

PHAINOPEPLA: The basic biology of this distinctive winter-spring visitor is summarized by Chu and Walsberg (2020). Its reproduction and population structure are described by Baldassarre et al. (2019), Chu (2002), and Walsberg (1978). Its digestion and physiology are discussed by Weathers and Nagy (1980), Walsberg (1975, 1982), and Walsberg and Thompson (1990). The evolution of passerine social systems is discussed by Akcay and Roughgarden (2007); Brouwer and Griffith (2019); Griffith, Owens, and Thuman (2002); and Kvarnemo (2018). Its evolution is discussed by Oliveros et al. (2019) and Spellman et al. (2008).

HOW MANY EGGS ARE IN YOUR BASKET?

My sources for this discussion include Begon, Townsend, and Harper (2006); Ehrlich, Dobkin, and Wheye (1988); Gill (1990); and Lack (1947b).

SONORAN DESERT MAMMALS

ROUND-TAILED GROUND SQUIRREL: The population ecology and social behavior of this common colonial rodent has been described by Dunford (1977a, 1977b) and Munroe and Koprowski (2011). Its estivation was studied by Walker et al. (1979). Its alarm calls are described by Dunford (1977c), and the evolution of these kinds of calls is discussed by Pollard and Blumstein (2012) and Shelley and Blumstein (2005). The theory of altruistic behavior was pioneered by Hamilton (1964). Evolution of ground squirrels is discussed by Fabre et al. (2012), Harrison et al. (2003), Helgen et al. (2009), and Zelditch et al. (2015).

MERRIAM'S KANGAROO RAT: Because this handsome, bipedal rodent has been the subject of many studies, we know a lot about its basic biology and evolution. Studies dealing with its ecology and behavior include Behrensmeyer, Daly, and Wilson (1986); Bowers (1990); Bradley and Mauer (1971); Jenkins, Rothstein, and Green (1995); Jones (1989); Koontz, Shepherd, and Marshall (2001); Longland and Price (1991); Newmark and Jenkins (2000); and Reynolds (1958). Its physiology has been studied by Nagy (2004), Nagy and Gruchacz (1994), Schmidt-Nielsen and Schmidt-Nielsen (1949), Soholt (1976), Tracy and Walsberg (2000). Ekdale (2016), Kotler and Brown (1988), Mason (2006), Thompson (1982), and Webster and Webster (1980) have studied its hearing. Studies of the community ecology of desert rodents include Brown (1975), Brown (1989), M'Closkey (1981), and Munger and Brown (1981). Finally, evolution of family Heteromyidae has been described by Alexander and Riddle (2005) and Hafner et al. (2007).

WHITE-THROATED WOODRAT: In addition to a detailed Wikipedia account, the ecology and behavior of this rodent is described by Macedo and Mares (1988). Detailed studies of pack rat physiology can be found in Brown (1968), Brown and Lee (1969), Dearing et al. (2008), Meyer and Karasov (1989), and Smith and Betancourt (2006). Packrat body size evolution is discussed by Smith, Betancourt, and Brown (1995) and Smith et al. (2014). Pack rat diets and how they deal with toxic plant chemicals are discussed by Justice (1985); McLister, Sorensen, and Dearing (2004); Miller, Dale, and Dearing (2014); Miller et al. (2016); Skopec, Haley, and Dearing (2007); and Sorenson, Turnbull, and Dearing (2004). Evolution of pack rats is described by Edwards, Fulhorst, and Bradley (2001); Martin (1980); Matocq, Shurtliv, and Feldman (2007); and Riddle and Hafner (1999).

LESSER LONG-NOSED BAT: This is the most common nectar-feeding bat in the Sonoran Desert. Summaries of much of its ecology, diet, behavior, and physiology can be found in several of my publications: Fleming (2004); Fleming and Nassar (2002); Fleming, Fenton, and Fenton (2020); Fleming, Nunez, and Sternberg (1993); and Fleming, Richardson, and Scobie (2021), in addition to two books (Fleming 2003, 2017). The genetic structure of its populations is discussed by Wilkinson and Fleming (1996). Its sensory biology is described by Gonzalez-Terrazas et al. (2016a, 2016b). Tschapka, Gonzales-Terrazas, and Knornschild (2015) describe how its tongue works. Fleming and Kress (2013, chap. 7) and Flores-Abreu et al. (2019) discuss its coevolution with its food plants, particularly columnar cacti and paniculate agaves. The evolution of nectar-feeding phyllostomids is described by Datzmann, Von Helversen, and Mayer (2010); Rojas, Warsi, and Davalos (2016); and Simmons and Wetterer (2002).

COYOTE: This medium-sized carnivore has been studied extensively throughout its range in North America, including urban Tucson. We thus know a lot about many aspects of its biology, which is summarized by Bekoff (1977). Other studies of its ecology and behavior include Bekoff and Wells (1980); Bounds and Shaw (1997); Golightly and Ohmart (1983); Grubbs and Krausmann (2009); Knowlton, Gese, and Jaeger (1999); McKinney and Smith (2007); McClure, Smith, and Shaw (1995); and Wells and Bekoff (1982). Its sensory biology is discussed by Arias-Del Razo et al. (2011); Baker, Shivik, and Jordan (2011); Bender, Bayne, and Brigham (1996); and Jacobs, Deegan, and Crognale (1993). Rosenzweig (1966) discusses the community structure of North American carnivores. The evolution of canids is described by Hody and Kays (2018), Nyakatura and Bininda-Emonds (2012), and Sinding et al. (2018).

BOBCAT: This relatively small felid is widespread in North America. Many features of its basic biology are summarized in Hansen (2007) and Lariviere and Walton (1997). Studies dealing with its ecology and behavior include Cavanaugh (2013), Haynes et al. (2010), Janacek et al. (2006), Jones and Smith (1979), Lawhead (1984), and Riley et al. (2003). Its coexistence with other carnivores is discussed by Hass (2009) and Rosenzweig (1966), among others. Felid evolution is discussed by Cuff et al. (2015), Piras et al. (2013), and Werdelin et al. (2010).

JAVELINA: This sociable, piglike mammal is a recent arrival in the Sonoran Desert. Studies dealing with its ecology and behavior include Bellantoni and Krausman (1993), Bigler (1974), Eddy (1961), Gabor and Hellgren (2000), Ilse and Helgren (1995), and Romero et al. (2013). Its population genetics are described by Biondo et al. (2014) and Cooper et al. (2010, 2011). Its physiology is discussed by Zervanos and Hadley (1973) and Zervanos and Day (1977). Discussions of its diet include

Lochmiller, Hellgren, and Grant (1986); Neal (1959); Nogueira-Filho (2005); and Theimer and Bateman (1992). Its evolution is discussed by Dutra et al. (2017).

SONORAN DESERT PLANTS

SAGUARO CACTUS: This icon of the Sonoran Desert has an extensive literature so that its biology is well known. David Yetman and colleagues (2020) provide a summary of much of this literature. My research on this species is summarized in Fleming (2002) and Fleming et al. (2001). Studies of its demography, seed germination, and nurse plant relationships include Alcorn and Kurtz (1959); Drezner (2006, 2007); Pierson and Turner (1998); Pierson, Turner, and Betancourt (2013); Rojas-Arechiga and Vazquez-Yanes (2000); Sosa and Fleming (2002); and Steenburgh and Lowe (1968). Its basic physiology and water storage are discussed by Gibson and Nobel (1986) and McAuliffe and Janzen (1986). Its role as a keystone species is discussed by Drezner (2014) and Renzi, Peachey, and Gerst et al. (2019). Evolution of Cactaceae is described by Hernandez-Hernandez et al. (2011, 2014) and Wallace (2002).

FOOTHILLS PALO VERDE: This common green-stemmed tree is closely associated with saguaro cacti and often serves as its nurse plant. The book by Turner, Bowers, and Burgess (1995) provides an overview of the ecology of this species. Additional studies dealing with its ecology include Bowers and Turner (2001); Bowers, Turner, and Burgess (2004); Eilts and Huxman (2013); Goldberg and Turner (1986); McAuliffe and Hammerlynck (2010); Munson et al. (2012); and Stuart, Gries, and Hope (2006). Its nurse plant ecology is discussed by Drezner (2006, 2007), McAuliffe (1984), and Tewksbury and Lloyd (2001). Its physiology is discussed by Bossard and Rejmanek (1992), Gibson (1998), Guo et al. (2018), Szarek and Woodhouse (1978a, 1978b), and Shaw (2015). Allelopathy is treated by Mahall and Calloway (1992) and Schafer et al. (2012). The evolution of Fabaceae is discussed by Bruneau et al. (2008), the Legume Phylogeny Working Group (2013, 2017), and Soltis et al. (2018).

DESERT MISTLETOE: These hemiparasites have an interesting lifestyle and interact with many other desert organisms. As a result, the literature on their biology is quite extensive. Accounts of their ecology include papers by Aukema (2001, 2003), Aukema and Martinez del Rio (2002a, 2002b), Lei (2000, 2001), Lira-Noriega and Peterson (2014), Lira-Noriega et al. (2015), Mathiasen et al. (2008), Spurrier and Smith (2006), and Wiesenborn (2016). Studies of mistletoe host specificity include Lara and Perez (2009), Rodl and Ward (2002), and Yule and Bronstein (2018). Its physiology is discussed by Ehleringer and Marshall

(1995), Glatzel and Geils (2009), and Schulze and Ehleringer (1984). The evolution of mistletoes is described by Kuijt (1997), Magallon et al. (2015), Nickrent (2020), and Overton (1997), among others.

A REVIEW OF SONORAN DESERT ECOSYSTEM PROCESSES AND THE EVOLUTION OF SOME OF ITS ANIMALS AND PLANTS

My general discussion of energy flow through ecosystems is based on material that can be found in any ecology textbook (e.g., Ricklefs [1990], chap. 11; Begon, Townsend, and Harper [2006], chap. 17). Hadley and Szarek (1981) discuss biological productivity in deserts. Martinez del Rio, Wolf, and Haughey (2004) and Fleming (2002) discuss adaptations involved in the mutualistic interaction between white-winged doves and saguaros, respectively. Darwin's famous "grandeur" quote comes from *The Origin of Species* (1859, 478).

HUMANS IN THE SONORAN DESERT

My overview of the history of humans in the Sonoran Desert comes from Niethammer (2020). Felger and Moser (1985) describe in detail the lives of Seri Indians. Recent discussions of the ecology and activities of Native Americans in Arizona and Sonora include Hill et al. (2015), Mitchell et al. (2020), and Rea (1981). Population trends in Phoenix, Tucson, and Hermosillo come from the website https://www.macrotrends.net.

3. CONSERVATION CONCERNS IN THE NORTHERN SONORAN DESERT

THE CONSERVATION STATUS OF SOME SONORAN DESERT VERTEBRATES

The current status of certain Sonoran Desert vertebrates comes from the website https://www.iucnredlist.org.

MAJOR THREATS TO THIS DESERT

This section is based on the review by Marazzi et al. (2015). Papers discussing the effects of urbanization (sensu lato) on Sonoran Desert vertebrates and plants include Ackley et al. (2015); Germaine, Schweinsburg, and Germaine (2001); Green and Baker (2003); Kwaitkowski et al. (2008); Mills, Dunning, and Bates (1989); Sullivan, Leavitt, and Sullivan (2017); and Walker et al. (2009). The effects of livestock on habitats in the U.S. southwest are discussed by Blydenstein et al. (1957), Fleischner (1994), and Turner (1990). Observations on the effects of agriculture on Sonoran Desert plants occur in Castellanos et al. (2005) and Lewis, Kaye, and Kinzig (2014), among others.

Climate trends and their effects on Sonoran Desert organisms have an extensive literature. Papers on climate trends include Notaro, Mauss, and Williams (2012); Pierson, Turner, and Betancourt (2013); and Weiss and Overpeck (2005). Effects of climate change on reptiles are discussed by Barrows et al. (2016); Flesch, Rosen, and Holm (2017); and Griffs-Kyle et al. (2018). Papers on birds include Bateman et al. (2020), Iknayan and Beissinger (2018), McCreedy and Van Riper (2015), Riddel et al. (2019), and Smith et al. (2017). Papers on mammals include Moritz et al. (2008); Moses, Frey, and Roemer (2012); Parra and Monahan (2008); and Riddell et al. (2021). Papers on plants include Batchelet et al. (2016) and Kimball et al. (2010).

CONSERVATION OF THE SONORAN DESERT

An example of a futurist is Kaku (2018). Wilson (2016) discusses the concept of saving one-half of Earth to conserve its biodiversity.

THE EXTENT OF PROTECTED LANDS: This information comes from Wikipedia accounts of the protected lands in Arizona and Sonora. Aslan (2021) and Gray, Dickson, and Zachmann (2014) discuss Sonoran Desert management issues and fire regimes, respectively.

THE SONORAN DESERT CONSERVATION PLAN: This plan is described by Cohn (2001) and Huckleberry (2002). Further information about this plan can be found on the website of the Coalition for Sonoran Desert Protection (https://www.sonorandesert.org).

SOME FINAL WORDS FROM THE THREE AUTHORS THAT INSPIRED ME TO WRITE THIS BOOK

These quotes come from their books (*The Immense Journey, A Sand County Almanac,* and *The Meaning of Evolution*). The song "Evolution" is the third track on Kitty Margolis's 1994 album *Evolution.* It can be heard at https://www.all-music.com/album/evolution-mw0000114949.

BIBLIOGRAPHY

Abrahamczyk, S., and S. S. Renner. 2015. "The Temporal Build-Up of Hummingbird/Plant Mutualisms in North America and Temperate South America." *BMC Evolutionary Biology* 15.

Ackley, J. W., J. Wu, M. J. Angilletta, S. W. Myint, and B. Sullivan. 2015. "Rich Lizards: How Affluence and Land Cover Influence the Diversity and Abundance of Desert Reptiles Persisting in an Urban Landscape." *Biological Conservation* 182:87–92.

Akcay, E., and J. Roughgarden. 2007. "Extra-Pair Paternity in Birds: Review of the Genetic Benefits." *Evolutionary Ecology Research* 9 (5): 855–68.

Alcorn, S. M., and J. Kurtz, E.B. 1959. "Some Factors Affecting the Germination of Seed of the Saguaro Cactus (*Carnegiea gigantea*)." *American Journal of Botany* 46:526–29.

Alexander, L. F., and B. R. Riddle. 2005. "Phylogenetics of the New World Rodent Family Heteromyidae." *Journal of Mammalogy* 86:366–79.

Altshuler, D. L., and D. R. Wiley. 2020. "Hummingbird Vision." *Current Biology* 30:R95–R111.

Alvarez, L. W., W. Alvarez, F. Asaro, and H. V. Michel. 1980. "Extraterrestrial Cause for the Cretaceous-Tertiary Extinction." *Science* 208:1095–108.

Anderson, A., and A. A. Anderson. 1973. *The Cactus Wren.* Tucson: University of Arizona Press.

Andersson, M., and R. A. Norberg. 1981. "Evolution of Reversed Sexual Size Dimorphism and Role Partitioning Among Predatory Birds, with a Size Scaling of Flight Performance." *Biological Journal of the Linnean Society* 15:105–30.

Angilletta, M. J., Jr., and M. W. Sears. 2003. "Is Parental Care the Key to Understanding Endothermy in Birds and Mammals?" *American Naturalist* 162:821–25.

Arias–Del Razo, I., L. Hernandez, J. W. Laundre, and O. Myers. 2011. "Do Predator and Prey Foraging Activity Patterns Match? A Study of Coyotes (*Canis latrans*), and Lagomorphs (*Lepus californicus* and *Sylvilagus audobonii*)." *Journal of Arid Environments* 75:112–18.

Arnold, K. E., and I. P. F. Owens. 1999. "Cooperative Breeding in Birds: The Role of Ecology." *Behavioral Ecology* 10:465–71.

Artuso, C., C. S. Houston, D. G. Smith, and C. Rohner. 2020. "Great Horned Owl (*Bubo virginianus*)." Birds of the World. Last modified March 4, 2020. https://doi.org/10.2173/bow.grhowl.01.

Aslan, C. E. 2021. "Land Management Objectives and Activities in the Face of Projected Fire Regime Change in the Sonoran Desert." *Journal of Environmental Management* 280:1–10.

Audsley, B. W., C. E. Bock, Z. F. Jones, J. H. Bock, and H. M. Smith. 2006. "Lizard Abundance in an Exurban Southwestern Savanna, and the Possible Importance of Roadrunner Predation." *American Naturalist* 155:395–401.

Aukema, J. A. 2001. "Dispersal and Spatial Distribution of the Desert Mistletoe, *Phoradendron californicum*, at Multiple Scales: Patterns, Processes, and Mechanisms." PhD diss., University of Arizona.

Aukema, J. A. 2003. "Vectors, Viscin, and Viscaceae: Mistletoes as Parasites, Mutualists, and Resources." *Frontiers in Ecology and the Environment* 1:212–19.

Aukema, J. A., and C. Martinez del Rio. 2002a. "Where Does a Fruit-Eating Bird Deposit Mistletoe Seeds? Seed Deposition Patterns and an Experiment." *Ecology* 83:3489–96.

Aukema, J. A., and C. Martinez del Rio. 2002b. "Variation in Mistletoe Seed Deposition: Effects of Intra- and Interspecific Host Characteristics." *Ecography* 25:139–44.

Austin, G. T. 1974. "Nesting Success of the Cactus Wren in Relation to Nest Orientation." *Condor* 76:216–17.

Averill-Murray, R. C., C. R. Darst, K. J. Field, and L. J. Allison. 2012. "A New Approach to Conservation of the Mojave Desert Tortoise." *Bioscience* 62:893–99.

Averill-Murray, R. C., C. R. Darst, N. Strout, and M. Wong. 2013. "Conserving Population Linkages for the Mojave Desert Tortoise (*Gopherus agassizii*)." *Herpetological Conservation and Biology* 8:1–15.

Avise, J. C. 2004. *Molecular Markers, Natural History, and Evolution*. 2nd ed. Sunderland, Mass.: Sinauer Associates.

Avise, J. C. 2015. "Evolutionary Perspectives on Clonal Reproduction in Vertebrate Animals." *Proceedings of the National Academy of Sciences of the United States of America* 112:8867–73.

Baker, J. M., J. Shivik, and K. E. Jordan. 2011. "Tracking of Food Quantity by Coyotes (*Canis latrans*)." *Behavioural Processes* 88:72–75.

Bakken, B. H., and P. Sabat. 2008. "The Mechanisms and Ecology of Water Balance in Hummingbirds." *Ornitologia Neotropical* 19:501–9.

Baldassarre, D. T., L. Campagna, H. A. Thomassen, J. W. Atwell, M. Chu, L. H. Crampton, R. C. Fleischer, and C. Riehl. 2019. "GPS Tracking and Population Genomics Suggest Itinerant Breeding Across Drastically Different Habitats in the Phainopepla." *Auk* 136:1–12.

Baltosser, W. H., and P. E. Scott. 2020. "Costa's Hummingbird (*Calypte costae*)." Birds of the World. Last modified March 4, 2020. https://doi.org/10.2173/bow.coshum.01.

Barker, F. K., K. J. Burns, J. Klicka, S. M. Lanyon, and I. J. Lovette. 2013. "Going to Extremes: Contrasting Rates of Diversification in a Recent Radiation of New World Passerine Birds." *Systematic Biology* 62:298–320.

Barrows, C. W., J. Hoines, M. S. Varnstad, M. Murphy-Mariscal, K. Lalumiere, and J. Heintz. 2016. "Using Citizen Scientists to Assess Climate Change Shifts in Desert Reptile Communities." *Biological Conservation* 195:82–88.

Batchelet, D., K. Ferschweiler, T. Sheehan, and J. Strittholt. 2016. "Climate Change Effects on Southern California Deserts." *Journal of Arid Environments* 127:17–29.

Bateman, B. L., C. Wilsey, L. Talor, J. Wu, G. S. LeBaron, and G. Langham. 2020. "North American Birds Require Mitigation and Adaptation to Reduce Vulnerability to Climate Change." *Conservation Science and Practice* 2:e242.

Beck, D. D. 1990. "Ecology and Behavior of the Gila Monster in Southwestern Utah." *Journal of Herpetology* 24:54–68.

Beck, D. D. 1995. "Ecology and Energetics of Three Sympatric Rattlesnake Species in the Sonoran Desert." *Journal of Herpetology* 29:211–23.

Beck, D. D., and R. D. Jennings. 2003. "Habitat Use by Gila Monsters: The Importance of Shelters." *Herpetological Monographs* 17:111–29.

Bednarz, J. C. 1987. "Pair and Group Reproductive Success, Polyandry, and Cooperative Breeding in Harris's Hawks." *Auk* 104:393–404.

Bednarz, J. C. 1988. "Cooperative Hunting Harris' Hawks (*Parabuteo unicinctus*)." *Science* 239:1525–27.

Bednarz, J. C., and J. D. Ligon. 1988. "A Study of the Ecological Bases of Cooperative Breeding in the Harris' Hawk." *Ecology* 69:1176–87.

Begon, M., C. R. Townsend, and J. L. Harper. 2006. *Ecology from Individuals to Populations*. 4th ed. Malden, Mass.: Blackwell.

Behrensmeyer, P., M. Daly, and M. I. Wilson. 1986. "Range Use Patterns and Spatial Relationships of Merriam's Kangaroo Rats (*Dipodomys merriami*)." *Behaviour* 96:187–209.

Bekoff, M. 1977. "*Canis latrans* Say 1823." *Mammalian Species* 79:1–9.

Bekoff, M., and M. C. Wells. 1980. "The Social Ecology of Coyotes." *Scientific American* 242:130–48.

Bellantoni, E. S., and P. R. Krausman. 1993. "Habitat Use by Collared Peccaries in an Urban Environment." *Southwestern Naturalist* 38:345–51.

Bender, D. J., E. M. Bayne, and R. M. Brigham. 1996. "Lunar Condition Influences Coyote (*Canis latrans*) Howling." *American Midland Naturalist* 136:413–17.

Bennett, A. F., and J. A. Ruben. 1986. "The Metabolic and Thermoregulatory Status of Therapsids." In *The Ecology and Biology of Mammal-Like Reptiles*, edited by N. Hotton III, P. D. MacLean, J. Roth, and E. C. Roth, 207–18. Washington, D.C.: Smithsonian Institution Press.

Benoit, J., V. Fernandez, P. R. Manger, and B. S. Rubidge. 2017. "Endocranial Casts of Pre-Mammalian Therapsids Reveal an Unexpected Neurological Diversity at the Deep Evolutionary Root of Mammals." *Brain, Behavior, and Evolution* 90 (4): 311–33. https://doi.org/10.1159/000481525.

Bergamo, P. J. 2016. "Flower Colour and Visitation Rates of *Costus arabicus* Support the 'Bee Avoidance' Hypothesis for Red-Reflecting Hummingbird-Pollinated Flowers." *Functional Ecology* 30:710–20.

Bergamo, P. J., A. R. Rech, V. L. G. Brito, and M. Sazima. 2016. "Flower Colour and Visitation Rates of *Costus arabicus* Support the 'Bee Avoidance' Hypothesis for Red-Reflecting Hummingbird-Pollinated Flowers." *Functional Ecology* 30:710–20.

Bergamo, P. J., M. Wolowski, F. J. Telles, V. L. Garcia de Britos, I. G. Varassin, and M. Sazima. 2019. "Bracts and Long-Tube Flowers of Hummingbird-Pollinated Plants Are Conspicuous to Hummingbirds but Not to Bees." *Biological Journal of the Linnean Society* 126:533–44.

Berry, K. H. 1986. "Desert Tortoise (*Gopherus agassizii*) Relocation: Implications of Social Behavior and Movements." *Herpetologica* 42:113–25.

Bhullar, B-A. S., and K. T. Smith. 2008. "Helodermatid Lizard from the Miocene of Florida, the Evolution of the Dentary in Helodermatidae, and Comments on Dentary Morphology in Varanoidea." *Journal of Herpetology* 42:286–302.

Bigler, W. J. 1974. "Seasonal Movements and Activity Patterns of the Collared Peccary." *Journal of Mammalogy* 55:851–55.

Bininda-Emonds, O. R. P., M. Cardillo, K. E. Jones, R. D. MacPhee, R. M. D. Beck, R. Grenyer, S. A. Price, R. A. Vos, J. L. Gittleman, and A. Purvis. 2007. "The Delayed Rise of Present-Day Mammals." *Nature* 446:507–12.

Biondo, C., P. Izar, C. Y. Miyakib, and V. S. R. Bussaba. 2014. "Social Structure of Collared Peccaries (*Pecari tajacu*): Does Relatedness Matter?" *Behavioural Processes* 109:70–78.

Bjorndal, K. A., and A. Carr. 1989. "Variation in Clutch Size and Egg Size in the Green Turtle Nesting Population at Tortuguero, Costa Rica." *Herpetologica* 45:181–89.

Bjurlin, C. D., and J. A. Bissonette. 2004. "Survival During Early Life Stages of the Desert Tortoise (*Gopherus agassizii*) in the South-Central Mojave Desert." *Journal of Herpetology* 38:527–35.

Blydenstein, J., C. R. Hungerford, G. I. Day, and R. R. Humphrey. 1957. "Effect of Domestic Livestock Exclusion on Vegetation in the Sonoran Desert." *Ecology* 38:522–26.

Boal, C. W. 2001. "Nonrandom Mating and Productivity of Adult and Subadult Cooper's Hawks." *Condor* 103:381–85.

Boal, C. W., and R. W. Mannan. 1998. "Nest-Site Selection by Cooper's Hawks in an Urban Environment." *Journal of Wildlife Management* 62:864–71.

Boal, C. W., and R. W. Mannan. 1999. "Comparative Breeding Ecology of Cooper's Hawks in Urban and Exurban Areas of Southeastern Arizona." *Journal of Wildlife Management* 63:77–84.

Bock, W. J. 1999. "Functional and Evolutionary Morphology of Woodpeckers." *Ostrich* 70:23–31.

Bossard, C. C., and M. Rejmanek. 1992. "Why Have Green Stems?" *Functional Ecology* 6:197–205.

Boucherie, P. H., M.-C. Loretto, J. J. M. Massen, and T. Bugyar. 2019. "What Constitutes 'Social Complexity' and 'Social Intelligence' in Birds? Lessons From Ravens." *Behavioral Ecology and Sociobiology* 73.

Bounds, D. L., and W. W. Shaw. 1997. "Movements of Suburban and Rural Coyotes at Saguaro National Park, Arizona." *Southwestern Naturalist* 42:94–99.

Bowers, J. E., and R. M. Turner. 2001. "Dieback and Episodic Mortality of *Cercidium microphyllum* (Foothill Paloverde), a Dominant Sonoran Desert Tree." *Journal of the Torrey Botanical Society* 128:128–40.

Bowers, J. E., R. M. Turner, and T. L. Burgess. 2004. "Temporal and Spatial Patterns in Emergence and Early Survival of Perennial Plants in the Sonoran Desert." *Plant Ecology* 172:107–19.

Bowers, M. A. 1990. "Exploitation of Seed Aggregates by Merriam's Kangaroo Rat: Harvesting Rates and Predatory Risk." *Ecology* 71:2334–44.

Bradley, W. G., and R. A. Mauer. 1971. "Reproduction and Food Habits of Merriam's Kangaroo Rat, *Dipodomys merriami*." *Journal of Mammalogy* 52:497–507.

Braun, E. J. 1969. "Metabolism and Water Balance of the Gila Woodpecker and Gilded Flicker in the Sonoran Desert." PhD diss., University of Arizona.

Brennan, T. C., and A. T. Holycross. 2006. *Amphibians and Reptiles in Arizona*. Phoenix: Arizona Game and Fish Department.

Brouwer, L., and S. C. Griffith. 2019. "Extra-Pair Paternity in Birds." *Molecular Ecology* 28:4864–82.

Brown, J. H. 1968. *Adaptation to Environmental Temperature in Two Species of Woodrats*, Neotoma cinerea *and* N. albigula. Miscellaneous Publications 135. Ann Arbor: Museum of Zoology, University of Michigan.

Brown, J. H. 1975. "Geographical Ecology of Desert Rodents." In *Ecology and Evolution of Communities*, edited by M. L. Cody and J. M. Diamond, 315–41. Cambridge, Mass: Belknap Press.

Brown, J. H., and A. Kodric-Brown. 1979. Convergence, competition, and mimicry in a temperate community of hummingbird-pollinated flowers. Ecology 60:1022-1035.

Brown, J. H., and A. K. Lee. 1969. "Bergmann's Rule and Climatic Adaptation in Woodrats (*Neotoma*)." *Evolution* 23:329–38.

Brown, J. S. 1989. "Desert Rodent Community Structure: A Test of Four Mechanisms of Coexistence." *Ecological Monographs* 59:1–20.

Bruneau, A., M. Mercure, G. P. Lewis, and P. S. Herendeen. 2008. "Phylogenetic Patterns and Diversification in the Caesalpinioid Legumes." *Botany-Botanique* 86:697–718.

Brusatte, S. L. 2016. "Evolution: How Some Birds Survived While All Other Dinosaurs Died." *Current Biology* 26 (10):R415–R417.

Brusatte, S. L. 2018. *The Rise and Fall of the Dinosaurs*. New York: William Morrow.

Brusatte, S. L., J. K. O'Connor, and E. D. Jarvis. 2015. "The Origin and Diversification of Birds." *Current Biology* 25 (19):R888–R898.

Bull, J. J. 1980. "Sex Determination in Reptiles." *Quarterly Review of Biology* 55:3–21.

Burns, K. J., S. J. Hackett, and N. K. Klein. 2002. "Phylogenetic Relationships and Morphological Diversity in Darwin's Finches and Their Relatives." *Evolution* 56:1240–52.

Burt, W. H., and R. P. Grossenheider. 1964. *A Field Guide to the Mammals*. Boston: Houghton Mifflin.

Caccone, A., G. Gentile, J. P. Gibbs, T. H. Fritts, H. L. Snell, J. Betts, and J. R. Powell. 2002. "Phylogeography and History of Giant Galapagos Tortoises." *Evolution* 56:2052–66.

Caccone, A., J. P. Gibbs, V. Ketmaier, E. Suatoni, and J. R. Powell. 1999. "Origin and Evolutionary Relationships of Giant Galapagos Tortoises." *Proceedings of the National Academy of Sciences of the United States of America* 96:13223–28.

Calder, W. A., III. 1984. *Size, Function, and Life History*. Cambridge, Mass.: Harvard University Press.

Calder, W. A., and K. Schmidt-Nielsen. 1967. "Temperature Regulation and Evaporation in the Pigeon and the Roadrunner." *American Journal of Physiology* 213:883–89.

Carey, C., and M. L. Morton. 1971. "A Comparison of Salt and Water Regulation in California Quail (*Lophortyx californicus*) and Gambel's Quail (*Lophortyx gambelii*)." *Comparative Biochemistry and Physiology A* 39A:75–101.

Carr, A. 1980. "Some Problems of Sea Turtle Ecology." *American Zoologist* 20:489–98.

Castellanos, A. E., M. J. Martinez, J. M. Llanoa, W. L. Halvorson, M. Espiricueta, and I. Espejel. 2005. "Successional Trends in Sonoran Desert Abandoned Agricultural Fields in Northern Mexico." *Journal of Arid Environments* 60:437–55.

Castoe, T. A., and C. L. Parkinson. 2006. "Bayesian Mixed Models and the Phylogeny of Pitvipers (Viperidae: Serpentes)." *Molecular Phylogenetics and Evolution* 39:91–110.

Castoe, T. A., C. L. Spencer, and C. L. Parkinson. 2007. "Phylogeographic Structure and Historical Demography of the Western Diamondback Rattlesnake (*Crotalus atrox*): A Perspective on North American Desert Biogeography." *Molecular Phylogenetics and Evolution* 42:193–212.

Cavanaugh, C. C. 2013. "Perceptions of Urban Bobcats by Residents of the Tucson Area: Assessing the Effectiveness of Education and Community Outreach." Bachelor's thesis, University of Arizona, Tucson. http://hdl.handle.net/10150/297525.

Chase, M. W., J. M. Christenhuiz, M. F. Fay, J. W. Byng, W. S. Judd, D. E. Soltis, D. J. Mabberley, et al. 2016. "An Update of the Angiosperm Phylogeny Group Classification for the Orders and Families of Flowering Plants: APG IV." *Botanical Journal of the Linnean Society* 181 (1): 1–20.

Chitka, L., J. Spaethe, A. Schimdt, and A. Hickelsberger. 2001. "Adaptation, Constraint, and Chance in the Evolution of Flower Color and Pollinator Color Vision." In *Cognitive Ecology of Pollination*, edited by L. Chitka and J. D. Thompson, 106–26. Cambridge: Cambridge University Press.

Chu, M. 2002. "Social and Genetic Monogamy in Territorial and Loosely Colonial Populations of Phainopepla (*Phainopepla nitens*)." *Auk* 119:770–77.

Chu, M., and G. Walsberg. 2020. "Phainopepla (*Phainopepla nitens*)." Birds of the World. Last modified March 4, 2020. https://doi.org/10.2173/bow.phaino.01.

Clark, C. J., and S. M. Russell. 2020. "Anna's Hummingbird (*Calypte anna*)." Birds of the World. Last modified March 4, 2020. https://doi.org/10.2173/bow.annhum.01.

Clark, R. W., G. W. Schuett, R. A. Repp, M. Amarello, C. F. Smith, and H.-W. Hermann. 2014. "Mating Systems, Reproductive Success, and Sexual Selection in Secretive Species: A Case Study of the Western Diamond-Backed Rattlesnake, *Crotalus atrox*." *Plos One* 9:e90616, 1–12.

Cohn, J. P. 2001. "Sonoran Desert Conservation." *Bioscience* 51:606–10.

Conniff, R. 2009. *The Species Seekers: Heroes, Fools, and the Mad Pursuit of Life on Earth.* New York: Norton.

Cooper, J. D., P. M. Waser, D. Gopurenko, E. C. Hellgren, T. M. Gabor, and J. A. DeWoody. 2010. "Measuring Sex-Biased Dispersal in Social Mammals: Comparisons of Nuclear and Mitochondrial Genes in Collared Peccaries." *Journal of Mammalogy* 91:1413–24.

Cooper, J. D., P. M. Waser, E. C. Hellgren, T. M. Gabor, and J. A. Dewoody. 2011. "Is Sexual Monomorphism a Predictor of Polygynandry? Evidence from a Social Mammal, the Collared Peccary." *Behavioral Ecology and Sociobiology* 65:775–85.

Cooper, W. E. 2009. "Flight Initiation Distance Decreases During Social Activity in Lizards (*Sceloporus virgatus*)." *Behavioral Ecology and Sociobiology* 63:1765–71.

Cooper, W. E., Jr., and N. Burns. 1987. "Social Significance of Ventrolateral Coloration in the Fence Lizard, *Sceloporus undulatus*." *Animal Behaviour* 35:526–32.

Cooper, W. E., Jr., C. S. Deperno, and J. Arnett. 1994. "Prolonged Poststrike Elevation in Tongue Flicking Rate with Rapid Onset in Gila Monster, *Heloderma suspectum*: Relation to Diet and Foraging and Implications for Evolution of Chemosensory Searching." *Journal of Chemical Ecology* 20:2867–80.

Coulson, J. O., and T. D. Coulson. 2013. "Reexamining Cooperative Hunting in Harris's Hawk (*Parabuteo unicinctus*): Large Prey or Challenging Habitats?" *Auk* 130:548–52.

Crews, D., and K. T. Fitzgerald. 1980. "'Sexual' Behavior in Parthenogenetic Lizards (*Cnemidophorus*)." *Proceedings of the National Academy of Sciences of the United States of America* 77:499–502.

Crews, D., M. Grassman, and J. Lindzey. 1987. "Behavioral Facilitation of Reproduction in Sexual and Unisexual Whiptail Lizards." *Proceedings of the National Academy of Sciences of the United States of America* 83:9547–50.

Cuellar, O. 1977. "Animal Parthenogenesis." *Science* 197:837–43.

Cuff, A. R., M. Randau, J. Head, J. R. Hutchinson, S. E. Pierce, and A. Goswami. 2015. "Big Cat, Small Cat: Reconstructing Body Size Evolution in Living and Extinct Felidae." *Journal of Evolutionary Biology* 28:1516–25.

Cunningham, J. D. 1959. "Reproduction and Food of Some California Snakes." *Herpetologica* 15:17–19.

Dahn, H. A., J. L. Strickland, A. Osorioa, T. J. Colston, and C. L. Parkinson. 2018. "Hidden Diversity Within the Depauperate Genera of the Snake Tribe Lampropeltini (Serpentes, Colubridae)." *Molecular Phylogenetics and Evolution* 129:214–25.

Darlington, P. J., Jr. 1957. *Zoogeography: The Geographical Distribution of Animals.* New York: John Wiley & Sons.

Darwin, C. 1839. *The Voyage of the Beagle.* London: John Murray.

Darwin, C. 1859. *The Origin of Species.* London: John Murray.

Darwin, C. 1871. *The Descent of Man and Selection in Relation to Sex.* London: John Murray.

Datzmann, T., O. Von Helversen, and F. Mayer. 2010. "Evolution of Nectarivory in Phyllostomid Bats (Phyllostomidae Gray, 1825, Chiroptera: Mammalia)." *BMC Evolutionary Biology* 10.

Davis, H. T., A. M. Long, T. A. Campbell, and M. L. Morrison. 2018. "Nest Defense Behavior of Greater Roadrunners (*Geococcyx californianus*) in South Texas." *Wilson Journal of Ornithology* 130:788–92.

Davis, J. R., and D. F. Denardo. 2009. "Water Supplementation Affects the Behavioral and Physiological Ecology of Gila Monsters (*Heloderma suspectum*) in the Sonoran Desert." *Physiological and Biochemical Zoology* 82:739–48.

Davis, J. R., and D. F. Denardo. 2010. "Seasonal Patterns of Body Condition, Hydration State, and Activity of Gila Monsters (*Heloderma suspectum*) at a Sonoran Desert Site." *Journal of Herpetology* 44:83–93.

Dawson, J. W., and R. W. Mannan. 1991. "Dominance Hierarchies and Helper Contributions in Harris' Hawks." *Auk* 108:649–60.

Dawson, W. R. 1982. "Evaporative Losses of Water by Birds." *Comparative Biochemistry and Physiology A* 71A:495–509.

Dearing, M. D., J. S. Forbey, J. D. McLister, and L. Santos. 2008. "Ambient Temperature Influences Diet Selection and Physiology of an Herbivorous Mammal, *Neotoma albigula*." *Physiological and Biochemical Zoology* 81:891–97.

Diaz de la Vega-Perez, A. H., V. H. Jimenez-Arcos, N. L. Manriquez-Moran, and F. R. Mendez de la Xruz. 2013. "Conservatism of Thermal Preferences Between Parthenogenetic *Aspidoscelis cozumela* Complex (Squamata: Teiidae) and Their Parental Species." *Herpetological Journal* 23:93–104.

Diller, L. V., and R. L. Wallace. 1996. "Comparative Ecology of Two Snake Species (*Crotalus viridis* and *Pituophis melanoleucus*) in Southwestern Idaho." *Herpetologica* 52:343–60.

Dimmitt, M. A. 2015. "Biomes and Communities of the Sonoran Desert Region." In *A Natural History of the Sonoran Desert*, edited by S. J. Phillips, M. A. Dimmitt, P. W. Comus, and L. M. Brewer, 5–19. Tucson: Arizona-Sonora Desert Museum Press.

Dimmitt, M. A., P. W. Comus, and L. M. Brewer, eds. 2015. *A Natural History of the Sonoran Desert*. 2nd ed. Tucson: Arizona-Sonora Desert Press.

Doak, D., P. Kareiva, and B. Klepetka. 1994. "Modeling Population Viability for the Desert Tortoise in the Western Mojave Desert." *Ecological Applications* 4:444–60.

Douglas, M. E., M. R. Douglas, G. W. Schuett, and L. W. Porras. 2006. "Evolution of Rattlesnakes (Viperidae; *Crotalus*) in the Warm Deserts of Western North America Shaped by Neogene Vicariance and Quaternary Climate Change." *Molecular Ecology* 15:3353–74.

Drezner, T. D. 2006. "Plant Facilitation in Extreme Environments: The Non-Random Distribution of Saguaro Cacti (*Carnegiea gigantea*) Under Their Nurse Associates and the Relationship to Nurse Architecture." *Journal of Arid Environments* 65:46–61.

Drezner, T. D. 2007. "An Analysis of Winter Temperature and Dew Point Under the Canopy of a Common Sonoran Desert Nurse and the Implications for Positive Plant Interactions." *Journal of Arid Environments* 69:554–68.

Drezner, T. D. 2014. "The Keystone Saguaro (*Carnegiea gigantea*, Cactaceae): A Review of Its Ecology, Associations, Reproduction, Limits, and Demographics." *Plant Ecology* 215:581–95.

Ducatez, S., J. Clave, and L. Lefebvre. 2015. "Ecological Generalism and Behavioural Innovation in Birds: Technical Intelligence or the Simple Incorporation of New Foods?" *Journal of Animal Ecology* 84:79–89.

Dunford, C. 1977a. "Behavioral Limitation of Round-Tailed Ground Squirrel Density." *Ecology* 58:1254–68.

Dunford, C. 1977b. "Social System of Round-Tailed Ground Squirrels." *Animal Behaviour* 25:885–906.

Dunford, C. 1977c. "Kin Selection for Ground Squirrel Alarm Calls." *American Naturalist* 111:782–85.

Dunson, W. A., M. K. Dunson, and R. D. Ohmart. 1976. "Evidence for the Presence of Nasal Salt Glands in the Roadrunner and the Coturnix Quail." *Journal of Experimental Zoology* 198:209–16.

Dutra, R. P., D. de Melo Casali, R. V. Missagia, G. M. Gasparini, F. A. Perini, and M. A. Cozzuol. 2017. "Phylogenetic Systematics of Peccaries (Tayassuidae: Artiodactyla) and a Classification of South American Tayassuids." *Journal of Mammalian Evolution* 24:345–58.

Duvall, D. 1979. "Western Fence Lizard (*Sceloporus occidentalis*) Chemical Signals." *Journal of Experimental Zoology* 210:321–26.

Dwyer, J. F., and J. C. Bednarz. 2020. "Harris's Hawk (*Parabuteo unicinctus*)." Birds of the World. Last modified March 4, 2020. https://doi.org/10.2173/bow.hrshaw.01.

Eddy, T. A. 1961. "Foods and Feeding Patterns of the Collared Peccary in Southern Arizona." *Journal of Wildlife Management* 25:248–57.

Edwards, C. W., C. F. Fulhorst, and R. D. Bradley. 2001. "Molecular Phylogenetics of the *Neotoma albigula* Species Group: Further Evidence of a Paraphyletic Assemblage." *Journal of Mammalogy* 82:267–79.

Edwards, H. H., and G. D. Schnell. 2020. "Gila Woodpecker (*Melanerpes uropygialis*)." Birds of the World. Last modified March 4, 2020. https://doi.org/10.2173/bow.gilwoo.01.

Ehleringer, J. R., and J. D. Marshall. 1995. "Water Relations." In *Parasitic Plants*, edited by M. C. Press and J. D. Graves, 125–40. London: Chapman and Hall.

Ehrlich, P. R., D. S. Dobkin, and D. Wheye. 1988. *The Birders Handbook*. New York: Simon and Schuster.

Eichholz, M. W., and W. D. Koenig. 1992. "Gopher Snake Attraction to Birds' Nests." *Southwestern Naturalist* 37:293–98.

Eifler, D. A., and M. A. Eifler. 1998. "Foraging Behavior and Spacing Patterns of the Lizard *Cnemidophorus uniparens*." *Journal of Herpetology* 32:24–33.

Eilts, J. A., and T. E. Huxman. 2013. "Invasion by an Exotic, Perennial Grass Alters Responses of a Native Woody Species in an Arid System." *Journal of Arid Environments* 88:206–12.

Eiseley, L. 1957. *The Immense Journey*. New York: Random House.

Eiseley, L. 1958. *Darwin's Century*. New York: Doubleday.

Ekdale, E. G. 2016. "Form and Function of the Mammalian Inner Ear." *Journal of Anatomy* 228:324–37.

Emery, N. J. 2006. "Cognitive Ornithology: The Evolution of Avian Intelligence." *Philosophical Transactions of the Royal Society B-Biological Sciences* 361:23–43.

Erickson, W. A., R. E. Marsh, and T. P. Salmon. 1990. "A Review of Falconry as a Bird-Hazing Technique." In *Proceedings of the Fourteenth Vertebrate Pest Conference*, edited by L. R. Davis and R. E. Marsh, 314–16. Davis: University of California.

Ericson, P. G. P. 2012. "Evolution of Terrestrial Birds in Three Continents: Biogeography and Parallel Radiations." *Journal of Biogeography* 39:813–24.

Esque, T. C., K. E. Nussear, K. K. Drake, A. D. Walde, K. H. Berry, R. C. Averill-Murray, A. P. Woodman, et al. 2010. "Effects of Subsidized Predators, Resource Variability, and

Human Population Density on Desert Tortoise Populations in the Mojave Desert, USA." *Endangered Species Research* 12:167–77.

Estes, W. A., and R. W. Mannan. 2003. "Feeding Behavior of Cooper's Hawks at Urban and Rural Nests in Southeastern Arizona." *Condor* 105.

Fabre, P.-H., L. Hautier, D. Dimitrov, and E. J. P. Douzery. 2012. "A Glimpse on the Pattern of Rodent Diversification: A Phylogenetic Approach." *BMC Evolutionary Biology* 12.

Facemire, C. F., M. E. Facemire, and M. C. Facemire. 1990. "Wind as a Factor in the Orientation of Entrances of Cactus Wren Nests." *Condor* 92:1073–75.

Felger, R. S., and M. B. Moser. 1985. *People of the Desert and Sea.* Tucson: University of Arizona Press.

Figueroa, A., A. D. McKelvy, L. L. Grismer, C. D. Bell, and S. P. Lailvaux. 2016. "A Species-Level Phylogeny of Extant Snakes with a Description of a New Colubrid Subfamily and Genus." *Plos One* 11 (9): e0161070.

Fisler, G. F. 1977. "Interspecific Hierarchy at an Artificial Food Source." *Animal Behaviour* 25:240–44.

Fitch, H. S. 1949. "Study of Snake Populations in Central California." *American Midland Naturalist* 41:513–79.

Fite, K. V. 1973. "Anatomical and Behavioral Correlates of Visual Acuity in the Great Horned Owl." *Vision Research* 13:219–30.

Fleischner, T. L. 1994. "Ecological Costs of Livestock Grazing in Western North America." *Conservation Biology* 8:629–44.

Fleming, T. H. 2002. "The Pollination Biology of Sonoran Desert Columnar Cacti." In *Columnar Cacti and Their Mutualists: Evolution, Ecology, and Conservation,* edited by T. H. Fleming and A. Valiente-Banuet, 207–24. Tucson: University of Arizona Press.

Fleming, T. H. 2003. *A Bat Man in the Tropics: Chasing el duende.* Berkeley: University of California Press.

Fleming, T. H. 2004. "Nectar Corridors: Migration and the Annual Cycle of Lesser Long-Nosed Bats." In *Conserving Migratory Pollinators and Nectar Corridors in Western North America,* edited by G. P. Nabhan, 23–42. Tucson: University of Arizona Press.

Fleming, T. H. 2017. *No Species Is an Island.* Tucson: University of Arizona Press.

Fleming, T. H., M. B. Fenton, and S. L. Fenton. 2020. "Hummingbird and Bat Pollinators of the Chiricahuas." *American Scientist* 108:362–69.

Fleming, T. H., and W. J. Kress. 2013. *The Ornaments of Life: Coevolution and Conservation in the Tropics.* Chicago: University of Chicago Press.

Fleming, T. H., and J. Nassar. 2002. "Population Biology of the Lesser Long-Nosed Bat, *Leptonycteris curasoae,* in Mexico and Northern South America." In *Columnar Cacti and Their Mutualists: Evolution, Ecology, and Conservation,* edited by T. H. Fleming and A. Valiente-Banuet, 283–305. Tucson: University of Arizona Press.

Fleming, T. H., R. A. Nunez, and L. S. L. Sternberg. 1993. "Seasonal Changes in the Diets of Migrant and Non-Migrant Nectarivorous Bats as Revealed by Carbon Stable Isotope Analysis." *Oecologia* 94:72–75.

Fleming, T. H., S. R. Richardson, and E. M. Scobie. 2021. "'Free Food:' Nectar Bats at Hummingbird Feeders in Southern Arizona." *Journal of Mammalogy* 102:1128–37.

Fleming, T. H., C. T. Sahley, J. N. Holland, J. D. Nason, and J. L. Hamrick. 2001. "Sonoran Desert Columnar Cacti and the Evolution of Generalized Pollination Systems." *Ecological Monographs* 71:511–30.

Flesch, A. D., P. C. Rosen, and P. Holm. 2017. "Long-Term Changes in Abundances of Sonoran Desert Lizards Reveal Complex Responses to Climatic Variation." *Global Change Biology* 23:5492–508.

Flores-Abreu, I. N., R. E. Trejo-Salazar, L. Sanchez-Reyes, S. V. Good, S. Magallon, A. Garcia-Mendoza, and L. E. Eguiarte. 2019. "Tempo and Mode in Coevolution of *Agave sensu lato* (Agavoideae, Asparagaceae) and Its Bat Pollinators, Glossophaginae (Phyllostomidae)." *Molecular Phylogenetics and Evolution* 133:176–88.

Friedman, N. R., and V. Remes. 2015. "Global Geographic Patterns of Sexual Size Dimorphism in Birds: Support for a Latitudinal Trend?" *Ecography* 39:17–35.

Friedman, W. E. 2009. "The Meaning of Darwin's 'Abominable Mystery.'" *American Journal of Botany* 96:5–21.

Frith, C. B., and B. M. Beehler. 1998. *The Birds of Paradise.* Oxford: Oxford University Press.

Futuyma, D. J. 1986. *Evolutionary Biology.* 2nd ed. Sunderland, Mass.: Sinauer Associates.

Gabor, T. M., and E. C. Hellgren. 2000. "Variation in Peccary Populations: Landscape Composition or Competition by an Invader?" *Ecology* 81:2509–24.

Galetti, M. 2013. "Functional Extinction of Birds Drives Rapid Evolutionary Changes in Seed Size (Vol 340, Pg 1086, 2013)." *Science* 342:1316.

Ganey, J. L., R. P. Balda, and R. M. King. 1993. "Metabolic Rate and Evaporative Water Loss of Mexican Spotted and Great Horned Owls." *Wilson Bulletin* 105:645–56.

Garcia-Trejo, E. A., A. Espinosa do los Monteros, A. del Coro Arizmendi, and A. G. Navarro-Siguenza. 2009. "Molecular Systematics of the Red-Bellied and Golden-Fronted Woodpeckers." *Condor* 111:442–52.

Gee, J. M., D. E. Brown, J. C. Hagelin, M. Taylor, and J. Calloway. 2020. "Gambel's Quail (*Callipepla gambelii*)." Birds of the World. Last modified March 4, 2020. https://doi.org/10.2173/bow.gamqua.01.

Germaine, S. S., R. E. Schweinsburg, and H. L. Germaine. 2001. "Effects of Residential Density on Sonoran Desert Nocturnal Rodents." *Urban Ecosystems* 5:179–85.

Gerson, A. R., A. E. McKechnie, B. Smit, M. C. Whitfield, E. K. Smith, W. A. Talbot, T. J. McWhorter, and B. O. Wolf. 2018. "The Functional Significance of Facultative Hyperthermia Varies with Body Size and Phylogeny in Birds." *Functional Ecology* 33:597–607.

Gibson, A. C. 1998. "Photosynthetic Organs of Desert Plants." *Bioscience* 48:911–20.

Gibson, A. C., and P. S. Nobel. 1986. *The Cactus Primer.* Cambridge, Mass.: Harvard University Press.

Gibson, L. J. 2006. "Woodpecker Pecking: How Woodpeckers Avoid Brain Injury." *Journal of Zoology* 270:462–65.

Gienger, C. M. 2009. "Ecological Interactions Between Gila Monsters (*Heloderma suspectum*) and Desert Tortoises (*Gopherus agassizii*)." *Southwestern Naturalist* 53:265–68.

Gienger, C. M., C. R. Tracy, and K. A. Nagy. 2014. "Life in the Lizard Slow Lane: Gila Monsters Have Low Rates of Energy Use and Water Flux." *Copeia* 2014:279–87.

Gill, F. B. 1990. *Ornithology.* New York: W. H. Freeman.

Gillingham, J. C., C. C. Carpenter, and J. B. Murphy. 1983. "Courtship, Male Combat and Dominance in the Western Diamondback Rattlesnake, *Crotalus atrox*." *Journal of Herpetology* 17:265–70.

Gillooly, J. F., J. P. Gomez, and E. Mavrodiev. 2017. "A Broad-Scale Comparison of Aerobic Activity Levels in Vertebrates: Endotherms Versus Ectotherms." *Proceedings of the Royal Society B-Biological Sciences* 284.

Gillooly, J. F., and M. W. McCoy. 2014. "Brain Size Varies with Temperature in Vertebrates." *PeerJ* 2:e301.

Giugliano, L. G., R. G. Collevatti, and G. R. Colli. 2007. "Molecular Dating and Phylogenetic Relationships Among Teiidae (Squamata) Inferred by Molecular and Morphological Data." *Molecular Phylogenetics and Evolution* 45:168–79.

Glatzel, G., and B. W. Geils. 2009. "Mistletoe Ecophysiology: Host–Parasite Interactions." *Botany-Botanique* 87:10–15.

Goldberg, D. E., and R. M. Turner. 1986. "Vegetation Change and Plant Demography in Permanent Plots in the Sonoran Desert." *Ecology* 67:695–712.

Goldstein, D. L., and K. A. Nagy. 1985. "Resource Utilization by Desert Quail: Time and Energy, Food and Water." *Ecology* 66:378–87.

Golightly, R. T., Jr., and R. D. Ohmart. 1983. "Metabolism and Body Temperature of Two Desert Canids: Coyotes and Kit Foxes." *Journal of Mammalogy* 64:624–35.

Goller, B., T. K. Fellows, R. Dakin, L. Tyrell, E. Fernandez-Juricic, and D. L. Altshuler. 2019. "Spatial and Temporal Resolution of the Visual System of the Anna's Hummingbird (*Calypte anna*) Relative to Other Birds." *Physiological and Biochemical Zoology* 92:481–95.

Gonzalez-Terrazas, T. P., J. C. Koblitz, T. H. Fleming, R. A. Medellin, E. K. V. Kalko, H. U. Schnitzler, and M. Tschapka. 2016a. "How Nectar-Feeding Bats Localize Their Food: Echolocation Behavior of *Leptonycteris yerbabuenae* Approaching Cactus Flowers." *Plos One* 11:e0163492.

Gonzalez-Terrazas, T. P., C. Martel, P. Milet-Pinheiro, M. Ayasse, E. K. V. Kalko, and M. Tschapka. 2016b. "Finding Flowers in the Dark: Nectar-Feeding Bats Integrate Olfaction and Echolocation While Foraging for Nectar." *Royal Society Open Science* 3 (8): 160199.

Grant, P. R. 1986. *Ecology and Evolution of Darwin's Finches*. Princeton, N.J.: Princeton University Press.

Grant, P. R., ed. 1998a. *Evolution on Islands*. Oxford: Oxford University Press.

Grant, P. R. 1998b. "Speciation." In *Evolution on Islands*, edited by P. R. Grant, 83–101. Oxford: Oxford University Press.

Gray, M. E., B. G. Dickson, and L. J. Zachmann. 2014. "Modelling and Mapping Dynamic Variability in Large Fire Probability in the Lower Sonoran Desert of South-Western Arizona." *International Journal of Wildland Fire* 23:1108–18.

Green, D. M., and M. J. Baker. 2003. "Urbanization Impacts on Habitat and Bird Communities in a Sonoran Desert Ecosystem." *Landscape and Urban Planning* 63:225–39.

Greene, H. W. 1997. *Snakes: The Evolution of Mystery in Nature*. Berkeley: University of California Press.

Greenwald, O. E. 1971. "The Effect of Body Temperature on Oxygen Consumption and Heart Rate in the Sonora Gopher Snake, *Pituophis catenifer affinis* Hallowell." *Copeia* 1971:98–106.

Greenwald, O. E. 1974. "Thermal Dependence of Striking and Prey Capture by Gopher Snakes." *Copeia* 1974:141–48.

Griffith, S. C., I. P. F. Owens, and K. A. Thuman. 2002. "Extra Pair Paternity in Birds: A Review of Interspecific Variation and Adaptive Function." *Molecular Ecology* 11:2195–212.

Griffiths, C. S., G. F. Barrowclough, J. G. Groth, and L. A. Mertz. 2007. "Phylogeny, Diversity, and Classification of the Accipitridae Based on DNA Sequences of the RAG-1 Exon." *Journal of Avian Biology* 38:587–602.

Griffs-Kyle, K. L., K. Mougeya, M. Vanlandeghema, S. Swain, and J. C. Drakea. 2018. "Comparison of Climate Vulnerability Among Desert Herpetofauna." *Biological Conservation* 225:164–75.

Grigg, G. C., L. A. Beard, and M. L. Augee. 2004. "The Evolution of Endothermy and Its Diversity in Mammals and Birds." *Physiological and Biochemical Zoology* 77:982–97.

Grubbs, S. E., and P. R. Krausman. 2009. "Use of Urban Landscape by Coyotes." *Southwestern Naturalist* 54:1–12.

Gullion, G. W. 1960. "The Ecology of Gambel's Quail in Nevada and the Arid Southwest." *Ecology* 41:518–36.

Guo, J. S., B. A. Hungate, T. E. Kolb, and G. W. Koch. 2018. "Water Source Niche Overlap Increases with Site Moisture Availability in Woody Perennials." *Plant Ecology* 219:719–35.

Gutierrez-Ibanez, C., A. N. Iwaniuk, and D. R. Wylie. 2011. "Relative Size of Auditory Pathways in Symmetrically and Asymmetrically Eared Owls." *Brain Behavior and Evolution* 78:286–301.

Hadley, N. F., and S. R. Szarek. 1981. "Productivity of Desert Ecosystems." *Bioscience* 31:747–53.

Hafner, J. C., J. E. Light, D. J. Hafner, M. S. Hafner, E. Reddington, D. S. Rogers, and B. R. Riddle. 2007. "Basal Clades and Molecular Systematics of Heteromyid Rodents." *Journal of Mammalogy* 88:1129–45.

Hagelin, J. C. 2001. "Castration in Gambel's and Scaled Quail: Ornate Plumage and Dominance Persist, but Courtship and Threat Behaviors Do Not." *Hormones and Behavior* 39:1–10.

Hagelin, J. C. 2002. "The Kinds of Traits Involved in Male–Male Competition: A Comparison of Plumage, Behavior, and Body Size in Quail." *Behavioral Ecology* 13:32–41.

Hagelin, J. C. 2003. "A Field Study of Ornaments, Body Size, and Mating Behavior of the Gambel's Quail." *Wilson Bulletin* 115:246–57.

Hagelin, J. C., and J. D. Ligon. 2001. "Female Quail Prefer Testosterone-Mediated Traits, Rather Than the Ornate Plumage of Males." *Animal Behaviour* 61:465–476.

Hamilton, R. A., G. A. Proudfoot, D. A. Sherry, and S. L. Johnson. 2020. "Cactus Wren (*Campylorhynchus brunneicapillus*)." Birds of the World. Last modified March 4, 2020. https://doi.org/10.2173/bow.cacwre.01.

Hamilton, W. D. 1964. "The Evolution of Social Behavior." *Journal of Theoretical Biology* 7:1–52.

Hansen, K. 2007. *Bobcat*. New York: Oxford University Press.

Harari, Y. N. 2018. *Sapiens: A Brief History of Mankind*. New York: Harper Perennial.

Harrison, R. G., S. M. Bogdanowicz, R. S. Hoffmann, E. Yensen, and P. W. Sherman. 2003. "Phylogeny and Evolutionary History of the Ground Squirrels (Rodentia: Marmotinae)." *Journal of Mammalian Evolution* 10:249–76.

Harvey, M. B., G. N. Ugueto, and R. L. Gutberlet, Jr. 2012. "Review of Teiid Morphology With a Revised Taxonomy and Phylogeny of the Teiidae (Lepidosauria: Squamata)." *Zootaxa* 3459.

Hass, C. C. 2009. "Competition and Coexistence in Sympatric Bobcats and Pumas." *Journal of Zoology* 278:174–80.

Haynes, L., J. Lamberton, C. Craddock, S. Prendergast, C. Prendergast, M. Colvin, B. Isaacs, et al. 2010. *Mountain Lions and Bobcats of the Tucson Mountains: Monitoring Population Status and Landscape Connectivity*. Tucson: University of Arizona.

Hedges, S. B. 2012. "Amniote Phylogeny and the Position of Turtles." *BMC Biology* 10 (64): 1–2.

Hedges, S. B., and L. L. Poling. 1999. "A Molecular Phylogeny of Reptiles." *Science* 283:998–1001.

Heffelfinger, J. R., F. S. Guthery, R. J. Olding, C. L. Cochran, and C. M. McMullen. 1999. "Influence of Precipitation Timing and Summer Temperatures on Reproduction of Gambel's Quail." *Journal of Wildlife Management* 63:154–61.

Helgen, K. M., F. R. Cole, L. E. Helgen, and D. E. Wilson. 2009. "Generic Revision in the Holarctic Ground Squirrel Genus *Spermophilus*." *Journal of Mammalogy* 90:270–305.

Henderson, C. W. 1961. "Comparative Temperature and Moisture Responses in Gambel and Scaled Quail." *Condor* 73:430–36.

Hernandez-Hernandez, T., J. W. Brown, B. Schlumpberger, L. E. Eguiarte, and S. Magallon. 2014. "Beyond Aridification: Multiple Explanations for the Elevated Diversification of Cacti in the New World Succulent Biome." *New Phytologist* 202:1382–97.

Hernandez-Hernandez, T., H. M. Hernandes, J. A. DeNova, R. Puente, L. E. Eguiarte, and S. Magallon. 2011. "Phylogenetic Relationships and Evolution of Growth Form in Cactaceae (Caryophyllales, Eudicotyledoneae)." *American Journal of Botany* 98:44–68.

Hill, J. B., P. D. Lyons, J. J. Clark, and W. H. Doelle. 2015. "The 'Collapse' of Cooperative Hohokam Irrigation in the Lower Salt River Valley." *Journal of the Southwest* 57:609–74.

Hody, J. W., and R. Kays. 2018. "Mapping the Expansion of Coyotes (*Canis latrans*) Across North and Central America." *ZooKeys* 759:81–97.

Hoffmeister, D. F. 1986. *Mammals of Arizona*. Tucson: University of Arizona Press.

Hopson, J. A. 1977. "Relative Brain Size and Behavior in Archosaurian Reptiles." *Annual Review of Ecology and Systematics* 8:429–48.

Hosner, P. A., E. L. Braun, and R. T. Kimball. 2015. "Land Connectivity Changes and Global Cooling Shaped the Colonization History and Diversification of New World Quail (Aves: Galliformes: Odontophoridae)." *Journal of Biogeography* 42:1883–95.

Huckleberry, C. 2002. "The Sonoran Desert Conservation Plan." *Endangered Species Bulletin* 27:12–15.

Hughes, J. M. 2020. "Greater Roadrunner (*Geococcyx californianus*)." Birds of the World. Last modified March 4, 2020. https://doi.org/10.2173/bow.greroa.01.

Iknayan, K. J., and S. R. Beissinger. 2018. "Collapse of a Desert Bird Community over the Past Century Driven by Climate Change." *Proceedings of the National Academy of Sciences of the United States of America* 115:8597–602.

Ilse, L. M., and E. C. Helgren. 1995. "Spatial Use and Group Dynamics of Sympatric Collared Peccaries and Feral Hogs in Southern Texas." *Journal of Mammalogy* 76:993–1002.

Ilsoe, S. K., W. D. Kissling, J. Fjeldsa, B. Sandel, and J. C. Svenning. 2017. "Global Variation in Woodpecker Species Richness Shaped by Tree Availability." *Journal of Biogeography* 2017:1–12.

Inouye, R. S., N. J. Huntley, and D. W. Inouye. 1982. "Non-Random Orientation of Gila Woodpecker Nest Entrances in Saguaro Cacti." *Condor* 83:88–89.

Isler, K., and C. P. van Schaik. 2006. "Metabolic Costs of Brain Size Evolution." *Biology Letters* 2:557–60.

Jacobs, G. H., J. F. Deegan, and M. A. Crognale. 1993. "Photopigments of Dogs and Foxes and Their Implications for Canid Vision." *Visual Neuroscience* 10:173–80.

Janacek, J. E., T. L. Blankenship, D. H. Hirth, M. E. Tewes, C. W. Kilpatrick, and L. I. Grassman, Jr. 2006. "Kinship and Social Structure of Bobcats (*Lynx rufus*) Inferred from Microsatellite and Radio-Telemetry Data." *Journal of Zoology* 269:494–501.

Janzen, F. J. 1991. "Environmental Sex Determination in Reptiles: Ecology, Evolution, and Experimental Design." *Quarterly Review of Biology* 66:149–79.

Jarvis, E. D., S. Mirarab, A. J. Aberer, B. Li, P. Houde, C. Li, S. Y. W. Ho, et al. 2014. "Whole-Genome Analyses Resolve Early Branches in the Tree of Life of Modern Birds." *Science* 346:1320–31.

Jarvis, E. D., G. Onur, L. Bruce, A. Csillag, H. Karten, W. Kuenzel, L. Medina, et al. 2005. "Avian Brains and a New Understanding of Vertebrate Brain Evolution." *Nature Review of Neuroscience* 6:151–59.

Jenkins, S. H., A. Rothstein, and W. C. H. Green. 1995. "Food Hoarding by Merriam's Kangaroo Rats: A Test of Alternative Hypotheses." *Ecology* 76:2470–81.

Jerison, H. J. 2004. "Dinosaur Brain Size." In *Encyclopedia of Neuroscience*, edited by G. Adelman and B. H. Smith, 1–6. 3rd ed. Netherlands: Elsevier Science.

Johnsgard, P. A. 1997. *The Hummingbirds of North America*. 2nd ed. Washington, D.C.: Smithsonian Institution Press.

Johnson, K. P., S. M. Goodman, and S. M. Lanyon. 2000. "A Phylogenetic Study of the Malagasy Couas with Insights into Cuckoo Relationships." *Molecular Phylogenetics and Evolution* 14:436–44.

Johnson, K. P., and J. D. Weckstein. 2011. "The Central American Land Bridge as an Engine of Diversification in New World Doves." *Journal of Biogeography* 38:1069–78.

Johnston, R. F., and R. K. Selander. 1964. "House Sparrows: Rapid Evolution of Races in North America." *Science* 144:548–50.

Johnston, R. F., and R. K. Selander. 1971. "Evolution in the House Sparrow: II: Adaptive Variation in North American Populations." *Evolution* 25:1–28.

Jones, J. H., and N. S. Smith. 1979. "Bobcat Density and Prey Selection in Central Arizona." *Journal of Wildlife Management* 43 (3): 666–72.

Jones, K. B. 1983. "Movement Patterns and Foraging Ecology of Gila Monsters (*Heloderma suspectum cope*) in Northwestern Arizona." *Herpetologica* 39:247–53.

Jones, W. T. 1989. "Dispersal Distance and the Range of Nightly Movements in Merriam's Kangaroo Rats." *Journal of Mammalogy* 70:27–34.

Jung, J.-Y., A. Pissarenko, A. A. Trikanad, D. Restrepo, F. Y. Su, A. Marquez, D. Gonzalez, et al. 2019. "A Natural Stress Deflector on the Head? Mechanical and Functional Evaluation of the Woodpecker Skull Bones." *Advances in Theory and Simulation* 2.

Justice, K. E. 1985. "Oxalate Digestibility in *Neotoma albigula* and *Neotoma mexicana*." *Oecologia* 67:231–34.

Kaku, M. 2018. *The Future of Humanity*. New York: Doubleday.

Kang, H., B. Liang, X. Maa, and Y. Xua. 2018. "Evolutionary Progression of Mitochondrial Gene Rearrangements and Phylogenetic Relationships in Strigidae (Strigiformes)." *Gene* 674:8–14.

Kardong, K. V., and T. L. Smith. 2002. "Proximate Factors Involved in Rattlesnake Predatory Behavior: A Review." In *Biology of the Vipers*, edited by G. W. Schuett, M. Hoggren, M. E. Douglas, and H. W. Greene, 253–66. Eagle Mountain, Utah: Eagle Mountain.

Kelley, S. W., D. Ransom, J. A. Butcher, G. G. Schulz, B. W. Surber, W. E. Pinchak, C. A. Santamaria, et al. 2011. "Home Range Dynamics, Habitat Selection, and Survival of Greater Roadrunners." *Journal of Field Ornithology* 82:165–74.

Kemp, T. S. 2005. *The Origin and Evolution of Mammals*. Oxford: Oxford University Press.

Kenward, R. E. 2009. "Conservation Values from Falconry." In *Recreational Hunting, Conservation and Rural Livelihoods: Science and Practice*, edited by B. Dickson, J. Hutton, and B. Adams, 181–96. Oxford: Blackwell.

Kerpez, T. A., and N. S. Smith. 1990. "Nest-Site Selection and Nest-Cavity Characteristics of Gila Woodpeckers and Northern Flickers." *Condor* 92:193–98.

Kimball, R. T., E. L. Braun, B. Liang, and Z. Zhang. 2013. "Assessing Phylogenetic Relationships Among Galliformes: A Multigene Phylogeny with Expanded Taxon Sampling in Phasianidae." *Plos One* 8:e64312.

Kimball, R. T., P. G. Parker, and J. C. Bednarz. 2003. "Occurrence and Evolution of Cooperative Breeding Among Diurnal Raptors (Accipitridae and Falconidae)." *Auk* 120:717–29.

Kimball, S., M. L. Angert, T. E. Huxman, and D. L. Venable. 2010. "Contemporary Climate Change in the Sonoran Desert Favors Cold-Adapted Species." *Global Change Biology* 16:1555–65.

Knowlton, F. F., E. M. Gese, and M. M. Jaeger. 1999. "Coyote Depredation Control: An Interface Between Biology and Management." *Journal of Range Management* 52:398–413.

Kolbert, E. 2014. *The Sixth Extinction*. New York: Picador.

Koontz, T. L., U. L. Shepherd, and D. Marshall. 2001. "The Effects of Climate Change on Merriam's Kangaroo Rat, *Dipodomys merriami*." *Journal of Arid Environments* 49:581–91.

Kotaka, N. 2004. "The Evolution of Concepts on the Evolution of Endothermy in Birds and Mammals." *Physiological and Biochemical Zoology* 77:1043–50.

Koteja, P. 2000. "Energy Assimilation, Parental Care and the Evolution of Endothermy." *Proceedings of the Royal Society B-Biological Sciences* 267:479–84.

Kotler, B. P., and J. S. Brown. 1988. "Environmental Heterogeneity and the Coexistence of Desert Rodents." *Annual Review of Ecology and Systematics* 19:281–307.

Krenz, J. G., G. J. P. Naylor, B. Shaffer, and F. J. Janzen. 2005. "Molecular Phylogenetics and Evolution of Turtles." *Molecular Phylogenetics and Evolution* 37:178–91.

Kruger, O. 2005. "The Evolution of Reversed Sexual Size Dimorphism in Hawks, Falcons, and Owls: A Comparative Study." *Evolutionary Ecology* 19:467–86.

Kruger, O., and N. B. Davies. 2001. "The Evolution of Cuckoo Parasitism: A Comparative Analysis." *Proceedings of the Royal Society B-Biological Sciences* 269:375–81.

Kruger, O., M. D. Sorenson, and N. B. Davies. 2009. "Does Coevolution Promote Species Richness in Parasitic Cuckoos?" *Proceedings of the Royal Society B-Biological Sciences* 276:3871–79.

Ksepka, D. T. 2017. "Early Paleocene Landbird Supports Rapid Phylogenetic and Morphological Diversification of Crown Birds After the K–Pg Mass Extinction." *Proceedings of the National Academy of Sciences of the United States of America* 114:8047–52.

Kuijt, J. 1997. "*Phoradendron olae* Kuijt, a New Species from Mexico Pivotal in the Taxonomy of the Genus, with Comments on *P. Californicum* Nutt." *Brittonia* 49:181–88.

Kvarnemo, C. 2018. "Why Do Some Animals Mate with One Partner Rather Than Many? A Review of Causes and Consequences of Monogamy." *Biological Reviews* 93:1795–812.

Kwiatkowski, M. A., G. W. Schuett, R. A. Repp, E. M. Nowak, and B. K. Sullivan. 2008. "Does Urbanization Influence the Spatial Ecology of Gila Monsters in the Sonoran Desert?" *Journal of Zoology* 276:350–57.

Lack, D. 1947a. *Darwn's Finches.* Cambridge: Cambridge University Press.

Lack, D. 1947b. "The Significance of Clutch Size, I–II." *Ibis* 89:302–52.

Laman, T., and E. Scholes. 2012. *Birds of Paradise.* Washington, D.C.: National Geographic Society.

Lamichhaney, S., J. Berglund, M. Sa¨llman Alme´n, K. Maqbool, M. Grabherr, A. Martinez-Barrio, M. Promerova, et al. 2015. "Evolution of Darwin's Finches and Beaks as Revealed by Genome Sequencing." *Nature* 518:371–86.

Lara, C., and F. Perez. 2009. "Provenance, Guts, and Fate: Field and Experimental Evidence in a Host-Mistletoe-Bird system." *Ecoscience* 16:399–407.

Lariviere, S., and L. R. Walton. 1997. "*Lynx rufus.*" *Mammalian Species* 563:1–8.

Lawhead, D. N. 1984. "Bobcat *Lynx rufus* Home Range, Density and Habitat Preference in South-Central Arizona." *Southwestern Naturalist* 29:105–13.

Leache, A. D., A. S. Chavez, L. N. Jones, J. A. Grummer, A. D. Gottscho, and C. W. Linkem. 2015. "Phylogenomics of Phrynosomatid Lizards: Conflicting Signals from Sequence Capture Versus Restriction Site Associated DNA Sequencing." *Genome Biology and Evolution* 7:706–19.

Lee, M. S. Y., A. F. Hugall, R. Lawson, and J. D. Scanlon. 2007. "Phylogeny of Snakes (Serpentes): Combining Morphological and Molecular Data in Likelihood, Bayesian and Parsimony Analyses." *Systematics and Biodiversity* 5:371–89.

Legume Phylogeny Working Group. 2013. "Legume Phylogeny and Classification in the 21st Century: Progress, Prospects and Lessons for Other Species-Rich Clades." *Taxon* 62:217–48.

Legume Phylogeny Working Group. 2017. "A New Subfamily Classification of the Leguminosae Based on a Taxonomically Comprehensive Phylogeny." *Taxon* 66:44–77.

Lei, S. A. 2000. "Age and Size of *Acacia* and *Cercidium* Influencing the Infection Success of Parasitic and Autoparasitic *Phoradendron.*" *California Academy of Sciences* 99:45–54.

Lei, S. A. 2001. "Survival and Development of *Phoradendron californicum* and *Acacia greggii* During a Drought." *Western North American Naturalist* 61:78–84.

Lele, A., M. S. Rand, and S. G. Zweifel. 2016. "Sequencing and Analysis of the Mitochondrial Genome of *Pituophis catenifer sayi* (Squamata: Colubridae)." *Mitochondrial DNA Part B: Resources* 1:483–84.

Leopold, A. 1949. *A Sand County Almanac and Sketches of Here and There.* New York: Oxford University Press.

Leopold, A. 1972. *Round River.* Edited by L. Leopold. New York: Oxford University Press.

Lerner, R. L., M. C. Klaver, and D. P. Mindell. 2008. "Molecular Phylogenetics of the Buteonine Birds of Prey (Accipitridae)." *Auk* 125:304–15.

Lerner, R. L., and D. P. Mindell. 2005. "Phylogeny of Eagles, Old World Vultures, and Other Accipitridae Based on Nuclear and Mitochondrial DNA." *Molecular Phylogenetics and Evolution* 37:327–46.

Lewis, D. B., J. P. Kaye, and A. P. Kinzig. 2014. "Legacies of Agriculture and Urbanization in Labile and Stable Organic Carbon and Nitrogen in Sonoran Desert Soils." *Ecosphere* 5 (5): 1–18.

Licht, P., and A. F. Bennett. 1972. "A Scaleless Snake: Tests of the Role of Reptilian Scales in Water Loss and Heat Transfer." *Copeia* 1972:702–7.

Lira-Noriega, A., and A. T. Peterson. 2014. "Range-Wide Ecological Niche Comparisons of Parasite, Hosts and Dispersers in a Vectorborne Plant Parasite System." *Journal of Biogeography* 41:1664–73.

Lira-Noriega, A., O. Toro-Nuñez, J. R. Oaks, and M. E. Mort. 2015. "The Roles of History and Ecology in Chloroplast Phylogeographic Patterns of the Bird-Dispersed Plant Parasite *Phoradendron californicum* (Viscaceae) in the Sonoran Desert." *American Journal of Botany* 102:149–64.

Lochmiller, R. L., E. C. Hellgren, and W. E. Grant. 1986. "Reproductive Responses to Nutritional Stress in Adult Female Collared Peccaries." *Journal of Wildlife Management* 50:295–300.

Longland, W. S., and M. V. Price. 1991. "Direct Observations of Owls and Heteromyid Rodents: Can Predation Risk Explain Microhabitat Use?" *Ecology* 72:2261–73.

Longrich, N. R., T. Tokarykb, and D. J. Fielda. 2011. "Mass Extinction of Birds at the Cretaceous–Paleogene (K–Pg) Boundary." *Proceedings of the National Academy of Sciences of the United States of America* 108:15252–57.

Lovegrove, B. G. 2012. "The Evolution of Endothermy in Cenozoic Mammals: A Plesiomorphic-Apomorphic Continuum." *Biological Reviews* 87:128–62.

Lovegrove, B. G. 2017. "A Phenology of the Evolution of Endothermy in Birds and Mammals." *Biological Reviews* 92:1213–40.

Lueck, B. E. 1985. "Comparative Social Behavior of Bisexual and Unisexual Whiptail Lizards (*Cnemidophorus*)." *Journal of Herpetology* 19:492–506.

Macedo, R. H., and M. A. Mares. 1988. "*Neotoma albigula.*" *Mammalian Species* 310:1–7.

Magallon, S., S. Gomez-Acevedo, L. L. Sanchez-Reyes, and T. Hernandez-Hernandez. 2015. "A Metacalibrated Time-Tree Documents the Early Rise of Flowering Plant Phylogenetic Diversity." *New Phytologist* 207:437–53.

Mahall, B. E., and R. M. Calloway. 1992. "Root Communication Mechanisms and Intracommunity Distributions of Two Mojave Desert Shrubs." *Ecology* 73:2145–51.

Malam, J., and S. Parker. 2002. *Encyclopedia of Dinosaurs and Other Prehistoric Creatures*. New York: Sandy Creek.

Mannan, R. W., and C. W. Boal. 2000. "Home Range Characteristics of Male Cooper's Hawks in an Urban Environment." *Wilson Bulletin* 112:21–27.

Mannan, R. W., R. N. Mannan, C. A. Schmidt, W. A. Estes-Zumpf, and C. W. Boal. 2007. "Influence of Natal Experience on Nest-Site Selection by Urban-Nesting Cooper's Hawks." *Journal of Wildlife Management* 71:64–68.

Mannan, R. W., R. J. Steidl, and C. W. Boal. 2008. "Identifying Habitat Sinks: A Case Study of Cooper's Hawks in an Urban Environment." *Urban Ecosystems* 11:141–48.

Manriquez-Moran, N. L., M. Villagran-Santa Cruz, and F. R. Mendez-de la Cruz. 2000. "Origin and Evolution of the Parthenogenetic Lizards, *Cnemidophorus maslini* and *C. cozumela*." *Journal of Herpetology* 34:634–37.

Marazzi, B., J. L. Bronstein, P. N. Sommers, B. R. Lopez, E. B. Ortega, A. Burquez, R. A. Medellin, et al. 2015. "Plant Biotic Interactions in the Sonoran Desert." *Journal of the Southwest* 57:457–502.

Martin, G. R. 1986. "Sensory Capacities and the Nocturnal Habit of Owls (Strigiformes)." *Ibis* 128:266–77.

Martin, L. D. 1980. "The Early Evolution of the Cricetidae in North America." *Paleontological Contributions from the University of Kansas* 102:1–42.

Martin, T., J. Marugan-Lobo, R. Vuillo, H. Martin-Abad, Z. X. Luo, and A. D. Buscalioni. 2017. "A Cretaceous Eutriconodont and Integument Evolution in Early Mammals." *Nature* 526:380–84.

Martindale, S. 1983. "Foraging Patterns of Nesting Gila Woodpeckers." *Ecology* 64:888–98.

Martinez del Rio, C., B. O. Wolf, and R. A. Haughey. 2004. "Saguaros and White-Winged Doves: The Natural History on an Uneasy Partnership." In *Conserving Migratory Pollinators and Nectar Corridors in Western North America*, edited by G. P. Nabhan, 122–43. Tucson: University of Arizona Press and Arizona-Sonora Desert Museum.

Mason, M. J. 2006. "Middle Ear Structures in Fossorial Mammals: A Comparison with Non-Fossorial Species." *Journal of Zoology* 255:467–86.

Mathiasen, R. L., J. R. Shaw, D. L. Nickrent, and D. M. Watson. 2008. "Mistletoes: Pathology, Systematics, Ecology, and Management." *Plant Disease* 92:988–1006.

Matocq, M. D., Q. R. Shurtliv, and C. R. Feldman. 2007. "Phylogenetics of the Woodrat Genus *Neotoma* (Rodentia: Muridae): Implications for the Evolution of Phenotypic Variation in Male External Genitalia." *Molecular Phylogenetics and Evolution* 42:637–52.

Mayr, E. 1942. *Systematics and the Origin of Species*. New York: Columbia University Press.

Mayr, E. 1982. *The Growth of Biological Thought*. Cambridge, Mass.: Belknap.

Mayr, G. 2004. "Old World Fossil Record of Modern-Type Hummingbirds." *Science* 304:861–64.

McAuliffe, J. R. 1984. "Sahuaro-Nurse Tree Associations in the Sonoran Desert: Competitive Effects of Sahuaros." *Oecologia* 64:319–21.

McAuliffe, J. R., and E. P. Hammerlynck. 2010. "Perennial Plant Mortality in the Sonoran and Mojave Deserts in Response to Severe, Multi-Year Drought." *Journal of Arid Environments* 74:884–96.

McAuliffe, J. R., and F. J. Janzen. 1986. "Effects of Intraspecific Crowding on Water Uptake, Water Storage, Apical Growth, and Reproductive Potential in the Sahuaro Cactus, *Carnegiea gigantea*." *Botanical Gazette* 147:334–41.

McClure, M. F., N. S. Smith, and W. W. Shaw. 1995. "Diets of Coyotes near the Boundary of Saguaro National Monument and Tucson, Arizona." *Southwestern Naturalist* 40:101–4.

McCreedy, C., and I. Van Riper, C. 2015. "Drought-Caused Delay in Nesting of Sonoran Desert Birds and Its Facilitation of Parasite- and Predator-Mediated Variation in Reproductive Success." *Auk* 132:235–47.

McCue, M. D. 2007. "Western Diamondback Rattlesnakes Demonstrate Physiological and Biochemical Strategies for Tolerating Prolonged Starvation." *Physiological and Biochemical Zoology* 80.

McGuire, J. A., C. C. Witt, J. V. Remsen, Jr., A. Corl, D. L. Rabosky, D. L. Altshuler, and R. Dudley. 2014. "Molecular Phylogenetics and the Diversification of Hummingbirds." *Current Biology* 24:910–16.

McKinney, T., and T. W. Smith. 2007. "Diets of Sympatric Bobcats and Coyotes During Years of Varying Rainfall in Central Arizona." *Western North American Naturalist* 67:8–15.

McLister, J. D., J. S. Sorensen, and M. D. Dearing. 2004. "Effects of Consumption of *Juniper* (*Juniperus monosperma*) on Cost of Thermoregulation in the Woodrats *Neotoma albigula* and *Neotoma stephensi* at Different Acclimation Temperatures." *Physiological and Biochemical Zoology* 77:305–12.

M'Closkey, R. T. 1981. "Microhabitat Use in Coexisting Desert Rodents—the Role of Population Density." *Oecologia* 50:310–15.

McNab, B. K. 1978. "The Evolution of Endothermy in the Phylogeny of Mammals." *American Naturalist* 112:1–21.

Mead, J. L., T. R. Van Devender, and K. L. Cole. 1983. "Late Quaternary Small Mammals from Sonoran Desert Packrat Middens, Arizona and California." *Journal of Mammalogy* 64:170–80.

Mendez-de la Cruz, F. R., M. Villagran-Santa Cruz, and R. M. Andrews. 1998. "Evolution of Viviparity in the Lizard Genus *Sceloporus*." *Herpetologica* 54:521–32.

Meyer, A., and R. Zardoya. 2003. "Recent Advances in the (Molecular) Phylogeny of Vertebrates." *Annual Review of Ecology and Systematics* 34:311–38.

Meyer, M. M., and W. H. Karasov. 1989. "Antiherbivore Chemistry of *Larrea tridentata*: Effects on Woodrat (*Neotoma lepida*) Feeding and Nutrition." *Ecology* 70:953–61.

Miller, A. W., C. Dale, and M. D. Dearing. 2014. "Microbiota Diversification and Crash Induced by Dietary Oxalate in the Mammalian Herbivore *Neotoma albigula*." *mSphere* 2:e00428-17.

Miller, A. W., K. F. Oakeson, C. Dale, and M. D. Dearing. 2016. "Effect of Dietary Oxalate on the Gut Microbiota of the Mammalian Herbivore *Neotoma albigula*." *Applied and Environmental Microbiology* 82:2669–75.

Mills, G. S., J. B. Dunning, and J. M. Bates. 1989. "Effects of Urbanization on Breeding Bird Community Structure in Southwestern Desert Habitats." *Condor* 91:416–28.

Milner, A. C., and S. A. Walsh. 2009. "Avian Brain Evolution: New Data from Palaeogene Birds (Lower Eocene) from England." *Zoological Journal of the Linnean Society* 155:198–219.

Mitchell, D. R., J. B. Mabry, N. M. Tagueña, G. Huckleberry, R. C. Brusca, and M. S. Shackley. 2020. "Prehistoric Adaptation, Identity, and Interaction Along the Northern Gulf of California." *California Archeology* 12:163–95.

Montalvo, A. E., J. Ransome, D., and R. R. Lopez. 2014. "Greater Roadrunner (*Geococcyx californianus*) Home Range and Habitat Selection in West Texas." *Western North American Naturalist* 74:201–7.

Moritz, C., J. L. Patton, C. J. Conroy, J. L. Parra, G. C. White, and S. R. Beissinger. 2008. "Impact of a Century of Climate Change on Small-Mammal Communities in Yosemite National Park, USA." *Science* 322:261–64.

Moses, M. R., J. K. Frey, and G. W. Roemer. 2012. "Elevated Surface Temperature Depresses Survival of Banner-Tailed Kangaroo Rats: Will Climate Change Cook a Desert Icon?" *Oecologia* 168:257–68.

Munger, J. C., and J. H. Brown. 1981. "Competition in Desert Rodents: An Experiment with Semipermeable Exclosures." *Science* 211:510–12.

Munroe, K. E., and J. L. Koprowski. 2011. "Sociality, Bateman's Gradients, and the Polygynandrous Genetic Mating System of Round-Tailed Ground Squirrels (*Xerospermophilus tereticaudus*)." *Behavioral Ecology and Sociobiology* 65:1811–24.

Munsey, L. D. 1972. "Water Loss in Five Species of Lizards." *Comparative Biochemistry and Physiology A* 43A:781–94.

Munson, S. M., R. H. Webb, J. Belnap, J. A. Hubbard, D. E. Swann, and S. Rutman. 2012. "Forecasting Climate Change Impacts to Plant Community Composition in the Sonoran Desert Region." *Global Change Biology* 18:1083–95.

Murphy, R. W., J. Fu, A. Lathrop, J. V. Feltham, and V. Kovac. 2002. "Phylogeny of the Rattlesnakes (*Crotalus* and *Sistrurus*) Inferred from Sequences of Five Mitochondrial DNA Genes." In *Biology of the Vipers*, edited by G. W. Schuett, M. Hoggren, M. E. Douglas, and H. W. Greene, 69–92. Eagle Mountain, Utah: Eagle Mountain.

Nagy, K. A. 1987. "Field Metabolic Rate and Food Requirement Scaling in Mammals and Birds." *Ecological Monographs* 57:111–28.

Nagy, K. A. 2004. "Water Economy of Free-Living Desert Animals." *International Congress Series* 1275:291–97.

Nagy, K. A. 2018. "Food Requirements of Wild Animals: Predictive Equations for Free-Living Mammals, Reptiles, and Birds." *Nutrition Abstracts and Reviews, Series B* 71:21R–31R.

Nagy, K. A., and M. J. Gruchacz. 1994. "Seasonal Water and Energy Metabolism of the Desert-Dwelling Kangaroo Rat (*Dipodomys merriami*)." *Physiological Zoology* 67:1461–78.

Nagy, K. A., and P. A. Medica. 1986. "Physiological Ecology of Desert Tortoises in Southern Nevada." *Herpetologica* 42:73–92.

Navarro-Siguenza, A. G., H. Vazquez-Miranda, G. Hernandez-Alonso, E. A. Garcia-Trejo, and L. A. Sanchez-Gonzalez. 2017. "Complex Biogeographic Scenarios Revealed in the

Diversification of the Largest Woodpecker Radiation in the New World." *Molecular Phylogenetics and Evolution* 112:53–67.

Neal, B. J. 1959. "A Contribution on the Life History of the Collared Peccary in Arizona." *American Midland Naturalist* 61:177–90.

Neff, J. A. 1940. "Population, and Game Status of the Western White-Winged Dove in Arizona." *Journal of Wildlife Management* 4:117–27.

Newmark, J. E., and S. H. Jenkins. 2000. "Sex Differences in Agonistic Behavior of Merriam's Kangaroo Rats (*Dipodomys merriami*)." *American Midland Naturalist* 143:377–88.

Niblick, H. A., D. C. Rostal, and T. Classen. 1994. "Role of Male-Male Interactions and Female Choice in the Mating System of the Desert Tortoise (*Gopherus agassizii*)." *Herpetological Monographs* 8:124–32.

Nickrent, D. L. 2020. "Parasitic Angiosperms: How Often and How Many?" *Taxon* 69:5–27.

Niethammer, C. 2020. *A Desert Feast*. Tucson: University of Arizona Press.

Nogueira-Filho, S. L. G. 2005. "The Effects of Increasing Levels of Roughage on Coefficients of Nutrient Digestibility in the Collared Peccary (*Tayassu tajacu*)." *Animal Feed Science and Technology* 120:151–57.

Notaro, M., A. Mauss, and J. W. Williams. 2012. "Projected Vegetation Changes for the American Southwest: Combined Dynamic Modeling and Bioclimatic-Envelope Approach." *Ecological Applications* 22:1365–88.

Nyakatura, K., and O. R. P. Bininda-Emonds. 2012. "Updating the Evolutionary History of Carnivora (Mammalia): A New Species-Level Supertree Complete with Divergence Time Estimates." *BMC Biology* 10.

O'Leary, M. A., J. I. Bloch, J. J. Flynn, T. J. Gaudin, A. Giallombardo, N. P. Giannini, S. L. Goldberg, et al. 2013. "The Placental Mammal Ancestor and the Post–K-Pg Radiation of Placentals." *Science* 339:662–67.

Ohmart, R. D. 1972. "Physiological and Ecological Observations Concerning the Salt-Secreting Nasal Glands of the Roadrunner." *Comparative Biochemistry and Physiology A* 43A:311–16.

Ohmart, R. D. 1973. "Observations on the Breeding Adaptations of the Roadrunner." *Condor* 75.

Ohmart, R. D., and R. C. Lasiewski. 1971. "Roadrunners: Energy Conservation by Hypothermia and Absorption of Sunlight." *Science* 172:67–69.

Oliveros, C. H., D. J. Field, D. T. Ksepka, F. K. Barker, A. Aleixo, M. J. Andersen, P. Alstrom, et al. 2019. "Earth History and the Passerine Superradiation." *Proceedings of the National Academy of Sciences of the United States of America* 116:7916–25.

Orlowski, J., W. Harmening, and H. Wagner. 2012. "Night Vision in Barn Owls: Visual Acuity and Contrast Sensitivity Under Dark Adaptation." *Journal of Vision* 12:1–8.

O'Rourke, C. T., M. I. Hall, T. Pitlik, and E. Fernandez-Juricic. 2010. "Hawk Eyes I: Diurnal Raptors Differ in Visual Fields and Degree of Eye Movement." *Plos One* 5:e12802, 12801–8.

Overton, J. M. 1997. "Host Specialization and Partial Reproductive Isolation in Desert Mistletoe (*Phoradendron californicum*)." *Southwestern Naturalist* 42:201–9.

Pana, Y., W. Zhengb, R. H. Sawyer, M. W. Penningfond, X. Zhenge, X. Wange, M. Wangg, et al. 2019. "The Molecular Evolution of Feathers with Direct Evidence from Fossils." *Proceedings of the National Academy of Sciences of the United States of America* 116:3018–23.

Parker, E. D., Jr. 1979a. "Phenotypic Consequences of Parthenogenesis in *Cnemidophorus* Lizards: I: Variability in Parthenogenetic and Sexual Populations." *Evolution* 33:1150–66.

Parker, E. D., Jr. 1979b. "Phenotypic Consequences of Parthenogenesis in *Cnemidophorus* Lizards: II: Similarity of *C. tesselatus* to Its Sexual Parental Species." *Evolution* 33:1167–79.

Parker, E. D., Jr., and R. K. Selander. 1976. "The Organization of Genetic Diversity in the Parthenogenetic Lizard *Cnemidophorus tesselatus*." *Genetics* 84:791–805.

Parra, J. L., and W. B. Monahan. 2008. "Variability in 20th Century Climate Change Reconstructions and Its Consequences for Predicting Geographic Responses of California Mammals." *Global Change Biology* 14:2215–31.

Pereira, A. G., J. Sterli, F. R. R. Moreira, and C. G. Schrago. 2017. "Multilocus Phylogeny and Statistical Biogeography Clarify the Evolutionary History of Major Lineages of Turtles." *Molecular Phylogenetics and Evolution* 113:59–66.

Peterson, C. C. 1996. "Anhomeostasis: Seasonal Water and Solute Relations in Two Populations of the Desert Tortoise (*Gopherus agassizii*) During Chronic Drought." *Physiological Zoology* 69:1324–58.

Phillips, S. J., and P. W. Comus. 2000. *A Natural History of the Sonoran Desert*. Tucson: Arizona-Sonora Desert Press.

Pianka, E. R. 1989. "Desert Lizard Diversity: Additional Comments and Some Data." *American Naturalist* 134:344–64.

Pianka, E. R., and L. J. Vitt. 2003. *Lizards, Windows to the Evolution of Diversity*. Berkeley: University of California Press.

Pierson, E. A., and R. M. Turner. 1998. "An 85-Year Study of Saguaro (*Carnegiea gigantea*) Demography." *Ecology* 79:2676–93.

Pierson, E. A., R. M. Turner, and J. L. Betancourt. 2013. "Regional Demographic Trends from Long-Term Studies of Saguaro (*Carnegiea gigantea*) Across the Northern Sonoran Desert." *Journal of Arid Environments* 88:58–69.

Piras, P., L. Majorino, L. Teres, C. Meloros, F. Lucc, T. Kotsakis, and P. Rajas. 2013. "Bite of the Cats: Relationships Between Functional Integration and Mechanical Performance as Revealed by Mandible Geometry." *Systematic Biology* 62:878–900.

Pollard, K. A., and D. T. Blumstein. 2012. "Evolving Communicative Complexity: Insights from Rodents and Beyond." *Philosophical Transactions of the Royal Society B Biology* 367:1869–78.

Pough, F. H., R. M. Andrews, M. L. Crump, A. H. Savitzky, K. D. Wells, and M. C. Brandley. 2016. *Herpetology*. 4th ed. Sunderland, Mass.: Sinauer Associates.

Powers, D. R. 1991. "Diurnal Variation in Mass, Metabolic Rate, and Respiratory Quotient in Anna's and Costa's Hummingbirds." George Fox University Faculty Publications—Department of Biology and Chemistry 14. Newberg, Ore.: George Fox University.

Powers, D. R. 1992. "Effect of Temperature and Humidity on Evaporative Water Loss in Anna's Hummingbird (*Calypte anna*)." George Fox University Faculty Publications—Department of Biology and Chemistry 13. Newberg, Ore.: George Fox University.

Powers, D. R., and K. A. Nagy. 1988. "Field Metabolic Rate and Food Consumption by Free-Living Anna's Hummingbirds (*Calypte anna*)." *Physiological Zoology* 61:500–6.

Powers, D. R., and S. M. Wethington. 2021. "Broad-Billed Hummingbird (*Cynanthus latirostris*)." Birds of the World. Last modified August 18, 2021. https://doi.org/10.2173/bow.brbhum.01.1.

Prum, R. O., J. S. Berv, A. Dornburg, D. J. Field, J. P. Townsend, E. M. Lemmon, and A. R. Lemmon. 2015. "A Comprehensive Phylogeny of Birds (Aves) Using Targeted Next-Generation DNA Sequencing." *Nature* 526:569–73.

Pyron, R. A., F. T. Burbrink, and J. J. Wiens. 2013. "A Phylogeny and Revised Classification of Squamata, Including 4161 Species of Lizards and Snakes." *BMC Evolutionary Biology* 13.

Rabe, M. J., and T. A. Sanders. 2010. "White-Winged Dove Population Status, 2010." U.S. Fish and Wildlife Publications 431. Washington, D.C.: U.S. Fish and Wildlife Service, Division of Migratory Bird Management.

Raitt, R. J., and R. D. Ohmart. 1966. "Annual Cycle of Reproduction and Molt in Gambel Quail of the Rio Grande Valley, Southern New Mexico." *Condor* 68:541–61.

Raposo do Amaral, F., F. H. Sheldon, A. Gamauf, E. Haring, M. Riesing, L. F. Silveira, and A. Wajntal. 2009. "Patterns and Processes of Diversification in a Widespread and Ecologically Diverse Avian Group, the Buteonine Hawks (Aves, Accipitridae)." *Molecular Phylogenetics and Evolution* 53:703–15.

Rea, A. M. 1981. "Resource Utilization and Food Taboos of Sonoran Desert Peoples." *Journal of Ethnobiology* 1:69–83.

Reeder, T. W., C. J. Cole, and H. C. Dessauer. 2002. "Phylogenetic Relationships of Whiptail Lizards of the Genus *Cnemidophorus* (Squamata: Teiidae): A Test of Monophyly, Reevaluation of Karyotypic Evolution, and Review of Hybrid Origins." American Museum Novitates 3365. New York: American Museum of Natural History.

Renzi, J. J., W. D. Peachey, and K. L. Gerst. 2019. "A Decade of Flowering Phenology of the Keystone Saguaro Cactus (*Carnegiea gigantea*)." *American Journal of Botany* 106:199–210.

Reynolds, H. G. 1958. "The Ecology of the Merriam Kangaroo Rat (*Dipodomys merriami* Mearns) on the Grazing Lands of Southern Arizona." *Ecological Monographs* 28:111–27.

Ricklefs, R. E. 1990. *Ecology*. 3rd ed. New York: W. H. Freeman.

Ricklefs, R. E., and F. R. Hainsworth. 1968. "Temperature Dependent Behavior of the Cactus Wren." *Ecology* 49:227–33.

Ricklefs, R. E., and F. R. Hainsworth. 1969. "Temperature Regulation in Nestling Cactus Wrens: The Nest Environment." *Condor* 71:32–37.

Ricklefs, R. E., M. Konarzewski, and S. Daan. 1996. "The Relationship Between Basal Metabolic Rate and Daily Energy Expenditure in Birds and Mammals." *American Naturalist* 147:1047–71.

Riddell, E. A., K. J. Iknayan, L. Hargrove, S. Tremor, J. L. Patton, R. Ramirez, B.O. Wolf, and S. R. Beissinger. 2021. "Exposure to Climate Change Drives Stability or Collapse of Desert Mammal and Bird Communities." *Science* 371:633–36.

Riddell, E. A., K. J. Iknayan, B. O. Wolf, B. Sinervo, and S. R. Beissinger. 2019. "Cooling Requirements Fueled the Collapse of a Desert Bird Community from Climate Change." *Proceedings of the National Academy of Sciences of the United States of America* 116:21609–15.

Riddle, B. R., and D. J. Hafner. 1999. "Species as Units of Analysis in Ecology and Biogeography: Time to Take the Blinders Off." *Global Ecology and Biogeography* 8:433–41.

Rieppel, O., and R. R. Reisz. 1999. "The Origin and Early Evolution of Turtles." *Annual Review of Ecology and Systematics* 30:1–22.

Riley, S. D., R. M. Sauvajot, T. K. Fuller, E. C. York, D. A. Kamradt, C. Bromley, and R. K. Wayne. 2003. "Effects of Urbanization and Habitat Fragmentation on Bobcats and Coyotes in Southern California." *Conservation Biology* 17:566–76.

Rodl, T., and D. Ward. 2002. "Host Recognition in a Desert Mistletoe: Early Stages of Development Are Influenced by Substrate and Host Origin." *Functional Ecology* 16:128–34.

Rodriguez-Robles, J. A. 2002. "Feeding Ecology of North American Gopher Snakes (*Pituophis catenifer*, Colubridae)." *Biological Journal of the Linnean Society* 77:165–83.

Rodriguez-Robles, J. A. 2003. "Home Ranges of Gopher Snakes (*Pituophis catenifer*, Colubridae) in Central California." *Copeia* 2003:391–96.

Rodriguez-Robles, J. A., and J. M. De Jesus-Escobar. 2000. "Molecular Systematics of New World Gopher, Bull, and Pinesnakes (*Pituophis*: Colubridae), a Transcontinental Species Complex." *Molecular Phylogenetics and Evolution* 14:35–50.

Rojas, D., O. M. Warsi, and L. M. Davalos. 2016. "Bats (Chiroptera: Noctilionoidea) Challenge a Recent Origin of Extant Neotropical Diversity." *Systematic Biology* 65:432–48.

Rojas-Arechiga, M., and C. Vazquez-Yanes. 2000. "Cactus Seed Germination: A Review." *Journal of Arid Environments* 44:85–104.

Romero, A., B. J. O'Neill, R. M. Timm, K. G. Gerow, and D. McClearn. 2013. "Group Dynamics, Behavior, and Current and Historical Abundance of Peccaries in Costa Rica's Caribbean Lowlands." *Journal of Mammalogy* 94:771–91.

Rosenfeld, R. N., K. K. Madden, J. Bielefeldt, and O. E. Curtis. 2020. "Cooper's hawk (*Accipiter cooperii*)." *Birds of the World*. Last modified March 4, 2020. https://doi.org/10.2173/bow.coohaw.01.

Rosenzweig, M. L. 1966. "Community Structure in Sympatric Carnivora." *Journal of Mammalogy* 47:602–12.

Ruben, J. 1995. "The Evolution of Endothermy in Mammals and Birds: From Physiology to Fossils." *Annual Review of Physiology* 57:69–95.

Ruby, D. E. 1978. "Seasonal Changes in the Territorial Behavior of the Iguanid Lizard *Sceloporus jarrovi*." *Copeia* 1978:430–38.

Ruggiero, M. A., D. P. Gordon, T. M. Orrell, N. Bailly, T. Bourgoin, R. C. Brusca, T. Cavalier-Smith, et al. 2015. "A Higher Level Classification of All Living Organisms." *Plos One* 10:e0119248.

Russell, S. M., and G. Monson. 1998. *The Birds of Sonora*. Tucson: University of Arizona Press.

Salter, J. F., C. H. Oliveros, P. A. Hosner, J. D. Manthey, J. D. Robbins, R. G. Moyle, R. T. Brumfield, et al. 2020. "Extensive Paraphyly in the Typical Owl Family (Strigidae)." *Auk* 137:1–15.

Salvatti, A. P., L. P. Gonzaga, C. Augusta, and C. A. de Moraes Russo. 2015. "A Paleogene Origin for Crown Passerines and the Diversification of the Oscines in the New World." *Molecular Phylogenetics and Evolution* 88:1–15.

Sato, A., C. O'huigin, F. Figueroa, P. R. Grant, B. R. Grant, H. Tichy, and J. Klein. 1999. "Phylogeny of Darwin's Finches as Revealed by mtDNA Sequences." *Proceedings of the National Academy of Sciences of the United States of America* 96:5101–6.

Scarborough, R., and R. C. Brusca. 2015. "Geologic Origin of the Sonoran Desert." In *A Natural History of the Sonoran Desert*, edited by M. A. Dimmitt, P. W. Comus, and L. M. Brewer, 71–84. Tucson: Arizona-Sonora Desert Museum Press.

Schafer, J. L., E. L. Mudrak, C. E. Haines, H. A. Paraga, K. A. Moloney, and C. Holzapfel. 2012. "The Association of Native and Non-Native Annual Plants with *Larrea tridentata* (Creosote Bush) in the Mojave and Sonoran Deserts." *Journal of Arid Environments* 87:129–35.

Schmidt-Nielsen, B., and K. Schmidt-Nielsen. 1949. "The Water Economy of Desert Mammals." *Scientific Monthly* 69:180–85.

Schoenjahn, J., C. R. Pavey, and G. H. Walter. 2020. "Why Female Birds of Prey Are Larger Than Males." *Biological Journal of the Linnean Society* 129:532–42.

Scholander, P. F., R. Hock, J. R. Walters, and L. Irving. 1950b. "Adaptation to Cold in Arctic and Tropical Mammals and Birds in Relation to Body Temperature, Insulation, and Basal Metabolic Rate." *Biological Bulletin* 99:259–71.

Scholander, P. F., V. Walters, R. Hock, and L. Irving. 1950a. "Body Insulation of Some Arctic and Tropical Mammals and Birds." *Biological Bulletin* 99:225–36.

Schulze, E.-D., and J. R. Ehleringer. 1984. "The Effect of Nitrogen Supply on Growth and Water-Use Efficiency of Xylem-Tapping Mistletoes." *Planta* 162:268–75.

Schwertner, T. W., H. A. Mathewson, J. A. Roberson, and G. L. Waggerman. 2020. "White-Winged Dove (*Zenaida asiatica*)." Birds of the World. Last modified March 4, 2020. https://doi.org/10.2173/bow.whwdov.01.

Shakya, S. B., J. Fuchs, J. M. Pons, and F. H. Sheldon. 2017. "Tapping the Woodpecker Tree for Evolutionary Insight." *Molecular Phylogenetics and Evolution* 116:183–91.

Shaw, J. R. 2015. "Multi-Scale Drivers of Riparian Vegetation Form and Function in Ephemeral Stream Networks of the Sonoran Desert." PhD diss., Colorado State University.

Shelley, E. L., and D. T. Blumstein. 2005. "The Evolution of Vocal Alarm Communication in Rodents." *Behavioral Ecology* 16:169–77.

Sibley, D. A. 2000. *The Sibley Guide to Birds*. New York: Knopf.

Simmons, L. S., and T. E. Martin. 1990. "Food Limitation of Avian Reproduction: An Experiment with the Cactus Wren." *Ecology* 71:869–76.

Simmons, N. B., and A. L. Wetterer. 2002. "Phylogeny and Convergence in Cactophilic Bats." In *Columnar Cacti and Their Mutualists: Evolution, Ecology, and Conservation*, edited by T. H. Fleming and A. Valiente-Banuet, 87–121. Tucson: University of Arizona Press.

Simon, C. A., K. Gravelle, B. E. Bissinger, I. Eiss, and R. Ruibal. 1981. "The Role of Chemoreception in the Iguanid Lizard *Sceloporus jarrovi*." *Animal Behaviour* 29:46–54.

Simpson, G. G. 1945. "The Principles of Classification and the Classification of Mammals." *Bulletin of the American Museum of Natural History* 85:1–350.

Simpson, G. G. 1949. *The Meaning of Evolution*. New Haven, Conn.: Yale University Press.

Simpson, G. G. 1953. *The Major Features of Evolution*. New York: Columbia University Press.

Sinding, M.-H. S., S. Gopalakrishan, F. G. Vieral, J. A. Sananiego Castruita, K. Raundrup, M. P. H. Jørgensen, M. Meldgaard, et al. 2018. "Population Genomics of Grey Wolves and Wolflike Canids in North America." *PLOS Genetics* 14 (11): e1007745.

Sinervo, B. 1990. "Evolution of Thermal Physiology and Growth Rate Between Populations of the Western Fence Lizard (*Sceloporus occidentalis*)." *Oecologia* 83:228–37.

Skopec, M. M., S. Haley, and M. D. Dearing. 2007. "Differential Hepatic Gene Expression of a Dietary Specialist (*Neotoma stephensi*) and Generalist (*Neotoma albigula*) in Response to Juniper (*Juniperus monosperma*) Ingestion." *Comparative Biochemistry and Physiology Part D* 2007:34–43.

Small, M. F., J. T. Baccus, and T. W. Schwertner. 2010. "Productivity in an Urban White-Winged Dove Population on the Edwards Plateau, Texas." *Bulletin of the Texas Ornithological Society* 43:61–66.

Smit, B., M. C. Whitfield, W. A. Talbot, A. R. Gerson, A. E. McKechnie, and B. O. Wolf. 2018. "Avian Thermoregulation in the Heat: Phylogenetic Variation Among Avian Orders in Evaporative Cooling Capacity and Heat Tolerance." *Journal of Experimental Biology* 221:1–10.

Smith, E. K., J. O. O'Neill, A. R. Gerson, A. E. McKechnie, and B. O. Wolf. 2017. "Avian Thermoregulation in the Heat: Resting Metabolism, Evaporative Cooling and Heat Tolerance in Sonoran Desert Songbirds." *Journal of Experimental Biology* 220:3290–300.

Smith, E. K., J. O. O'Neill, A. R. Gerson, and B. O. Wolf. 2015. "Avian Thermoregulation in the Heat: Resting Metabolism, Evaporative Cooling and Heat Tolerance in Sonoran Desert Doves and Quail." *Journal of Experimental Biology* 218:3636–46.

Smith, F. A., and J. L. Betancourt. 2006. "Predicting Woodrat (*Neotoma*) Responses to Anthropogenic Warming from Studies of the Palaeomidden Record." *Journal of Biogeography* 33:2061–76.

Smith, F. A., J. L. Betancourt, and J. H. Brown. 1995. "Evolution of Body Size in the Woodrat over the Past 25,000 Years of Climate Change." *Science* 270.

Smith, F. A., A. W. Murray, L. E. Harding, H. M. Lease, and J. Martin. 2014. "Life in an Extreme Environment: A Historical Perspective on the Influence of Temperature on the Ecology and Evolution of Woodrats." *Journal of Mammalogy* 95:1128–43.

Smith, L. C., and H. B. John-Alder. 1999. "Seasonal Specificity of Hormonal, Behavioral, and Coloration Responses to Within- and Between-Sex Encounters in Male Lizards (*Sceloporus undulatus*)." *Hormones and Behavior* 36:39–52.

Soares, A. E. R., B. J. Novak, J. Haile, T. H. Heupink, J. Fjeldsa, T. P. Gilbert, H. Poinar, et al 2016. "Complete Mitochondrial Genomes of Living and Extinct Pigeons Revise the Timing of the Columbiform Radiation." *BMC Evolutionary Biology* 16 (230): 1–9.

Soholt, L. F. 1976. "Development of Thermoregulation in Merriam's Kangaroo Rat, *Dipodomys merriami*." *Physiological Zoology* 49:152–57.

Soltis, D. E., P. S. Soltis, P. K. Endress, M. W. Chase, S. Manchester, W. Judd, L. Majure, and E. Mavrodiev. 2018. *Phylogeny and Evolution of the Angiosperms*. Chicago: University of Chicago Press.

Sonerud, G. A., R. Steen, L. M. Low, L. T. Roed, K. Skar, V. Selas, and T. Slagsvold. 2012. "Size-Biased Allocation of Prey from Male to Offspring via Female: Family Conflicts, Prey Selection, and the Evolution of Size Dimorphism in Raptors." *Oecologia* 172:93–107. https://doi.org/10.1007/s00442-012-2491-9.

Sorenson, J. S., C. A. Turnbull, and M. D. Dearing. 2004. "A Specialist Herbivore (*Neotoma stephensi*) Absorbs Fewer Plant Toxins Than Does a Generalist (*Neotoma albigula*)." *Physiological and Biochemical Zoology* 77:139–48.

Sosa, V. J., and T. H. Fleming. 2002. "Why Are Columnar Cacti Associated with Nurse Plants?" In *Columnar Cacti and Their Mutualists: Evolution, Ecology, and Conservation*, edited by T. H. Fleming and A. Valiente-Banuet, 306–23. Tucson: University of Arizona Press.

Spellman, G. M., A. Cibois, R. G. Moyle, K. Winker, and F. K. Barker. 2008. "Clarifying the Systematics of an Enigmatic Avian Lineage: What Is a Bombycillid?" *Molecular Phylogenetics and Evolution* 49:1036–40.

Spotila, J. R., L. C. Zimmerman, C. A. Binckley, J. S. Grumbles, D. C. Rostal, A. List, E. Beyer, et al. 1994. "Effects of Incubation Conditions on Sex Determination, Hatching Success, and Growth of Hatchling Desert Tortoises, *Gopherus agassizii*." *Herpetological Monographs* 8:105–18.

Spring, L. W. 1965. "Climbing and Pecking Adaptations in Some North American Woodpeckers." *Condor* 67:457–88.

Spurrier, S. E., and K. G. Smith. 2006. "Watering Blue Palo Verde (*Cercidium floridum*) Affects Berry Maturation of Parasitic Desert Mistletoe (*Phoradendron californicum*) During an Extreme Drought in the Mojave Desert." *Journal of Arid Environments* 64:369–73.

Steenburgh, W. F., and C. H. Lowe. 1968. "Critical Factors During the First Years of Life of the Saguaro (*Cereus Giganteus*) at Saguaro National Monument, Arizona." *Ecology* 50:825–34.

Stuart, G., C. Gries, and D. Hope. 2006. "The Relationship Between Pollen and Extant Vegetation Across an Arid Urban Ecosystem and Surrounding Desert in Southwest USA." *Journal of Biogeography* 33:573–91.

Sullivan, B. K., D. J. Leavitt, and K. O. Sullivan. 2017. "Snake Communities on the Urban Fringe in the Sonoran Desert: Influences on Species Richness and Abundance." *Urban Ecosystems* 20:199–206.

Sweet, S. S. 1985. "Geographic Variation, Convergent Crypsis and Mimicry in Gopher Snakes (*Pituophis melanoleucus*) and Western Rattlesnakes (*Crotalus viridis*)." *Journal of Herpetology* 19:55–67.

Szarek, S. R., and R. M. Woodhouse. 1978a. "Ecophysiological Studies of Sonoran Desert Plants: III: The Daily Course of Photosynthesis for *Acacia greggii* and *Cercidium microphyllum*." *Oecologia* 35:285–94.

Szarek, S. R., and R. M. Woodhouse. 1978b. "Ecophysiological Studies of Sonoran Desert Plants: IV: Seasonal Photosynthetic Capacities of *Acacia greggii* and *Cercidium microphyllum*." *Oecologia* 37:221–29.

Taylor, E. N., and D. F. Denardo. 2005. "Reproductive Ecology of Western Diamond-Backed Rattlesnakes (*Crotalus atrox*) in the Sonoran Desert." *Copeia* 2005:152–58.

Tewksbury, J. J., and J. D. Lloyd. 2001. "Positive Interactions Under Nurse-Plants: Spatial Scale, Stress Gradients and Benefactor Size." *Oecologia* 127:425–34.

Theimer, T. C., and J. C. Bateman. 1992. "Patterns of Prickly-Pear Herbivory by Collared Peccaries." *Journal of Wildlife Management* 56:234–40.

Thompson, J. N. 2013. *Relentless Evolution*. Chicago: University of Chicago Press.

Thompson, S. D. 1982. "Microhabitat Utilization and Foraging Behavior of Bipedal and Quadrupedal Heteromyid Rodents." *Ecology* 63:1303–12.

Townsend, T. M., A. Larson, E. Louis, and J. R. Macey. 2004. "Molecular Phylogenetics of Squamata: The Position of Snakes, Amphisbaenians, and Dibamids, and the Root of the Squamate Tree." *Systematic Biology* 53:735–57.

Tracy, R. L., and G. Walsberg. 2000. "Prevalence of Cutaneous Evaporation in Merriam's Kangaroo Rat and Its Adaptive Variation at the Subspecific Level." *Journal of Experimental Biology* 203:773–81.

Tschapka, M., T. P. Gonzalez-Terrazas, and M. Knornschild. 2015. "Nectar Uptake in Bats Using a Pumping-Tongue Mechanism." *Science Advances* 2015 (1): 1500525.

Turner, F. B., P. Hayden, B. L. Burge, and J. B. Roberson. 1986. "Egg Production by the Desert Tortoise (*Gopherus agassizii*) in California." *Herpetologica* 42:93–104.

Turner, R. M. 1990. "Long-Term Vegetation Change at a Fully Protected Sonoran Desert Site." *Ecology* 71:464–77.

Turner, R. M., J. E. Bowers, and T. L. Burgess. 1995. *Sonoran Desert Plants.* Tucson: University of Arizona.

Upham, N. S., J. A. Esselstyn, and W. Jetz. 2019. "Inferring the Mammal Tree: Species-Level Sets of Phylogenies for Questions in Ecology, Evolution, and Conservation." *Plos Biology* 17.

Utiger, U., N. Helfenberger, B. Schatti, C. Schmidt, M. Ruf, and V. Ziswiler. 2002. "Molecular Systematics and Phylogeny of Old World and New World Ratsnakes, *Elaphe* Auct., and Related Genera (Reptilia, Squamata, Colubridae)." *Russian Journal of Herpetology* 9:105–24.

Uvaa, V., M. Packertb, A. Ciboisic, L. Fumagallia, and A. Roulina. 2018. "Comprehensive Molecular Phylogeny of Barn Owls and Relatives (Family: Tytonidae), and Their Six Major Pleistocene Radiations." *Molecular Phylogenetics and Evolution* 125:127–37.

Van Devender, T. R. 1973. "Late Pleistocene Plants and Animals of the Sonoran Desert: A Survey of Ancient Packrat Middens in Southwestern Arizona." PhD diss., University of Arizona.

Van Devender, T. R. 2002. "Environmental History of the Sonoran Desert." In *Columnar Cacti and Their Mutualists: Evolution, Ecology, and Conservation*, edited by T. H. Fleming and A. Valiente-Banuet, 3–24. Tucson: University of Arizona Press.

Van Devender, T. R., and R. C. Brusca. 2015. "Deep History of the Sonoran Desert." In *A Natural History of the Sonoran Desert*, edited by M. A. Dimmitt, P. W. Comus, and L. M. Brewer, 63–70. Tucson: Arizona-Sonora Desert Museum Press.

Van Dongen, P. A. M. 1998. "Brain Size in Vertebrates." In *The Central Nervous System of Vertebrates*, vol. 3, edited by R. Nieuwenhuys, H. J. ten Donkelaar, and C. Nicholson, 2099–2134. Berlin: Springer.

Vaughan, T. N., J. M. Ryan, and N. J. Czaplewski. 2000. *Mammalogy.* 4th ed. Fort Worth, Tex.: Saunders College.

Vidal, N., and S. B. Hedges. 2005. "The Phylogeny of Squamate Reptiles (Lizards, Snakes, and Amphisbaenians) Inferred from Nine Nuclear Protein-Coding Genes." *Comptes Rendus Biologies* 328:1000–8.

Walker, J. M., A. Garber, R. J. Berger, and H. C. Heller. 1979. "Sleep and Estivation (Shallow Torpor): Continuous Processes of Energy Conservation." *Science* 204 (4397): 1098–1100.

Walker, J. S., N. B. Grimm, J. M. Briggs, C. Bries, and L. Dugan. 2009. "Effects of Urbanization on Plant Species Diversity in Central Arizona." *Frontiers in Ecology and the Environment* 7:465–70.

Wallace, R. S. 2002. "The Phylogeny and Systematics of Columnar Cacti: An Overview." In *Columnar Cacti and Their Mutualists: Evolution, Ecology, and Conservation*, edited by T. H. Fleming and A. Valiente-Banuet, 42–65. Tucson: University of Arizona Press.

Walsberg, G. 1975. "Digestive Adaptations of *Phainopepla nitens* Associated with the Eating of Mistletoe Berries." *Condor* 77:169–74.

Walsberg, G. 1978. "Brood Size and the Use of Time and Energy by the Phainopepla." *Ecology* 59:147–53.

Walsberg, G. 1982. "Coat Color, Solar Heat Gain, and Conspicuousness in the Phainopepla." *Auk* 99:495–502.

Walsberg, G., and C. W. Thompson. 1990. "Annual Changes in Gizzard Size and Function in a Frugivorous Bird." *Condor* 92:794–95.

Wang, N., R. T. Kimball, E. L. Braun, B. Liang, and Z. Zhang. 2013. "Assessing Phylogenetic Relationships Among Galliformes: A Multigene Phylogeny with Expanded Taxon Sampling in Phasianidae." *Plos One* 8 (5): e64312.

Weathers, W. W. 1981. "Physiological Thermoregulation in Heat-Stressed Birds: Consequences of Body Size." *Physiological Zoology* 54:345–61.

Weathers, W. W., and K. A. Nagy. 1980. "Simultaneous Doubly Labeled Water ($^3HH^{18}O$) and Time-Budget Energy Estimates of Daily Energy Expenditures in *Phainopepla nitens*." *Auk* 97:861–67.

Webster, D. B., and M. Webster. 1980. "Morphological Adaptations of the Ear in the Rodent Family Heteromyidae." *American Zoologist* 20:247–54.

Weiss, J. L., and J. T. Overpeck. 2005. "Is the Sonoran Desert Losing Its Cool?" *Global Change Biology* 11: 2065–77.

Welch, K. C., Jr., D. L. Altshuler, and R. K. Suarez. 2007. "Oxygen Consumption Rates in Hovering Hummingbirds Reflect Substrate-Dependent Differences in P/O Ratios: Carbohydrate as a 'Premium' Fuel." *Journal of Experimental Biology* 210:2146–53.

Wells, M. C., and M. Bekoff. 1982. "Predation by Wild Coyotes: Behavioral and Ecological Analyses." *Journal of Mammalogy* 63:118–27.

Werdelin, L., N. Yamaguchi, W. E. Johnson, and S. J. O'Brien. 2010. "Phylogeny and Evolution of Cats (Felidae)." In *Biology and Conservation of Wild Felids*, edited by D. W. MacDonald and A. J. Loveridge, 59–82. New York: Oxford University Press.

Wetterer, A. I., M. V. Rockman, and N. B. Simmons. 2000. "Phylogeny of Phyllostomid Bats (Mammalia: Chiroptera): Data from Diverse Morphological Systems, Sex Chromosomes, and Restriction Sites." Bulletin of the American Museum of Natural History 248. New York: American Museum of Natural History.

Whaley, W. H. 1979. "The Ecology and Status of the Harris' Hawk (*Parabuteo unicinctus*) in Arizona." PhD diss., University of Arizona.

Whitson, M. A. 1971. "Field and Laboratory Investigations of the Ethology of Courtship and Copulation in the Greater Roadrunner (*Geococcyx californianus*—Aves, Cuculidae)." PhD diss., University of Oklahoma.

Whittaker, R. H. 1969. "New Concepts of Kingdoms of Organisms." *Science* 163:150–60.

Wiens, J. J., K. H. Kozak, and N. Silva. 2012. "Diversity and Niche Evolution Along Aridity Gradients in North American Lizards (Phrynosomatidae)." *Evolution* 67:1715–28.

Wiens, J. J., C. A. Kuczynski, S. Aril, and T. W. Reeder. 2010. "Phylogenetic Relationships of Phrynosomatid Lizards Based on Nuclear and Mitochondrial Data, and a Revised Phylogeny for *Sceloporus*." *Molecular Phylogenetics and Evolution* 54:150–61.

Wiesenborn, W. D. 2016. "Conspecific Pollen Loads on Insects Visiting Female Flowers on Parasitic *Phoradendron californicum* (Viscaceae)." *Western North American Naturalist* 76:113–21.

Wilkinson, G. S., and T. H. Fleming. 1996. "Migration and Evolution of Lesser Long-Nosed Bats *Leptonycteris curasoae*, Inferred from Mitochondrial DNA." *Molecular Ecology* 5:329–39.

Williams, J. B., M. M. Pacelli, and E. J. Braun. 1991. "The Effect of Water Deprivation on Renal Function in Conscious Unrestrained Gambel's Quail (*Callipepla gambelii*)." *Physiological Zoology* 64:1200–16.

Williams, K. E., K. E. Hodges, and C. A. Bishop. 2012. "Small Reserves Around Hibernation Sites May Not Adequately Protect Mobile Snakes: The Example of Great Basin Gophersnakes (*Pituophis catenifer deserticola*) in British Columbia." *Canadian Journal of Zoology* 90:304–12.

Williamson, S. L. 2001. *A Field Guide to the Hummingbirds of North America*. Boston: Houghton Mifflin.

Wilson, E. O. 2016. *Half-Earth*. New York: Liveright.

Wink, M., A.-A. El-Sayed, H. Sauer-Gurth, and J. Gonzalez. 2009. "Molecular Phylogeny of Owls (Strigiformes) Inferred from DNA Sequences of the Mitochondrial Cytochrome B and the Nuclear RAG-1 Gene." *Ardea* 97:581–91.

Winne, C. T., and M. B. Keck. 2004. "Daily Activity Patterns of Whiptail Lizards (Squamata: Teiidae: *Aspidoscelis*): A Proximate Response to Environmental Conditions or an Endogenous Rhythm?" *Functional Ecology* 18:314–21.

Woese, C. R., and G. E. Fox. 1977. "Phylogenetic Structure of the Prokaryotic Domain: The Primary Kingdoms." *Proceedings of the National Academy of Sciences of the United States of America* 54:5088–90.

Wolf, B. O., and C. Martinez del Rio. 2000. "Use of Saguaro Fruit by White-Winged Doves: Isotopic Evidence of a Tight Ecological Association." *Oecologia* 124:536–43.

Wolf, B. O., and C. Martinez del Rio. 2003. "How Important Are Columnar Cacti as Sources of Water and Nutrients for Desert Consumers? A Review." *Isotopes and Environmental Health* 39:53–67.

Wolf, B. O., C. Martinez del Rio, and J. Babson. 2002. "Stable Isotopes Reveal That Saguaro Fruit Provides Different Resources to Two Desert Dove Species." *Ecology* 83:1286–93.

Woodbury, A. M., and R. Hardy. 1948. "Studies of the Desert Tortoise, *Gopherus agassizii*." *Ecological Monographs* 18:145–200.

Wu, C. W., Z. D. Zhu, and W. Zhang. 2015. "How Woodpecker Avoids Brain Injury?" *Journal of Physics: Conference Series* 628. https://doi.org/10.1088/1742-6596/628/1/012007.

Wuster, W., L. Peppin, C. E. Pook, and D. E. Walker. 2008. "A Nesting of Vipers: Phylogeny and Historical Biogeography of the Viperidae (Squamata: Serpentes)." *Molecular Phylogenetics and Evolution* 49:445–59.

Wylie, D. R. W., C. Gutierrez-Ibanez, and A. N. Iwaniuk. 2015. "Integrating Brain, Behavior, and Phylogeny to Understand the Evolution of Sensory Systems in Birds." *Frontiers in Neuroscience* 9:1–17.

Yetman, D., A. Burquez, D. Hultine, and M. J. Sanderson. 2020. *The Saguaro Cactus: A Natural History*. Tucson: Southwest Center.

Yule, K. M., and J. L. Bronstein. 2018. "Reproductive Ecology of a Parasitic Plant Differs by Host Species: Vector Interactions and the Maintenance of Host Races." *Oecologia* 186:471–82.

Zelditch, M. L., J. Li, L. A. P. Tran, and D. L. Swiderski. 2015. "Relationships of Diversity, Disparity, and Their Evolutionary Rates in Squirrels (Sciuridae)." *Evolution* 69:1284–300.

Zervanos, S. M., and G. I. Day. 1977. "Water and Energy Requirements of Captive and Free-Living Collared Peccaries." *Journal of Wildlife Management* 41:527–32.

Zervanos, S. M., and N. F. Hadley. 1973. "Adaptational Biology and Energy Relationships of the Collared Peccary (*Tayassu tajacu*)." *Ecology* 54:759–74.

Zimmer, C. 2001. *Evolution*. New York: HarperCollins.

Zimmerman, L. C., M. P. O'Connor, S. J. Bulova, J. R. Spotila, S. Kemp, and C. J. Salice. 1994. "Thermal Ecology of Desert Tortoises in the Eastern Mojave Desert: Seasonal Patterns of Operative and Body Temperatures, and Microhabitat Utilization." *Herpetological Monographs* 8:45–59.

INDEX

ABOUT THE AUTHOR

Theodore H. Fleming is a professor emeritus of biology at the University of Miami. He spent thirty-nine years in academia at the University of Missouri -St. Louis and the University of Miami, teaching ecology courses and conducting research on tropical rodent populations and plant-visiting bats and their food plants in Panama, Costa Rica, Australia, Mexico, and Arizona. He lives in Tucson.